business economics

Second edition

Andrew Gillespie

OXFORD

UNIVERSITY PRESS

Great Clarendon Street, Oxford, OX2 6DP,
United Kingdom

Oxford University Press is a department of the University of Oxford.
It furthers the University's objective of excellence in research, scholarship,
and education by publishing worldwide. Oxford is a registered trade mark of
Oxford University Press in the UK and in certain other countries

British Library Cataloguing in Publication Data
Data available

ISBN 978–0–19–965799–5

Printed in UK by
Bell and Bain Ltd, Glasgow

Kristy Elias.

business economics

PUTTING ECONOMICS TO WORK

What is the value of economics in everyday business life? Take advantage of our fantastic new features accompanying this book in order to:

- ○ Help you understand how economics can be used in your future **careers**
- ○ Learn what **essential skills** and attributes employers value in the workplace
- ○ Improve your prospects of **employment**

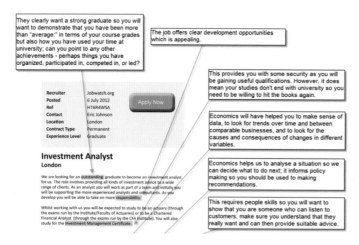

Jobwatch

Online

Unique annotated job adverts identifying the skills required for various graduate jobs, and most importantly, how you can articulate and demonstrate such skills.

Economics and employability

What is your name
Robin Cohen

Tell us about your role at Deloitte?
I am a partner within the economic consulting practice at Deloitte. The main responsibilities of a partner are leading the many different aspects of our economic consulting practice. This includes leading client projects, building long-term relationships with clients, and developing our practice alongside the many other practices within Deloitte both in the UK and overseas.

What is economic consulting and why do clients use you?
Economic consulting applies economics to provide advice principally on the interactions between governments (or regulators) and firms, and between firms and the markets in which they compete. We do so to help our clients understand their economic issues and inform optimum business and policy decisions. In doing so, we apply a variety of economic concepts which are built upon those introduced in this book. Our clients use us to obtain credible economic analysis, which is well founded and uses reliable data.

Economics & Employability

In text

Top business practitioners from organizations including Deloitte, PricewaterhouseCoopers, Simon-Kucher & Partners and Mission Burrito explain how economics is used in their day to day work, and why it is relevant to your future careers.

Thank you to Tor and John for support from the start and to Ali, Seth, Romily, and Clemency for all their smiles and sparkle.

Brief contents

Detailed contents

New to this edition

- New insights from top business practitioners explaining how economics is used in their day to day work
- Tips from business practitioners on the essential skills and attributes they value in the workplace
- Updated coverage of the financial crisis
- Increased coverage of macroeconomics and game theory
- 90% of examples and cases have been updated to illustrate economics in business.

How to use this book

Learning objectives
Each chapter contains a bulleted list of the key economic concepts and tools.

Opening case study
A topical business case study at the beginning of each chapter provides you with an introduction to the subject and helps to set the scene. As you progress through the chapter you will find the answers to the case study questions.

In-text features

Comprehensive solutions and guidance for each of these features can be found online at www.oxfordtextbooks.co.uk/orc/gillespiebusiness2e/

Think about it
Short reflective questions help you to consider the significance of the theory you have covered and apply your learning to a new problem.

Economics and employability
Insights from business practitioners demonstrate how the chapter topics are relevant to their job, and why economics is useful in their role. The practitioners also discuss what attributes and skills are needed to succeed in their business.

You and economics
This feature looks at how economics is relevant to your everyday life, and highlights how you can use your understanding of economics in practice to make decisions.

Data analysis
Provides you with economic data to analyse and interpret.

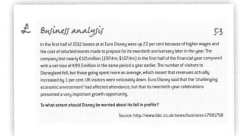

£ *Business analysis* 5.3

In the first half of 2012 losses at Euro Disney were up 22 per cent because of higher wages and the cost of refurbishments made to prepare for its twentieth anniversary later in the year. The company lost nearly €121 million (£97.4m; $157.4m) in the first half of the financial year compared with a net loss of €99.5million in the same period a year earlier. The number of visitors to Disneyland fell, but those going spent more on average, which meant that revenues actually increased by 1 per cent. UK visitors were noticeably down. Euro Disney said that the 'challenging economic environment' had affected attendance, but that its twentieth-year celebrations presented a very important growth opportunity.

To what extent should Disney be worried about its fall in profits?

Source: http://www.bbc.co.uk/news/business-17981798

Business analysis

Real life business examples highlight how economics works in action. Economics is based on essential theory, but as a business student or practitioner you need to know how this applies to the real world and what is happening around you.

}{ *People and economics: Neoclassical economists*

Neoclassical economic thinking dominates mainstream economics. It assumes that households seek to maximize their utility, given their incomes, and that businesses seek to maximize their profits, given the revenue and cost conditions. It assumes that people make rational decisions and highlights the way in which decisions are made using marginal conditions (such as marginal revenue and marginal cost).

People and economics

Here you are provided with useful details on the key people and organizations in economics.

End of chapter features

Checklist

Having read this chapter, you should now understand:

- the different types of cost and the relationship between them;
- the link between costs and productivity;
- why managers want to keep costs low and how they might do this;
- the different types of revenue (for example, total revenue, marginal revenue, and average revenue);
- the difference between the short run and the long run, and why it matters;

Checklist

A checklist at the end of each chapter helps you review the work you have covered.

Discussion questions

1. To what extent do economies of scale matter?
2. Discuss the potential cost advantages and disadvantages to a business of expanding.
3. Why do marginal costs matter?

Discussion questions

These discussion questions are an opportunity for you to explore wider business economics issues.

Summary

A supply curve shows the quantity supplied at each and every price, all other factors held constant. A change in price leads to a movement along the supply curve and a change in the quantity supplied; a change in the other factors, such as technology or the number of producers, leads to a shift in the supply curve. The sensitivity of the quantity supplied to a change in price is measured by the price elasticity of supply. An increase in indirect taxes adds to the costs of a supplier; a subsidy reduces the costs of a supplier.

Managers need to understand the determinants of supply, because an increase in supply might make the market much more competitive. Managers may also try to increase

Summary

Chapters conclude with a brief summary of the key concepts and points made within the chapter.

Short answer questions

1. Define profit. Explain why an accountant's understanding of profit is different from that of an economist.
2. Is it true or false that fixed costs never change? Explain your answer.
3. Is it true or false that the shutdown point for a business in the short run occurs when the price equals the average variable cost? Explain your answer.
4. Explain three types of internal economy of scale.

Short answer questions

Questions at the end of each chapter test your grasp of the key concepts.

One step further

🌐 Visit our Online Resource Centre at **www.oxfordtextbooks.co.uk/orc/gillespiebusiness2e/** to test your understanding, watch video walk-throughs, and access further information on topics covered in this chapter.

One step further

At the end of particular chapters you'll find a link pointing you to the Online Resource Centre where you will find more challenging material to expand your knowledge.

Online Resource Centre

www.oxfordtextbooks.co.uk/orc/gillespiebusiness2e/

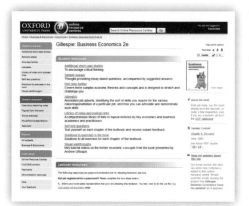

The Online Resource Centre (ORC) comprises resources for both lecturers and students.

Free and open-access material available to students

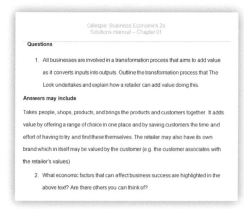

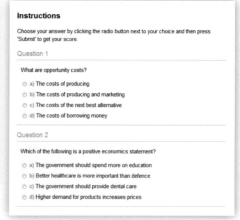

Solutions to questions in book

After you've answered the questions raised in the textbook, you'll be able to check your answers online. Here you'll find over 100 solutions, enabling you to monitor your own learning.

Additional short cases

Extra case studies help to highlight how business economics can be applied in real business situations.

Sample essays

Essay questions and suggested answers provide you with guidance on how to tackle essays.

Self-test questions

These provide a quick and easy way to test your understanding, with instant feedback.

Library of video and podcast links

A comprehensive library of links to topical lectures by key economics and business academics and practitioners.

One step further

This material covers more complex economic theories and concepts and is designed to stretch and challenge you.

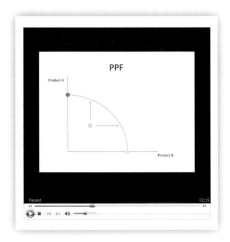

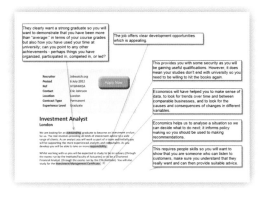

Visual walkthroughs

Using screen capture software, the author offers a mini tutorial on some of the trickier economic concepts discussed in the text, allowing you to watch these in your own time.

Jobwatch

This unique feature provides you with annotated job adverts, identifying the sort of skills you require for the various roles/responsibilities of a particular job, and how you can articulate and demonstrate such skills.

Free for all lecturers who adopt the textbook

PowerPoint slides

A suite of customizable PowerPoint slides has been provided to use in your lecture presentations.

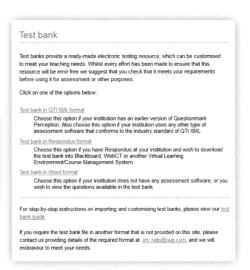

Case study teaching notes

Notes and guide answers are provided for each chapter's opening case.

Group exercises

Ideas for group activities to set students are provided.

Test bank

A ready-made electronic testing resource which is fully customizable and contains feedback for students will help you to save time creating assessments. There are 20 questions per chapter, each with feedback.

Acknowledgements

Many thanks to everyone at OUP especially Sarah Lodge, Kirsty Reade, and Helen Cook for all their support, tolerance, and help in developing this latest edition.

Preface

Welcome to the second edition of *Business Economics*. We were delighted with the response to the first edition but saw this updating of the book as an opportunity to add some new features. We have updated nearly all of the case studies and examples so that the data are fresh and contemporary and relate very much to what is happening in the business world around you. We have also tried to make this edition even more relevant to you and demonstrate how the subject can help you in your career.

Two key aims of this book have always been to make studying economics accessible and also to show how an understanding of this subject can be valuable in everyday and business life. To help achieve this we have rewritten the opening case studies to consider those issues being debated on an almost daily basis at the moment. Should the government intervene more in the economy and markets? Is the government programme of cutbacks a good or a bad thing? Can businesses be trusted? Does it matter if the pound is weak or strong? We hope that these will provoke much discussion.

We have also asked a number of people in business, ranging from consultants to entrepreneurs to managers, to write about how economics helps them in their jobs. These profiles showing economics in the workplace demonstrate how an understanding of economic theory directly relates to decision-making in business and can help you in your career. Now more than ever, with so much economic turmoil and debate, you will want to be able to understand these issues when you apply for jobs and start work.

Other features that are new to this edition are as follows.

You and economics   These show how much of your everyday life is affected by economics and economic theory—everything from your choice to go to university as opposed to getting a job straight from school, the impact of government policy on your standard of living, the prices you pay in the shops for different products, and even whether you will be able to afford a holiday abroad this year all involve the economic issues which are highlighted here.

Economics and organizations   This short feature at the end of each chapter offers a brief overview of the main organizations we think you would benefit from knowing about, such as the Bank of England, the World Trade Organization, and the Competition Commission. You will hear these organizations mentioned on the news regularly, so we thought it would be helpful to know something about them. We also give a link to their websites so you can find out more.

People and organizations   So often we study famous economists such as John Maynard Keynes and Milton Friedman and yet know nothing about them as people. In this feature we give you a little background information on leading economists.

Features which we have maintained from the first edition are as follows.

Business analysis   These features occur throughout each chapter and provide you with a short case to analyse. They allow you to apply the economic theory you have been studying in the chapter to a real-life context.

Data analysis   This is an opportunity to examine data and use your theory to explain the causes and effects of changes in it.

Think about it   These are reflective questions that get you to think about the material you have just read and consider whether it is always true, when it does not apply, and other factors that might also be significant.

End of chapter questions   These include some short answer questions to help you review your understanding of the chapter. There are also some discussion questions to review some of the key areas that have been covered.

We hope that you enjoy *Business Economics* and that the new features help you see the relevance of the subject. By the end of the textbook we hope that you will feel more comfortable analysing economic data, explaining the causes and effects of changes in economic variables, and making recommendations—all important skills in today's workplace.

If you have any feedback on this edition and/or suggestions for future ones we would love to hear from you. You can contact us on wattgill@aol.com

Introduction

1

Learning objectives

In this chapter, we provide an overview of the whole book. We also introduce some of the key tools that are used by economists, and hopefully we will start to show how you can think like an economist and why you might want to! These tools and this way of thinking will help you with your analysis of a wide range of topics which you are likely to want to come back to at various points in your studies. Get the basics right and everything follows from this.

By the end of this chapter, you should:

- ✓ appreciate the importance for managers of studying economics;
- ✓ understand what is meant by the external environment of business and PESTEL analysis;
- ✓ appreciate the difference between microeconomics and macroeconomics.

© **Case study**

Alison Mitchell joined The Look three months ago. The Look is a high street clothes retailer that is mainly based in the UK, but has some stores in continental Europe. Alison is a management trainee who recently finished her history degree at university. She has just come back from a management presentation in which the annual results of the company were announced. She left feeling slightly worried and a little confused.

'I know the economy has been doing badly and this has hit customer spending. Customers are worried about their jobs, which is not surprising given the high unemployment figures, and many of them have had their wealth hit hard by falling house prices. The economic climate is making everyone a little more cautious. This year's profits for the company were nearly £6 million, which is higher than our competitors. But the board of directors is apparently unhappy with this return, given the investment that has been made into the business. It wants a significant improvement in the coming year and stressed our role in making sure this happens. Six million is hardly a small number, but apparently it's not enough! We're now looking at cost-cutting measures including switching more to suppliers based in Vietnam. There are also plans for revenue growth by opening up stores in emerging markets, such as Russia and India. The growth rates of these economies are much faster than the UK and the board thinks that this opens up opportunities, although I don't think the weak value of the pound will help the expansion plans. In the UK, we've been told to prepare for a difficult future and look for ways of working more closely with our **stakeholders** to push up our profit margins.

What I don't understand is why none of the economists seemed to predict this downturn. What's the point of studying economics if you can't do anything with it?'

Questions

1. All businesses are involved in a transformation process that aims to add value as it converts inputs into outputs. Outline the transformation process that The Look undertakes and explain how a retailer can add value doing this.

2. What economic factors that can affect business success are highlighted in the above text? Are there others that you can think of?

3. What about other external, non-economic, factors?

4. Which other types of business do you think are likely to want to target economies such as India and Russia? Why?

5. If economists failed to predict the global downturn of 2008, is Alison right to say that there is no point studying economics?

What is an economy?

In the time it will take you to read this sentence billions of households and businesses around the world will have made trillions of decisions which will have helped to create millions of products to meet customers' needs which are sold to generate income. Households will be making decisions about where to shop, what to buy, where to work, and how much to work; businesses will be making decisions about what to produce and how best to produce it. These decisions come together in markets where buyers and sellers negotiate to decide on what is sold and at what price. There are markets for almost everything—food, gold, oil, labour, shares, and even carbon emission permits. Buyers and sellers negotiate, haggle, plead, and bargain to get the best deal for themselves. Businesses will be pursuing goals such as increasing their profits, while consumers will be trying to maximize their own satisfaction. To produce the output there are billions of other transactions being made to determine who works where for how much, what suppliers are used, and where production is going to take place. Therefore an economy is the result of trillions of decisions made individually by people acting as households, employees, employers, and managers trading in markets involving products, labour services, land and other resources. In some economies these transactions are relatively unregulated—people and businesses are left to decide for themselves what to do; in other economies they may be regulated or controlled by a government. This is because governments may wish to limit or control what is produced or how it is produced or who consumes it; they may even want to take control of the production themselves.

The decisions occurring in one country will also be affected by what is happening abroad—changes in overseas markets may influence decisions such as where you sell, where you work, what you can buy, and what you pay.

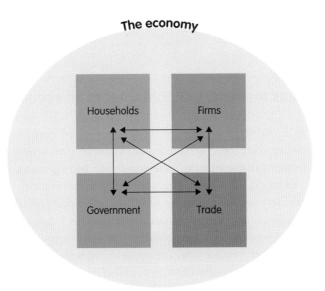

Figure 1.1 The economy

There are then four elements to an economy: households that provide the workforce and who consume products, businesses that employ and produce, governments that regulate and intervene, and trade-markets abroad that influence production and consumption in a country. These four elements interact via markets where they are buyers and sellers making rational choices to pursue their own interests.

 ## You and economics

You wake up early thanks to an alarm clock that you were bought when you first came to university. Your parents thought that you should have one and chose what they thought was the best value for money. It is a well-known American brand but was produced in China along with most of the consumer products you have. You are living in a student house not far from where your lectures are. Living there costs a little more than some of the other places you looked at, but you can get up 20 minutes later if you need to and still make lectures on time. To cover the rent you have a part-time job in a bar in the city centre. You earn the minimum wage but the hours are fairly flexible and you get to meet lots of people which you enjoy. You are studying for a management degree because you think that this will help you when it comes to getting a job later on. You work to a budget each week. Most of your money goes on food and rent, but you are trying to save for a new laptop for your studies.

With reference to the case study above, in what ways are you part of the economy:

a) as a consumer;

b) as part of the production process.

Think about what you did last week. In what ways were you interacting with businesses? The government? Foreign markets? Consumers?

Why all business managers should want to be economists

As we can see, an economy is a complex entity made up of decision-makers making choices and bargaining with others to find a deal. The role of an economist is to try and understand the decisions that are made, understand their consequences, and think about how to influence them. As a business manager you will also want to understand how these markets work. You will be overseeing an organization that provides goods and services, and to do this you must buy the resources you need; as a manager you are also an employee selling your services. Not surprisingly, you will try to understand the forces shaping the various markets you are in to anticipate changes and the impact of change. In recent years, there have been massive changes in global economies, leading to economies shrinking, banks closing, governments spending billions of pounds to try to save particular industries, and share prices collapsing. The result has been dramatic and frightening change in the business environment for many managers. Change may be the one constant of business, but the shocks that have occurred with economies shrinking in 2008 and many governments facing major debt crises have led most businesses to reconsider their strategies. Nothing highlights better that managers should not only want to be economists, but, in fact, cannot afford not to be. How badly would your sales be affected if you were to increase your price? Is the government's decision to change income tax for high-income earners going to have an impact on your sales? What effect would a higher interest rate have on your business? Which overseas markets are the ones to focus on? These are all important economic issues and, not surprisingly, managers should and will want to know the answers to such questions. And if you want to become a manager why not find out now so that you are one step ahead?

What is economics about?

Economics studies the way in which choices are made within an economy—for example, what products are made, what **resources** are used, and who gets what in an economy. By understanding economic theory, managers are able to make more sense of the business environment around them and make better decisions for their organizations. A failure to understand the economic environment leaves managers without a clear view of what is, or has been, happening in their markets and what is likely to happen in the future.

Managers need to understand how changes in economic conditions can affect the demand for their products and their costs. They need to understand economic theory to appreciate why changes have occurred, what the possible impact of changes might be, and how they should prepare for or respond to them. Gaining an understanding of economics provides managers with more insight into their environment, enabling them to develop more effective strategies to exploit the opportunities and helping them to make the best choices to use their resources most effectively and protect themselves from threats.

Business as a transformation process

All businesses are involved in a transformation process (see Figure 1.2), and managers oversee this process by planning, organizing, coordinating, and controlling it to ensure that it achieves the organization's objectives. They take resources, such as people, ideas, and land, and turn them into goods and services to provide to customers. The aim of this transformation process is to add value so that the outputs provided are worth more than the inputs used up in producing them. All around the world, millions of businesses identify different customer needs and wants, and transform resources in different ways to meet these needs so that they can meet their own objectives. For example:

- Fedex moves products around the world safely and quickly for their customers;
- Sony produces cameras, laptops, and makes films and music;
- Disneyland provides an entertainment experience;

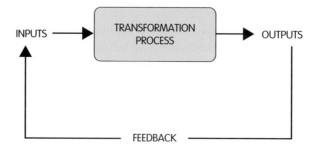

Figure 1.2 The transformation process

- Fox produces films;
- Management consultants McKinsey provide advice;
- Toni & Guy cuts hair.

The transformation process will be constantly reviewed as feedback suggests whether or not it is effective; a failure to sell or to make a profit may make managers review the inputs used or the nature of the process itself. With a fall in profits, for example, managers may move resources out of one type of business into another. Over the last fifty years in the UK, for example, resources have been shifted out of sectors such as farming, whilst other sectors such as education and finance have grown significantly. An economist is interested in issues such as why businesses choose to produce the products they do and what determines the best method of production—where should the business produce and what combination of different resources should it use? Similarly, the manager wants to know what to provide and how best to provide it.

The resources available to a business to use in the transformation process include the following.

- **Land** This refers to the physical resources in an economy and includes the minerals, climate, and natural resources in the area. What matters here is the quantity and also the quality of resources available: some countries have much more physical space than others (compare China with the UK, for example); some have more of some natural resources than others (think of oil in Saudi Arabia and diamonds in South Africa); some have warmer climates (think of Brazil compared with Norway). Therefore the land resources of different economies vary considerably at any time, and this will affect what can be produced in each region. Land is relatively fixed, although countries do sometimes try to expand the amount of land they have, for example by reclaiming land from the sea as countries such as Holland and the United Arab Emirates have done.

- **Population** The impact of the population on the amount that a country can produce will depend on the quantity of people, but also on their 'quality' in terms of contributing to the transformation process; this means that you need to consider factors such as their number, age, health, and skills. Changes in the population structure will affect the resources available to businesses in a country as well as affecting demand. In 2004, eight Eastern European countries (including Latvia, Lithuania, and Poland, as well as Malta and Cyprus), joined the **European Union** (EU), which made the movement of people to the UK far easier. Between May 2004 and December 2006, this led to over half a million people from these accession countries coming into the UK. This provided a source of cheap labour in the UK, particularly in factories, bars, cafés, restaurants and hotels, and construction, thereby providing a valuable resource. Another population issue facing many developed economies is an ageing population, which means that the working population has to support more retired people.

- *Capital* This refers to the quantity and quality of capital goods in an economy. A 'capital good' is one that is used to produce other goods in the future: for example, factories, office premises, machines, and equipment. The value of this resource depends on the amount and quality of the capital goods which, in turn, depends on the level of technology. Investment is essential to the growth of an economy; it can lead to more efficient processes, innovation, and greater **productivity**. Imagine trying to build a house using only your hands; now imagine using tools such as a bulldozer and a crane, and you will see the benefits of investment. Investment provides the equipment that can fuel economic growth. If a business within an economy focuses on consuming now rather than investing in capital equipment, it is likely to experience slower economic growth in the future.

- *Ideas and enterprise* Economies benefit from entrepreneurs—that is, people who have ideas and think of new business opportunities. Entrepreneurs set up new businesses, which create jobs and provide more goods and services for customers. Entrepreneurs identify new possibilities for products and processes that help move an economy forward. This is why governments often encourage start-ups.

These different resources can be transformed into goods and services in an enormous variety of ways, such as refining, manufacturing, transporting, teaching, designing, and building. Look at all of the businesses in your local area and you will appreciate the many different ways in which resources are combined.

? *Think about it ...*   1.1

Dubai is situated on the Persian Gulf coast of the United Arab Emirates. The Emirate of Dubai shares borders with Abu Dhabi in the south, Sharjah in the northeast, and the Sultanate of Oman in the southeast. Dubai covers an area of 1,588 square miles (4,110 km²), which represents a significant expansion beyond its initial designation of 1,500 square miles (3,900 km²) due to land reclamation from the sea. What factors do you think determine whether land reclamation is worthwhile?

The aim of these transformation processes is to create products that are worth more than the cost of the resources used up in the process of providing the products. The worth of a product and the costs of providing it are usually (not always) measured in monetary terms—that is, the aim is to produce a product for which customers are willing to pay more than it costs to provide, thus generating a profit for the business. To add value and meet their own needs, businesses try to enable customers to meet their needs as well, highlighting the interdependence that occurs in an economy.

Opportunity cost

To make the transformation process happen, investors and managers must make a number of decisions such as who to produce for and exactly what to produce. Managers are constantly making decisions about which projects to invest in and which business ideas to pursue. To decide on the best option, they need to measure the likely returns on a project in relation to the investment. For example, if a particular project would cost more than it is likely to earn, it should not be pursued; the resources should be used elsewhere.

This highlights the concept of **opportunity cost**. Opportunity cost measures the benefits given up in relation to the next best alternative. For example, a decision to put more money into advertising a product means that this money cannot be used to modify the product. This alternative has been sacrificed. The alternatives to any action need to be considered before choosing which ideas or projects to pursue. For example, investing in a new marketing campaign might make a £2 million profit, but it might be that, with the same investment, you could develop a new product and make £3 million profit. Opportunity cost is a fundamentally important concept in business and economics: whenever a decision is made, another option has been given up; just because one choice offers a reward does not make it the right choice, because of what is being sacrificed. When making a decision a manager should also consider the risk involved and the consequences of failure. This is the probability of the project going wrong and an assessment of the damage this might cause. A decision that offers high potential returns but with an extremely high risk involved may be less appealing than one that has reasonable returns with very low risk.

 ## You and economics

There always seems to be too much to do—assignments to research and hand in, people to see, places to go, films to watch, and music to download. But fitting it all in is not easy and you are forced to make choices between what is the best use of your time. If you don't get the assignment done today, you know that you'll need to catch up later and won't be able to go to Marie's party on Saturday. That's opportunity cost.

Questioning the most effective use of resources is a key management skill. Are the resources that are being used **adding value** sufficiently and helping to generate a high enough return for the business, given the risk involved and the opportunity costs? Should they be used elsewhere instead? Understanding how resources should be allocated efficiently (that is, how they are used without wastage) and effectively (that is, ensuring that they are used for the right purpose) is at the heart of business management and economics.

The most common measure of how effectively resources are being used in business is profit. This shows that the value of the output sold is greater than the costs of providing it. But when measuring the performance of other, less financially driven, organizations such as hospitals, community centres, or political parties, other measures of performance are required. Even when assessing business performance many stakeholders use a range of measures. For example, Elkington put forward a model suggesting that businesses should measure People, Planet and Profits—that is, the financial rewards earned and the impact of the business on the environment and on its staff. If you look at the websites of most large companies you will see a wide range of indicators of business performance.

? Think about it ...   1.2

1. What do you think is the best way of deciding how well a university is performing?

2. What about a hospital?

3. In what ways, apart from profit, might a business such as BP, the multinational energy company, measure its success?

4. If you worked for a business, how would you measure the success of your employer?

As economic conditions change, the inputs you use, the way in which you transform your resources or even what you actually produce may need to change as well.

- Higher wages or rents in the UK may encourage businesses to relocate aspects of production abroad.

- Lower costs of borrowing may encourage investment in new technology.

- Changes in the levels of demand in the economy may affect your sales and your expansion plans.

- Falling incomes might lead you to introduce a budget line of products.

- New entrants may force you to modify and improve your product.

Therefore managers must prepare for, and react to, economic change. This change can be at a local, national, or international level: for example, the community council tax in the UK is set by local authorities, the income tax rate paid by employees is set by the national government, and taxes on foreign products are set by the European Union.

Classifying production

Businesses produce many different types of product. These can be classified in different ways, as follows.

- *Goods versus services* Goods are physical items, such as iPhones and guitars; they are tangible. Goods can be stored by businesses in anticipation of future demand. The customer can touch them and inspect them before buying. Services are intangible items, such as a karate class or medical advice. These cannot be stockpiled and customers cannot physically see what they are buying; consequently they rely on other indicators, such as word of recommendation or inspections by regulating bodies, to provide a stamp of approval.

The distinction between a good and service is not always clear. When you visit a restaurant, you are buying the food (a good) and the environment of the restaurant (a service). When you choose where to shop, you are influenced by the items that are stocked, but also the quality of the service. When you study for a degree, the lectures are a service, but elements, such as the lecture handouts and the degree certificate, are physical products. When you visit a theme park, the physical goods are the tickets and food that you buy; the service is the experience that you get on the rides.

- *Economic versus free goods* To produce the vast majority of products, resources have to be used up; these resources could be used elsewhere and therefore have an opportunity cost. For example, to produce more cars it is necessary to sacrifice something else, such as the production of furniture, because resources will have been diverted into one sector rather than another. When sacrifices have to be made to increase production of a particular product, that item is known as an 'economic good'. By comparison, in some rare cases, a product is provided 'free of charge'; no sacrifices have to be made, and so there is no opportunity cost. For example, air simply exists and no sacrifice is needed to provide it. This type of product is known as a 'free good'.

- *Capital versus consumption products* Capital items are products that are bought to help in the production process and create more products in the long term. They represent an investment for the future: for example, a company may invest in new technology. These goods are not bought to consume themselves, but because of their contribution to the transformation process and their ability to create consumption products in the future. Consumption items, by comparison, are products that are for immediate use, such as food and holidays. If all spending in an economy were to be on consumption products, there would be no investment for the future.

? *Think about it ...*   1.3

You have earned £1,000 from some part-time work. What might be an example of how you used this money (a) for short run consumption and (b) for long-term investment?

You and economics

You have won £40,000 on the lottery. Do you spend it all now and enjoy yourself or save it and try to earn more money for later? This is the sort of decision—choosing between now and the future—that all individuals and businesses, and indeed governments, make. The more you enjoy yourself now, the less money you are putting aside for the future, so what's it to be—some great nights out, some fantastic holidays, and a lot more taxis, or more money in your pension fund?

Sectors of the economy

There are many ways in which businesses can transform resources. To assess how different businesses are performing and to monitor changes in their performance over time, it is useful to categorize businesses in some way.

For example, we can distinguish between the following.

- *Primary, secondary, and tertiary businesses* The primary sector comprises businesses involved in the extraction of, and production using, natural resources—for example, farming, oil extraction, and forestry. The secondary sector refers to manufacturing and construction—these take materials and turn them into finished and semi-finished products. The tertiary sector refers to services such as finance and tourism. Economies can differ significantly in the composition of their business. For example, the UK is now dominated by the tertiary sector, whereas many developing economies depend on the primary sector.

- *The size of businesses* The size of a business can be measured in several ways. For example, you could measure the value of sales, the number of employees, or the number of outlets. In most economies, there are far more smaller enterprises than larger ones. In the European Union, small and medium-sized enterprises (SMEs) comprise approximately 99 per cent of all businesses and employ between them about 65 million people.

- *Private and public sector businesses* Businesses that are owned by private individuals and organizations are part of the private sector; for example, BT, Ford, and IBM are private sector organizations. Businesses that are owned by the government are part of the public sector. Some organizations are part-owned by the government and private owners; for example, the UK government bought a controlling interest in the Royal Bank of Scotland in 2008 when this bank was in difficulty. In the UK, there are also a number of public–private partnerships (PPPs) in which both sectors work together to provide a service. Private sector businesses tend to pursue profit to reward their investors and owners. Public sector organizations are overseen by government ministers and committees, but are ultimately owned by everyone in the country. These organizations are more likely to have social objectives, such as improving the welfare of the country's citizens, even if this does not maximize profits.

Think about it...   1.4

1. Think of three large private sector organizations in your economy. What do you think their objectives are?
2. How might these objectives differ from those of much smaller organizations?
3. Can you think of organizations in your economy that are owned by the government. What do you think their objectives are?

Business analysis   1.1

Table 1.1 Biggest companies in the world based on sales, profits, assets, and market value

Rank	Company	Country	Sales (US$ bn)	Profits (US$ bn)	Assets (US$ bn)	Market value (US$ bn)
1	Exxon Mobil	USA	433.5	41.1	331.1	407.4
2	JPMorgan Chase	USA	110.8	19	2,265.8	170.1
3	General Electric	USA	147.3	14.2	717.2	213.7
4	Royal Dutch Shell	Netherlands	470.2	30.9	340.5	227.6
5	ICBC	China	82.6	25.1	2,039.1	237.4
6	HSBC Holdings	UK	102	16.2	2,550	164.3
7	PetroChina	China	310.1	20.6	304.7	294.7
8	Berkshire Hathaway	USA	143.7	10.3	392.6	202.2
9	Wells Fargo	USA	87.6	15.9	1,313.9	178.7
10	Petrobras-Petróleo Brasil	Brazil	145.9	20.1	319.4	180

Source: Forbes 2012

1. Why do you think so many of the biggest businesses in the world are involved in oil and gas operations?
2. Why do you think so many are from the USA or China?
3. Can you think of other industries that tend to have large companies?

Business as an open system

A business can be regarded as a system. This is because it comprises a number of different elements that need to work together for success. Within an organization there are, for example:

- *marketing activities*, which focus on understanding the market and customer, developing a marketing strategy, and developing a set of marketing plans (such as developing the product, setting the price, developing the promotional mix, and developing the distribution channels);

- *operations activities*, which focus on decisions such as location, new product development, developing the method of production, managing stock levels, maintaining quality, and deciding on the best way of delivering the products;

- *financial activities*, which are involved in raising finance, budgeting, managing cash flow, and producing financial reports;

- *human resources (HR) activities*, which involve decisions relating to the recruitment and selection of staff, developing remuneration systems, training, and career development.

All these activities must combine to contribute towards the overall corporate strategy. For example, a decision to expand the business may require an increased marketing effort to boost demand while also increasing the capacity to be able to provide necessary products; this, in turn, may need investment provided by the finance function and the recruitment of staff to produce the products required.

Businesses are open systems because they interact with their environment. Business activities will be affected by, for example, changes in legislation or the population. At the same time, business behaviour will influence the external environment, such as the wealth of the local community or levels of pollution.

Therefore it is important for managers to analyse the external environment and understand their place within in. This can be undertaken using **PESTEL analysis** (see Figure 1.3).

PESTEL analysis

PESTEL analysis provides a framework for managers when examining the external environment. It helps managers to categorize the relevant issues in their environment, so that they can assess their relative importance and develop an appropriate strategy (see Figure 1.4).

The letters in the acronym stand for the following factors.

- *Political* For example, a government may sign a treaty with another country that makes trade easier or more difficult. Over the last fifty years, the European Union has expanded considerably, which makes it easier for British firms to export within Europe. It started with six member countries in 1951 and now has twenty-seven members, with other countries wanting to join.

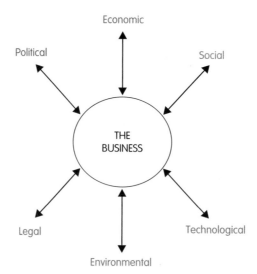

Figure 1.3 PESTEL analysis examines the relationship between a business and political, economic, social, technological, environmental, and legal factors

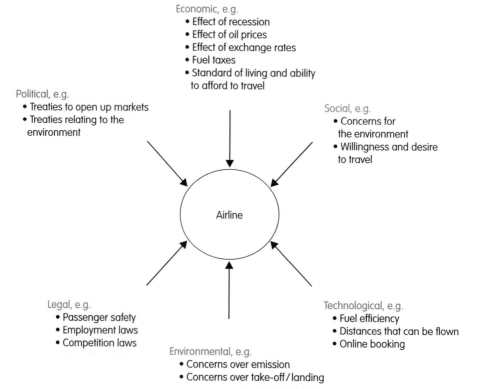

Figure 1.4 PESTEL analysis for an airline

- *Economic* These refer to local, national, or international economic conditions, which can affect a business in terms of its supply and demand conditions. For example, a change in the cost of borrowing money may affect the ability of a business to expand and influence the amount that customers are willing to spend.

- *Social* These include factors such as population size and the age of the population. For example, in the UK the average age of the population is increasing, which will affect the demand for different goods and services (e.g. blood pressure tablets and care homes).

- *Technological* This refers to changes, such as developments in the speed of accessing the internet, which can create business opportunities, such as online banking and video streaming.

- *Environmental* This refers to changes, such as global warming, which influence what is produced, as well as the production methods that a business will use as it tries to be more environmentally friendly in its approach.

- *Legal* This refers to factors such as national or local government legislation. For example, changes in the national minimum wage may affect the costs of a business.

£ Business analysis — 1.2

Table 1.2 Demography in China and the USA

	China	USA
Total fertility rate, 2010	1.56	2.08
Population growth, 2010–50 (%)*	−3.4	+30.0
Peak population year	2026	NA†
Median age, 2010	34.5	36.9
Median age, 2050*	48.7	40.0
Population aged 20–24, 2010 (million)	120	22
Population aged 20–24, 2050 (million)*	63	25
Change in share of population (% points) 2010–50		
Under 15	−5.5	−1.3
15–64	−11.4	−6.9
Over 65	+17.4	+8.1*

*UN projection (medium variant)

†Population still rising

Source: United Nations

What do you think are the possible business implications of the demographic data above for US and Chinese businesses?

Monitoring the external environment is an important part of a manager's job. Managers should be looking for future changes in the environment that create opportunities and threats. Using your own sales team and analysing your own data can help you to do this, as well as studying other sources, such as government publications and information provided by industry associations.

An 'opportunity' is a change that is potentially beneficial for a business. A 'threat' is a change that is potentially damaging to a business. Whether a change is an opportunity or a threat depends on the nature of the change, and on the strengths and weaknesses of the business. The development of e-books may be an opportunity for companies, such as Amazon and Apple, which already have the appropriate skills and resources in electronic markets. It could be a threat to traditional publishers, such as Penguin, which may not have the same experience in producing electronic products. The growth of mobile phone usage might be a threat to the calculator and watch industries because mobile phones have calculators and clocks as one of their features, but may be an opportunity to the network operators.

Understanding, predicting, and preparing for external change is very important for managers so that they can exploit opportunities as they arise and protect themselves against potential threats. For example, the **exchange rate** is vitally important for any business involved in trading with customers or other companies abroad because it influences the price of products sold to, or bought from, other countries. If the exchange rate is US$1.5 : £1, a £100 product costs US$150; if the exchange rate changes to US$1.8 : £1, the same product will now cost US$180 simply because of the exchange rate movement. Over 50 per cent of the Minis produced in Oxford by BMW are sold in the USA; imagine how important changes in the value of the pound relative to the dollar are to the company and its success. If you were to fail to understand the implications of a change in the exchange rate, this would most likely mean that you would miss opportunities to target particular countries or fail to plan properly for price increases. Therefore an understanding of economics should help managers to understand the relevant issues in their environment and plan more effectively to help the business to succeed.

 ## You and economics

You are regularly getting information about the external environment from a range of sources—television, radio, online media, your friends, your lectures. From this you hear about a range of economic factors, such as the latest figures on unemployment and growth of the economy, what the government plans are, and the latest offers at the supermarket. All this data might influence your decisions, such as where to shop and what you should expect as wages. You are also picking up information directly when you shop—for example, you immediately see what is happening to prices and you can decide what is good value for money.

Stakeholders

All business activities affect, and are affected by, other individuals and organizations. These individuals and groups are called **stakeholders**, and they include the community, suppliers, employees, investors, the government, and distributors. These groups may try to change a firm's behaviour; for example, suppliers may request faster payment to improve their cash flow and employees may ask for better working conditions (see Table 1.3). Managers' decisions will also have a direct effect on them. Expansion of a business may put pressure on local amenities, such as the road system, and a decision to relocate may cost local jobs.

When considering whether a decision is fair (not necessarily whether it is economically efficient), managers may want to consider the impact on the different stakeholder groups. Some managers adopt what is called a 'stakeholder approach'—that is, they believe that a partnership approach with these groups will enable all of them to benefit. Better relationships with staff may cost more in the **short run**, but can lead to greater productivity and better performance in the **long run**. Similarly, working closely with suppliers may mean higher and faster payment for them, but can also help to ensure quality and continuity of supply. Other managers adopt a stakeholder approach that focuses only on the rewards to investors; this type of manager believes that the views and interests of other stakeholders should not be considered. The only thing to focus on is profit; everything else is a distraction. There are of course a range of ways of dealing with stakeholders (see Figure 1.5). The way managers treat different groups may depend on their strength and their level of interest in the business. The more interested and the more powerful a group is, the more managers may want to cooperate with them.

Business analysis   1.3

In 2012 Prime Minister David Cameron said that the UK needs to build an economy that is fairer. He argued that the economy needs to allow everyone to share in the success of business and the markets and criticized the bonus culture that had been prevalent in the financial sector and which Cameron said had been out of control.

The Prime Minister wants to encourage firms to show greater social responsibility and used John Lewis as an example of best practice. John Lewis is an employee cooperative. This means that it is owned by its employees (called partners), all of whom have one vote in the organization.

1. Do you think markets promote morality?
2. Do you think cooperatives are desirable?

Table 1.3 Stakeholder objectives

Stakeholder	Possible objective
Investors	High share price, good dividends
Employees	Job security, career development, good pay
Suppliers	Reasonable terms, payment on time, long-term contracts
Community	Jobs, environmentally friendly production
Government	Exports, jobs, environmentally friendly production

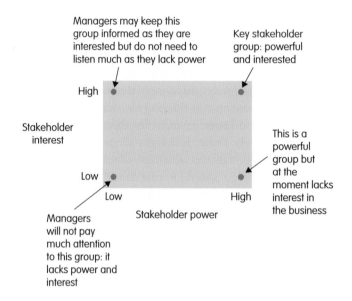

Figure 1.5 Stakeholder map

 You and economics

Who is affected by your decisions regarding shopping, working, studying? Do you keep these groups informed?

Draw a stakeholder map of your different stakeholder groups.

The economic environment

As we have seen, the economic environment is an element of the external environment. Economic change can affect businesses on both the demand and supply side.

- On the *demand* side, economic change can affect factors such as the income and confidence of customers, which in turn affects their spending and levels of demand;

- On the *supply* side, economic changes can affect factors such as the price of resources and therefore costs, which in turn will affect profits.

Changes in factors such as the income of the country, the value of a currency, the prices of resources, the degree of competition in a market, levels of unemployment, and the cost of borrowing are all examples of economic factors that can play a very important role in the success or failure of a business.

Economic changes can be very dramatic. Most people did not expect the sudden collapse of many banks across the world in 2008 and 2009. In such situations, managers often have to make important decisions on the basis of imperfect information. In other cases, the change may happen over a much longer period of time. For example, the decline of the mining sector in the UK has happened over many years as it became uncompetitive relative to other countries. In this situation, managers have more time to understand the issues and plan ahead; in theory, this should make managing change easier.

? Think about it ...   1.5

What are the main economic issues being debated at the moment?

What do you think are significant changes that have occurred in your economy over the last five years?

Economics and employability

Tell us your name and a little bit about your degree.
My name is Anastasia Butakova and I'm studying at London School of Economics, doing a degree in pure economics. I've just finished my first year in which I've covered four subjects: economics, mathematics, statistics, and political science.

What made you choose to study economics at university?
I chose economics because I have a real passion for the subject. I first studied economics as one of my A-level subjects and that is when my interest in the discipline started to develop. My teacher made the lessons really fun and interesting, so I started reading around the subject. The first books I read were *Freakonomics* and *Undercover Economist* which give me an idea of what economics is by applying it to everyday life. Afterwards, I moved on to Paul Krugman's blog and his various books in order to broaden my knowledge. Once I had covered a good grasp of theoretical concepts, I started reading *The Economist* so that I could identify the models and theories and see whether they are working in real-world economics. As a result I've become interested in current affairs.

Another important reason why I chose economics as my major is to have good career prospects once I graduate. Studying economics helps to develop the skills which will come in useful in many jobs: consulting, investment banking, financial advisory, risk management, auditing, setting up a business or helping to maintain or redeem the existing one, or doing academic work. Also, studying economics provides a good balance of both mathematical and evaluative skills; I'm being taught how to follow a familiar set of rules, yet also how to argue my own point of view given the facts and evidence. I think these are the qualities that many employers are looking for.

Finally, it goes without saying that economics is everywhere. Its importance is growing, as real-world economics is becoming less easy to predict; more people become interested and aware of what's going on in the economic world.

In what ways do you think the subject is useful?
Fundamentally, economics is useful for policy-making, for improving the economies in the world, and helping to create more economic prosperity. Even though economic models are often criticized for being imperfect, by constantly updating and improving our knowledge of economics we can avoid making mistakes in the future and create models that will help to make the right decisions.

Economics improves the understanding of the real world, and allows people to form their own opinions on current affairs and to really understand what the government is doing and what targets it is pursuing.

Besides developing essay-writing skills, economics also helps to develop a more analytical way of thinking: rather than just applying a familiar algorithm to the same situation, in economics you have to evaluate a model, situation, or theory. Therefore economics teaches us to think logically and independently and provides a good lesson in decision-making.

Microeconomics and macroeconomics

The study of economics can be divided into two sections, although these are interrelated.

- *Microeconomics* ('micro' meaning small) focuses on the study of specific markets—for example, the markets for oil, for clothes, or for computer games. Managers may be interested in how much competition there is in their markets, how easy it is for other firms to enter, and the projected growth of the market. Analysing conditions in a given market can help to explain changes such as the price, output, quality, and likely profits in a market.

- *Macroeconomics* ('macro' meaning large) analyses the economy as a whole—that is, all the different markets combined. Whereas microeconomics focuses on the price of one product, macroeconomics focuses on the general price level in the economy. Whereas microeconomics examines the output in one market, macroeconomics examines the total output of the economy. Each individual may make a decision about what to buy and where to work; each business may decide what to produce and what price to sell its output at. When these decisions are all combined (aggregated), this forms the macroeconomy.

Managers will be interested in what happens in both their own market (microeconomics) and the economy as a whole (macroeconomics). An understanding of microeconomic analysis may help them to predict what will happen to their costs or the prices in the markets in which they compete. An understanding of macroeconomics might help them to understand what is happening to broader factors in the economy, such as the average income level, the general level of prices, and the rate of growth in the economy.

 ## Business analysis   1.4

The Cuban economy has been struggling badly in recent years. It has suffered as a result of the global economic crisis of 2008 and its aftermath because this reduced incomes abroad and led to less tourism to Cuba. At the same time lower levels of economic growth reduced demand for and the price of oil, which hit Venezuela which relies on oil exports. Unfortunately for Cuba, Venezuela is a major financial supporter and so when its income was hurt it cut back on its aid. Then, to make matters worse, a hurricane wiped out a lot of Cuba's crops, making it dependent on food imports. This happened at a time when world food prices were increasing and the price of nickel, Cuba's main export, was falling.

Identify the various factors in Cuba's external environment that might have hindered the growth of the Cuban economy.

People and economics

Alfred Marshall (1842–1924) was a British economist and one of the most important writers of his time. His book *Principles of Economics* (1890) provided one of the most comprehensive analysis of supply, demand and marginal utility, and the cost of production there had ever been. He is known as one of the founders of economics. In his book he writes:

> Economics is a study of man in the ordinary business of life. It enquires how he gets his income and how he uses it. Thus, it is on the one side, the study of wealth and on the other and more important side, a part of the study of man.

Marshall was the first economist to explain that demand falls as price increases, and that the demand curve slopes downwards from left to right. He was also first to explain the concept of the price elasticity of demand and the concept of consumer surplus.

Current issues

Once you start studying economics you will realize that it relates to all aspects of the world around us. It helps us to understand issues and also to decide what actions should be taken. However, there is still plenty of room for debate in terms of what the priorities should be, what's the best policy to adopt, what the possible consequences of a policy may be, and what the long-term effects might be. Economics relates to decision-making and allocating resources. Policy decisions may want to influence what is consumed, how it is produced, and who gets the output. Just look at some of these issues below, all of which may require government intervention. Economics helps us decide what the priorities are and the best policies to adopt. Current economic issues include the following.

- What is the best way of protecting the environment whilst enabling economic growth?
- Should smokers be entitled to healthcare?
- Should prostitution be legalized? What about cannabis?
- Should drivers be taxed according to how many miles they drive?
- Should we build nuclear power stations or can we use wind power?

Economists help policy-makers to decide whether to subsidise, tax, ban, or encourage different activities. Therefore economists are key members of any government, and indeed any business. In the next chapter we shall see how economists analyse data to make decisions.

Summary

Businesses undertake a transformation process, taking resources and adding value to these to produce goods and services worth more than the inputs used up in the process. Businesses are an open system in which managers are affected by the external environment.

This environment can be analysed using PESTEL analysis, which examines political, economic, social, technological, environmental, and legal factors.

Economists build models to understand how markets and economies work. They aim to understand how choices are made and how resources are allocated. To build these models, they make assumptions about the objectives of individuals, employees, and managers. To construct and use these models, economists must be able to interpret data, which requires an understanding of concepts such as marginals, averages, totals, index numbers, and weighted indices.

Checklist

Having read this chapter, you should now understand:

- [ ] the importance of economics to managers;
- [ ] the transformation process;
- [ ] the difference between micro- and macroeconomics;
- [ ] the difference between capital and consumption goods;
- [ ] the difference between primary, secondary, and tertiary sectors;
- [ ] the difference between the private and public sectors;
- [ ] the meaning of business as an open system.

Short answer questions

1. What's the difference between micro- and macroeconomics?
2. What is meant by the external environment of business?
3. What is meant by PESTEL analysis?
4. What is the level of unemployment in your country at the moment?
5. What is the growth rate of your economy at the moment?
6. Is the cost of borrowing money (the interest rate) at the moment fairly high or low?
7. Explain two economic factors that might affect the success of a business.
8. Why do managers need to understand economics?
9. Are businesses in your economy mainly operating in the primary, secondary, or tertiary sector?
10. What is the difference between the private and the public sector?

Discussion questions

1. To what extent is the economy likely to be the key external factor determining the success of businesses?
2. Discuss the possible value to managers of undertaking PESTEL analysis.

3. What two changes in your economy in recent years do you think are likely to be most important for businesses? Justify your choices.

One step further

Visit our Online Resource Centre at **www.oxfordtextbooks.co.uk/orc/gillespiebusiness2e/** to test your understanding, watch video walk-throughs, and access further information on topics covered in this chapter.

Thinking like an economist

2

Learning objectives

In this chapter, we highlight some of the ways that economists look at the world and introduce some of the key tools that they use. Hopefully, we will start to show you how you can think like an economist.

By the end of this chapter, you should:

- ☑ understand the meaning of index numbers;
- ☑ understand the difference between nominal and real values;
- ☑ understand the difference between absolute figures and growth rates;
- ☑ understand averages and totals;
- ☑ understand the marginal condition;
- ☑ be able to explain the reasons why economists produce models;
- ☑ understand the value of index numbers and weighted indices;
- ☑ understand the difference between normative and positive economics;
- ☑ understand the difference between fairness and efficiency.

© **Case study**

'To be honest there's an awful lot I don't understand—and the older I get the more I realize I don't know! I sometimes wish I had studied economics instead of music at university,' said George.

George was talking to Chloe who was an economist at Merrill Lynch bank. 'For example, on the news they say that inflation is falling, but when I go shopping I can see that prices are going up. How does that work? Then they say that China is growing fast, but when I was travelling there last year I could see an awful lot of people on very low incomes. And how can the Chinese economy have a higher income than the UK if people there are living on such low wages?'

'Having said that, they say that people in the UK generally earn something like £24,000 but lots of the people I know don't earn that. Then the boss of my orchestra company told us all last week that we should be grateful for a pay increase of 1 per cent in these difficult times. I am not sure why I should be grateful—I know I feel worse off. The accounts show that the orchestra made a profit of £40,000 last year so how come she said she was disappointed that it was not enough? She started muttering something about the return on investment, but I had no idea what that was. I know for a fact that we only made £39,000 the year before, but my boss said that was not a real increase. Seems real to me! And when I challenged her on the fact that her salary was nearly twice mine she told me that was the way that markets worked and it was perfectly efficient. It may be efficient but it's not fair—I work just as hard as her if not harder! I tell you Chloe, the world's crazy enough as it is without economists confusing us even more.'

Chloe listened patiently. 'Let me begin at the beginning,' she said.

Questions

1. How can your wages increase but you end up worse off?
2. What is meant by a 'return on investment'? Why do you think that this is an important concept?
3. Why might the boss of the orchestra earn more than twice as much as George? Do you think that this is efficient? Is it fair?
4. Can you have inflation and lower prices?
5. Can China be growing faster than the UK but have less income per person?

Introduction

In the first chapter we examined the role of business and its interrelationship with the economic environment. In this chapter, we consider how economists think and what tools they have at their disposal to examine a given situation and understand the causes and consequences of change. These tools enable economists and managers to understand a problem more fully, and thereby to understand the potential effects and how best to react to, or prepare for, change. This chapter provides a background to the rest of the book, and you may well want to refer back to it at various points later on.

While it is important for managers to understand economic issues, they also need to think like economists to analyse and make judgements. Economics involves the study of choices; so does management. Economics looks at how resources are allocated and the returns are generated in different market conditions. Therefore the key tools used by economists are also vital for managers.

What does an economist do?

An economist studies all the different transactions and decisions occurring within an economy and thinks about how decisions are made, whether they lead to a desirable outcome, and what else could have been done instead. An economist tries to build models to make sense of the real world and, having explained what has happened, he/she wants to be able to predict what will happen next. An economist is always learning because conditions and behaviours change and so he/she will be improving the models he/she uses. An economist is interested in the choices that are made. At any point in time households have limited budgets, employees have limited skills and time, and businesses have limited funds. This means that they all have to make choices about how to use these resources most effectively in order to meet their own objectives as successfully as possible. What to buy? Where to work? What to invest in? Economists examine these decisions and their outcomes, and analyse what happens in different markets and countries.

? Think about it...   2.1

1. Many economic models assume we are rational and therefore that the 'principle of transitivity' holds. This principle states that if A is better than B and B is better than C, then A must be better than C. Is this true of our behaviour? If you prefer band X to band Y, and band Y to band Z, does this automatically mean you prefer X to Z? Or if football team A beats B and B beats C, will A always beat C?

2. A 50 per cent increase in quantity offered to customers as a special offer is the same as a 33 per cent discount in price. A rational consumer would realize this. Which do you think most customers would choose?

Business analysis 2.1

Interpreting data

An important skill for economists is the ability to analyse data and understand trends and links between different pieces of information. This can help make sense of the past and help improve decision-making in the future. An economist needs to be able to look at data and explain what might have caused changes in it and what the effects of such changes might be, as well as being able to make a judgement on the relative importance of a given change. For example, when considering the effects of a change in the overall income of a particular economy, you might want to know why it has occurred, what is likely to happen in the future, and how sensitive demand for your product is to changes in the income of this specific region.

When analysing data, an economist may consider the following.

Absolute versus relative numbers

Some data may be presented in absolute terms. For example, the profits of a business may be £250,000 this year—that is, an absolute number. But to know whether this is a 'good' level of profit, you might want to compare it with something else—that is, you might want to think about the scale of it *relative* to another figure.

For example, you may want to compare the profit figure with the level of sales that generated it: if sales were £5 million and profits were £250,000, this means that profits were 5 per cent of sales. This is known as the 'profit margin' and is calculated as

$$\text{profit margin} = (\text{profit/sales}) \times 100\%$$

In this case

$$\text{profit margin} = (£250,000/£5,000,000) \times 100 = 5\%$$

You might also want to know how your profits relate to the number of people you employ. For example, if you have ten employees and your profits were £250,000, your profits per employee were £25,000. Profits per employee are calculated as

$$\text{profit per employee} = \text{profit/number of employees}$$

In this case

$$\text{profit per employee} = £250,000/10 = £25,000$$

You might also want to know about your profits in relation to the investment that has been made in the project or the business. For example, if the investment was £2.5 million and profits were £250,000, this means that the return on investment (ROI) is 10 per cent. ROI is calculated as

$$\text{ROI} = (\text{profit/investment}) \times 100\%$$

In this case

$$\text{ROI} = (£250,000/£2,500,000) \times 100 = 10\%$$

Data analysis   2.1

The data in Figure 2.1 shows UK government spending. The spending on education was £91 billion in this financial year.

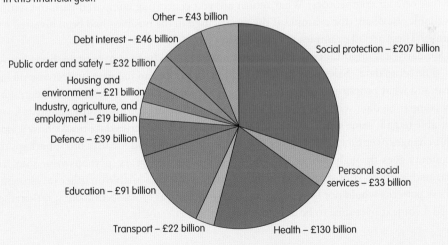

Figure 2.1 Government spending and government taxes
Source: HM Treasury. Crown Copyright

1. Why is it useful to see spending on other items?
2. What else do you think you would want to know to decide whether the government was spending enough on education in this year?

Data analysis   2.2

Marks and Spencer plc (M&S) is a leading UK retailer. For the financial year ending 2012:

turnover (revenue)	£9.9 billion
profit before tax	£0.65 billion
number of employees	81,000
capital invested in the business	£7.8 billion

To assess the profits of the business, you may want to compare it with other data such as the level of sales or investment.

1. Calculate its profit margin (i.e. the profit per sale). This shows the profit that M&S makes for every pound spent in its stores.
2. Calculate the profit per employee.
3. Calculate the company's ROI.

Trends and comparisons (time series and cross-section data)

When analysing data, it is often useful to relate it to other organizations or countries. Analysing data for different businesses or countries at a particular point in time is known as 'cross-section data': you are gaining an insight into a business, an industry, or an economy in comparison with others at a specific date. How high is your profit margin relative to that of your competitors? What return are you generating compared with the returns available elsewhere (for example, if the money used in the business had been invested in a bank)? These are all examples of cross-section data.

Similarly, it is important to look at how a variable has changed over time; this is known as 'time series data'. Sales may be £200 million, but is this an increase or decrease on last year and what proportion of the total sales in the market as a whole does this represent? By comparing data with the past or with other similar organizations (or countries), you are able to gain some sense of its relative significance. Time series data tracks how a variable changes over time. This enables you to identify trends and identify links: perhaps the economy goes through periods of slow growth every few years; perhaps your sales are seasonal; perhaps your share price is linked to the returns available on other investments. These patterns would not be spotted by simply looking at cross-section data; rather, they need a context over time to be able to identify them effectively.

Data analysis   2.3

The profit margin for M&S in 2012 was 6.62 per cent, meaning that the profit before tax for every £1 spent in its stores was 6.62 pence. Without any other information, it is difficult to know whether this is good or bad. Therefore we might want to use cross-section data for a comparison with its competitors. We might also want to compare this figure with those for previous years.

In this case:

- in 2012, the profit margin was 6.62 per cent;
- in 2011, it was 8.01 per cent;
- in 2010, it was 7.37 per cent;
- in 2009, it was 7.79 per cent;
- in 2008, it was 12.51 per cent;
- in 2007, 10.91 per cent;
- in 2006, it was 9.6 percent.

Before making any final judgements it is important to consider the context of this performance. For example, was this part of an overall strategy to cut prices and boost sales?

How could a business have a lower profit margin but a higher overall level of profit?

 ## Business analysis   2.2

Rate of return of different sectors of the UK economy

In what ways do you think the profitability (that is, the profits of the business in relation to the amount invested) of different business sectors might be affected by external factors?

Summarize the changes in profitability shown in Figure 2.2.

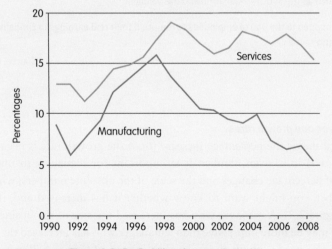

Figure 2.2 Profitability of sectors in the UK

Why do think the profitability of manufacturing is typically lower than that of the service sector?

Nominal and real data

Another factor to consider when looking at data is the possible impact of price increases. When there is a sustained increase in the general price level, this is called **inflation**. For example, if annual inflation is 3 per cent, this means that prices, in general, have increased by 3 per cent over the last twelve months. This is important when considering other changes, such as wage increases. Assume that employees receive a pay increase of 2 per cent. In **nominal** terms (that is, the amount received at the given time), employees have 2 per cent more money. But in terms of what this can actually buy, given that prices are generally going up by 3 per cent, this means that employees are worse off. This means that, in **real** terms, they cannot buy as much as they could last year and their earnings have actually fallen in terms of their purchasing power.

Similarly, if you receive interest at 1 per cent on your savings in the bank, but when you go shopping, you find that prices are 3 per cent higher, in real terms the interest rate that you have received is negative. Therefore real figures are numbers that have been adjusted to take account of inflation.

 ## Data analysis   2.4

Inflation in Zimbabwe in July 2008 was estimated to be 231 million per cent! In January 2009, it was estimated to be 5 sextillion per cent (that is, 5,000 million million million). Prices were more than doubling in a single day, and this made banknotes useless very quickly. As a result, local banknotes were hardly used and people preferred to use overseas currencies if they had them. In January 2009, a new series of banknotes was issued, including a Z$100 trillion (that is, 100 million million) note. This incredibly high rate of inflation is known as hyperinflation. Since 2009 the local currency has been abandoned and now individuals and businesses trade in other currencies such as the South African rand and the US dollar.

What had to happen to the pay of employees to maintain their real earnings in Zimbabwe during 2008 and 2009?

Source: CIA Factbook

Absolute figures and growth rates

A growth rate shows the percentage increase (or, if the growth rate is negative, the percentage decrease) in a given number. It is important for managers to understand the importance of percentage changes and the scale of the absolute numbers; when analysing a given number, you might want to know whether it has increased and, if so, by how much (see Figure 2.3). A manager who has increased the size of the business by 20 per cent in a year may be more impressive than a manager who has increased the size by 5 per cent. But you also need to think about the absolute size of figures: a 20 per cent increase on sales of £2,000 may be a lot easier to achieve than a increase of 2 per cent on sales of £2,000 million (and would be smaller in absolute terms).

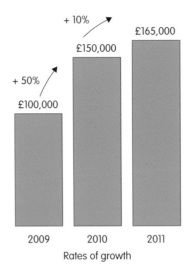

Figure 2.3 Rates of growth

It is also important to consider the rate of growth (Figure 2.4). If your sales are grow-ing by 10 per cent, this means that they are 10 per cent higher by the end of the period than they were at the start. If the subsequent growth rate is 5 per cent, this means that sales have continued to grow, but by 5 per cent, not 10 per cent. The rate of growth has fallen, but sales are still rising.

Similarly, if inflation falls from 3 per cent to 2 per cent, this means that prices are still growing, but at a slower rate. It does not mean that prices have fallen; a price would only fall in value if the growth rate were negative.

 Business analysis   **2.3**

If one grain of rice was put on the first square of a chessboard and doubled every square (i.e. two grains of rice on square 2, four on square 3, etc.), how many grains of the rice would there be on the last square of the chessboard?

Answer: 18,446,744,073,709,551,61!!

This highlights the impact of cumulative growth. If you can double profits every year for 64 years you'll be very rich!

Averages and totals

The difference between average numbers and totals is another important distinction to consider when analysing data. When considering costs, for example, it is important to

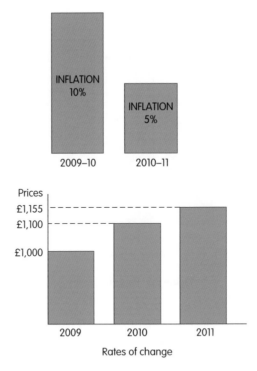

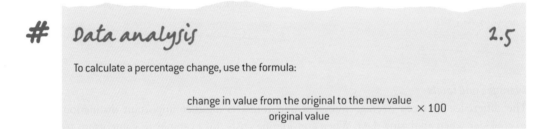

Figure 2.4 Rates of change. If prices generally increase by 10 per cent in one year and 5 per cent in the next year, the rate of growth of prices (called inflation) has decreased but prices are still going up. For example, they would have increased from £1,000 to £1,100 to £1,155 over the two years.

distinguish between the **total cost** of producing a product and the **average cost** (the cost per unit). When mass producing bottled water, for example, the total costs will be high, but if enough bottles are produced, the cost per bottle (that is, the average cost) may be relatively low. The cost per unit of producing Rolls Royce cars may be more than that of producing Toyotas, but the total cost of producing Toyotas is much higher because they are produced on a much larger scale. On average, a business might not make a high profit per item (its profit margin may be low), but if it sells a high volume of items, the total profit may be high. In 2011 Tesco's profit margin was just 5.8 per cent (that is, 5.8 pence in every pound), but given that its sales were £60.9 billion the profit added up to £3.5 billion before tax.

Data analysis   *2.5*

To calculate a percentage change, use the formula:

$$\frac{\text{change in value from the original to the new value}}{\text{original value}} \times 100$$

For example, if profits increase from £10 million to £12 million, the percentage change is calculated as:

$$\frac{(12-10)}{10} \times 100 = 20\%$$

1. If sales increase from £250 million to £300 million, what is the percentage increase in sales?
2. If sales fall from £300 million to £250 million, what is the percentage fall in sales?

To calculate the percentage of a number, use the formula:

$$X\% \text{ of } Y = (X/100) \times Y$$

For example, 5 per cent of 250 is:

$$(5/100) \times 250 = 12.5$$

3. What is a 10 per cent change in sales of twenty units?
4. If the growth rate for your sales was −2 per cent last year, what does this mean?
5. If the growth rate for your sales is predicted to be 5 per cent next year, and 2 per cent the year after, what will happen to your sales be in two years time?
6. If the sales of a business have increased across three years from £200,000, to £220,000, to £230,000, calculate the growth rates over the three years.

When looking at the performance of an economy, it may not be enough to consider the total income of the country; you may also want to consider the population size to calculate the income per person. According to the International Monetary Fund (IMF), the top five countries in terms of total income of the country were the USA, Japan, China, Germany, and France. The top five in terms of income per person were Qatar, Luxembourg, Norway, Singapore, and Brunei.

 ## Data analysis   2.6

According to the IMF, Luxembourg had the highest gross domestic product (GDP) per person in 2011, but its total income ranked it 93rd in the world. China was second in the world for national income, but 92nd for income per person.

How can this be?

Index numbers

As we have seen, when making business and economic decisions it is often important to analyse relative changes in data—that is, to calculate the percentage change in a given variable. If someone receives a pay increase of £50 a week, is this a big increase or not? The answer is that it depends on the amount that the person was receiving before—that is, how much the increase is as a percentage of the original pay. Similarly, if a business increases the price of its products by £10, is this significant or not? This depends on whether it is 0.0001 per cent or 10 per cent of the original price. Again, calculating the percentage change can be helpful in gaining some sense of the significance of any change.

To help them to analyse data, economists often use **index numbers**. Index numbers make it easier to identify a percentage change quickly. Therefore index numbers are designed to help decision-makers analyse data more easily.

When calculating percentage changes, you need to choose a starting point—that is, you need to compare whether something has increased or decreased relative to a given point. This point is called the 'base'. It is usually given a value of 100 (sometimes 1,000). Any change in the variable is calculated in percentages and converted into an index number. If the index number is 105, this represents 5 per cent more than the base (because it is five points more than 100). If the index number is 125, this is 25 per cent more than the base. If the index is 95, this is 5 per cent less than the base.

% Worked example

Assume that you are trying to convert a country's national income figures into index numbers and want to compare these figures over four years (Table 2.1).

Table 2.1 National income and index number

	National income (£m)	Index number
2009	5,000	100
2010	5,100	102
2011	5,200	104
2012	5,500	110

If we were given only the first two columns, we could, of course, work out the percentage changes between 2010 and 2009, 2011 and 2009, and 2012 and 2009. But if the index has been calculated already, the percentage changes are easier to identify. For example, we can see there is a 2 per cent increase in GDP from 2010 to 2009, a 4 per cent increase from 2011 to 2009, and a 10 per cent increase from 2012 to 2009. Using the index numbers, percentage changes can quickly be seen without needing to calculate anything.

In some instances, you may only be given the index numbers and not the underlying data (Table 2.2).

Table 2.2 Index numbers

	Index of unit costs
2009	100
2010	99
2011	97
2012	94

What we can see from this is that unit costs have fallen over the period relative to 2010: in 2011, they are 3 per cent lower; in 2012, they are 6 per cent lower. Note that, in this instance, we do not know what the unit costs actually are, but we do know how much they have changed.

Weighted indices

A weighted index shows percentage changes, but when working these out the relative importance of the variables being considered is taken into account. For example, when working out inflation, economists are interested in how much prices have increased in a typical basket of goods. However, not all goods in your shopping basket are equal in terms of their relative importance, because you spend much more each week on some items than others, and so this needs to be reflected in the calculation. The weight given to an item reflects its relative importance. In this case, each item is given a 'weight', which depends on how much is spent on that item.

In the example in Table 2.3, there are three products. A has increased in price by 20 per cent, while B and C have each increased by 10 per cent; this is shown by the index number. The relative importance of these items in terms of the individual's expenditure is given by the relative weights. A accounts for 60 per cent of his/her spending, B accounts for 30 per cent, and C accounts for 10 per cent. This means that the change in price of A is relatively more important than the change in price of B and C. This is seen when the weighted index is calculated.

Table 2.3 Prices 2012

Item	Index in 2012	Weight	Weight × index
A	120	60	7,200
B	110	30	3,300
C	110	10	1,100
Total		100	11,600

Base in 2012 = 100

The following formula is used to calculate a weighted index:

$$\frac{(\text{index of A} \times \text{weight of A}) + (\text{index of B} \times \text{weight of B}) + (\text{index of C} \times \text{weight of C})}{\text{total of the weights}}$$

In this case

$$[(120 \times 60) + (110 \times 30) + (110 \times 10)]/100 = (7{,}200 + 3{,}300 + 1{,}100)/100$$

$$= 11{,}600/100 = 116$$

This means the weighted index is 116 up from the base of 100, that is a 16 per cent increase.

The weighted index in this instance is 16 per cent; this means that, taking account of the relevant importance of the different items, prices have increased by 16 per cent on average.

Obviously the same method would be used if there were more items in the basket—adding the sum of all the index numbers multiplied by the weights and dividing the answer by the sum of the weights.

 # Data analysis 2.7

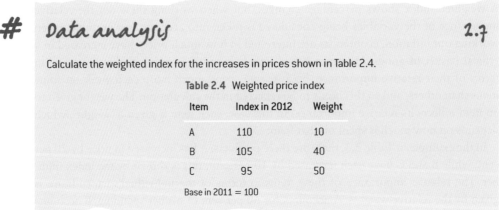

Calculate the weighted index for the increases in prices shown in Table 2.4.

Table 2.4 Weighted price index

Item	Index in 2012	Weight
A	110	10
B	105	40
C	95	50

Base in 2011 = 100

Analysing diagrams

Quite a lot of economics data is presented in the form of diagrams. The data relating to two variables may be plotted to see if there is any relationship. Do sales of your products appear to be linked to the average income in the economy? What about your spending on marketing? Diagrams provide a visual representation of data and can be a useful way in which to help economists to analyse trends and relationships.

When examining a chart, be sure to look carefully at the following.

■ Its *title*—what exactly is it showing? Is it past data or a projection? What period does it cover?

- Its *scale*—a change in the scale of a chart can create a very different impression (see Figure 2.5);

- Its *source*—how reliable is the data? Forecast sales figures produced internally for a sales conference to inspire employees may be more optimistic and less reliable than audited figures checked by an outside agency to present to shareholders. This is very important advice for you when researching a topic: check where the data is from, because some sources are not very reliable;

- *Missing data*—sometimes what is interesting is not only what a diagram shows, but also what it does *not* show; that is, what information is missing. Your overall profits might have increased, but what about the performance of different divisions?

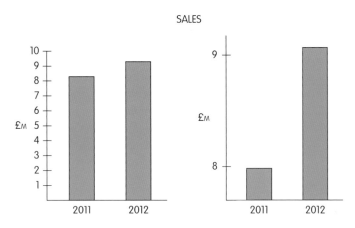

SALES

Figure 2.5 Impact of a change of scale. In both diagrams sales have increased from £8 million to £9 million between 2011 and 2012. However, when the scale is changed (right-hand diagram), the increase looks much greater

Economic models

To analyse the effects of changes in the economy, economists have to build models to explain how the economy works. A model is a simplified framework to help to organize the way in which we think about a problem. These models make assumptions about, for example, what motivates the various groups in society, such as employees, businesses, and consumers. The aim of a model is to explain changes that have occurred and to predict future changes in key variables. A model involves a set of assumptions; for example, if we were trying to estimate future customer spending, we might make assumptions about the factors that influence this expenditure.

The model that is constructed when trying to analyse a situation may not necessarily predict the behaviour of one individual household, firm, or employee, but the aim is to be able to predict the behaviour of these groups in general; one individual may not act in the way predicted, but if the majority do, the model will still be valid.

Economic theory generally assumes that the various groups involved in decision-making act in a rational way and aim to maximize their own welfare:

- businesses aim to maximize profit when deciding what to produce and how to produce it;
- customers aim to maximize their **utility** (satisfaction) when deciding how to spend their money and what to buy;
- employees aim to maximize their satisfaction when choosing between work and leisure.

When analysing a market, economists will look for the results that would maximize the outcomes for those involved; the value of the model will depend, in part, on how appropriate this assumption is.

Of course, models may prove accurate for a given situation but, over time, turn out to be ineffective when it comes to explaining or predicting what is happening in an economy. This may be because conditions have changed. Consider the present-day labour market compared with that of your grandparents: employees are generally better educated; the workforce is more diverse, in terms of gender and ethnic origin; there is more information available on job opportunities; and employees are more likely to move area and jobs during the course of their careers. This means that any model of labour markets would need to be modified over time to reflect a changing world.

Economics and employability

What is your name?
Tom Woodhouse.

Tell us about your role at PwC.
My job title is Audit and Assurance Associate and I'm currently splitting my time between college and client work. For around 35 per cent of the past year, I've been studying to become a Chartered Accountant with the Institute of Chartered Accountants in England and Wales (ICAEW). The rest of the time, I join teams working at client sites as part of PwC's mainstream audit business. Curiosity is key—it's investigative work that often involves one-to-one meetings, analysing records, and also writing reports on everything from bank records to customers, from company property to personnel.

In what ways is an understanding of economics useful in your work?
It is more than useful—it is essential! PwC is a diverse group of experts, advisors, auditors, and consultants, but we all work to deliver distinctive insights that lead to sustained increases in value. This would not be possible without first understanding the immediate economic environment that surrounds each of our clients—their strengths and weaknesses, opportunities and threats. At the same time we must balance this in-depth knowledge with an awareness of wider economic issues—for example, national growth or depression, laws, and regulation.

How does economic change affect your work?

At PwC you need to be extremely agile when circumstances change. Whether it is new compliance rules and regulations, the under- or over-performance of a client, or more general developments in the local and national economy, these must all be acknowledged and incorporated into your work. If, for instance, in an effort to increase efficiency following the recent financial crisis, one client installed a more sophisticated secure computer system, you could potentially take comfort over these new controls and thus reduce the level of detailed testing (which most often means agreeing client records to third-party documentation, i.e. purchase invoices) which would need to be performed during the audit.

In what ways does economic change affect your clients?

Economic change, whether brought about by crisis, regulatory change, competition, or ethical concerns, must be managed and mitigated by all businesses. Failing this, growth and perhaps even survival may be jeopardized. Therefore an important part of all audits is helping clients to become agile with change and more resilient to risk—working to identify emerging risks and managing existing risks more effectively. Emphasis is placed on learning from what has happened and preparing for, and even better avoiding, potential issues in the future.

Did you study economics at university as part of your studies, and, if so, how has it helped you in your work? If not, do you wish that you had and why?

I actually studied history at Durham University. Economics is meaningless without its historical context. I may have focused less on theory and more on practice, but I quickly learnt that profit, growth, and achievement are constants of human action, regardless of whether you are concerned with the past or the present.

What skills are important in your role?

Making a positive impact on the client, shrewd judgement, and the ability to take on new challenges with flexibility and intelligence is vital. Being good with detail and highly numerate is also key, as is the capacity to build strong working relationships with both fellow team members and client personnel.

}{ *People and economics: Behavioural economists*

These economists focus on how people make decisions in practice, i.e. what determines behaviour. Behaviourists question traditional ideas of economic rationality (*homo economicus*) with decision-making models more closely linked to psychology. For example, they highlight that people are heavily influenced by a fear of regret and so may sacrifice potentially high rewards to avoid the fear of failure. Other features of decision-making are that people:

- have cognitive dissonance which means that they tend to disregard new evidence which does not fit with their existing understanding of things;
- prefer things as they are, and so they take bigger risks to keep things as they are than they would to get them to that position in the first place!

People and economics: Kahneman and Tversky (1979)

Kahneman and Tversky proposed 'prospect theory', which suggested that decision-making may not be entirely rational after all. According to their research, how you make decisions varies according to the possible gains and losses relative to the precise position you are in at the moment. For example, rationally there is no difference between winning £50 or winning £100 and then losing £50. In both cases you end up with £50 at the end, but in the second case having won more than that you don't like to lose any! Imagine, for example, that you have £1,000 and have to pick one of two choices:

A: There is a 50 per cent chance of winning £1,000 and a 50 per cent chance of gaining £0
B: You have a 100 per cent chance of gaining £500.

Which would you choose?

Now imagine that you have £2,000 and you must pick either:

A: you have a 50 per cent chance of losing £1,000, and a 50 per cent of losing £0.
B: You have a 100 per cent chance of losing £500.

Logically, according to the laws of probability, there is no difference between A and B in either case, but most people choose A in the first situation and B in the second situation. This shows that when we might gain money we prefer certainty (even of there is a chance of more), but when we might lose money we are more willing to take risks to reduce the losses.

The marginal condition

When trying to identify the output that maximizes the returns to any particular group, economists often consider 'marginal benefit' and '**marginal cost**'. Marginal benefit refers to the extra rewards from selling or consuming another unit; marginal cost refers to the extra cost involved in providing another unit. If you have ever been in a pub and thought whether you should stay for 'just one more', you are considering the marginal benefit; when you start to worry about how much harder staying will make getting up in the morning, this is the marginal cost. If the marginal benefit from producing or consuming a unit is greater than the marginal cost, then the firm or household will benefit from it and it should be provided or consumed; total welfare will increase. However, if the marginal benefit is less than the marginal cost, this unit should not be made or consumed; total welfare will fall (see Figure 2.6). To maximize the returns (when the extra benefit exceeds the extra costs), all units should be made up to the point at which the extra benefit equals the extra cost—that is, the point at which there are no additional rewards to be gained. This is known as 'equating at the margin'.

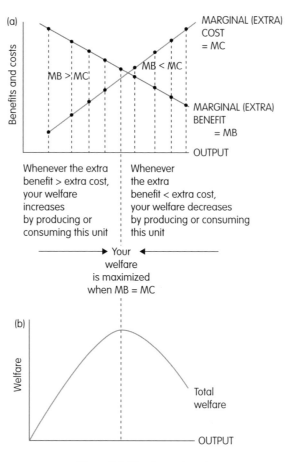

Figure 2.6 Margins and totals

The concept of 'equating at the margin' is important in many areas of economics (and, indeed, life). For example, many people complain about levels of pollution and want it removed completely, but this would be economically inefficient. Pollution is generated by production, which brings benefits to people (such as more products to consume); production needs to be continued up to the point at which the marginal benefit is equal to the marginal costs (including the pollution), which does not mean that all pollution will disappear.

Rational decision-making

Economics also assumes that employees, consumers, and managers act rationally—that is, that they make logical decisions to maximize their benefits. This is why the marginal condition applies. If the extra benefit of an activity is greater than the extra cost, the individual will undertake that activity to increase his/her welfare. While some individuals may act irrationally, a model will still have value if the majority act rationally; a problem arises if the majority act irrationally.

Data analysis   2.8

Table 2.5 Welfare maximising output

Units	Extra benefit (MB)	Extra cost (MC)	Impact on total welfare (MB–MC)	Total welfare
0	0	0	?	0
1	20	9	?	?
2	18	11	?	18
3	16	13	?	21
4	14	14	?	?
5	12	17	?	?

1. Complete Table 2.5
2. At what level of output is welfare maximized and why?
3. What is the relationship between the extra increase in welfare obtained by consuming a unit and the total welfare?

? Think about it…   2.2

1. When you are deciding where to go on holiday, how logical is your decision-making process? Do you do lots of research to choose the location and resort?
2. What about when you chose the university at which you are studying: did you do a high level of research to ensure that a logical decision was made?
3. What about when you decided which car to buy?
4. If your decision-making was not rational, does this undermine the study of economics?

Normative and positive economics

When analysing economic issues, managers need to distinguish between decisions based on assumptions that can be tested and decisions based on what they think is right. For example, it is possible to test whether a cut in price leads to a significant rise in sales—managers can cut the price and see what happens. This is an example of **positive economics**, because it can be tested to see if the assumptions or theories are right or not.

However, if managers believe that they should invest more in the local community rather than pay out profits to shareholders, this is an opinion—that is, their view of what they think is right—and therefore is an example of **normative economics**.

This distinction is extremely important when listening to debate about economic policy. Are the politicians arguing about what they think the priority should be, which is normative economics, or are they arguing about what the most effective policy to bring about an agreed aim should be, which is positive economics? Even if we understood the workings of households, employees, and businesses perfectly and could analyse the effects of any change exactly, there would still be differences of opinion in terms of what the government's priority should be.

? Think about it...   2.3

In recent years in the UK, the coalition government has pursued an austerity programme to reduce government spending. The view it takes is that reducing spending will reduce the deficit and this should be the priority of the government. Opposition parties have tended to agree that reducing spending is necessary, but have argued that reducing it too fast actually damages growth and may lead to the government spending more because of increased benefit payments. Opposition parties have tended to argue that the spending cuts need to be less severe and less quick.

Which elements of the different views stated above are positive economics and which are normative?

You and economics

You want to find out how studying economics could help you in your career, so you have been asking your friends and looking at the track record of graduates from your university. What has impressed you is the breadth of careers they have gone into in both the private and public sectors. Economics students seem to work in all kinds of areas including:

- accountancy
- banking and finance
- government departments and ministries
- law
- management
- economics consultancy and analysis
- charities

- the foreign service
- journalism
- marketing

It seems like a good choice and that the skills of an economist are transferable and valued.

Distinguishing fairness and efficiency

Positive economics focuses on evidence-based and testable analysis. It examines issues to identify the most efficient solution; this does not necessarily mean that this is the decision that a manager would want to make in terms of what he/she feels is fair. For example, it may be efficient to pay an employee £100 a week, because this is what he/she is prepared to work for, and this might be the profit-maximizing decision. But if the employee has worked for you for many years, you may feel that it is only fair to pay him/her more. Similarly, it may be efficient to make redundancies, but managers may feel, out of a sense of responsibility, that they should not do this if it can be avoided. Therefore there will be times when the economist's desire to be efficient may clash with a manager's desire to be fair: what may seem right may not be efficient. This might be increasingly true given the growing interest in corporate social responsibility (CSR). This takes the view that businesses should view themselves as corporate citizens and consider how they help their stakeholders. This may lead to decisions which are seen as 'right' even if they are not necessarily profit-maximizing.

? *Think about it ...*   2.4

In 2012 many political and business commentators criticized bankers for receiving high bonuses. The pressure was so great that some high-profile bankers, such as Stephen Hester of the Royal Bank of Scotland, refused their bonuses. However, several bankers argued that these high rewards were essential to retain talent and prevent the best people from leaving the country, and even leaving the banking sector.

Is the debate over bankers' pay an example of normative or positive economics?

Why might high pay for bankers be efficient but unfair? Which do you think is more important?

Distinguishing cause and effect

Economists often look for links between different variables—for example, what causes property prices to increase? What affects how much households spend? There is a

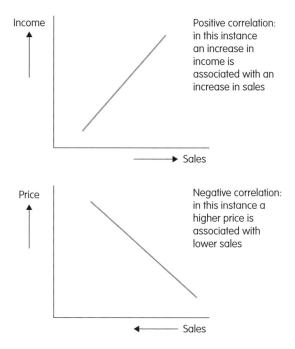

Figure 2.7 Positive and negative correlation

correlation when there is an apparent link between different variables: if the two varia-bles move in the same direction, this is a 'positive correlation'; if they move in different directions, this is known as a 'negative correlation' (see Figure 2.7). For example, there might be a positive correlation between the amount of income that people have and the amount that they spend. There might be a negative correlation between the price of an item and the quantity demanded.

Economists are constantly analysing data to understand how the economy works; after all, the economy is like a complex machine with trillions of interconnected parts. Even when a relationship appears to be understood, it is capable of change because there are so many different factors and the mix is always changing and developing.

It is also important to be careful not to assume that a correlation shows that there is a direct effect between two variables or that one factor leads to another. Correlation is not the same as 'causation'. When income in the economy is falling, governments often lower interest rates to make borrowing cheaper. A simple observation of numerous instances of falling income and low interest rates may make you think that low interest rates cause falling income, whereas, in fact, they are a reaction to it.

However, if a correlation can be identified, this can obviously be of value to managers. For example, if the sales of their products are linked to the income in the economy and a growth in the economy is predicted, then they should prepare for higher sales by recruit-ing staff and making sure that they have the capacity that they need.

? *Think about it...*   2.5

1. There are more shark attacks on people when the weather is hot. Does this mean that hot weather causes more sharks to attack people?
2. There are often more people employed at the government's Treasury (that is, the department that controls its finances) when the economic situation is poor. Does this mean that these economists cause the poor economic situation?

Are economists scientists?

Economists look to build models and quantify factors to make the optimal decisions. They seek out the maximizing solution in a given situation; for example, what would maximize consumer satisfaction or business profits. They seek to explain what has happened in the past and to predict what might happen in the future to help policy-makers make better decisions. To do this, they analyse data so that they can base decisions on evidence. In this sense, they are like scientists—analysing data to find relationships and, hopefully, fundamental truths.

 You and economics

Next time you go shopping think of the decisions you are taking. At any moment you have a limited budget and are having to make choices. What are you doing to maximize your satisfaction?

However, there are some problems with treating economics as if it were a science.

- Economics deals with highly complex relationships between millions of groups of producers, consumers, and employees. It can be difficult to build a model that illustrates how all these relationships interact.
- Economics deals with people who are not always as rational as the models predict; predicting behaviour is always difficult. For example, people's decisions will be influenced by many factors, such as their expectations, which are not necessarily easy to incorporate in models.
- Data can be difficult to gather quickly and accurately, given the scale of economies and the number of organizations that belong to them. Making the right decisions can be difficult if the data is wrong, even if the model is right.

■ It is not possible to undertake large-scale experiments on economies to test relation-ships, so learning often comes after an event has happened and the findings can be incorporated into the models, which may already be out of date.

This does not mean that studying economics is useless for managers; rather, its findings and models need to be reviewed as new issues develop and new thinking emerges. This makes it all the more interesting to study as our understanding evolves and, hopefully, improves over time.

Why do economists disagree?

Building models to try to explain the complexities of trillions of interrelationships between households, governments, businesses, and employees is understandably difficult. Not surprisingly, economists will sometimes build different models that make different predictions. Furthermore, the data that they use to build their models will sometimes dif-fer simply because it can be difficult to gather information on this scale accurately and because identifying causation is not always straightforward.

Even if their models were the same, there would still be plenty of room for debate because of normative economics. We might all agree how the economy works, but still have completely different views of what the priorities should be in terms of economic policy. Is lower unemployment more important than stable prices? Should the govern-ment be aiming for a more equal income distribution? These views of what we should be aiming to achieve provide plenty of opportunities for disagreement. The same is true within a business. Managers may disagree about the relative importance of new product development, training, promotional campaigns, and improved production systems—given limited resources at any moment, a decision will have to be made about what the priority is.

 ## Business analysis   2.4

The value of a degree

Table 2.6 Mean salaries of full-time first-degree leavers entering employment or self-employment

Subject	Graduate	Non-graduate
Dentistry	£30,293	–
Medicine	£29,132	–
Chemical engineering	£27,195	£16,571
General engineering	£26,542	£17,781
Economics	£25,722	£16,237

(Continued)

Table 2.6 (*Continued*)

Subject	Graduate	Non-graduate
Veterinary medicine	£25,387	£18,273
Geology	£24,766	£14,437
Mechanical engineering	£24,726	£16,621
Social work	£24,297	£14,346
Mathematics	£24,259	£15,582
Russian	£23,967	
Physics and astronomy	£23,675	£14,966
Civil engineering	£23,667	£15,503
Aeronautical and manufacturing engineering	£23,268	£15,946
Electrical and electronic engineering	£23,132	£15,183
Nursing	£22,485	£17,203
Computer science	£22,311	£15,370
Building	£21,695	£15,339
Politics	£21,582	£15,127
Business studies	£21,329	£15,672

Source: HESA 2009–10

Based on the data in Table 2.6, should all politics students become economists? Should all economists become medics?

 You and economics

You have heard a lot in the news about the state of many economies in Europe. It seems as if many governments are in debt and having to spend huge sums just repaying the interest on their loans. Several governments have announced measures to cut spending to try to significantly reduce their debts and get back into a healthier financial position. This seems to make sense to you—after all, if you have overspent for a couple of months, you know you need to cut back to get your borrowing under control again. However, you heard a couple of economists on the news this morning arguing that if governments cut their spending too much this causes high levels of unemployment and slow growth, and this ends up reducing their tax revenue so that the governments are not better off at all. The economists argued that governments needed to keep spending to promote growth and this would eventually bring in more revenue. You're not sure what you believe now—cut spending or increase it?

Summary

As an economist you will gain many skills. You will learn how to analyse data, and how to understand the cause and effect of economic change and consider how this might affect the decisions of households, firms, and government. In this chapter you have seen some of aspects of data analysis that will help you understand issues better and make better decisions. For example, you have examined the difference between nominal and real data, the use of index numbers to show percentage changes, and the use of the marginal condition to maximize outcomes.

Checklist

Having read this chapter, you should now understand:

- [ ] index numbers;
- [ ] nominal and real values;
- [ ] the rational aims of producers, households, and employees;
- [ ] normative and positive economics;
- [ ] percentage changes;
- [ ] economic models;
- [ ] absolute and relative numbers.

Short answer questions

1. If you receive a 10 per cent bonus, what determines whether you are better off in real terms?

2. If sales of your product increase from 200,000 units to 220,000 units a year, what is the percentage increase in sales? If sales fall from 220,000 units to 200,000 units, what is the percentage decrease in sales?

3. 'Lower interest rates lead to more spending.' Is this an example of positive or normative economics?

4. If the base value of your share prices was 100 in 2011 and the index is now 86, what does this mean has happened to the share price?

5. Sales of your product two years ago were 300,000 units. The growth rate last year was 8 per cent and has been 5 per cent this year. How many units did you sell this year?

6. Your profits two years ago were £2 million; they then increased to £2.4 million the following year and to £2.6 million the year after that. What were the growth rates for each of the two years?

7. If the extra revenue from selling a unit is £8 and the extra cost is £5, would profit increase or decrease if the unit were sold?

8. If the extra revenue from selling an additional unit equals the extra cost of producing it, does this mean that no profit is being made? Explain your answer.

9. What is a model and why do economists create them?

10. Your business made a profit of £300,000 last year. Is this a good level of profit or not? Explain your answer.

Discussion questions

1. Why do you think that it is vital to understand the difference between nominal and real values?

2. Why is normative economics so important and so subject to debate?

3. Is economics a science or an art?

One step further

Visit our Online Resource Centre at **www.oxfordtextbooks.co.uk/orc/gillespiebusiness2e/** to test your understanding, watch video walk-throughs, and access further information on topics covered in this chapter.

The fundamental economic problems

3

Learning objectives

In this chapter, we consider the fundamental economic problems facing every economy, and the different ways in which decisions about what to produce, how to produce, and for whom to produce the products are answered.

By the end of this chapter, you should:

- ✓ understand the meaning of scarcity and choice;
- ✓ understand the key economic problems in society;
- ✓ be able to explain the difference between a free market, a planned economy, and a mixed economy;
- ✓ be able to outline the key advantages and disadvantages of each type of economy;
- ✓ understand the meaning of the production possibility frontier and productive efficiency.

© *Case study*

'I see that the government are trying to introduce changes to the National Health Service. I don't care what they say—I think it's the beginning of end of state healthcare. It won't be long before we all have to pay to get treated,' said Susie who was chatting to her friend Jessie. 'You're right. First they start making us pay to use a motorway and next it will be doctors. Just look at what happened with dentists—it's almost impossible to get treated by a National Health dentist these days; you have to go private and I don't know about you, but I can't afford it so I don't go. The dentists want to make money out of you anyway so I wouldn't trust them when they say what work has to be done,' moaned Jessie. 'The amount of money the government takes off us in taxes, it should have no problems paying for healthcare but treatment seems to get worse each year. And there are fewer police on the streets and smaller pensions.' Jessie nodded. She knew that the government had many failings having worked in the Civil Service. Three years ago she had left that job and set up her own business as a consultant. She loved working for herself and the fact that if the business did well she kept the rewards. She thought this was a great incentive to be more effective than her competitors. Sometimes her earnings were a bit variable and she knew that many of her friends who had set up on their own had ended up unemployed, but she thought she could make a go of it. 'You've got to work hard to get anywhere but if you keep improving what you offer and how you promote yourself I think you'll get there. Of course you need to keep your eyes open—a lot of your competitors will do anything to win business and I have been shocked by some of the prices they have charged their customers who had no idea they were being ripped off.'

Questions

1. What goods and services does your government provide in your economy? Do you think your government should provide more or less goods and services? Why?

2. Do you think you should pay for medical care? Explain your answer.

3. What do you think should be the priorities for government spending in your country? Why?

4. Most businesses in the UK are people working for themselves. What do you think is the attraction of this? What problems do you think it brings?

5. Do you think businesses can be trusted to behave properly if left to themselves?

Introduction

In this chapter, we examine the fundamental economic questions that face every economy and compare these with the issues facing business managers. We then consider the range of approaches to solving these questions found in different economies, and compare their advantages and disadvantages.

Economic resources

In Chapter 1 we saw how a business takes resources and transforms them into outputs. Think of a construction project and imagine all of these resources combining as part of a transformation process.

■ A manager has the idea to develop a piece of land and so acquires this property. The money used to do this could have been used on another project, so this highlights the concept of opportunity cost.

■ The manager then employs an architect to design the building, making use of his/her creativity, imagination, and technical skills and experience.

■ The next stage is to build the building, which involves employing staff and using capital equipment. This stage will involve many other businesses providing the construction materials used and, in some cases, undertaking some of the specialist work, such as installing the gas supply and electrics. This highlights how businesses in an economy are interrelated and how the success or failure of one will affect others. All businesses are part of a supply chain taking inputs and finally transforming them into the final goods and services.

■ Once constructed, the building has to be sold, which requires the skills and ability of the marketing function.

Therefore the construction project involves the careful coordination of many factors of production to produce a building that can be sold and can generate a profit for the business. Factors of production are used to produce the building, and managers will aim to use resources efficiently to avoid waste and help achieve the objective of generating a final product that is worth more than the costs of providing it. This in turn requires an understanding of the market and what customers want and are willing to pay for. Throughout this process each group involved will be seeking to fulfill their own objectives. For example, customers will want to maximize their satisfaction, employees will want to maximize their satisfaction through their earnings at work, and businesses will want to maximize their profits. This profit must be high enough to justify the use of the resources in this way; after all, using resources has an opportunity cost, and they could have been used for a completely different project.

Given that the quantity and quality of resources (i.e. land, labour, capital, and enterprise) available in an economy is fixed at any moment in time, managers are competing for these to use in their production processes. Given the limited resources, this constrains the maximum amount that an economy can produce, and so decisions about using resources for one project means that something else will not be produced. Having said this, not every economy has the same resources: some economies have more or better quality resources, either because of natural endowment or due to investment in the past, and this enables them to produce more than other economies.

Scarcity and choice

At any point in time the quantity and quality of resources in an economy are limited, and this restricts the number of products that can be produced. Like any business, the economy has a capacity at any moment given the resources and technology available. However, the wants of customers are unlimited: whatever we have at the moment, we want more. This means that there is a scarcity of products relative to what we would like to have—unfortunately, we cannot have everything. As a result, choices have to be made in terms of how the resources of an economy are allocated. Just as an individual manager must decide how to allocate the people, equipment, and funds that he/she has within the business, decisions must be made within an economy in terms of where the country's resources are used. Should the available land be used for a health club or should flats be built on it? Should employees be used to work in hotels or insurance? Decisions need to be made to determine how resources are used. These concepts of 'scarcity' and 'choice' lie at the heart of economics—because of the scarcity of resources all the different parties in an economy must make choices.

Businesses have limited resources and have to decide on how to use these efficiently and effectively to maximize their returns. Households have limited income and have to decide how to allocate their spending to maximize their satisfaction (utility). Employees have limited time, and have to decide how to allocate this time between leisure and work to maximize their welfare. Therefore all the different groups in society face constraints and have to make choices to try to maximize their returns. These decisions are interrelated; labour's decisions about how much to work affects what can be produced and what employees will earn and will be able to spend. The interrelated nature of an economy can be seen in the circular flow model in Figure 3.1. Households work for firms in

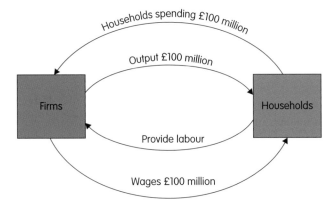

Figure 3.1 Circular flow: simple model

return for income. This income is spent buying products from businesses. (The circular flow model is developed more in Chapter 12.)

 You and economics

You have a limited amount of money from your student loan and part-time job. You have had to think carefully about how many hours you could work without damaging your studies and completely destroying your social life. You shop around for the best deals, although you need to balance the time spent shopping around with the possible savings you make. You have a scarcity of money and time and so have to make choices. Can you think of other examples where the concept of scarcity and choice is relevant to you?

The production possibility frontier (PPF)

The limited availability of resources in an economy at any moment in time determines its capacity—that is, the maximum output that it can produce given its resources and technology. The maximum combination of products that can be produced given the existing resources in the economy is illustrated by a **production possibility frontier (PPF)**.

The PPF shown in Figure 3.2 highlights an economy that is choosing between only two products (this makes it easier to illustrate the key issues in a diagram). If all the resources in the economy were dedicated to the production of product A, then output Q1 can be produced. If resources are transferred out of the production of A and into the production of B, then less of A is produced, but more of B is produced. The extra output of B is achieved at the expense of some of A, which again highlights the concept of opportunity cost. The opportunity cost of the extra units of B is the amount of A that has to be given

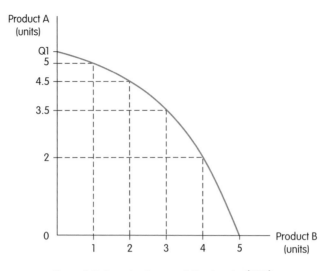

Figure 3.2 A production possibility frontier (PPF)

up as resources are transferred from one industry to another. For example, to produce the second unit of B, resources are transferred out of product A and the amount of A produced falls from 5 to 4.5; this means that the opportunity cost of the second B is 0.5 units of A. Similarly, the opportunity cost of the third B is one unit of A, and that of the fourth B is 1.5 units of A.

 Data analysis   3.1

Table 3.1 shows combinations of products on an economy's production possibility frontier.

Complete the column showing the opportunity cost of each extra unit of B in terms of the number of units of A sacrificed.

Table 3.1 Opportunity cost

A	B	Opportunity cost of extra B
100	0	?
90	1	?
75	2	?
55	3	?
32	4	?
0	5	?

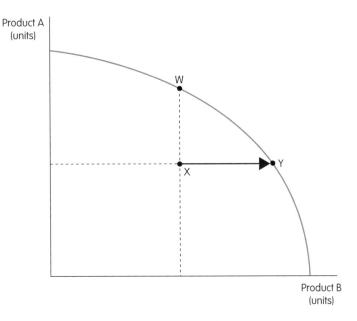

Figure 3.3 Productive inefficiency

Any combination of products on the PPF displays **productive efficiency** (see Figure 3.3). This is because the resources of the economy are fully employed and more of one product can only be produced if less of another product is made. The only way to increase production in one sector is to transfer resources out of another, thereby making a sacrifice and generating an opportunity cost.

Any combination of products produced inside the frontier, such as X, is productively inefficient. This is because more of one product could be made without less of another if resources were to be used more efficiently. For example, an economy could have the same amount of product A as it has at X, but have more units of B if resources were used more efficiently and production occurred at Y. Similarly, W has more of A than X and so, if resources were used more efficiently, the economy could produce at this point.

An economy producing at X is the equivalent of a business producing less than its maximum capacity. A business that is producing less than it can, given its current resources, is under-utilizing its capacity; it is being inefficient, because people or machines are sitting idle. A business solution to this would be to try to boost demand to increase sales. Similarly, if an economy is at X, a government may want to try to increase demand in the economy for goods and services, and thereby reduce the levels of unemployment.

 Business analysis   3.1

The combination of goods and services and the value of these can vary considerably from one economy to another. Look at the examples in Table 3.2 showing data for 2011.

Table 3.2 Differences in the structure of economics

	National income	Proportion of income from agriculture (%)	Proportion of income from industry (%)	Proportion of income from services (%)
USA	$15trn	1.2	19.2	79.6
India	$4.46trn	17.2	26.4	56.4
UK	$2.4trn	0.7	21.4	77.8
Netherlands	$705.7bn	2.7	24.2	73.1
Vietnam	$400bn	22	40.3	37.7

Source: CIA Factbook

Why do you think the size of economies and the composition of economies varies so much?

You and economics

You finish your degree and start looking for work. You find that all the jobs in your area require different skills from the ones you have developed. The jobs available require very practical skills—plumbing, carpentry, electrics. The job centre says that something will come up soon, but for the short term you are not working and the economy is not producing on its PPF.

Economics and employability

What is your name?
Hugh Angle.

What is your role?
Gallery owner in Stow-on-the-Wold.

What made you go into the art world?
After university, like most people, I didn't know what I really wanted to do. I wanted to race in F1 but unfortunately I didn't have a spare £2,000,000 lying around to promote me in order to even take the gamble that I might be spotted or good enough! However, I did have my love of art, which had started from a very young age. I went to California and spent some time learning from a great art dealer and soon knew that this was the job for me. I then joined Sotheby's, knowing before I started that ultimately the aim was to set up my own gallery.

Why did you chose Stow-on-the-Wold as a location for your gallery?

I chose Stow-on-the-Wold for my gallery because it is a fantastic art hub outside London's thriving art community. The need to remain within a prominent and lucrative microeconomy is crucial when establishing any brand in a market which is saturated with direct competition. Finding a niche within the market has been hard, but I am slowly finding my way. The hardest thing is just trying to keep my head above water in this economy. Given the state of the economy at the moment, people are sitting on their hands and not making luxury purchases or investing in commodities such as art.

How has an understanding of economic theory been relevant to you?

I have to weigh up the opportunity costs of whatever I decide to do. The pressure of being the person who makes all the decisions can be quite stressful at times. For example, this might be as simple as budgeting for an advertising piece in a magazine, and if so, which magazine should I choose and which will provide the best exposure. It could also be choosing one artist over another to exhibit on the walls in the gallery, as there is a finite amount of space and time available at the gallery. Choosing one artist over another may cost me money, be it shipping, advertising, or lost sales. One such example is where I decided to take on an impressionist artist, only to find that his work was not selling well. I was left with his work in the storage room (taking up space) and needed to spend money on getting it back to the artist. On the other hand, I decided to exhibit the work of Paul Bennett, a great semi-abstract artist who is becoming increasingly popular on an international level, and he has been selling very well.

What are you plans for the future of your business?

In time I would like to see an expansion of the business, perhaps on an international scale where I might open on the east coast of the USA, or perhaps look to the Far East within a developing economy. Nevertheless, I am a long way from this and first need to establish my brand in the ranks of galleries across the country and eventually the world.

The shape of the production possibility frontier

The shape of the PPF (see Figure 3.4) will depend on what happens as resources are transferred from one industry to another. If the transfer has constant returns—that is, if, every time a resource is transferred from industry A to B, the same amount of output is sacrificed in A and the same amount is gained in B—then the PPF would be a straight line.

However, if increasingly fewer units of B were produced each time a given amount of resources were switched out of industry A and into B, this would lead to a PPF that was concave to the origin (Figure 3.5). This could occur due to the **law of diminishing returns**.

The law of diminishing returns focuses on the short run which, in economics, is defined as the time period when there is at least one fixed factor of production. The law of diminishing returns states that, in the short run, the extra output produced from adding a variable factor (such as labour) to the fixed factor (such as machinery) will eventually

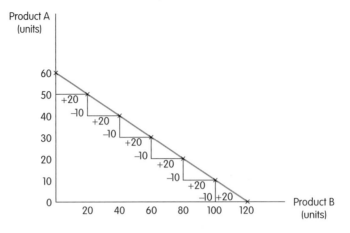

Figure 3.4 Straight-line production possibility frontier

diminish. This law occurs because, at some point, the variable factors of production will get in the way of each other and become less efficient. Imagine recruiting more staff to your insurance office or your travel agency, but not increasing the number of computers or desks; the extra people would struggle to be as productive as the first few, because they would not have the resources that they need to work. The extra employees are not any less efficient in themselves, but the conditions and the lack of additional equipment restricts the contribution that they are able to make to production. This means that the extra output (also called the 'marginal product') of additional employees will fall.

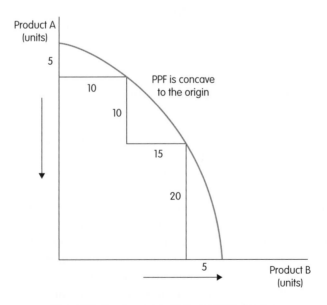

Figure 3.5 Concave production possibility frontier

As a result of the law of diminishing returns, when resources are transferred from one industry to another, the extra output achieved will eventually diminish with each additional unit of a variable factor, causing the PPF to be concave to the origin. In fact, if the law of diminishing returns is assumed to apply in both industries, as factors of production are transferred from one to the other, successively more units of one product are given up for successively fewer units of the other product, which makes the PPF even more concave to the origin. At first relatively unproductive factors are taken from industry A and they have a big impact on output as they move into B; however, increasingly more output is sacrificed as resources are moved out of A, and these have increasingly less effect on output in B due to the law of diminishing returns.

 ## Data analysis 3.2

Table 3.3 Summary of income elasticity of demand

Number of employees in A	Units produced		Number of employees in B
	Product A	Product B	
5	100	0	0
4	90	50	1
3	75	90	2
2	55	125	3
1	30	150	4
0	0	170	5

1. Plot the PPF for the data shown in Table 3.3.
2. Calculate the number of units sacrificed as each employee is transferred from industry A to industry B.
3. Calculate the number of units gained as each employee is transferred from industry A to industry B.
4. Is the law of diminishing returns operating in both these industries? Explain your answer.

 ## You and economics

As the exams get closer you realize that you need to revise. You have decided to cut back on your job to free up time for your studies. However, you are not sure exactly how many hours to drop. Experience suggests that the first hour of revision can be very productive, but sitting there hour after hour becomes less effective. You feel lucky to have a job at all at the moment, given the high levels of unemployment in the country. This level of unemployment seems like a significant waste of resources. Just imagine what the economy could produce if these people who wanted to work had a job.

Outside the production possibility frontier

Given the resources available in an economy at any moment, an economy cannot produce combinations of products outside its frontier. This is because the PPF shows the maximum combination of products that it is possible to make. However, it may be possible to consume outside the frontier via trade. A country can produce products where it has an advantage over another economy and export these in return for other products from abroad. For example, assume that an economy is at X producing Q1 of A and Q1 of B. If within the economy the country switched resources out of A and into B, it might move to Y. This means it has given up Q1Q2 of A and in return produced Q1Q2 of B. However, if instead it exports Q1Q2 of A (i.e. sells these abroad) and in return is able to receive Q1Q3 of B from another country, it can consume at Z which is outside the frontier. Its ability to do this obviously depends on finding countries it can export to and the price they are willing to pay. (For more on the benefits of trade see Chapter 16).

 ## Business analysis   3.2

The Confederation of British Industry (CBI) is an organization which represents UK businesses. In 2012 it asked the UK government to reorientate the UK economy towards exports, arguing that this could add £20 billion to the UK economy by 2020. The CBI wants Britain to match the European Union with an average of one in four small to medium-sized enterprises exporting by 2020. The CBI wants exports to rise from 29 per cent of the UK's income in 2010 to 36 per cent by 2016. In a recent report it said that the sectors in the UK with high export growth potential are construction services, communication services, electrical goods, optical and high-tech goods, creative industries, and financial services. It argues that UK exporters have failed to exploit the full potential of the BRIC nations (Brazil, Russia, India, and China) and of many other emerging markets such as Indonesia, Mexico, South Korea, and Turkey.

Discuss the ways in which the UK government might help to encourage exports.

Source: CBI

Economic growth

Over time, as the resources available in an economy increase or improve in quality, the amount of products of A and B that can be produced will increase, leading to economic growth. Economic growth occurs when there is an increase in the quantity of goods and services available in an economy. This growth can be caused by changes such as:

- improvements in technology enabling capital equipment to be more productive;
- a better educated or better trained workforce, or a better approach to managing people;
- an increase in the land available, perhaps because new technology allows more land to be reclaimed or used more productively.

This economic growth is shown by an outward shift of the PPF (see Figure 3.6). The economy can now produce more of both product A and product B and increase the country's potential output. This growth is similar to a business increasing its capacity over time through investment, training, or the acquisition of more land.

Many governments will pursue economic growth as an economic objective because it provides more goods and services for its people. If the population does not increase, this means more products on average per person which may be politically popular. However, there may be drawbacks with economic growth. For example, it may create pollution and damage the environment. It may also involve more hours being worked and a less attractive quality of life even though more products are available.

Looking at the growth of an economy will be important to managers who are examining potential markets in which they might compete. More growth may create more demand. Managers will be interested in the following factors.

- ***The maximum output of a country now and in the future*** Is it a large potential market? If so, it may be worth targeting this market. The emerging markets, such as Brazil,

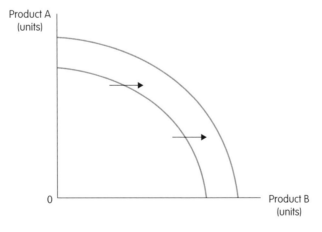

Figure 3.6 Outward shift in the production possibility frontier

Russia, India, and China (these are known as the BRIC economies), have been growing very rapidly in recent years, and many multinationals, such as Unilever, are targeting these regions for future expansion because they offer the potential of much faster growth than more developed and mature economies such as the UK. The next group of countries tipped for fast growth in the coming years are known as CIVETS: Cambodia, Indonesia, Vietnam, Egypt, Turkey, and South Africa. Managers will already be looking to develop an understanding of these markets and assess the appeal of these countries in terms of production and sales.

■ *The combination of goods and services produced in the economy, and the opportunities and threats that this creates* Is an economy mainly producing consumption goods? If so, this might provide sales opportunities for producers of consumer electronics. Or is it more focused on capital goods? If so, this might create opportunities for producers of machinery.

The output gap

The **output gap** measures the difference between the amount that an economy is able to produce if its resources are fully employed (its potential output) and the actual level of output at a given moment.

If the demand in an economy is too low, the output being produced will be below the potential output (that is, the economy is producing within the PPF). This is called a 'negative output gap'.

However, if the actual output in the economy is above the level that can be sustained in the long term (for example, demand is only being met by employees working overtime, firms working extra shifts, and machines being used far more than is usually recommended), this will put pressure on prices to increase. This is because, if there are very high levels of demand and businesses are struggling to meet all of the orders that they have, managers may feel that they can, and have to, increase their prices to ration the demand. This is known as a 'positive output gap'.

Estimates indicate positive output gaps in the UK during the 'booms' in economic activity of the early 1970s and the late 1980s. There were negative output gaps when demand was falling in the mid-1970s, the early 1980s, the early 1990s, and 2008–9. In 2008–9 the Treasury estimate of output was nearly 4 per cent lower than the potential output of the economy.

? *Think about it...* 3.2

'For the economy to flourish, people, good and information must move freely. Businesses across all regions and industries need the right conditions to grow. Reliable infrastructure is essential to achieving this. Ensuring networks are integrated and resilient is vital. Failure to make the right choices at the right time, or pausing investment, risks not only growth but also the UK's international competitiveness.

Over the centuries, the UK has had a great record of investing in world class infrastructure to underpin economic growth. From the earliest days, infrastructure has been built by a combination of public and private money, in ventures involving business and both national and local government. Private capital was given the incentive to invest in often cutting-edge technology, by prospect of earning proper returns.

The role of the government is to specify the infrastructure that is needed, identify the key barriers to achieving investment and mobilise resources, both public and private, to make it happen.'

Source: http://www.hm-treasury.gov.uk/infrastructure_index.htm

In what way do you think that the infrastructure of a country can help economic growth?

? Think about it... 3.3

Which of the following statements relating to the PPF are true and which are false?

A: All combinations of goods on the frontier are productively inefficient.

B: Economic growth can shift the frontier outwards.

C: With a negative output gap, an economy will produce inside the frontier.

D: As resources are moved from one industry to another, there is an opportunity cost.

How might a negative output gap in an economy affect the marketing, finance, operations, and human resource (HR) functions of a business?

The three fundamental economic questions

The PPF highlights that it is not possible to produce more of all products at any given moment: more of one can only be produced if fewer of another are produced because of the limited resources in an economy at a particular point in time. Therefore what to produce with these resources is a fundamental question (see Figure 3.7). What combination of products should be produced? But decisions also have to be made regarding how these products are made. Given the constraint of limited resources, how should the factors of production available be used most efficiently? And who should benefit from the products produced?

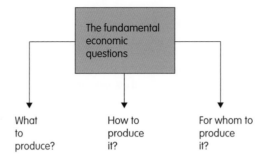

Figure 3.7 The fundamental economic questions

These fundamental economic problems (that is, what to produce, how to produce, and for whom to produce) can be solved in different ways, depending on the type of economy (see Figure 3.8). The solutions include the following.

- *The market mechanism* In what is known as a 'free market economy' the decisions about what and how to produce are determined by supply and demand. The levels of supply and demand in different markets affect what is produced in the economy, how it is made, and who gets what. In terms of what to produce, if there is a high level of demand for a particular item, this will attract businesses to produce it because of the profits that can be made. In terms of how to produce, the best way of producing the item will depend on the markets for different resources, such as the demand and supply of labour, which will affect its price. For example, if labour is scarce it is likely to be expensive and so there will be more incentive to switch to capital. In terms of who receives the products, this will depend on who can afford them—if you have enough money in the **free market**, you can buy the products that you want. If you are willing to pay enough, you can get whatever you want produced.

- *The government* An alternative to the free market is for the government to intervene and determine what is produced, how it is produced, and who receives the rewards of production. This is known as a **planned (or command) economy**. In this scenario, the state decides what products need to be made and how resources are allocated. People are directed to work in particular industries. The government also determines who gets what by determining how individuals are rewarded and how the products are distributed.

- *A mixed economy* A **mixed economy** exists when the basic economic problems are solved by a combination of the market system and the government. In reality, all economies are mixed—they all contain a public and private sector. Where they differ is the extent to which the government intervenes. For example, North Korea has a high level of government involvement in the provision of goods and services, whereas in Hong Kong

Figure 3.8 Range of economies

and the USA the free market dominates. The degree of intervention will change over time as governments change—in recent years the government has taken control of many businesses in Venezuela whilst in Cuba there has been a growth in free market activities.

These different types of economy are examined in more detail in the next three sections.

The free market

In a free market economy, decisions about what to produce depend on market forces. The combination of goods and services available in an economy (i.e. where the economy ends up on the production possibility frontier) is the result of the independent decisions of suppliers and buyers. The price changes to bring together these different decisions. At a particular moment in any market, there is supply (which shows what producers are willing and able to produce at different prices) and demand (which shows what customers are willing and able to purchase at different prices). These forces interact, and a price is found at which the quantity supplied and the quantity demanded are equal. This is known as 'equilibrium' in the market. Millions of producers and customers are making decisions to maximize their own returns (profits in the case of producers, and their own satisfaction in the case of consumers) in many different markets; the price mechanism adjusts to bring their decisions into line. For example, if demand for 3D televisions is high, this will increase demand in this sector. This will tend to increase the price that customers are willing to pay, which will encourage suppliers to produce more (and/or more producers to enter this industry). The result will be that more resources are shifted into this industry and pulled out of another one in which demand is falling, such as CDs. This could be seen as a movement along the production possibility curve.

Similarly, if demand falls for a product, such as fax machines, there will be fewer rewards available for producers in this industry and so some will move out, looking for higher rewards elsewhere such as smart phones. The free market is made up of interaction of all the different markets for goods, ideas, and services, with the price adjusting to equate demand and supply in each one and thereby determining what an economy produces.

Changes in the demand for a product will not only influence what is produced, but also affect how items are made. This is because the markets for the factors of production are linked to the markets for products. For example, an increase in the demand for leisure centres would increase demand for staff in this sector; the demand for labour is derived from demand for the product. An increased demand is likely to lead to higher wages and attract people to these jobs rather than to work in other sectors. Labour is attracted out of one use into another. Similarly, the demand for more leisure centres may increase demand for land in order to build more of this type of business and bid up the price, so that more of these centres are built instead of shops. Therefore land will be diverted into new uses. This highlights how interrelated markets are within an economy—changes in demand and supply conditions in one market have a knock-on effect in other markets.

Changes in market conditions within the factor markets will affect how products are produced. For example, an improvement in technology that reduces the costs of using machinery would encourage the use of this resource relative to labour. An increase in supply of labour, perhaps because of immigration, may lead to more of this resource being used as it becomes relatively cheaper.

The beauty of the free market system is that it is the result of millions of independent decisions by managers, employees, landowners, banks, and other organizations, all serving their own interests and looking for the highest rewards that they can get. If you have a business idea and want to pursue it, you set up a business and, if it meets customer needs and generates enough income, you can make a profit. If you are a household, you can choose to spend your money on whatever maximizes your satisfaction (utility) and you work where you get the best rewards you can. As market conditions change, either in the markets for goods and services or in the markets for resources, the allocation of factors of production and the output of different products change; these changes are all driven by market forces. This approach is also known as *laissez-faire* because individuals and businesses are left to make their own decisions.

Managers may welcome the free market because it allows them to make decisions without any intervention. There are no government regulations and therefore no controls on their behaviour. Therefore they are able to do exactly what they want without needing government permission or meeting set regulations. There are no restrictions on what to produce, how to advertise, what price to charge, where to sell it, or how to produce it. This can lead to quick decision-making and a flexible approach. However, this lack of rules and regulation may also mean that some businesses may sell unsafe products, may mislead customers in terms of the ingredients or specifications of a product, or may force buyers to pay extremely high prices because of a lack of choice. This type of behaviour not only affects household shopping, but also affects any business that is buying from suppliers or competing against other firms. Managers will want to protect themselves against behaviour such as this from other firms. Therefore they may prefer to have some government intervention rather than a totally free market. There is also pressure from society and politicians to control business behaviour. In recent years a number of politicians have attacked 'predatory capitalism' and argued for more regulation of businesses to ensure better behaviour.

 ## Business analysis   3.3

In 2008, Bernard Madoff was accused of running a fraudulent investment scheme that lost up to US$50,000 million of his clients' money. These clients included the British bank HSBC, Santander of Spain, and BNP Paribas of France. Investors thought that they were receiving superb returns because of Madoff's skill at investing. In fact, he was allegedly paying these returns out using money from new investors in his fund.

As long as he kept attracting more investment into his scheme, Madoff could continue the impression of being an investment guru. But when the money coming in slowed up, he could not pay out and what appears to have been a huge fraud was eventually discovered. Even so, he seemed to have fooled investors and regulators for many years.

Do you think that fraud is likely to be inevitable when managers try to maximize profits?

 ## Data analysis   3.3

Table 3.4 Demand, supply, and the equilibrium price

Price (£)	Quantity demanded (units)	Quantity supplied (units)
10	100	270
9	120	220
8	150	170
7	170	130
6	200	90
5	250	0

Table 3.4 shows the quantity that consumers want to buy at different prices, all other things unchanged. It also shows what producers are willing and able to sell at different prices, all other things unchanged.

1. At which price do the decisions of producers and consumers match each other?
2. What quantity is supplied and demanded at a price of £10? What does the price need to do for the market to reach equilibrium?
3. What quantity is supplied and demanded at a price of £5? What does the price need to do for the market to reach equilibrium?

For more analysis of supply and demand, see Chapters 6–8.

3{ People and economics: Adam Smith

Adam Smith is a much quoted economist who highlighted the significance of market forces and the benefits for society as a whole in his book *Inquiry into the Nature and Causes of the Wealth of Nations* (usually abbreviated to *The Wealth of Nations*), published in 1776. One of the key points Smith made was that whilst individuals might pursue their own interests, society as a whole would still benefit.

The planned (or command) economy

In a fully planned economy, resources are all allocated by government directives. The government determines exactly what is produced in what quantities each year, how the products are produced, and how much people are rewarded.

In a planned economy, the government decides the key economic questions:

■ what to produce;
■ how the available resources are allocated to produce the goods and services that it has decided need producing;
■ who benefits from the economy by allocating the rewards (for example, by setting income levels for differing jobs).

There are advantages to this approach, in that it can avoid some things being produced that may be profitable, but which society as a whole may regard as undesirable (such as drugs and prostitution). It can also prevent unethical or unfair behaviour, such as mis-selling products, by imposing regulations in these areas.

In a planned economy, a government is able to focus on the production of socially desirable goods and services even if they are not necessarily the most profitable. Late-night bus services, school buses, opera performances, hosting the Olympics, and health education programmes may not be particularly profitable, but a government may decide that they are in the interests of their society and ensure that they are provided rather than violent films, reality television, disposable fashion items, and fuel-guzzling sports cars. It can also regulate undesirable behaviour such as excessive pollution and exploitation of staff. In a planned economy a government may be able to take a long-term view and invest in projects that might take twenty years to bring about returns; in a free market, pressure from investors may lead to a focus on short-term profit and a lack of investment in new product development and innovation.

However, there are disadvantages of a planned economy, not least that what is being produced may not match with what customers actually want. Customers may want to buy the latest computer software only to find shops' shelves full of economics textbooks that the government wants them to read. And people may end up having to work in industries in which they do not want to work, resulting in low job satisfaction.

The planned economy relies on a government making the major decisions in the economy and allocating all the available resources. This is a huge amount of planning for one organization (as opposed to the free market, which is decentralized and so does not rely on one body overseeing everything that happens). As a result, it may lead to slow decision-making and an overload of work, so that inefficient decisions are made. For example, if the production of products does not match what customers want, there may be stockpiles of items that are not wanted and **shortages** of ones that are in demand, but are not produced. Poor decision-making may also mean that employees and equipment may be used inefficiently, thus wasting resources. In particular, the absence of the profit motive may lead to inefficiency and a lack of innovation. In the free market, businesses keep the profits that they make, and this means that there is a desire to keep costs down and produce what is wanted; this may also encourage innovation to stay competitive. In the planned economy, all rewards belong to the state, so there may be less incentive to look for better and cheaper ways of doing things; indeed, this may encourage inefficiency because, if the government has decided that a certain amount of an item has to be produced, then it does not necessarily matter to managers how efficiently this is done because they will not personally gain from any savings made to the resources used. The role of central government in a planned economy may take away the ability, or willingness, of individual managers to respond quickly to market opportunities and reduce their desire to be efficient or provide a better customer service.

On the positive side, in a planned economy, employees may have job security and the provision of education and healthcare. They may be protected from exploitative businesses and know that the government will look after their interests. However, it may reduce the spark of innovation that involves new businesses, creates products, and

Table 3.5 Summary of the free market and the planned economy

Free market	Planned economy
Resources allocated by supply and demand	Resources allocated by government intervention
No control over what is produced, but responds to demand, so produces what is wanted	Government determines what is produced, so can plan for the economy as a whole and plan long term; can produce socially desirable products
Decisions taken by individual households, firms, and employees	Government can take an overview of the economy and its priorities, and can cross-subsidize production to provide some products cheaply or free
No need for central planning; lower administration costs	Central planning is expensive and can be bureaucratic
May be inequality because earnings depend on demand and supply	Can redistribute income to reduce inequality
Incentive to be efficient and innovative, because individuals and businesses directly gain	Individuals and businesses may lack incentive, because profits go to the state

contributes to economic growth. On the other hand, the free market can bring many problems, not least great inequality—some will be paid far more than others and if you don't have the money you are not able to buy the goods and services you might want and, more importantly, the products you may need to survive.

The characteristics of the free market and the planned economy are summarized in Table 3.5.

Business analysis   3.4

Household incomes, on average, more than doubled between 1977 and 2009–10 (the latest year for which comparable data are available). In monetary terms, people are twice as well off now as they were just 35 years ago. This increase in prosperity is shared by all types of families—pensioners, working-age people with children, and the working-age childless. However, there has also been a large increase in inequality. Up to 1977, income inequality had been on a long-term downward trend in the UK. The 1980s saw a historically unprecedented increase in inequality and this has been maintained. In 1977, the person 90 per cent of the way up the income distribution had an income 1.7 times as high as the person in the middle of the distribution and 3.0 times as high as the person just 10 per cent of the way up the distribution. By 2009–10, this person at the 90th percentile had an income more than twice the median and more than four times as high as the person at the 10th percentile. The income share of the richest 1 per cent has nearly trebled. Even after tax, in 2009–10 the richest 1 per cent of households took home nearly 9 per cent of all income compared with 3 per cent in 1977.

Source: Institute of Fiscal Studies: http://www.ifs.org.uk/

The mixed economy

The free market model and the planned economy approach outlined in the previous two sections are extremes to highlight what can happen as you move nearer to one or other of these, and to help decision-makers to determine how much they want the government to intervene in an economy. In reality, all economies are mixed to some degree. That means that there are some aspects of the economy in which market forces operate and the price mechanism determines what is produced, how it is produced, and who gets it, but there are other parts in which the government intervenes (see Figure 3.9). For example, laws might cover the way in which products are produced and sold. There may also be areas of the economy in which the government directly provides goods and services, such as education, health, or the military. The government may provide these products because it wants to keep control of key services—perhaps for security reasons or because the government wants to make sure that these products are more affordable for people than they would be in the free market. In other cases there may be private and public sector partnerships; for example private businesses build roads in return for toll income for a number of years before this revenue is transferred to the government. A government that regulates business activity heavily, and provides many goods and services itself, is said to be 'interventionist'; a government that leaves the market more to itself is said to be more free market.

While all countries are mixed economies, they vary in the relative size of the free market compared with the government sector (see Figure 3.10). This depends on the extent to which society wants the government to regulate business behaviour and be responsible for the direct provision of products. All managers will want some intervention—not least to protect themselves against other businesses and unfair competition—but they may want to restrict the extent of regulation, because of the costs of meeting its rules and because it may limit their actions.

Free market economy	Mixed economy	Planned (command) economy
=	=	=
Private sector	Private and public sectors	Public sector

Figure 3.9 The mixed economy

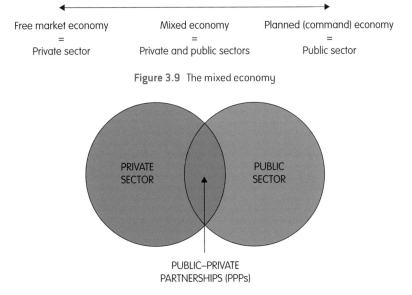

Figure 3.10 The private and public sectors

You and economics

You shop around to upgrade your mobile phone. You look at different deals as the retailers try to get you to buy specific phones and deals. They are competing with each other in a market with them as suppliers and you as the buyer. The way they describe the products, the type of finance they can offer you, and the hours they open their shops are all regulated by the government to protect you as a consumer. To get to the shops you catch a train; this is privately run and competes for your business with other options such as catching a bus, getting a taxi, buying a bike, or walking. The prices the rail operator can charge are controlled by a regulatory body that is overseen by the government to prevent the train companies exploiting their power. The number of seats available on the train and the frequency of the service are also controlled by the government.

In your part-time job you are paid above the minimum wage set by the government. You are protected by laws that prevent discrimination and ensure that the workplace is healthy and safe.

How else does government regulation affect you as a consumer and an employee?

 ## Business analysis   3.5

In 2012 the Japanese government invested 1 trillion yen ($12.5 billion) into Tokyo Electric Power (Tepco), the operator of the now closed Fukushima Dai-ichi nuclear power plant. This was a huge nationalization and the biggest state intervention into a private non-bank asset since America's bail-out of General Motors in 2009. It is particularly noteworthy in Japan where the electricity industry has always been in the private sector (except for during the Second World War). In return for this major investment, the government has gained a majority stake that enables it to choose board members.

Why do you think the government may have invested this much money into this business?

Summary

All economies have limited resources, but their population has unlimited wants. This means that all economies face the problems of scarcity and choice—resources are scarce and so choices have to be made to determine what is made, how it is made, and who gets the product. Choices will involve an opportunity cost. The solution to the basic economic questions could, in theory, be via a free market economy, a planned economy, or a mixed economy. In reality, all economies are mixed to some extent.

Checklist

Having read this chapter, you should now understand:

- [ ] what is meant by scarcity and choice;
- [ ] what is shown by the production possibility frontier (PPF);
- [ ] the effect of growth on the PPF;
- [ ] the determinants of the shape of the PPF;
- [ ] the meaning of productive efficiency;
- [ ] the meaning of the law of diminishing returns;
- [ ] the three fundamental economic problems;
- [ ] the differences between the free market, the planned economy, and the mixed economy;
- [ ] the meaning of opportunity cost;
- [ ] the meaning of the output gap.

Organizations and economics

Confederation of British Industry (CBI)

The CBI exists to represent businesses on a national and international level. It represents over 240,000 companies, ranging from small start-ups to well-established public limited companies, in every sector of the UK including agriculture, automotive, aerospace and defence, construction, creative and communications, financial services, IT and e-business, management consultancy, manufacturing, professional services, retail, transport, tourism, and utilities.

The mission of the CBI is:

'... to promote the conditions in which businesses of all sizes and sectors in the UK can compete and prosper for the benefit of all. To achieve this, we campaign in the UK, the EU and internationally for a competitive policy landscape.'

Source: http://www.cbi.org.uk

Adam Smith Institute

The Adam Smith Institute is one of the world's leading think tanks. Independent, non-profit, and non-partisan, it works to promote libertarian and free market ideas through research, publishing, media commentary, and educational programmes. Famous for its trail-blazing work on tax, privatization, and public service reform, the Institute is today at the forefront of making the case for free markets and a free society in the UK. It is named after the economist Adam Smith, who highlighted the benefits of the free market system.

The Institute defines a free market as follows: 'A free market is one in which all activities take place voluntarily, without anybody coercing anybody else—and that includes government.'

Source: http://www.adamsmith.org

Institute for Fiscal Studies (IFS)

The aim of the IFS is to promote more effective government economic and social policies by gaining an understanding of their potential impact on individuals, families, businesses, and the government. These findings are based on detailed research. IFS research includes work on tax, welfare, education, and public finances.

Source: http://www.ifs.org.uk/

Short answer questions

1. What is meant by scarcity and choice in economics?
2. What are the three basic economic questions?
3. What is shown by a production possibility frontier (PPF)?
4. What might cause an outward shift of the PPF?
5. What is meant by opportunity cost?
6. What is meant by productive efficiency?
7. How are resources allocated in the free market?
8. What is meant by the output gap?
9. What is meant by a mixed economy?
10. What problems might occur in a planned economy?

Discussion questions

1. Discuss the importance of opportunity cost in economics.
2. Is the free market the best solution to the fundamental economic questions?
3. Does the government need to regulate business behaviour more?

One step further

Visit our Online Resource Centre at **www.oxfordtextbooks.co.uk/orc/gillespiebusiness2e/** to test your understanding, watch video walk-throughs, and access further information on topics covered in this chapter.

Demand

4

Learning objectives

By the end of this chapter, you should:

- ✓ understand what influences the demand for products;
- ✓ understand why you should be interested in the demand for products;
- ✓ understand how an understanding of the concept of elasticity of demand can help you in your business decision-making;
- ✓ understand what actions you might have to take if demand changes.

Case study—Fountains fall

Alan Ceranti, the managing director of Fountains Construction plc, is looking at the company's latest sales figures. The business has been growing rapidly over the last few years. It has found good locations in the northwest to build its houses and apartments, and it has acquired a reputation in the region for high-quality premium properties. Market conditions in the last few years had been favourable and the properties have sold quickly. Money has been reinvested in the business to finance further growth and this has been supplemented by extensive borrowing.

But Alan is seriously worried by the company's latest sales figures. Sales are down 30 per cent and the business is sitting on a large number of unsold finished properties, as well as many others under construction. Worse still, UK property prices are down 8 per cent on average on last year, and the number of mortgages being taken out is at its lowest for ten years. The company's share price has fallen 40 per cent in the last three months and investors are demanding that action is taken.

Questions

1. Why do you think that the demand for houses and apartments might have fallen so significantly?

2. How sensitive do you think demand for houses and apartments is likely to be in relation to changes in price?

3. How sensitive do you think demand for houses and apartments is likely to be in relation to changes in income?

4. What do you think that the possible effects of the 30 per cent fall in sales might be on Fountains Construction plc?

5. What actions do you think Alan should take in this situation?

Introduction

A great deal of economic analysis focuses on how markets work, and senior managers spend a lot of their time trying to understand the way their markets are working now and how they might develop in the future. Given that resources in an economy are limited relative to individuals' wants, markets develop to determine who gets what for what price as well as determining how those products are produced. Whether these are individuals offering to barter different products and services to exchange goods, buyers and sellers haggling in a street market, customers and sellers meeting online, prisoners trading items in jail for cigarettes, or consumers shopping on the high street, economies are made up of many different markets, small and large, where individuals and organizations are exchanging goods and services. And every one of us is operating in many of these markets throughout our lives as either a buyer or a seller. For example, you will have chosen one university and course from among thousands of other options in higher education, and you will have chosen this rather than full-time work. You are a buyer in this market and the university is a seller. In a few years' time, you will enter the job market, where you will want to supply labour and find someone to employ you; you will then be trading in the labour market. Once employed, the organization for which you work will be selling its services in a marketplace competing against other providers for customers—another market. Outside work, you will choose how to spend your income and be a buyer in many different markets, such as the housing market, the food market, and the clothes market. All around us there are buyers and sellers exchanging goods, services, and even ideas, and you are part of many of these yourself.

In this chapter, we focus on the factors influencing demand. We then examine supply in Chapter 5, and bring the two sides of the market together in Chapter 6.

Understanding demand

The success of any business depends on its ability to the meet the needs of its customers. According to the very well-known management writer Peter Drucker (1954), 'there is only one valid definition of business purpose: to create a customer'. Customers bring in the revenue. A film company must produce movies that people want to watch; an airline must offer the right combinations of routes, times, and fares to attract passengers; and a band needs to make a sound that gets people to download. Whatever you do—whether you manage an insurance business, university, or leisure centre—you need customers to choose your products if you are to survive. To make sure that you win customers and keep them, you need to understand what they are willing and able to buy and what others are offering. It is not enough for customers to want a product (after all, there are many things that we want, but cannot have); they also need to have the purchasing power to buy it during the time period being considered, and they need to want your product and not someone else's. The amount customers are willing and able to buy in a given period is known as 'effective demand'.

Finding out what people want and how much they can afford to buy is the role of market research. Market research gathers and analyses data that is relevant to the marketing function; it helps a business to understand the drivers of demand for its product and enables it to make more effective marketing decisions. One of the key roles of the marketing function in a business is to provide information on existing and potential customers to help to ensure that the business provides what customers want, while also meeting the needs of the organization (for example, ensuring that it can make a profit). Marketing acts as the link between the customer and the operations of the business.

As a manager, you will want to understand what influences the demand for your product, so that you can plan how best to control it and anticipate changes in it so that you can be ready to take appropriate actions. For example, if you know that demand is going to fall, you may want to consider issues such as your staffing levels and how much stock to reorder; you may also want to delay any expansion plans.

Without demand, there are no customers; this means no revenue and no profit. Every year, thousands of businesses have to shut down because they are not meeting their customers' needs. In the UK in the last few years many businesses have struggled because of disappointing sales. Just think of Habitat, Thornton's, Game, and La Senza. As Kotler (1983) said: 'Companies produce what the consumers want and in this way they maximize their customer satisfaction and earn their profits.' If they fail to do this, they fail.

}{ People and economics: Philip Kotler

Philip Kotler (born 1931) is something of a marketing guru! He is the author of *Marketing Management* and numerous other marketing books that are used in university courses worldwide. Many of the models used to analyse markets and marketing approaches that are used by managers across the world are the result of Kotler's work. As a marketer, Kotler looks at how managers can shape the individual demand for their products, whereas economists tend to consider how changes in demand can affect businesses and industries. Kotler puts the manager much more in control of his/her destiny. Kotler is the S.C. Johnson & Son Distinguished Professor of International Marketing at the Kellogg School of Management at Northwestern University.

? Think about it ...   4.1

1. Why is it not enough to consider what customers want to buy when trying to measure the demand for a product?

2. Managers are not always aiming to increase demand; sometimes they might want to decrease it. Can you think of situations when this might be the case?

Marketing and demand

Your potential customers will have a given income at any moment in time and will have to decide how to allocate this among the variety of goods and services available. Imagine a student, who has a weekly allowance or grant of £200; he/she will have to make decisions on how best to spend this. This involves thinking about what types of product to buy, such as books, food, rent, films, and clothes. It also involves decisions about which specific products to buy. Which textbooks are essential? Where should he/she eat? Which music should he/she download? Your aim as a manager is to get customers to choose your product rather than that of a competitor; the aim of the customer is to maximize his/her satisfaction (or utility).

A customer's choice of whether to buy your product (as opposed to that of your rival) will depend on many factors, some of which are under your control and some of which are not.

The factors that managers can directly influence include the marketing activities. These can be summarized using what are known as the '4Ps' of the marketing mix (McCarthy 1960).

■ *Price* Obviously, given a limited income, the price will influence what is affordable and how much money is left for other items. How much did you pay for this book, for example? Would you have bought it if it were twice as expensive? Companies will have to think of pricing points in a market that they are targeting relative to the bene-fits that the product provides, and the products and prices of competitors. For exam-ple, Tesco has three product lines aimed at different market segments: Tesco Finest (premium), Tesco Standard, and Tesco Everyday Living (basic). Under the considera-tion of pricing, factors such as whether you can buy on credit, how much must to be given as a deposit, and whether there are discounts for bulk purchases may also be relevant.

■ *Product* This includes the tangible factors relating to the product, including its specifi-cations, quality, and design. For example, you might choose a particular television because of the size, the quality of the picture, or the thinness of its screen. The product also includes intangible factors, such as the brand image, the after-sales service, and the guarantees provided. For example, you may prefer Sony televisions because you trust the brand; you have bought Sony products before and have never been let down, or you have heard from a friend how good they were. Presumably, you bought this book because you think that it covers the material that you need for your studies. Was your decision affected by the design? The number of pages? The reputation of the pub-lisher? The online material?

■ *Promotion* This refers to the messages that the producer gives out about its product and the way in which the business communicates these messages (for example, via advertising, public relations, or a sales force). What made you buy this book? Was it recommended to you? Did you see an advert? What message about the book appealed to you most?

■ *Place* This refers to the distribution of the products. How accessible is it to the custom-ers? One of the strengths of Coca Cola, for example, is that it is so widely distributed that you can easily find it whenever you are thirsty. One of Coca Cola's aims is to be within 'an arm's length of desire'. Where did you buy this book? If it was not available in your nearest bookstore or online, would you have bought it?

The combination of factors such as price, product, promotion, and place all influence how much customers are likely to want to buy your product and whether they can afford it.

By changing these elements of the marketing mix, managers hope to shape, influence, and control demand.

Of course, this model can be extended to include other factors that can influence customers' buying decisions. For example, when considering services you might add factors such as:

- the physical environment—customers may choose a restaurant or café because of the nature of the store;
- the people—customers may choose some stores because of the expertise or helpfulness of the assistants;
- the process—customers may choose a drive-through because of the ease of service.

 ## You and economics

Look at your weekly shopping basket. Think about the store where you went to buy this—why did you choose this store? Was it the location—was it very convenient or was it somewhere easy to park? Was it the prices—did you choose this store because you know the prices will be low? Or is it the range of products that you like—you know that you have a good selection of a range of brands you like. Or perhaps you were influenced by other factors—it has a café where you like to have a cup of tea, its petrol is cheap, it has lots of checkouts so you can get in and out quickly.

Price and demand

Price is an important element of the marketing mix—just think how often you look at the price tag of an item or search online for the best deal. A decision facing many managers is, firstly, what price to set and, then, when and whether to change it up or down at a later stage. The importance of price in relation to customers' buying decisions can be analysed using a **demand curve**.

A demand curve shows how much customers are willing and able to buy at each and every price in a given time period, assuming that all other factors are unchanged. For most products, the demand curve is downward sloping. This is because as the price falls, the quantity demanded by customers increases, and vice versa (see Figure 4.1). Every unit that we consume generates a certain amount of satisfaction (also called 'utility') for the customer. The drink that you buy when you are thirsty, the meal that you buy when you are hungry, the film that you go to see when you want something to do in the evening, and the club to which you go with your friends all generate extra utility for which you are willing to pay. According to the law of diminishing marginal utility, each extra unit of consumption generates less additional (marginal) benefit: the second cup of tea consumed in a given period is not as satisfying as the first; the third sandwich is not as satisfying as the second; and the fifth Mars bar may add little to your well-being compared with the first. If you are rational and trying to maximize your utility, you will want to

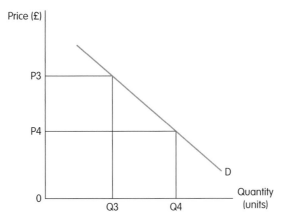

Figure 4.1 Price and quantity combinations

consume every unit that you can that generates utility with a greater value than the price charged, given your budget. With a lower price, there are now more additional units that create value that you think provides utility that is worth more, or at least the same, as the price that is being charged—that is, the quantity demanded increases.

? Think about it...   4.2

1. Can you think of anything you consume where the extra utility of a unit in a given time period does not fall as you consume more?

2. What would it imply if your extra utility from consuming a product always increased with more consumption?

3. If the extra (marginal) utility of consuming a product is falling, but positive, what is happening to your total utility?

4. Could the marginal utility be negative when you consume a unit? If so, what would happen to your total utility?

5. Choose a type of business you know. What could it do to increase the utility you get from consuming its products? What might be the difficulty of doing this?

 Business analysis   4.1

By 2012 more than a million British adults had subscribed to extra-marital affair dating websites, with up to 400,000 unique users logging on each week. These sites have experienced a steep increase in demand, especially from female users.

MaritalAffair.co.uk is one of the biggest sites, with nearly 600,000 members. Women using the site outnumber men by three to one.

The company said that it acquired more than 10,000 new users the day after Valentine's Day in 2012, and most of them were married women.

Discuss the factors that might affect demand for websites enabling extra-marital affairs.

Source: http://www.telegraph.co.uk/, March 2012

? Think about it ... 4.3

A Ferrari is less essential to life than water and yet the price of a Ferrari is much higher than ten gallons of water. Why do you think this is?

(Hint: think of the total utility and the marginal utility of these products.)

A change in price is shown as a movement along the demand curve (see Figure 4.2) and this changes the quantity demanded. A lower price usually leads to an increase in the quantity demanded because customers can afford to buy more with a given income and because more units of the product represent value for money at this price relative to alternative products (the utility gained on these units exceeds or is equal in value to the price

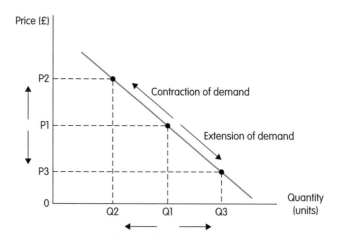

Figure 4.2 Effects of a price change on the demand curve

paid). An increase in the quantity demanded due to a price fall is known as an extension of demand. The movement along the curve can be analysed by dividing it into two parts.

- The substitution effect—this occurs because with a lower price the product is now relatively cheap compared with other products and therefore this inevitably increases the quantity demanded. Consumers substitute the cheaper product for more expensive alternatives.

- The income effect—this occurs because you have more purchasing power if the price of a product is lower but your income is the same. In real terms your income has increased. In most cases, the quantity demanded of a product will increase with increasing purchasing power.

A fall in price will usually lead to an increase in the quantity demanded owing to a combination of the substitution effect (which always increases the quantity demanded) and the income effect (which in the case of most products will reinforce the substitution effect and increase the quantity demanded).

Assuming that the demand curve is downward sloping, an increase in price will lead to a contraction in demand (a fall in quantity demanded). This is because less can be afforded with a given income and, in the customer's mind, fewer units are worth the higher price.

In some cases, a demand curve may be upward sloping (see Figure 4.3). This could be because the product is perceived to be of a better quality if the price is higher (when faced with an unfamiliar selection of wines, you might decide that the higher priced ones must be better). These products are known as 'ostentatious' goods; customers buy more because they want to be seen buying them, because they are more expensive—a practice known as 'conspicuous consumption' (Veblen 1899)—and/or because they feel confident that the more expensive products must be better quality.

Another type of an upward-sloping demand curve is known as a 'Giffen good'. Imagine an extremely low-income family in a poor country, who spends nearly all its money on rice and, very occasionally, can afford some meat. The rice is essential to live; the meat is

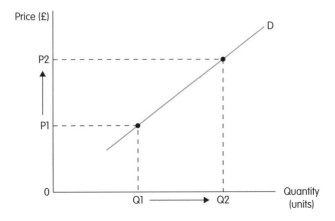

Figure 4.3 Upward-sloping demand curve

a luxury. If the price of rice increases, this will use up even more of the family's limited budget. It may be that the family can no longer afford the meat and so what money is left over, having been spent on the essential quantity of rice, is only enough to buy more rice. The higher price of rice has actually increased the quantity demanded.

${$ People and economics: Veblen

Thorstein Veblen (1857–1929) was an American economist and sociologist whose best known book was *The Theory of the Leisure Class* (1899). Veblen argued that there was a critical distinction between the productiveness of 'industry', run by engineers manufacturing goods, and 'business', which exists only to make profits for a leisure class. The main activity of the leisure class was 'conspicuous consumption', and their economic contribution is 'waste'—activity that contributes nothing to productivity.

${$ People and economics: Giffen

The work of Giffen was mentioned in the well-known book *Principles of Economics* by a famous economist Alfred Marshall. Marshall wrote

'As Mr Giffen has pointed out, a rise in the price of bread makes so large a drain on the resources of the poorer labouring families and raises so much the marginal utility of money to them, that they are forced to curtail their consumption of meat and the more expensive farinaceous foods: and, bread being still the cheapest food which they can get and will take, they consume more, and not less of it.'

Consumer surplus

In the transaction process between producers and consumers both parties are pursuing their own aims. Businesses generally want to make a profit and consumers are gaining utility from the good or service. If the value of the utility gained is greater than the amount of money paid, consumers will feel that the exchange was worthwhile. Ideally, consumers would like more utility for less expenditure.

The difference between what consumers are willing to pay for a unit (which depends on the marginal utility of an extra unit) and the price actually paid is called **consumer surplus**.

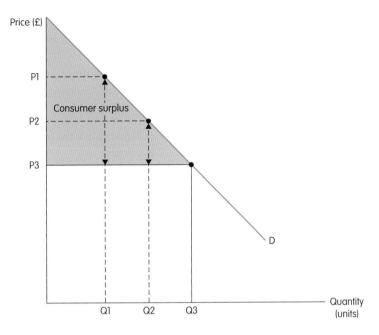

Figure 4.4 Consumer surplus

In Figure 4.4, a consumer is willing to pay P1 for unit Q1, as shown by the demand curve. For the next unit, it is assumed that there is diminishing marginal utility and therefore the customer is willing to pay only P2 for the extra unit. Because the second unit is less satisfying the consumer is only willing to pay P2. If he/she pays P2 for both units, the customer gains consumer surplus on the first unit, because he/she is willing to pay more for it because it gave more utility. As more units are demanded, the price that the consumer is willing to pay continues to fall because they are less satisfying; if all units are acquired at the same price, there is consumer surplus on all the preceding units. For example, at Q3 the shaded area represents the consumer surplus.

A consumer will be eager to benefit from consumer surplus because this represents utility for which he/she does not pay. But the ideal for a producer would be to get consumers to pay what they are willing to pay for each unit and thereby remove the consumer surplus. In one sense the shaded area in Figure 4.4 shows that customers are getting more for their money than they are paying for; producers will be eager to find ways of capturing this. Ways in which this can be done are examined when we consider **price discrimination** in Chapter 9.

To what extent is a change in price likely to affect demand for products?

A demand curve highlights that the amount that customers want, and are able, to buy depends on the price and shows that a change in price changes the quantity demanded, all other things unchanged. A change in price is shown as a movement along the demand curve. Of course, the sensitivity of demand to price changes varies from product to product; this sensitivity is measured by the **price elasticity of demand.**

The price elasticity of demand measures the extent to which the quantity demanded of a product changes following a change in price, all other things unchanged. It is calculated using the equation:

$$\frac{\text{Percentage change in the quantity demanded of the product}}{\text{Percentage change in price}}$$

If the change in quantity demanded is greater than the change in price, then demand is said to be 'price elastic'. Imagine that a 10 per cent increase in price leads to a 20 per cent fall in quantity demanded. This means that the price elasticity of demand is:

$$\frac{-20}{+10} = -2$$

The price change has had twice as much impact on the quantity demanded, meaning that demand is sensitive to price. When you see business promotions stressing special offers, winter and summer sales, and discounted products, this clearly suggests that managers think that these products are sensitive to prices.

If the change in quantity demanded is less than the change in price, demand is said to be 'price inelastic'. Assume that a 10 per cent increase in price leads to a 5 per cent fall in quantity demanded. This means that the price elasticity of demand is:

$$\frac{-5}{+10} = -0.5$$

The price change has had half as much impact on quantity demanded, meaning that demand is not sensitive to price.

When the demand curve is downward sloping, the price elasticity of demand is always negative. This is because the two variables move in different directions; when the price rises the quantity demanded falls, and vice versa. If the price elasticity of demand is positive, this means the demand curve is upward sloping (an increase in price increases the quantity demanded and vice versa; both variables move in the same direction giving a positive answer). The sign of the answer (positive or negative) shows whether the demand is downward or upward sloping. The size of the answer (regardless of the sign) shows whether demand is price elastic or inelastic.

Table 4.1 and Figure 4.5 illustrate the effect of price elasticity on demand. When the price elasticity of demand is zero, it means that demand is totally price inelastic—that is, a change in price has no impact on the quantity demanded. When the value of the price elasticity is <1, demand is price inelastic. (By value we mean the size of the number, ignoring the negative sign; e.g. −0.5 is less than 1 but −2 is more than 1.) When the price elasticity is 1, demand is unit elastic (that is, a change in price has the same percentage effect on the quantity demanded). When the price elasticity is >1, demand is price elastic (e.g. −3 has a value that is greater than 1 because we ignore the negative sign). When the price elasticity is infinity, a change in price has an infinite effect on the quantity demanded.

Table 4.1 Price elasticity and demand

Value of price	Elasticity	Effect on demand
0	Perfectly price inelastic	A change in price has no effect on quantity demanded
<1	Price inelastic	A change in price has a less than proportional effect on quantity demanded
1	Unit elasticity	A change in price has the same proportional effect on the quantity demanded
>1	Price elasticity	A change in price has a more than proportional effect on the quantity demanded
Infinity	Perfectly price elastic	A change in price leads to an infinite change in quantity demanded

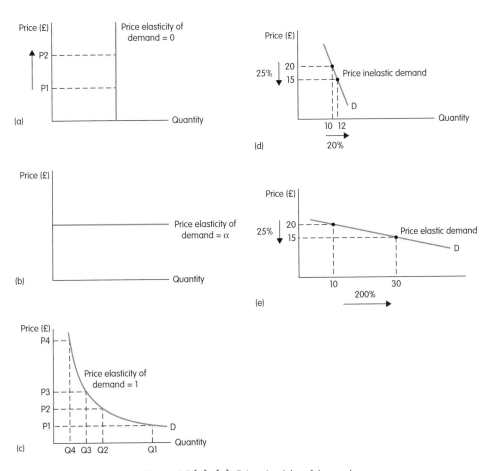

Figure 4.5 (a)–(e) Price elasticity of demand

The concept of the price elasticity of demand is very important to managers who might be considering whether to change the price of their products. For example, they will want to know the likely effect of a short-term promotional price cut on sales, because this will affect the amount of stock that needs to be held, the likelihood of queues or shortages

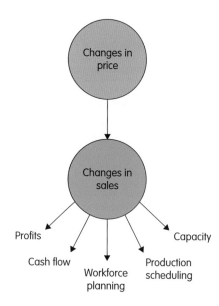

Figure 4.6 The effect of price on other functions

occurring, and whether extra staff may be required to help with sales. Therefore the effect of price changes affects all the different functions of a business, as Figure 4.6 illustrates.

 Data analysis 4.1

1. If the change in quantity demanded is an increase of 8 per cent following a decrease in price of 2 per cent, what is the price elasticity of demand? Is demand price elastic or inelastic? Explain your answer.
2. If the change in quantity demanded is an increase of 8 per cent following a decrease in price of 20 per cent, what is the price elasticity of demand? Is demand price elastic or inelastic? Explain your answer.

? **Think about it...** 4.4

1. What impact do you think a 1 per cent increase in the price would have on your demand for the following items? Think about why differences might occur.

   A: A daily newspaper
   B: A health club membership fee

C: The television licence fee

D: The bus fare into town

E: The price of a sandwich

F: Car insurance

2. Do you think that demand for the following is price elastic or inelastic?

A: Emergency plumbers

B: Children's school clothes

C: Tickets to music concerts

Data analysis   4.2

A price reduction from 40 to 38 pence increases sales of an energy bar from 200,000 to 210,000 units a week. Calculate the price elasticity of demand for these bars.

Economics and employability

What is your name?
Robin Cohen.

Tell us about your role at Deloitte.
I am a partner within the economic consulting practice at Deloitte. The main responsibilities of a partner are leading the many different aspects of our economic consulting practice. This includes leading client projects, building long-term relationships with clients, and developing our practice alongside the many other practices within Deloitte both in the UK and overseas.

What is economic consulting and why do clients use you?
Economic consulting applies economics to provide advice principally on the interactions between governments (or regulators) and firms, and between firms and the markets in which they compete. We do so to help our clients understand their economic issues and inform optimum business and policy decisions. In doing so, we apply a variety of economic concepts which are built upon those introduced in this book. Our clients use us to obtain credible economic analysis, which is well founded and uses reliable data.

What specific examples can you give of the application of economic concepts in your role?
Take, for example, the concept of price elasticity of demand. Our clients in the mobile telecommunications industry make decisions on their prices based on many different factors,

including any supply constraints they may have, the incremental cost of supply, the relative prices of their different types of services, and the prices of their competitors (and other substitutes, including fixed-line phones or email). For many products, operators may wish to increase demand in order to use up spare capacity in their network, but if prices are relatively inelastic then reducing the price will actually cause the overall revenue to fall, even if usage does increase.

Another good example of the application of price elasticity of demand is for our clients in the airline industry. When forming a business plan for a new flight route, an operator needs to have a very clear idea over its pricing and how this will relate to demand. It is very difficult and expensive for an operator to increase the supply of seats, and over-supplying can be a costly mistake. In addition, supply of seats is in many cases a stepped curve, with additional supply requiring the leasing or purchase of a new aeroplane, airport landing slots, and storage.

What skills are important in your role?

Having a comprehensive understanding of theoretical economics and concepts is obviously crucial to being a good economic consultant, but there are other skills that are also necessary.

We require our consultants to be good researchers. This means that they will need to be able to assemble facts and figures on markets and businesses quickly and accurately. We also require them to be excellent teamworkers. The deadlines that we have to meet to deliver our work often means that quite large teams are required that must work together in a coordinated and effective way. This also means that, as their careers progress, our consultants must become effective managers. Finally, and very importantly, communication skills are vital to applying economics outside the seminar room. This is because our success is measured by our ability to explain the results from our analysis to a wide audience, in particular non-economists.

How does the economic cycle affect your work?

The demand for economic consulting services is, to a large extent, acyclical—that is, it does not rise or fall substantially as a result of recessions or booms. This is because many of our clients, such as those in regulated industries, require our skills irrespective of the overall macroeconomic climate.

But some particular types of economic consulting work are more cyclical. For example, the reduction in both the profitability of firms and their credit availability during downturns typically reduces the number of mergers which clients undertake.

Sources: Robin Cohen, Tim Miller, Neil Marshall, and Ben Watts

Price and revenue

The **total revenue** that a business receives has many different possible names. It can be called its 'revenue', 'sales', or 'turnover'. Out of this revenue a business will pay costs; what it is then left with is profit. The total revenue that you earn will depend on the number of products sold and the average price of each one. For example, twenty products sold at £10 each generates a revenue of £200.

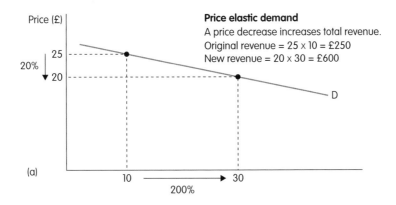

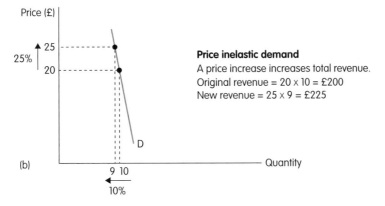

Figure 4.7 Prices, sales, and revenue

If demand is price elastic (see Figure 4.7a), a decrease in price will increase the total revenue earned by the business. This is because the fall in the price per unit leads to a bigger proportional increase in the quantity demanded; the increase in sales more than compensates for the lower unit price.

If demand is price inelastic (see Figure 4.7b), a decrease in price will lead to a fall in total revenue. This is because the increase in sales is less than the fall in price (in percentages). If demand is price inelastic, this means that managers can actually increase the price to boost turnover. Although sales will fall to some extent, this is more than offset by the increased price per unit and overall income will increase.

The effect of price changes on total revenue under different price elasticity of demand conditions is summarized in Table 4.2.

Table 4.2 Summary of price elasticity of demand

	Value	Effect on revenue of a price increase	Effect on revenue of a price decrease
Price inelastic	<1	Rises	Falls
Price elastic	>1	Falls	Rises

% Worked example

Last year, you were selling membership of your health club at £400 a year. You had 500 members. This year, you wanted to boost sales revenue and so you decided to reduce your membership fee to £360. The number of members has risen to 525.

1. Calculate the price elasticity of demand.

The percentage change in quantity demanded is:

$$\frac{(\text{Change in quantity})}{\text{Original quantity}} \times 100 = \frac{25}{500} \times 100 = +5\%$$

The percentage change in price is:

$$\frac{(\text{Change in price})}{\text{Original price}} \times 100 = \frac{-40}{400} \times 100 = -10\%$$

The price elasticity of demand is:

$$\frac{\text{Percentage change in quantity demanded}}{\text{Percentage change in price}} = \frac{+5\%}{-10\%} = -0.5\%$$

This is price inelastic (because the value is < 1).

2. Calculate the change in total revenue.

The total revenue last year was:

$$£400 \times 500 = £200,000$$

The total revenue this year is:

$$£360 \times 525 = £189,000$$

The change in total revenue is:

$$£200,000 - £189,000 = £11,000$$

3. Explain the link between price elasticity of demand and total revenue.

A fall in price has led to a fall in total revenue, because the demand is price inelastic; the increase in membership does not compensate for the lower membership fee.

Data analysis 4.3

1. What would the price elasticity of demand have been in the worked example if membership numbers were to have risen to 800?
2. What would have happened to total revenue?
3. What does this show about price changes, price elasticity, and revenue?

 Business analysis 4.2

The price elasticity of demand for tobacco

In 1999, a World Bank review concluded that, all else being equal, price rises of about 10 per cent would on average reduce tobacco consumption by about 4 per cent in developed countries and about 8 per cent in developing countries. In a more recent study of previous research, Gallet and List found that the average price elasticity of demand for tobacco products was −0.48. This means that, on average, a 10 per cent increase in price will be followed by a fall in consumption of 4.8 per cent.

Why might the price elasticity of demand for tobacco vary between developed and developing countries?

How do you think the price elasticity might vary between different age groups? What about different income groups?

If these estimates are correct, would a price increase lead to a rise or fall in revenue for tobacco companies? Explain your answer.

Source: http://www.tobaccoinaustralia.org.au/

How does the price elasticity of demand vary along a demand curve?

The price elasticity of demand will vary at different price points on a demand curve (see Figure 4.8). A customer's sensitivity to a 10 per cent increase in the price of a £1 newspaper may be very different from his/her sensitivity to a 10 per cent increase in a £500 suit.

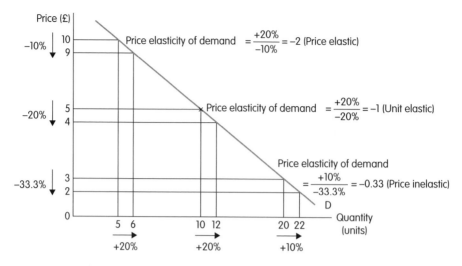

Figure 4.8 Changes in price elasticity along a demand curve

Generally, demand will not be sensitive to price changes at low prices, but at some price point customers will start to become more sensitive. This is reflected on a straight-line demand curve: demand is more price elastic at higher prices than at lower prices.

Therefore the price elasticity of demand for a product can change, and this highlights that managers need to be careful if they keep increasing the price. Demand may originally be price inelastic, in which case a price increase will lead to an increase in revenue. However, with successive increases in price, at some point demand will become price elastic and revenue will fall.

Determinants of the price elasticity of demand

The sensitivity of demand to a price change depends on how much the product is needed and how easily customers can switch to something else. The more that customers think you are offering something that provides them with a real benefit that cannot be provided easily in another way, the more price inelastic demand will be. San Pellegrino is not only bottled water, it is bottled water chosen by the very best restaurateurs, or so its publicity claims. However, if you offer something that customers think they can easily get somewhere else, then demand will be sensitive to price. An increase in your price will lead to a relatively large fall in quantity demanded as they switch to competitors. This is why companies work so hard to convince you of their unique selling proposition (USP) to lock you in and make you less sensitive to price, because, in your mind, 'there is no alternative'. Therefore when considering price elasticity the ease of switching and willingness to switch are significant.

Therefore the price elasticity of demand depends a great deal on the marketing activities of a business and the way in which a product is perceived. If a Sony product is seen as reliable and innovative, demand may be price inelastic. If you trust Hilton hotels, admire the Body Shop, feel warm about Google, respect Mont Blanc pens, and admire Nike trainers, these products are likely to be price inelastic. The greater the perceived uniqueness and the greater the brand loyalty, the more price inelastic is demand. Apple users often claim that their products are significantly different from other brands in terms of design, user-friendliness, and 'cool'; this makes demand price inelastic. If, by comparison, there are lots of alternative products that you rate as highly, demand is likely to be price elastic. Customers will also consider the costs of switching. Imagine that you have installed a particular database system in your business. To switch to another system may involve re-entering all the data, which could be very costly in terms of resources.

Therefore the value of the price elasticity of demand depends on factors such as the following.

- **The product itself** Does it offer something that people want and is it perceived to be unique in some ways? Newly developed drugs are often expensive because they are protected in law by a **patent** and so, if hospitals want such a drug, they have to pay quite a lot. Demand will be price inelastic if the product is effectively patented.

- **The availability of substitutes** The more of these there are, the more price elastic is demand. A substitute may be a rival product that is perceived to perform the same function (for example, a Toshiba laptop versus an HP laptop) or a product that is chosen instead of yours (for example, a Playstation rather than a bicycle as a Christmas present for your child). Managers may try to make it difficult to compare products to make demand for their product price inelastic; if you try to work out the best mobile phone deal, you can see the problems of comparing the price because of an enormous variety of offers, deals, and different features. However, if a business thinks that it can win sales by offering a lower price, it will try to make comparisons easier to encourage customers to change to it. For example, the food retailer Tesco regularly highlights which of its prices are cheaper than those of its rival Aldi.

- **Switching costs** Changing from one product to another may involve switching costs (for example, a fee to change mortgage providers, the time taken to organize a new internet provider, the time and effort needed to learn the features of a Mac compared with a PC, and the time needed to find out about and compare alternatives). The greater these costs are perceived to be, the greater the incentive is to stay put and continue with your existing products, making demand price inelastic.

- **Time** Over time, you have more opportunities to find substitutes, to research and test them, and to be sure that they will do the job properly. You also have time to organize a switch from one to the other, which makes demand more price elastic.

- **Who actually pays for the product** The demand for business travel on trains and planes is very price inelastic, because the businesses, rather than the individuals, tend to pay. This means that the individual is not particularly concerned about the price and so the providers can increase it. That is why business class or first-class tickets cost so much more than the standard fare.

- **The percentage of income spent on a product** If customers do not spend much of their income on your product, they may be less sensitive to price because it will have less effect on their overall spending power—a doubling in the price of chewing gum, for example, would not increase our overall spending considerably. How much would you be affected by a 5 per cent increase in the price of milk or sugar? What about your rent or your tuition fees?

Think about it...   4.5

1. What is likely to be the difference between the price elasticity of demand for a category of product (such as chocolate) and a particular brand of chocolate (such as Mars)? Explain your answer. (Note: Think about how easy it is to find a substitute for a brand compared with the product as a whole.)
2. What effect do you think the following actions are likely to have on the value of the price elasticity of demand for your product?
   A: Heavy investment in branding.
   B: The launch of a rival product by a competitor.
   C: A very favourable rating in a magazine.
3. Imagine that you are given £1,000. For what three things might you use the money? (Note: These alternatives are substitutes for each other even if they are very different products.)

What is the 'ideal' price elasticity of demand for a product?

The 'ideal' price elasticity of demand depends on what you are trying to achieve and how you want to market your product. In many cases, managers may want the demand for their products to become less sensitive to price. If you can make customers perceive that your product is different from that of the competition—that is, if you can make them think that there is something special about what you offer—the price becomes less significant and demand becomes more price inelastic. By promoting the particular features of your product, by highlighting how different it is from competitors, or by developing something that meets the customers' needs more precisely than anything else, you can make customers less sensitive to the price. They are buying the brand and the experience.

This type of strategy is known as a 'differentiation strategy' (Porter 1985): 'we deliver pizzas more quickly'; 'we use only organic products'; or 'we use only local suppliers'. In this situation, managers want demand to be price inelastic, enabling them to increase the price of their products: a Starbucks is not only a coffee, an iPhone is more than a mobile phone, and Chanel No. 5 is not only a nice smell.

An alternative approach to marketing is to focus on a low-price approach (this assumes that the business can get costs down so that it can still generate profits at low prices). Companies such as Primark and Ryanair have gained market share by offering products at a low price relative to competitors. In this case, managers would want demand to be price elastic—that is, they would want any cut in price to lead to a bigger increase in price (in percentages). Companies such as Poundstretcher, Primark, TK Maxx, Superdrug, and

Ikea all compete using a relatively low price as a factor, and therefore would want demand to be sensitive to price (price elastic).

Therefore the ideal pricing strategy for a business depends on the overall marketing strategy. This strategy may well change as market conditions alter. For example, when a product is first launched, it may have a unique feature such as its design (think of the first Dyson, the Blackberry, the Honda Prius, or the iPhone); this enables the business to charge a high price because demand is price inelastic. The first buyers are known as 'early adopters' in marketing terms, and the product may be a 'must have' item for buyers at this stage; in this case, demand is price inelastic and is likely to be set high. Over time, other firms may imitate the product, the original technology may no longer be cutting edge, and demand may become more price elastic. In marketing terms, the product may be entering the 'maturity phase' of its life cycle (see Figure 4.9).

Managers may want to cut the price at the maturity stage of the product life cycle to boost demand; this is known as an 'extension strategy'. When cutting price, the managers will want demand to be price elastic.

@ Go online to access a video walk-through of how to analyse the price elasticity of demand.

? *Think about it ...*   4.6

Which of the following statements about the price elasticity of demand are true and which are false?

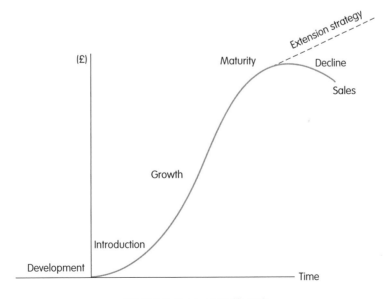

Figure 4.9 The product life cycle

A: If demand is price inelastic, a change in price does not change the quantity demanded.

B: If demand is price inelastic, a fall in price increases revenue.

C: A heavily branded product is likely to be price elastic.

D: If the price elasticity of demand is −2, an 8 per cent fall in price will lead to a 4 per cent rise in quantity demanded.

E: The price elasticity of demand along a demand curve is constant.

Apart from the price, what else can affect the demand for products?

Changes in the price will lead to a movement along the demand curve and a change in quantity demanded. But this is only one of many factors that might influence the demand for a product. There is, for example, the rest of the marketing mix to consider. Advertising plays an important role in generating many products, such as bottled water and cars, for example. Similarly, improvements in distribution can stimulate demand by making the product more visible. Just look at the rapid growth of Costa Coffee recently. The product itself is another key influence on demand—just look at the success of the Apple iPad, the BMW Mini, Lego bricks, Wagamama noodles, or the TetraPak carton.

   The demand for a product is also influenced by external factors that a manager cannot control, including the following.

- ■ *The income levels of the target market* The ability of the customer to buy a product at any given price depends on his/her income. With more income, he/she has more purchasing power and is able to buy more of a product if he/she wishes. But the impact of higher incomes on the demand for any given product can vary depending on its perceived nature. Some items may be regarded as luxury products; customers may aspire to these and, when their incomes increase by a given percentage, there is a relatively large effect on demand (think Burberry, Blackberry, Dolce and Gabbana, and Jimmy Choo). Other products may be perceived more as necessities and so demand for them will increase with more income, but not necessarily by very much. How much of any pay rise are you likely to spend on additional food flavourings, envelopes, or socks? Some items, known as inferior products, may actually see a fall in demand if income increases, as customers switch to what they regard as better products. If you win the National Lottery, you may find that you switch the moped for an Aston Martin, or a caravan holiday for an all-inclusive hotel holiday, so demand for mopeds and caravans falls as income increases.

- ■ *The population size* In marketing terms, the 'population' is the total number of people in the target market. This is not necessarily the same as the whole population of a country; rather, it is the total number of potential buyers. If you can gain access to new regions of the world, the size of your target market could increase, significantly boosting the possible demand for your products. This is why many well-known brands are trying to sell their goods and services in emerging markets, such as China and India. According to Unilever—the food, household goods, and personal care products giant—over 44 per cent of its income now comes from emerging markets. Your target population will also increase if you target a new **market segment**: for example, if you promote your moisturizer to men as well as women, or your aspirins to people with heart conditions as well as those with headaches.

- *The time of day, week, and year* Sales of many products will tend to increase in, for example, the build-up to Christmas. Sunglasses, travel insurance, and tennis equipment will tend to sell more in the summer. Clothes and music tend to sell more at the weekend; nightclubs will be busier on Friday evenings; and trains and buses will be busy at rush hour.

- *The actions of competitors* Naturally, the demand for your product will be influenced by what your competitors are doing. After all, in many markets, you will be fighting for customers and your rivals will be eager to take away your demand. They will try to do this through their own marketing activities: updating products; launching new models; cutting prices; and increasing their promotion. For example, BA and Virgin have fought very hard for many years to take customers from each other.

- *The effects of changes in prices of* complements The demand for your products will depend on other products that are linked to yours. A highly successful new computer game designed specifically for a particular console system may boost demand for that system (and vice versa). A fall in the price of contact lenses may increase sales of contact lens solution.

- *Changes in the law, or changes in government policy or advice* Smoking in public places is increasingly being banned (for example, it was banned in 2007 in the UK and in 2008 in most public places in The Netherlands). This led to a surge in the demand for patio heaters as customers were forced to smoke outside. With less smoke inside pubs, the smell of sweat became much more noticeable and so demand from pubs for air fresheners also increased.

- *The prices of other products* A fall in the price of a substitute product is likely to increase the quantity demanded of this product and reduce the quantity demanded of yours. An increase in the price of a complementary product is likely to reduce demand for this and for your product.

Shifts in demand

While a change in the price of a product can be shown as a movement along a demand curve, changes in any other factor lead to a shift in demand (see Figure 4.10). There is a change in the quantity demanded at each and every price. An increase in demand is shown by an outward shift in demand—more is demanded at each and every price (Figure 4.10a). A fall in demand is shown by an inward shift in demand—less is demanded at each and every price (Figure 4.10b).

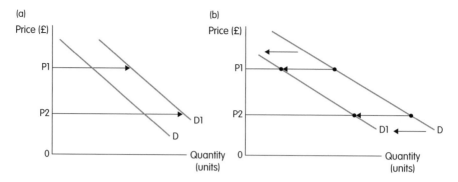

Figure 4.10 (a) An increase and (b) a decrease in demand

 Business analysis   4.3

In May 2012 the UK agreed a £50 million trade deal to sell British pork to China. Offal and trotters, and other pork parts appealing to Chinese but not to British consumers, will form the bulk of the meat. Pork consumption in China is estimated to have quadrupled over the last 20 years, creating a huge market opportunity.

What factors may be increasing demand for British pork?

Source: http://www.bbc.co.uk/news/business-18108545

 Go online to access a video walk-through of shift versus movements along the demand curve.

How might a fall in demand affect a business?

A fall in demand for your product might occur for a variety of reasons, such as a fall in income, a fall in competitors' prices, or a fall in the number of people in the buying population.

With a fall in demand, sales are very likely to fall as well. In the short term, you may not take action; you may wait to see if the fall in demand is going to last or not. As a result, stocks may build up as you continue to produce even though demand has fallen. But if you do think that the fall in demand will be sustained, you are likely to try to find ways to get demand to increase again or you might attempt to reduce costs because of the fall in income to try and maintain your profits.

Actions to boost demand might include:

■ new promotional strategies to make more customers aware of the products;

■ a relaunch of the products aimed at new markets or market segments;

■ finding new distribution channels to allow more people to access the products more easily.

Businesses may also try to reduce costs if sales are falling to try and reduce the impact on profits. Actions to reduce costs might include:

■ not replacing staff who leave (and, if necessary, making people redundant);

■ delaying new investment projects;

■ looking for ways of reducing waste;

■ looking to reduce capacity (for example, selling shops or shutting production).

The pressure on managers to take such action depends on how much demand has fallen and the existing financial position of the business.

 ## Business analysis   4.4

The number of pubs closing in the UK is around 12 a week according to the Campaign For Real Ale (Camra). Although this is slowing down, the total number of pubs that have closed since 2008 is over 4,500. The reasons are varied, but include the slow growth of the UK economy, high taxes on beer, and supermarkets selling beer cheaply. There may also have been a social change, so that going to the pub is no longer seen as part of a typical week. Around 55,000 pubs are left in the UK.

Explain three reasons for the decline in demand for pubs.

Do you think the decline in demand for pubs is likely to continue in the future?

The income elasticity of demand

One important factor influencing the demand for your products is likely to be the level of income of your customers. Changes in income will change demand and so you need to understand the relationship between the two.

The extent to which demand is affected by a given change in income is measured by the **income elasticity of demand**.

This is calculated using the equation:

$$\frac{\text{Percentage change in the quantity demanded}}{\text{Percentage change in income}}$$

Demand is said to be 'income elastic' if the percentage change in quantity demanded is greater than the percentage change in income. For example, if there is a 20 per cent increase in quantity demanded following a 10 per cent increase in income, this means that the income elasticity is:

$$\frac{+20}{+10} = +2$$

Demand is said to be 'income inelastic' if the percentage change in quantity demanded is less than the percentage change in income. For example, if there is a 2 per cent increase in quantity demanded following a 10 per cent increase in income, this means that the income elasticity is:

$$\frac{+2}{+10} = +0.2$$

In most cases, the demand for a product will increase with more income—hence the positive answer. But it is possible that demand might fall as customers switch to a more luxurious product. For example, there might be a fall of 20 per cent in quantity demanded when income increases by 10 per cent. In this case, the income elasticity of demand would be:

$$\frac{-20\%}{+10\%} = -2$$

The answer is negative because the variables move in different directions; an increase in income reduces the quantity demanded. Even though the number is negative, demand is still income elastic, because the change in quantity demanded is greater than the change in income (hence the value of 2). The sign of the answer shows whether demand increases or decreases when income increases.

If demand falls with more income, the product is known as an **inferior good**. If demand increases with an increase in income, this is known as a **normal good**. If demand is very sensitive to income (that is, a high value for the income elasticity), the product is known as a 'luxury product'. If demand is not very sensitive to income (that is, a low value for the income elasticity of demand), the product is known as a 'necessity product'. Following an income increase, the demand curve for a luxury good will shift more to the right than for a necessity product; demand for an inferior good will shift to the left (see Figure 4.11). When calculating the income elasticity of demand the sign shows whether demand increases or decreases when income increases, and the size of the answer shows whether demand is elastic or inelastic.

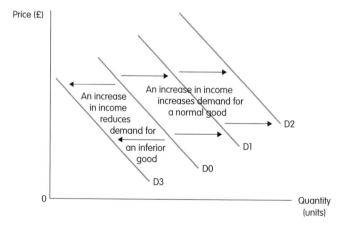

Figure 4.11 Income elasticity and shifts in demand

The effects of an increase in income on different types of product is shown on an Engels curve (Figure 4.12).

Income elasticity of demand is summarized in Table 4.3.

Data analysis   4.4

Table 4.3 Summary of income elasticity of demand

Product	Income elasticity of demand
Normal product	Positive
Inferior product	Negative
Necessity and normal	Value positive and <1
Luxury and normal	Value positive and >1

1. If income levels increase from £20,000 to £24,000 and sales of your furniture increase from 300 units a week to 330, what is the income elasticity of demand?
2. If the income elasticity of demand is +0.1 and incomes increase by 20 per cent, how much would the quantity demanded increase? If sales were originally 400 a week, how much would they be after the income increase?
3. If income levels increase from £20,000 to £24,000 and sales of your furniture fall from 300 units a week to 270, what is the income elasticity of demand?

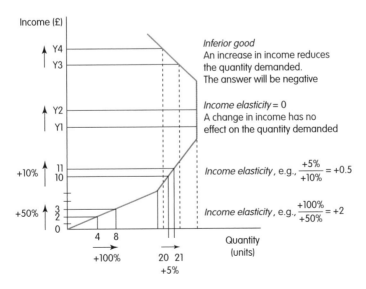

Figure 4.12 Example of an Engels curve

Business analysis   4.5

There are many goods and services that we bought in the 1970s that are no longer part of a typical shopping basket. When the Office for National Statistics (ONS) was constructing price statistics in 1977, it included cine film, radio licences, party containers of beer, luncheon meat, condensed milk, lard, and carpet tiles in its typical basket of goods. These have all gone, and have been replaced by products such as mobile phones, hair straighteners, low-alcohol lager, chicken nuggets, organic fruit and vegetables, and hardwood flooring.

There has also been a change in the relative importance of items in spending as incomes have increased. The greatest change has been in the importance of food in household spending. In the late 1970s, one pound in every four spent went on food. That has now fallen to less than 13 per cent. Alcohol and especially tobacco have also become less important elements of household budgets. The percentage of households spending money on tobacco has fallen dramatically from 60 to 24 per cent. However, spending on personal goods and services, motoring, and leisure services has grown. Car ownership is much more widespread, and much more income is spent on holidays. Spending on housing has also grown substantially.

Explain the reasons why

(a) the proportion of income spent on food has fallen
(b) the proportion of income spent on tobacco has fallen
(c) the proportion of income spent on cars and holidays has risen

as incomes have risen since 1977.

Source: Institute for Fiscal Studies: http://www.ifs.org.uk/

Why is the income elasticity of demand important to a manager?

If you can estimate the income elasticity of demand for your products, you can forecast the impact of expected changes in income. For example, if the income elasticity of demand for a product is +2 and an increase in income of 3 per cent is forecast, then you can expect an increase of 6 per cent in the quantity demanded. Based on this, you can order supplies, organize staffing, and decide whether this new level of demand is sufficient or whether you want additional promotions to boost sales further.

Therefore marketing managers should consider the income elasticity of their different products and the income growth in different regions; this may then lead to changes in the marketing approach. Imagine that you produce income elastic products, such as the latest washing machines and dishwashers: the fast economic growth in recent years of regions such as Brazil, Russia, India, and China (BRIC) would be appealing and you might want to focus on these areas in future. However, if you were operating in another country that was experiencing slower growth, you might decide to change your product mix to concentrate on more basic cheaper models that are less sensitive to income growth. Supermarkets, such as Tesco, have different ranges of products to meet different economic conditions. When incomes are growing fast, sales of the 'Tesco Finest' range will increase; when incomes are falling or growing slowly, the 'Tesco Everyday' range will do better.

 You and economics

Just imagine starting full-time work having been a student for the three years. Your income increases quite significantly (hopefully) and this will change some aspects of your consumption patterns. The amount you spend on deodorant and milk may not change very much, but you may buy more expensive perfume or aftershave, you may move to a more expensive flat, and you may increase the amount you spend on eating out and holidays. In some areas you may spend less; perhaps you catch the bus less often as you buy a car, you may buy less from Poundland, and you may finally get yourself a washing machine and stop using the launderette.

As you can see, some of the items you buy are normal and income elastic, some are income inelastic, and some are inferior.

The cross-price elasticity of demand

All businesses face competition. This means that you must be aware of what your rivals are doing and appreciate that your decisions will be affected by competitors' actions. This includes the effects of competitors changing their prices. At the same time, you must monitor changes in prices of products that are related to yours, because these will also have an impact on your demand.

Imagine that a customer is looking to buy a new digital camera: that customer is likely to look around at the various options, and compare models and prices. If a competitor offers a similar product at a lower price than yours, this is likely to reduce your sales; if the price of a complementary product falls, this might stimulate demand for your product. For example, lower prices for digital cameras might stimulate demand for photo printers.

The extent to which your demand is sensitive to a change in the price of another product is measured by the **cross-price elasticity of demand**.

The cross-price elasticity of demand is calculated using the equation:

$$\frac{\text{Percentage change in the quantity demanded of product A}}{\text{Percentage change in the price of product B}}$$

If the price of another product increases and the quantity demanded of your product increases, the two products are substitutes—customers are switching from that product to yours (think Pepsi and Coca Cola, Haagen Dazs and Ben and Jerry's ice cream, or

Mars and Kit Kat chocolate bars). The answer to the calculation will be positive because the increase in the price of product B leads to an increase in quantity demanded of product A; the two elements of the equation move in the same direction. For example:

$$\frac{+20\%}{+10\%} = +2$$

The size of the answer (in this case 2) shows the strength of the relationship. In this case the products are fairly close substitutes because an increase in the price of product B has twice the effect on the quantity demanded of product A.

However, if the products were complements, the cross-price elasticity of demand would be negative. For example, an increase in the price of coffee-making machines might lead to a fall in demand for coffee beans. Again, the size of the answer shows the strength of the relationship.

For example, if a 10 per cent increase in the price of product B leads to a 20 per cent fall in the quantity demanded of product A, the cross-price elasticity is:

$$\frac{-20\%}{+10\%} = -2$$

In this case, the two products are quite close complements because a price change for product B has twice the effect on the quantity demanded of product A.

An example of the significance of substitutes and complements is given by Frank (2008). Frank points out that many pubs and bars charge for water, but not for peanuts. The reason is that peanuts are a complement for beer and spirits. By getting you to eat more of these (which are usually salty), you will consume more alcohol—that is why they are given away. However, bottled water is a substitute for alcohol and so bars charge for this, otherwise they will lose income.

% Worked example

The Bengal Tiger and the Old Curry House are two Indian restaurants on the high street of a large town in southwest England. Last week, the Bengal Tiger introduced a special mid-week discount that reduced the average price of a meal from £20 to £18 per person. The number of customers on that evening at the Old Curry House fell by 20 per cent.

The price change at the Bengal Tiger is:

$$\frac{-2}{20} \times 100 = -10\%$$

The cross-price elasticity of demand for the Old Curry House is:

$$\frac{-20\%}{-10\%} = +2$$

This means that the products are substitutes (because a decrease in the price of one decreases demand for another) and are closely related (because the change in quantity demanded is twice the change in price).

 # *Data analysis* 4.5

1. Product A has increased in price from £2 to £2.50. As a result, sales of your product have fallen by 5 per cent. What is the cross-price elasticity of demand? Are the products complements or substitutes? Explain your answer.
2. The cross-price elasticity of demand for two products is −2. What is the effect on the quantity demanded of one if the price of the other decreases by 4 per cent?

Cross-price elasticity of demand is summarized in Table 4.4.

Table 4.4 Summary of cross-price elasticity of demand

Product	Cross-price elasticity of demand
Substitutes	Positive
Complements	Negative

Why is the cross-price elasticity of demand important to a manager?

All managers need to scan their environment to understand how changes in the marketing of other products might affect their success. By calculating the cross-price elasticity, managers can understand the relationship between different products more effectively. The relationship may not always be immediately obvious: when one supermarket increased the price of its wine, it found that its sales of cheese also fell; customers who bought wine also ate cheese, and so the products were complements. Understanding these relationships may determine what stores stock and even where products are displayed. Soft drinks and crisps are complements (along with DVDs—think of nights on which you stay in watching a film), and so are often put opposite each other in the supermarket aisles; the close relationship between these products influenced PepsiCo's decision to expand from drinks into crisps. The use of reward cards enables supermarkets to track very effectively who is buying what and the impact of different price changes on the buying patterns of different customer groups.

Equally, the cross-price elasticity of demand will show which products are substitutes. For example, top-up phone cards are a major substitute for sweets; when children are deciding how to spend their pocket money, they decide between these two products. A substitute for flowers is wine; people buy both as gifts for others. Understanding what is a substitute for your own products may influence how you promote your product, where you promote it, and with what messages.

Other forms of elasticity of demand

The concept of elasticity of demand examines the relationship (or correlation) between the quantity demanded of a product and other variables.

- The price elasticity of demand measures how sensitive demand is to changes in the price.
- The income elasticity measures how sensitive demand is to changes in income.
- The cross-price elasticity of demand measures how sensitive demand is to changes in the price of another product.

There are, of course, many other factors that can influence the demand for a particular product, such as changes in the temperature, interest rate changes, and changes in the population structure. For example, the amount of boiled sweets consumed in the UK is linked to the number of car journeys people take.

Managers will want to know the correlation between a specific factor and the demand for their product and therefore will want to calculate the relevant elasticity of demand. For example, the quantity demanded of lager, or the number of visitors to a garden centre, or the sales of sun cream may be related to the temperature; in this case, the manager of these products may measure the temperature elasticity of demand and use this to forecast changes in sales given expected weather patterns.

The weather elasticity of demand can be calculated using:

$$\frac{\text{Percentage change in the quantity demanded}}{\text{Percentage change in temperature}}$$

Similarly, managers might want to determine the relationship between the quantity demanded and spending on advertising. This could be calculated using:

$$\frac{\text{Percentage change in quantity demanded}}{\text{Percentage change in advertising expenditure}}$$

Therefore elasticity of demand is a powerful concept that can be used in a variety of situations to understand the drivers of demand for your product and the impact on demand as these variables change. Once these changes have been predicted, a business can plan in a variety of functional areas, such as producing a cash flow forecast, a workforce plan, or a marketing plan.

 Business analysis   4.6

In mid-2012 the UK supermarket Sainsbury's started a new stage in the petrol price war by announcing that it would reduce its petrol prices by 3 pence a litre. The cut was introduced at

Sainsbury's 266 petrol stations across the country. Asda, Tesco, and Morrison's had all announced price cuts in recent weeks.

Sainsbury's offered a 3 pence cut with a sales promotion giving a voucher for a further 5 pence off per litre for customers spending £50 in stores or online.

Sainsbury's Head of Fuel, said: 'We know that fuel continues to be a big part of many household budgets and we are committed to helping our customers cut down on cost whenever we can. Wholesale fuel prices have dropped across Europe and we are delighted to pass these savings on to our customers.'

Do you think Sainsbury's was right to cut its petrol prices?

Source: http://www.guardian.co.uk/uk/feedarticle/10250319

How much should you care if you lose one of your customers?

The total demand for your product is simply the sum of all of the individual demands of customers added together. Diagrammatically, we add together all the quantities demanded at each and every price (this is known as a 'horizontal summation'). In the same way, if we want the market demand for a product, we add up the demand for all the individual firms (see Figure 4.13).

If some customers switch to competitors, less will be demanded at each price, all other things being equal; this means that the market demand shifts to the left. If you operate in a mass market, the loss of one customer is unlikely to have much impact—one less person buying your chewing gum or drinking your tea may not affect the total sales very much. However, in some markets, one customer may be very significant indeed in terms of overall sales—for example, if you produce military aircraft and lose an order from a particular government, this may have a big impact.

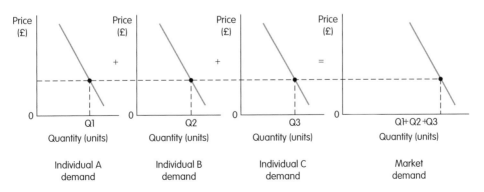

Figure 4.13 The market demand

The demand for a business and the market demand

Figure 4.13 can also be used to highlight the difference between the demand for one firm's products and the total market demand. A manager will be interested primarily in the demand for his/her products and how he/she can influence these. But the demand for all the businesses combined will make up the overall demand for that product. The actions by one business to shift its own demand outwards—perhaps through a better use of its salesforce or improved packaging—may have relatively little effect on the overall demand in a market. If the effect is simply to take demand away from other businesses, the total demand would stay the same.

Summary

Marketing managers will be very interested in the revenue that they can generate through sales. Often, they will have sales targets; these may be set in absolute terms or as market share (that is, the sales of one product as a percentage of the total market). To achieve a given level of sales, marketing managers must understand the factors that influence the demand for their products and how sensitive demand is to changes in these. Through their marketing activities, they can try to influence the demand for their products.

The concept of the elasticity of demand measures the sensitivity of demand to changes in these different variables. A manager can change some factors, such as the price of the product, to influence demand; other factors, such as income, are not directly under a manager's control. Effective marketing involves not only understanding the influences of demand now, but also preparing for how demand might change in the future.

Checklist

Having read this chapter, you should now understand:

- [ ] what is shown by a demand curve;
- [ ] the difference between a movement along and a shift in a demand curve;
- [ ] the meaning of the price elasticity of demand;
- [ ] the determinants of the price elasticity of demand;
- [ ] the difference between price elastic and price inelastic demand;
- [ ] how demand varies at different prices along a straight-line demand curve;
- [ ] the relationship between price changes, the price elasticity of demand, and total revenue;
- [ ] the difference between a substitute and a complement, with reference to the cross-price elasticity of demand;
- [ ] the difference between a normal and an inferior product, with reference to the income elasticity of demand.

Organizations and economics

Advertising Standards Authority

The ASA is an independent body set up by the government to regulate the advertising industry and ensure that organizations do not not mislead in their adverts. The role of the ASA is to ensure that all advertisements are 'legal, decent, honest and truthful'.

The ASA investigates complaints about adverts to ensure that misleading, harmful, or offensive adverts are withdrawn. This protects various stakeholders such as customers.

The need for the ASA highlights the potential dangers of markets that are left unregulated.

Source: http://www.asa.org.uk/

Short answer questions

1. What is stated by the law of diminishing marginal utility?

2. Distinguish between a change in quantity demanded and a change in demand.

3. Which of the following statements are true and which are false?
   A: A reduction in price always leads to an increase in total revenue.
   B: Total revenue = price + quantity sold.
   C: The price elasticity of demand for a downward-sloping demand curve is negative.
   D: If the value of the price elasticity of demand is <1, demand is price inelastic.
   E: A price elasticity of −0.5 means that a 10 per cent increase in price leads to a 20 per cent fall in quantity demanded.

4. Which of the following statements are true for a downward-sloping demand curve and which are false?
   A: An increase in price will increase revenue if demand is price elastic.
   B: The price elasticity of demand is constant along a straight-line demand curve.
   C: If the percentage change in quantity demanded is less than the percentage change in price, demand is price elastic.
   D: A price elasticity of demand of −1.5 means that a 10 per cent increase in price will lead to a fall in quantity demanded of 15 per cent.
   E: If demand is price inelastic, then the quantity demanded will not change with a change in price.

5. Explain two factors that influence the price elasticity of demand.

6. Distinguish between a substitute and a complement.

7. Distinguish between a normal good, an inferior good, and a luxury good.

8. If the income elasticity of demand is +1.5 and the income of a region increases by 20 per cent, and sales were 400 units, what will they be now? Is demand income elastic or income inelastic? Explain your answers.

9. What is the difference between marginal and total utility?

10. What is a Giffen good?

Discussion questions

1. To what extent do you think that price is the most important determinant of demand?

2. Discuss the ways in which the concept of the elasticity of demand might be of value to the managing director of an international supermarket chain.

3. To what extent is the demand for low-cost airlines under the control of the companies' managers?

One step further

Visit our Online Resource Centre at **www.oxfordtextbooks.co.uk/orc/gillespiebusiness2e/** to test your understanding, watch video walk-throughs, and access further information on topics covered in this chapter.

Costs and revenues

5

Learning objectives

In this chapter, we examine the factors that determine the costs and revenues of a business, and how these might affect a manager's decision-making. An understanding of costs and revenues is essential to understanding the decisions made by businesses in relation to the amount they are willing and able to supply at different prices. This is quite a complex chapter, but an understanding of productivity and costs underpins a great deal of microeconomic analysis and so it is a very important section.

By the end of this chapter, you should:

- ☑ understand the difference between fixed and variable costs;
- ☑ understand the difference between average variable, average fixed, and average costs;
- ☑ understand marginal, average, and total revenue;
- ☑ understand the difference between normal and abnormal profits;
- ☑ be able to explain what is meant by profit maximization;
- ☑ understand the marginal condition of profit maximization.

© *Case study*

Susannah is expecting a bleak Christmas. In the past, she had always hoped for a jump in sales in December as customers bought last-minute presents from her book shop. This year has been very quiet, however, and if things do not improve, she will have to think about selling up and find something else to generate income. She has owned the Summercity Book Shop for fifteen years and built up a good number of loyal customers.

Then, three years ago, Waterstones, a national book chain, opened up nearby; a few months ago, a major supermarket opened just minutes away and is selling best-sellers at prices that Susannah cannot match. Susannah just cannot see a way of competing with these larger businesses.

In the past, Susannah had considered expanding her own business and opening up more shops in the region, but she had always decided against this. She had worried about her ability to control a much bigger business and decided that she was happy running only the one shop, provided that it made her enough money. Now, she is sure that she has left any plans for expansion far too late; survival is the key issue at the moment. If only she had expanded years ago, she might have been in a much better position now.

Susannah has written to her local Member of Parliament (MP), complaining about the seemingly non-stop growth of the big stores at the expense of smaller businesses. The MP has been understanding, but has said that there is little that she can do to interfere with the plans of private businesses.

Questions

1. What problems might Susannah have competing against the bigger stores?

2. Is there anything that you think she could do to keep in business?

3. Do you think that expanding her business would have made good business sense?

4. What do you think influences the objectives of the owners of a business? What are Susannah's business objectives?

5. Do you think that the government should intervene to stop big businesses expanding further?

6. Is there anything else that Susannah could do to try to get the government to intervene to protect her business?

Introduction

Businesses are created for a purpose. The owners will combine resources to achieve an objective. An objective is a target for which to aim. To be effective an objective should be 'SMART'—this means that it should have the following features:

■ specific—it defines exactly what is being measured;

■ measurable—it sets out the amount to be achieved or the desired rate of return;

■ agreed—it should be agreed between superior and subordinate rather than forced to try and achieve it;

■ realistic—capable of being achieved; there is little point in setting a target that cannot be hit;

■ time specific—it sets out the time period within which the target needs to be achieved.

For example, an objective might be to double the sales of the business in the next five years.

The objective of many businesses is to make profits. For example, a business might have an objective of increasing profits by £2 million over the next five years or achieving a return on investment (ROI) of 10 per cent a year over the next five years.

The profits of a business are determined by the difference between its revenue and its costs. Revenue measures the value of its sales; costs measure the value of the inputs used up. The difference between revenues and costs represents the excess earnings generated from being in business; these profits belong to the owners of the business. In this chapter, we examine the factors that influence revenues and costs, and therefore the profits of a business. We will examine how costs and revenue can change at different outputs and prices and therefore how much businesses will want to supply. This will enable us to derive the supply curve in the next chapter and understand what determines how much is supplied at each price.

Profits

Profit measures the difference between revenue and costs. It is the difference between the value of the sales a business makes over a given period and the value of the inputs used up in generating those sales. It is an 'excess' that has been earned by selling the output produced. Profits are important to many businesses because:

■ they are used to reward the owners for taking the risk of investing;

■ they affect the value of the business—for example, high profits may boost demand for shares in the business, thereby increasing the share price and hence shareholders' wealth;

■ they can be used as an internal source of finance for further expansion, which is cheaper than borrowing money because the business does not have to pay interest.

Economics and employability

Tell us your name and a bit about your job.

My name is Ailsa Youngson and I run a small café based at the West Oxford Community Centre. I'm self-employed and license the café from the West Oxford Community Association, who run the Centre. As the sole employee of the business I'm responsible for everything that goes into running the café on a daily basis: menu planning, ordering, cooking, making coffee, clearing tables, event catering, accounts, marketing,and a lot of washing up!

In what ways is an understanding of economics useful in your work?

It's essential to have an understanding of economics—to put it simply, if you don't price the items on your menu at a level which more than covers the cost of making them (including labour costs and overheads as well as ingredients) you won't make a profit. But if you price them so high that you don't get any customers, you also won't make a profit. So you always need to bear in mind keeping your costs down and charging a reasonable amount—since I'm a community café, it's particularly important to me that my food is accessibly priced, though because I don't employ anyone and have a good arrangement with the Community Association, my overheads are also low, so that helps.

How does economic change affect your work?

I don't really have a sense of being affected by economic change—I think that eating out is a constant in people's lives, and particularly at the price level of my café I'm not sure that I'm really affected by people cutting back in the same way that perhaps a restaurant in a higher price range might be. Possibly over a longer period of time I might be able to detect more of an impact.

Did you study economics at university as part of your studies, and, if so, how has it helped you in your work?

No, I studied English at university which has not helped at all in my work, much as I enjoyed it! There was a small business component to the catering course I went on which was very helpful, but I think actively applying that knowledge is probably when it most makes sense, and a lot of what you learn, you learn as you go along. I had no idea when I went to university that I would end up running a café, and if I had I might have been more interested in economics.

What skills are important in your role?

The most important thing in my role is passion and enthusiasm—without this it would be hard to cope with the long hours and hard work. Cooking is obviously a key skill, but it's the fact that I continue to find cooking rewarding and engaging that makes it worthwhile. You also need to like people, as you are representing your business on a daily basis, and whether people feel welcome and comfortable is a big part of whether and how often they decide to come back, so you need to be polite and friendly no matter how tired you are or how bad your day has been, which can be easier said than done. It also obviously helps to be organized as there is a huge amount to juggle—not just the practical side but the admin and paperwork.

For managers, profits are often used as an indicator of their own performance and so, by increasing profits, they are helping their own careers (and possibly earning a bonus).

Economic profit compared with accounting profit

The profit of a business depends on the revenue it can earn and the costs it incurs. There are many different costs that a business has to pay—for example, staff costs, rent, and the costs of energy, materials, and equipment. These would all be measured by an accountant. But when economists think of costs, they also include the opportunity cost of the resources being used. They consider what these people, with these skills, and this land, and this machinery, and this finance, and all of the other resources that they have available, could be earning elsewhere and build this into the calculation of the costs. This is where accountants and economists differ in their calculations: an accountant measures the costs being paid (such as rent, wages, interest, and materials), but an economist also includes opportunity costs.

Normal and abnormal profit

If a business is just covering its economic costs, this means that it is making enough return to keep resources in their present use. This level of profit is called **normal profit**. There is no incentive for a business making normal profits to leave the industry for another one and there is no incentive for other firms to enter this industry; the profit being earned only covers the accounting costs and the opportunity cost of being there. Imagine that Tesco makes a profit of £1,000 million. This is a large sum of money, but it may simply be the amount of profit that these resources need to make to keep them being used by Tesco in the markets in which it operates. After all, Tesco is an extremely large organization with over 500,000 employees in 14 countries. In theory, it could use these resources to provide a completely different type of service and needs to consider how much it would then earn.

If the revenue being earned is greater than the economic costs, this means that an **abnormal profit** is being earned; this acts as an incentive or signal for other firms to try to come into this industry, because the existing businesses earn more than the opportunity cost of being there. Abnormal profits act as a signal for firms outside the industry to switch their efforts and enter new regions or develop new products to benefit from high returns. Whether they can actually enter the market depends on whether there are any barriers to entry.

? *Think about it ...*   *5.1*

There are many property programmes on television in which people redevelop and sell houses. Imagine a couple who give up their jobs and spend a year working very hard, six days a week, developing a house for an accounting profit of £30,000.

Why might an economist argue that this is a loss?

You and economics

You start work and you earn revenue. Out of this you need to pay costs—living expenses, phone bill, entertainment, bills, and repayments of loans. What's left over (if there is any!) is profit. You may decide to save this to use in the future or invest it now in something you need—perhaps a new motorbike or car. To stay in the job you are doing you need to earn a certain amount over and above your costs—this is the same as normal profits. If you earned less than this you would change your job! If you earn more than this you are making abnormal profit (although you wouldn't tell your boss that!).

The short run and long run

The cost and revenue conditions of any business, and the decisions that managers take as a result of these, will vary depending on the time period involved. At any minute, a manager will have to work with the resources he/she has available. Over time, however, managers are able to change the mix of resources they are using and can be more flexible in terms of the decisions that they can take—for example, they can recruit new staff and find new suppliers.

Also, over time, it is possible for the structure of markets to change as firms enter or leave the market and as technology changes. For example, Nokia started off producing paper before transforming itself into a telecommunications business, attracted by the higher rewards in this growing sector. 3M turned itself over time from 'Mining in Minnesota' to become a producer of products such as Post-It® notes. IBM used to be a major producer of computers but now concentrates mainly on computing services rather than the hardware.

Therefore it is important to distinguish between short-run and long-run decisions. The **short run** is defined in terms of production as the period during which at least one factor is fixed; in the **long run**, all factors of production are variable.

Therefore in the short run at least one factor of production acts as a constraint, and managers may not be able to use the resources in exactly the combination that they want. This means that, in the short run, the costs of the business may not be as low as they can be in the long run; this is because in the short run managers may have to try to minimize costs, given the technology and equipment that they have, whereas in the long run they can update this. Therefore in the long run, the manager can choose the optimal mix of resources to minimize costs for any level of output.

Another difference between the short run and the long run is that it may be possible for firms to enter or exit an industry over time. This means that managers may face more competition over time if other businesses enter the industry. It also means that managers may choose to reallocate their own resources to move into a different industry or market segment if they wish. As we saw in Chapter 2, when considering the production possibility frontier, resources may move out of one industry and into another, and this could be because businesses are pursuing higher profits.

How long the short run actually is will vary from industry to industry—for example, retail store managers may be committed to pay the rent on a building and not be able to change the firm's location for at least a year. Transferring data from an existing database system to a new one might take a few months, while opening a new factory might take over a year. Therefore the length of the 'short run' depends therefore on your commitment to existing resources.

? *Think about it...*   5.2

The long run is the period of time when all factors of production are variable. How long it takes to change all the factors of production will vary from industry to industry.

How long do you think it is likely to take to introduce a new production line in a car factory? What about the length of time to open a new hotel?

Types of costs

One of the most common ways of classifying costs is to examine what happens to them as output changes—that is, to distinguish between **variable costs** and **fixed costs**. 'Fixed costs' are costs that do not change with output—for example, the interest being paid on a debt or the rent on facilities may be fixed for any given period and are not related to the amount produced. Fixed costs can change over time, but they are not affected directly by how much you produce. By comparison, 'variable costs' do vary with the level of output—for example, the costs of materials and components used in providing the product would increase as more is produced. For example, as you build more houses, you use more bricks, slates, and electrical wire.

Therefore the total costs of a business can be analysed in terms of the fixed costs and variable costs combined, and calculated as:

$$\text{Total costs} = \text{Fixed costs} + \text{Variable costs}$$

As output increases, variable costs will increase as more of these resources are used up; fixed costs will not. The difference between total costs and fixed costs at any output is the amount of variable costs.

When running their businesses, managers must consider their cost structure. For example, if they have high fixed costs (perhaps because of expensive office locations or high salaries for staff), even if output falls to zero (meaning that no revenue will be coming in) they will have high financial commitments because the fixed costs still have to be paid in the short run. Therefore high fixed costs create a high risk if sales are lower than expected. Imagine that you have high levels of debt with high interest payments: if revenue falls, you may struggle to meet your loan commitments. Eurotunnel, the Channel Tunnel operator, suffered enormous financial problems for many years because of high interest repayments and a failure to hit its initial sales targets, thanks to low-cost airlines and the ferry companies.

The risk caused by high fixed costs explains why many businesses have attempted to become more flexible in their operations. They have tried to limit the number of salaried staff to the key employees and they have outsourced elements of production or used temporary or part-time staff when needed. If demand increases, more work is subcontracted or temporary staff are employed; if demand falls, less work is subcontracted or temporary staff are laid off. This makes the costs of the business more flexible and more responsive to changes in demand. A reduction in revenue is matched by a reduction in costs as the business quickly scales down. However, if many costs are fixed (for example, if all staff are permanent and on salaries), a fall in demand can cause far more difficulties because costs will not fall in line.

Even if most of the costs of a business are variable, managers will still be interested in controlling them. This may be by searching around to find the best-value supplier or finding ways of reducing waste. But, when reducing costs, they must be careful not to reduce the quality of the product and service, or they may end up reducing sales as a result. Cutting the number of crisps in your packet, or the quantity of soup in your can, may lead to customer dissatisfaction.

? *Think about it...*   **5.3**

Would it be better to employ all staff on short-term contracts?

Would it be better to link all staff pay directly to sales and abandon salaries?

Average and marginal costs

The total costs of a business are important when calculating profit, but managers and decision-makers are also interested in the average cost and the marginal cost.

- *Average costs* These are the costs per unit. Average cost is calculated as:

$$\frac{\text{Total costs}}{\text{Output}}$$

Managers will want to make sure that the price that they charge covers the average costs in the long run. If the price is higher than the average cost, abnormal profits are made on each unit. But when setting the price, the manager will consider the volume of sales as well as the profit per item. It may be better to make less profit per item and sell more than to have a high profit per item with low sales. The profit per sale for Tesco is around 5 per cent and for Amazon is about 3 per cent, but both businesses are able to generate high total profits because they have such a high level of sales overall.

- *Marginal costs* These represent the extra cost per unit. Marginal cost is calculated as:

$$\frac{\text{Change in total costs}}{\text{Change in output}}$$

If the marginal cost of the tenth unit is £5, for example, this means that the total costs have increased by £5 when the tenth unit is produced. In some industries, the marginal costs of production will be significant (for example, the cost of producing another gourmet meal in a top-class restaurant); in other industries, the costs of an additional customer (for example, another person on the bus or plane) will be negligible because the majority of the costs are fixed. Marginal costs are important because, as we shall see later, the profit-maximizing output can be found by comparing marginal costs and marginal revenue. When deciding whether to do something more it is the marginal (extra) benefit or cost you should consider.

The law of diminishing returns and marginal costs

In the short run, marginal costs are influenced by the law of diminishing returns. This law states that the extra output (also called the 'marginal product') from adding a variable factor, such as labour, to a fixed factor, such as machinery, will eventually diminish (see Figure 5.1). This means that total output will increase as more variable factors of production are added, but at a slower rate. With less productivity, the marginal costs of production will rise (see Figure 5.2). If each extra worker produces fewer units, but is paid the same amount of money as the original workers, the extra cost of the units in terms of labour will go up. For example, if one extra employee is paid £50 a day and produces fifty units, then the cost of these extra units is £1 a unit. If the next employee is paid £50 a day and produces only twenty-five units, the cost of these extra units in terms of labour is now £2. As the productivity of the additional employee falls, the extra cost of the units produced in terms of labour increases; therefore the marginal cost curve is the inverse of the marginal product curve in the short run.

Data analysis

5.1

Table 5.1 The relationship between marginal and total costs

Output (units)	Total cost (£)	Marginal costs (£)
1	20	–
2	50	30
3	90	?
4	140	?
5	?	60
6	?	80
7	400	?

Complete the missing figures for total cost and marginal cost in the table above. Explain the relationship between marginal and total costs.

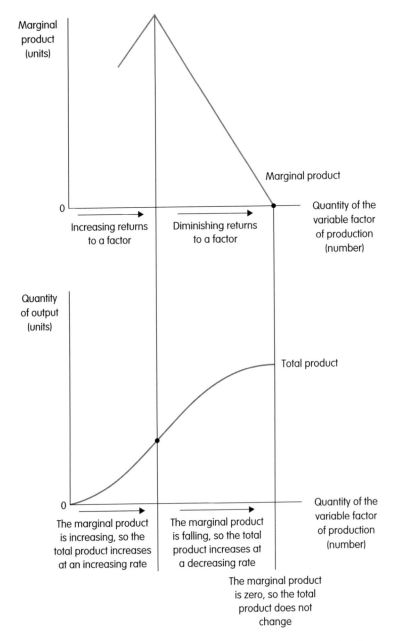

Figure 5.1 The relationship between the marginal product and the total product

Given the impact of the law of diminishing returns, the marginal costs will rise as the marginal product declines. This means that total costs will rise at a slower rate at first, due to falling marginal costs, but then start to rise at an increasing rate, due to increasing marginal costs (see Figure 5.3)

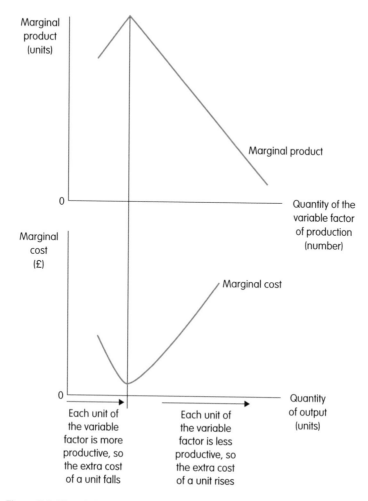

Figure 5.2 The relationship between the marginal product and the marginal cost

People and economics: David Ricardo (1772–1823)

Ricardo studied in London and Amsterdam and then set up as a stockbroker where he was extremely successful. In his *Essay on the Influence of a Low Price of Corn on the Profits of Stock* (1815), Ricardo set out what has become the law of diminishing marginal returns. In *The Principles of Political Economy*, published in 1817, he outlined his theory of economic rent. This is payment to landowners which is over and above the payment necessary to keep the farmland in its current state (i.e. it is abnormal profit).

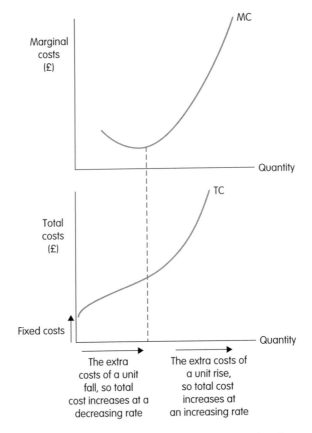

The extra
costs of a unit
fall, so total
cost increases at a
decreasing rate

The extra costs of
a unit rise,
so total cost
increases at
an increasing rate

Figure 5.3 The relationship between marginal costs and total costs

The relationship between average and marginal costs

If the marginal cost of another unit is below the existing average cost, the average cost will fall (see Figure 5.4). Assume that the average cost per unit is £10 and then you make an extra unit for £1; this will bring the average cost down.

However, if the marginal cost is above the average cost, the average will increase. Assume that the average cost per unit is £10 and then you make an extra unit for £12; this will pull the average cost up.

Table 5.2 demonstrates the relationship between the marginal cost and the average cost.

Managers will continually be trying to find ways of controlling their marginal and average costs to ensure that they remain competitive. An increase in costs is likely to mean fewer profits (or even a loss) or may require the business to try to push up prices if it can. Lower costs, by comparison, may increase profit margins and/or enable the business to reduce its prices, making it more price competitive.

 Go online to access a video walk-through of how to analyse marginal, average, and total costs.

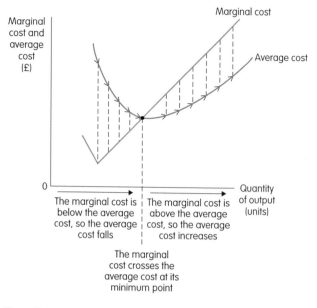

Figure 5.4 The relationship between marginal cost and average cost

 You and economics

It was a strange evening. You started off with a drink at home before you went. You had bought some beers from the supermarket so this worked out at about £2 each. Then you went to a nearby pub for happy hour where you paid £3 for a drink. You decided to stay for a while, but once Happy Hour had ended you were now paying £5 for a drink. Eventually you moved on to a nightclub—good venue and great music, but horrific prices. As the night had progressed the extra (marginal) costs of a drink increased, pulling up the average cost.

Analysing average costs

Total costs are made up of fixed costs plus variable costs. Average cost (the cost per unit, also called the average total cost) is made up of the fixed cost per unit and the variable cost per unit:

$$\text{Total cost} = \text{Fixed cost} + \text{Variable cost}$$

Therefore

$$\text{Total cost/output} = (\text{Fixed cost/output}) + (\text{Variable cost/output})$$
$$\text{Average cost} = \text{Average fixed cost} + \text{Average variable cost}$$

In the next section, we analyse the factors that determine the shape of these curves and how they influence the overall cost per unit.

Table 5.2 Average and marginal costs

Output (units)	Total cost (£)	Average cost (£)*	Marginal cost (£)	Consequence
1	100	100	–	–
2	180	90	80	The marginal cost is below the average cost, so the average cost falls
3	240	80	60	The marginal cost is below the average cost, so the average falls
4	280	70	40	The marginal cost is below the average cost, so the average falls
5	400	80	120	The marginal cost is above the average, so the average rises
6	600	100	200	The marginal cost is above the average so the average rises

*Calculated as (total cost/output)

Average fixed costs

The average fixed cost will continually fall as more units are produced. This is because the fixed costs can be 'shared out' over more units. Fixed costs of £100,000 with an output of one unit are £100,000 per unit; if 50,000 units are produced, they are only £2 per unit; if 100,000 units are produced, they are only £1 per unit. This explains why, in industries in which there are high fixed costs (such as the car industry, telecommunications, and transport companies), managers are very keen to keep outputs high so that the fixed costs are spread over more units.

If sales are low, managers will need to consider discounting their prices to promote sales; higher sales would reduce the average fixed cost and therefore may enable more profits to be made, even at the lower price. However, the danger is that, if sales do not increase, the business will make a loss due to the low price. The success of a price-cutting policy in these circumstances depends on the price elasticity of demand.

? Think about it ...   5.4

1. Can you think of two types of business likely to have high fixed costs?

2. If you were cutting price to increase sales significantly, would you want demand to be price elastic or inelastic? Explain your answer.

Average variable costs

The average variable cost shows the variable cost per unit, and its shape depends on the productivity of the variable factors. In the short run, the average product of the variable factor will tend to decrease at some point due to the law of diminishing returns. Employees are more productive on average at first, but at some point they become less productive because more workers are being added to fixed factors that limit their ability to produce. The average variable cost is the inverse of this; when employees are becoming more productive, the variable cost per unit falls and vice versa.

When the marginal product is above the average product, this pulls up the average product; when it is below, it pulls down the average product (see Figure 5.5). For example, if your employees handle fifty enquiries a day on average in your call centre and then the extra person only handles forty, this will bring down the average number of enquiries handled. If your employees handle fifty enquiries a day on average in your call centre and then the extra person handles sixty, this will increase the average. Therefore the marginal product cuts the average product at its maximum point.

Similarly, because of the relationship between marginal and average, if marginal cost is below the average variable cost, the latter will fall; if marginal cost is above the average variable cost, the latter will rise. This means that the marginal cost cuts the average variable cost at its minimum point.

Figure 5.6 highlights the inverse relationship between productivity and costs on a marginal and an average level. Essentially, if your variable factors are more productive, this reduces unit costs; if they are less productive, your unit costs rise. Again, this explains why managers should focus on productivity and make sure that this is improving, if possible.

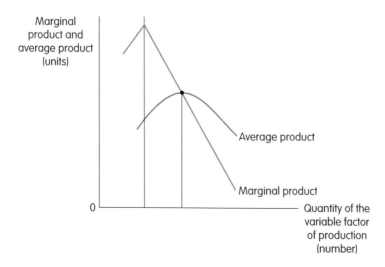

Figure 5.5 The relationship between the marginal product and the average product

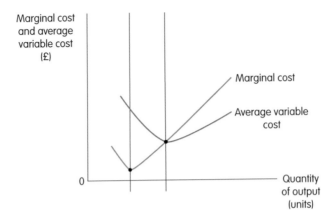

Figure 5.6 The relationship between the marginal cost and the average variable cost

 ## Data analysis 5.2

1. You employ ten employees who produce 500 units. What is the average product? If the marginal product of an eleventh worker is 100 units, what is the new average product?
2. If the marginal product of additional employees is falling, what is happening to total output?

Short-run average costs

Given that average fixed costs continually fall as output increases, this means that the average variable cost and average total costs get closer to each other as a business expands, i.e. they converge. At low output levels, costs are dominated by the fixed costs, but as output increases, the variable costs become more significant (see Figure 5.7). Again, this highlights the risk of having high fixed costs if sales are low; the cost per unit will be high because of your fixed costs, meaning that you will be making a loss.

 ## Data analysis 5.3

The fixed costs of a business are £80,000 a week. The variable costs are £20 a unit.

1. What is the average fixed cost and the average cost if:
   A: output is 200 units?
   B: output is 1,000 units?
   C: output is 5,000 units?
2. Would the business make a profit at 1,000 units if the price per unit were £50? Explain your findings.

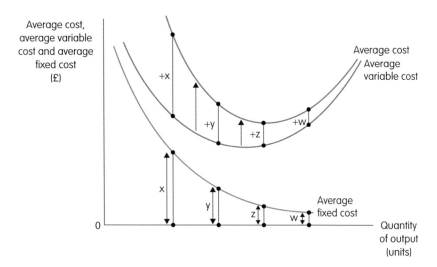

Figure 5.7 The relationship between the average cost, the average variable cost, and the average fixed cost

 ## You and economics

During the holidays you have many different temporary jobs. Last summer you worked on a summer language course as an assistant. This was a very labour intensive operation—the classes were small, the level of personal attention were very high, and the staff–student ratio was about 1:5. The staff wages made up a very high percentage of the total costs.

Last summer you were working at a bottling plant for Coca Cola. The investment in equipment was extraordinary, as was the scale of the whole operation, and you imagine that labour costs are a relatively small proportion of the total costs.

Long-run average costs

In the long run, managers can change all the factors of production; they are no longer constrained by having at least one factor fixed. With all the factors being variable, they can choose the ideal combination to minimize the average cost for any level of output. The lowest average cost for any output level is shown by the long-run average cost curve. This curve is actually derived from the short-run average cost curves.

A short-run average cost curve shows the lowest cost per unit given a level of fixed factor(s). Over time, the fixed factor can be changed (for example, more equipment can be acquired or bigger premises found), but then you are constrained again by this new level of fixed factor. Therefore another short-run average cost curve is constructed with a new level of fixed factors (for example, twelve machines rather than eleven). If the fixed factors are changed again, there is another short-run average cost curve, and so on. This means that there are different average cost curves in the short run for all the different levels of the fixed factor. The long-run average cost curve is derived by moving from one short-run average cost curve to another.

Assume that a business is producing at Q1 and has the optimal amount of capital equipment, so that its average costs are the lowest possible and therefore it is on the long-run average cost curve (see Figure 5.8). If the business expands to Q2 in the short run, it is constrained by the amount of capital it has and, in the short run, produces at X on SRAC1. Over time, it can increase its capital equipment to the optimal level and move on to a new short-run average cost curve at Y. If it expands again to Q3 in the short run, it moves along SRAC2 to Z but, over time, adjusts its capital equipment to reduce the unit costs to W on a new short-run average cost curve SRAC3.

The shape of the long-run average cost curve is important for managers when deciding whether or not to expand the business. If the long-run average cost falls, there will be an incentive to produce more over time, although this decision will obviously depend on demand as well.

Internal economies of scale

As a business moves to a larger scale of operations in the long run, it may experience falling average (unit) costs (as it moves from one short-run average cost curve to another). If the unit cost falls as the scale of operations increases, the business is said to be benefiting from **internal economies of scale.**

These internal economies of scale may be due to the following factors.

■ *Technical economies of scale* A business may invest in capital equipment, such as a production line. If this equipment is used only on a small scale, this will be expensive

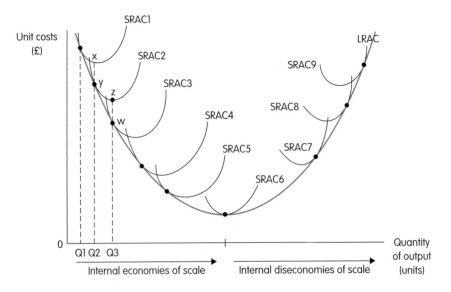

Figure 5.8 Internal economies and diseconomies of scale

(for example, the high costs of the production line may be spread only over a few hundred units of production). If production occurs on a larger scale, the cost per unit is likely to be lower because the costs of the investment are spread over more units. Some technology is designed for large-scale production and will be inefficient if used on a small scale. Think of farming: if you have only one field, but buy a tractor, this equipment is not used to its full potential. As you expand your farm, your tractor can be used more efficiently. This helps to explain why farming production is increasingly undertaken by fewer larger farms that are able to use their technology efficiently and spread costs in a way with which small farms cannot compete. Similarly, a production line will be inefficient if it is not used for the scale for which it has been designed: the production line at Coca Cola can produce 2,000 cans per minute. Imagine the impact on the cost per unit if it were to produce only one can per minute. Therefore to reduce unit costs machinery should be used fully.

■ *The law of increased dimensions* This economy of scale is most appropriate to businesses involved in transportation or warehousing. If the dimensions of a warehouse or container lorry are doubled, the volume that it can contain increases eight times (see Figure 5.9). This means that the cost per unit of storage or delivery is reduced. To build a container ship twice as large increases the surface area and therefore the material costs four times, but given that it can then hold eight times as much cargo the cost per unit being transported falls.

■ *Managerial economies of scale* These occur as a business grows, allowing it to use specialist managers. For example, larger organizations are more likely to be able to afford and justify specialist human resource (HR) managers. This may help to ensure that people are managed effectively, are motivated, and are used efficiently. Other areas in which specialists may be used might include finance, commercial law, and

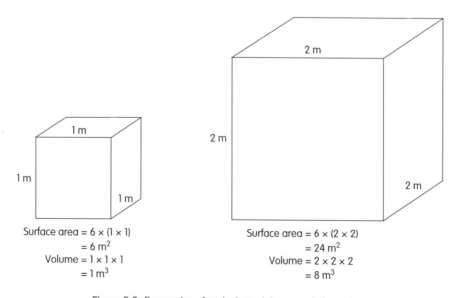

Figure 5.9 Economies of scale through increased dimensions

marketing. Entrepreneurs often try to manage all the areas of the business themselves and are unlikely to be experts in all these different fields. The employment of specialists can lead to better decisions and fewer mistakes being made. Managerial economies can also occur because the growth in the number of managers will not be as fast as the growth of the business as a whole. If a manager oversees four people, it is probably possible for the business to grow so that he/she is looking after seven or eight people without requiring an additional manager. This means that his/her salary costs can be spread over more people as the business grows.

- *Financial economies of scale* These occur if larger businesses are able to raise finance more cheaply than smaller businesses. Larger businesses are likely to have more assets to use as collateral than small firms, and this might mean that a bank believes that they are lower risk and therefore can be given lower rates of interest. The credit rating of a business (which is assessed by companies such as Standard & Poor's, and Moody's) has a big impact on the interest rate that it is charged; this does not depend only on the size of a business, but a larger firm with more collateral may be asked to pay less back overall.

- *Purchasing economies of scale* These occur when larger firms can negotiate better terms from suppliers and distributors. Given the scale of the orders, they can push prices down and achieve a lower cost per unit. They are the cost benefits that occur due to bulk buying. Large orders also enable suppliers to benefit from their own economies of scale, which can lead to lower unit costs, which can be passed on as lower prices.

The existence of internal economies of scale provides a reason for a business to expand to benefit from the cost advantages of large-scale operations.

?   Think about it...   5·5

Why do you think internal economies of scale are becoming more significant as markets become more global?

£   Business analysis   5.1

The *Emma Maersk* is one of the biggest ships ever built—almost 400 metres long, or the length of four football pitches, and another half-pitch wide. The ship can carry around 15,000 20-foot containers, each of which can hold around 140,000 T-shirts. This cargo can be moved from China to Europe in just over three weeks. To do this the *Emma Maersk* has the largest internal combustion engine ever built. Incredibly, the ship only needs 13 people to crew it.

Maersk Lines, the world's largest container shipping company and owner of the *Emma Maersk*, believes that scale is the key to success. It is now building 20 even larger ships with a capacity of 18,000 twenty-foot-equivalent units (TEUs).The new ships will cost $200 million each. Meanwhile, Singapore's Neptune Orient Lines has ordered ten vessels of 14,000 TEUs, and Orient Overseas Container Line has ordered ten of 13,000 TEUs.

However, the recent economic crisis has hit demand, meaning that there is over-supply and the price of moving freight has consequently fallen significantly. In 2011 Maersk said its container business had lost $297 million in the latest quarter. Competitors had also been losing money.

To improve the situation, companies are searching for new strategies to differentiate themselves from rivals, or merely to survive. Maersk has launched the 'Daily Maersk' service on the China–Europe run, deploying 70 vessels to promise daily deliveries to Felixstowe, Bremerhaven, and Rotterdam, the three main European container ports. The firm is hoping to deliver 95 per cent of these containers on time, up from 80 per cent for its own service on that route. This would be far higher than the industry average of about 65 per cent. If a container arrives more than a day late, Maersk pledges to compensate the customer. Orient Overseas, in contrast, is focusing on the quality of its cargo-handling.

Why do you think there is so much pressure on businesses to reduce their transportation costs?

Economies of scope

As well as internal economies of scale, larger businesses may benefit from 'economies of scope'. These are factors that make it cheaper per unit to produce a range of products in one business rather than for each of them to be produced by individual businesses. These economies include cost savings from centralized functions such as marketing. For example, Cadbury's markets all its chocolate under the one brand name, which means that it may need to spend less money on promotion to get a new product tried by customers, because the brand is known; it will also be cheaper to distribute all of its products together. Economies of scope will also include shared research into different products or processes.

Another advantage comes through cross-selling products from one business to others. For example, a travel company might sell travel insurance from one of its other divisions. This enables firms to access customers more cheaply. Just look at how banks have diversified into areas such as insurance, pensions, life assurance, and share trading.

A desire for economies of scope might encourage managers to diversify into different areas to share their skills in new areas. Historically, companies such as BTR and Hanson, in the UK, and ITT, in the USA, aggressively pursued expansion through acquisition, buying companies in very different markets, believing that there were gains from shared resources, however different the products. More recently, Tata has diversified into many different markets such as tea, cars, hotels, steel, and information technology. However, the problems of running many different types of business have tended to make conglomerates unpopular with managers and investors.

Internal diseconomies of scale

If managers keep expanding the business, at some level of output the long-run average costs may start to increase. If the average costs rise with an increase in scale, the business is experiencing internal diseconomies of scale.

The reasons why average costs might increase with a larger scale are generally linked to the problems of managing a bigger business, which include the following.

- *Coordination and control problems* Managing a small business is relatively simple, in that there may be relatively few people to organize and a limited number of products and customers with which to deal. As a business grows, it usually operates in more markets, with more decisions to make. Simply keeping track of what is happening when can be increasingly difficult and lead to inefficiency.

- *Motivational problems* With more people working within an organization, keeping everyone feeling as though they are part of the business and working towards the same aims can be difficult. Different departments, different divisions, and different regions can form their own ways of doing things, set their own priorities, and have their own values. This can lead to conflict, and can result in some people feeling as if their views are neglected. Absenteeism and labour turnover tend to be higher in larger organizations than smaller ones because of these problems of alienation.

? ## Think about it...   5.6

Unilever is a major manufacturer of food, homecare, healthcare, and personal care products. It has 400 brands spanning fourteen categories of home, personal care, and food products. Its brand portfolio ranges from global brands, such as Lipton, Knorr, Dove, and Omo, to trusted local brands, such as Blue Band and Suave.

1. To what extent do you think Unilever can develop a common set of values among all its employees and brands?

2. What problems might it face in achieving this?

To avoid diseconomies of scale, managers may adopt many management techniques, such as:

- the use of target setting to agree on objectives throughout the organization;
- the use of budgets to set financial targets for different parts of the business;
- the use of appraisals to review individuals' performances;
- ensuring that any one unit within the business is not too large—a policy adopted by the Virgin Group and Swedish company ABB;
- producing a mission statement to make it clear what the business believes in and what its values are, to try to get everyone thinking, believing, and acting in the same way.

A mission statement is meant to reflect the purpose of the business and the core values of its employees. It can provide a useful focus for employees by defining what the business represents.

All these techniques are adopted to try to ensure that all employees are aiming for the same goals and that they feel part of the business; hopefully, this can prevent the emergence of diseconomies of scale.

The minimum efficient scale

The level of output at which internal economies of scale stop occurring is known as the **minimum efficient scale (MES)** (see Figure 5.10). To benefit fully from internal economies of scale without incurring diseconomies, managers would want to produce at the MES. This level of output is likely to influence the number of firms competing in a market. If the MES is high relative to the total market sales, the market is likely to be dominated by just a few firms operating efficiently; if each firm becomes efficient and produces at the MES, it means that a few firms can supply the whole market. This may occur in markets such as banking, insurance, the car industry, pharmaceuticals, and aircraft manufacture.

However, if the MES is only a small proportion of the total market, the industry can have many relatively small, but nevertheless efficient, producers. This will result in a more competitive industry. This may occur in markets such as hairdressing, plumbing, and electricians.

However, the market structure will also depend on the cost disadvantage of *not* producing at the MES level (see Figure 5.11). For example, if the unit costs of producing at one-tenth of the MES level are only 0.01 per cent higher than being at the MES, the disadvantage of remaining small is not a major problem. You might find many inefficient firms surviving in this industry, and it might be possible for a new business to enter the market and compete even if it is relatively small and not operating at the MES.

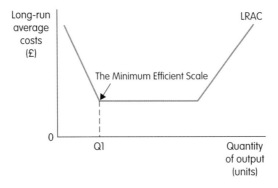

Figure 5.10 The minimum efficient scale

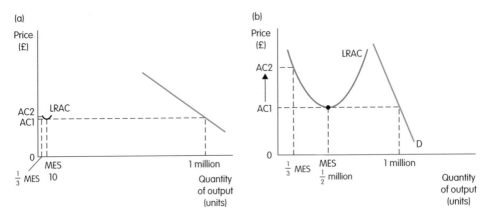

Figure 5.11 The relationship between the minimum efficient scale and market structure

However, if the cost disadvantage of operating at one-tenth of MES is 50 per cent, it is unlikely that inefficient firms will survive; trying to compete in this industry on a relatively small scale is likely to be difficult unless your product is different enough to justify a high price to cover the costs. On the left-hand side of Figure 5.11 there is a low MES relative to demand and a low cost disadvantage of operating below the MES; therefore you would expect many firms to be operating in this industry. In the industry on the right-hand side of Figure 5.11, the MES is high relative to the industry and the cost disadvantage of operating below this is high; this suggests that there will be relatively few businesses in this industry.

Therefore understanding internal economies and diseconomies of scale is important for managers because it will influence:

■ the level of output at which they might want to produce;

■ the likely structure of any market that they enter.

External economies and diseconomies of scale

As well as internal economies and diseconomies of scale, there are also external economies and diseconomies. These occur when a firm benefits from an external factor that increases or decreases the average costs at every level of output.

External economies of scale occur when the average costs fall at every level of output, for one of the following reasons.

■ *A location decision* By locating in a particular area near other similar businesses, this creates a demand for specialist services. Suppliers may locate nearby and local colleges may provide specialized training courses for this industry. This can reduce your own costs. These cost savings are also known as 'economies of agglomeration'. Silicon Valley is famous for its computing business and Hollywood for its films. Locate in an area like this and you can tap into a great deal of expertise and know-how.

- *The expansion of the industry* This creates more demand for suppliers, who might then benefit from internal economies of scale. As the suppliers gain lower unit costs, this may be passed on to their customers via lower prices.

External diseconomies of scale may occur if the industry expands, and this causes suppliers to grow and experience internal diseconomies of scale. They may then pass their higher average costs on in the form of higher prices.

Business analysis   5.2

Silicon Valley is in the southern part of the San Francisco bay area in the USA. This region is the centre of many of the world's largest technology corporations, such as silicon chip manufacturers and high technology businesses.

Why do you think Silicon Valley became such a hub for innovation?

What would be the advantage for a high tech business of locating there?

Problems reducing costs

Controlling costs is important to maximize profits, but this may require some painful decisions. For example, a reduction in output may require a reduction in the labour force—that is, it may be necessary to make some staff redundant. Such changes require consultation with employee representatives and may involve difficult decisions regarding who is to be made redundant. Managers will probably not want to rush to lay off employees if they can help it; after all, if demand increases, they may need those staff again. The business may try to negotiate wage freezes or temporary layoffs in the short term.

Reducing costs may also affect quality. For example, if a business switches to cheaper suppliers or cuts staff pay, it may find that the standard of materials or of the work done falls, and this may affect sales and the brand reputation in the future.

Table 5.3 Summary

Item	Meaning	Equation	Label
Total product	Total output	–	TP
Marginal product	Extra output gained by employing an additional factor of production	Change in output/change in factor of production	MP
Average product	Output per factor of production (e.g. output per employee)	Total output/number of units of factor of production	AP

(Continued)

Table 5.3 (*Continued*)

Item	Meaning	Equation	Label
Marginal cost	Extra cost of a unit	Change in total costs/change in output	MC
Average cost	The cost per unit	Total costs/output	AC
Average fixed cost	The fixed cost per unit	Fixed costs/output	AFC
Average variable cost	Variable cost per unit	Variable costs/output	AVC

Revenue

Controlling costs is obviously an important aspect of management and will affect all areas of the business. For example, the overall levels of spending that a business can afford will affect the marketing budget, the amount spent on supplies, the production costs, and the firm's approach to managing people. But the other element of profit is revenue, and managers will want to consider the likely revenue at different levels of output and compare this with the costs to decide on the profit-maximizing level of output. When analysing the accounts of a business, the revenue is called the 'top line'; the profits are called the 'bottom line', because this is the final figure after costs are deducted. Profits can be increased by increasing revenue or lowering costs.

Producing very low levels of output may have low costs, but if there is relatively little to sell, the profits may not be very high. Producing on a larger scale will cost more in total, but if sales are high and the business benefits from internal economies of scale, profits might increase as well. Therefore the optimal output depends not only on an analysis of costs, but also on an analysis of revenue.

The revenue of a business measures the value of its sales. It is also called the 'total revenue' or 'turnover', and is calculated as:

$$\text{Total revenue} = \text{Price} \times \text{Quantity sold}$$

For example, if a business sells 1,000 units at £20 each, then its revenue is £20,000 (see Figure 5.12).

Most businesses have a range of products and these are often sold at different prices in different markets. The total revenue of the business is the combination of all the different revenues from the various products. Costs then have to be deducted to calculate the profit that has been made:

$$\text{Total revenue} - \text{Total costs} = \text{Profit}$$

Marginal and average revenue

Managers will be interested in total revenue for any level of sales, but they will also be interested in analysing marginal and average revenue. Managers need to understand marginal and average revenue to decide whether to produce an additional unit, and to calculate the profits for any level of sales.

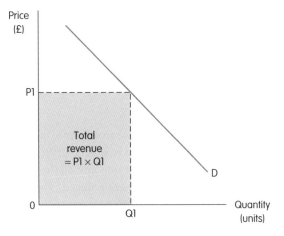

Figure 5.12 Total revenue

- Average revenue is the amount of income per unit—that is, the price. If each unit is sold for £20, then the average revenue per unit is £20.
- Marginal revenue is the extra revenue generated from selling another unit. If all units are sold at the same price, the marginal revenue is the same as the average revenue. For example, if all units are sold at £20, then the extra revenue is £20; when the price has to be cut to sell more, the marginal revenue and average revenue start to diverge.

Assume that you are able to sell one unit at £20, but you want to sell two units instead. If you are facing a downward-sloping demand curve, then, to sell more, you will need to lower the price. Assume that, to sell two units, you have to lower the price to £18. The average revenue (that is, the price) is now £18 per unit, but the marginal revenue is only £16. This is because you lowered the price to £18 for the second unit; you also had to reduce the price of the first unit from £20 to £18. Therefore the extra revenue is:

£18 (the second unit price) – £2 (the 'loss' or lost revenue on the first unit) = £16

Alternatively, you can see this from calculating the change in total revenue:

$$\text{Total revenue for one unit} = £20 \times 1 = £20$$
$$\text{Total revenue from two units} = £18 \times 2 = £36$$

The marginal revenue from selling the second unit is the extra revenue generated:

$$£36 – £20 = £16$$

Supposing that you want to sell three units rather than two and, to do so, you have to lower the price to £16? The extra revenue from the third unit is £16, but you have lowered the price on the first two by £2 each. The marginal revenue is:

$$£16 – £4 = £12$$

Calculating the total revenue, we can see that:

$$\text{Total revenue for two units} = £18 \times 2 = £36$$
$$\text{Total revenue for three units} = £16 \times 3 = £48$$

Therefore the marginal revenue from selling the third unit is:

$$£48 - £36 = £12$$

You can see from this that, as you lower the price to sell more units, the marginal revenue starts to diverge from the average revenue (that is, it gets further and further away). This is because you are lowering the price on the last unit and all the previous units. The more you sell, the more units that will have their prices reduced. Therefore marginal revenue equals the price of the last unit minus the reductions in price on all the preceding units.

It is important for managers to remember this. If they are going to set a higher sales target, they may have to reduce the price and sell all the units at the same price; the extra benefit should recognize that the prices will be lower on all the previous units than they were before. Think of a bank manager wanting to offer lower interest rates to new borrowers; if this has to be extended to the existing borrowers as well as the new ones, the lost revenue must be taken into account.

 ## Data analysis   5.4

You run a car dealership in Scotland. Assume that you can sell twenty cars this week at £20,000 each. To sell twenty-one cars and hit your sales target, you estimate that you will need to drop the price to £19,000.

1. What is the marginal revenue of the twenty-first car? What is the total revenue?
2. You calculate that, to sell twenty-two cars, you would need to drop the price as low as £6,000. What is the total revenue of twenty-two cars?
3. What is the marginal revenue of the twenty-second car?

 ## Think about it...   5.7

If all products were sold at the same price (for example, £10), what would the marginal revenue be? What is the average revenue? What is the total revenue if sales are 60 units?

Calculating marginal average revenue and total revenue

Between one and five units in Table 5.4, the price is lowered to sell more and is lowered on all previous units, meaning that marginal revenue falls. The more units that are sold,

Table 5.4 Marginal average revenue and total revenue

Output	Average revenue = price	Total revenue = price × quantity	Marginal revenue = change in total revenue/change in output
1	£10	£10	–
2	£9	£18	£8
3	£8	£24	£6
4	£7	£28	£4
5	£6	£30	£2
6	£5	£30	£0
7	£4	£28	–£2
8	£3	£24	–£4

the more units are affected by the price cut, and the bigger the difference between price and marginal revenue. As marginal revenue falls, total revenue increases at a slower rate. At the output of six units, marginal revenue is zero, meaning that total revenue does not change. To sell the seventh unit, the price cut on the previous unit exceeds the gain from the last unit and overall revenue falls (that is, marginal revenue is negative).

? Think about it... 5.8

Would you be prepared to pay different prices for different units? Imagine your first drink in the pub was one price but the price changed for each extra drink.

The divergence of average and marginal revenue can be seen in Table 5.4. You can also see the relationship between total revenue and marginal revenue in Figure 5.13. When marginal revenue is positive but falling, the total revenue will be increasing, but at a slower rate. When marginal revenue is zero, total revenue does not change and is at its maximum point. When marginal revenue is negative, the total revenue will be falling (a negative marginal revenue occurs when the price is reduced by so much or on so many previous units that this outweighs the gains of the extra unit).

The marginal revenue shows how much the total revenue changes and therefore is the gradient of the total revenue curve.

If demand is price elastic, a cut in price leads to a bigger percentage increase in the quantity demanded, so the gains from the new sales outweigh the revenue lost on those before. Therefore marginal revenue is positive and total revenue increases with a price cut (see Figure 5.14).

If demand is price inelastic, a price cut has relatively little effect on the quantity demanded and so the gain from new sales does not outweigh the lost revenue on the previous units. Therefore marginal revenue is negative and total revenue falls.

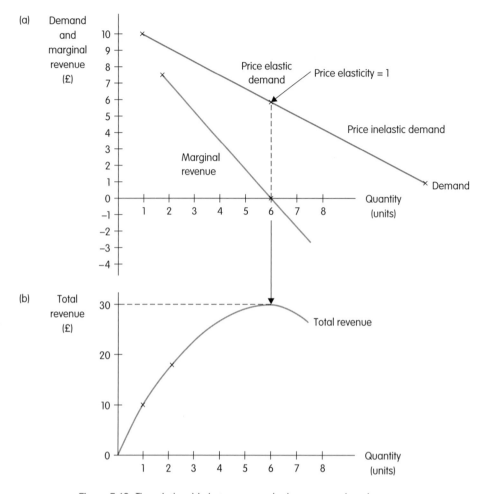

Figure 5.13 The relationship between marginal revenue and total revenue

@ **You and economics**

Last year you started helping a friend run student nights at a local club. You were charging £10 a ticket and managed to get an average of about 300 people into a venue with a capacity of 450. You are now trying to decide whether to change the price to earn more money. Your friend thinks that you could push the price up, but you wonder if you should cut the price. In the end you convince him to cut the price to £8 and end up filling the club. It was a good decision as revenue went from £3,000 to £3,600. Your friend had not believed that demand was very sensitive to price, but as someone living on a tight budget you knew better!

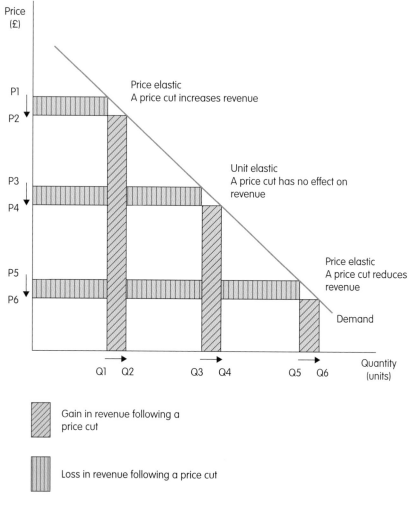

Figure 5.14 The relationship between price cuts and total revenue

Determining the profit-maximizing price and output—the marginal condition

Having analysed the costs and demand conditions at different levels of output, managers can determine the price at which they want to sell, and the output that they want to produce and sell.

The 'right' price and output will depend on managers' objectives. If the aim is to maximize profit, the manager will want the largest positive difference between total revenue and costs. This level of output can be identified using what is known as the 'marginal condition' (see Figure 5.15).

The marginal revenue is the extra revenue earned by selling another unit; the marginal cost is the extra cost of producing another unit.

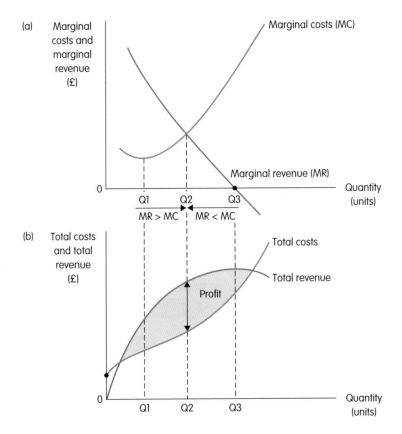

Figure 5.15 The profit-maximizing output

If a firm is producing at the point at which the marginal revenue is greater than the marginal cost, selling another unit would earn additional profits. This means that this unit and any others like it should be produced and sold to increase profits.

If the marginal revenue of selling another unit is less than the marginal cost, a loss would be made on this extra unit; as a result, this extra unit should not be sold, because the overall profits would fall. If the marginal revenue of an extra unit equals the marginal cost, profit would not change and so if it cannot be increased it must be maximized.

To maximize profits, a manager needs to make sure that the business is selling all the units for which marginal revenue is greater than the marginal cost, up to the point at which the marginal revenue equals the marginal cost; this means that every unit for which there is extra profit to be gained has been sold, up to the point at which there is no extra profit and so profits are the greatest that they can be.

Profit maximization occurs when there is the greatest positive difference between revenue and costs—that is, when marginal revenue equals marginal cost. This is the output for which there will be the greatest positive difference between revenue and total costs. This occurs at an output when marginal revenue equals marginal cost.

When marginal costs fall, the total cost rises at a slower rate (see Figure 5.15). This occurs up to Q1; after this, marginal cost rises and the total cost increases at a faster rate (the slope of the total cost, which reflects the marginal costs, gets steeper). Marginal revenue is falling as more output is sold, which means that total revenue increases at a slower rate up to Q3. At Q3, marginal revenue is zero, so there is no extra revenue and total revenue is maximized. After Q3, marginal revenue is negative and this means that total revenue falls. A business profit maximizes when marginal revenue equals marginal cost, which is the point at which there is the greatest positive difference between total revenue and total cost at Q2.

You and economics

You have decided to take up running to keep fit. You have been trying to increase the amount you run each week by adding half a kilometre each time. You find that every time you increase the distance the pain goes up, but there is also an increased sense of achievement. However, now you have got to 10 kilometres it feels as if the additional pain may be beginning to exceed the additional satisfaction, so you have decided to stick at this distance.

People and economics: Neoclassical economists

Neoclassical economic thinking dominates mainstream economics. It assumes that households seek to maximize their utility, given their incomes, and that businesses seek to maximize their profits, given the revenue and cost conditions. It assumes that people make rational decisions and highlights the way in which decisions are made using marginal conditions (such as marginal revenue and marginal cost).

Measuring the profits or losses made—the average condition

When a firm produces at the highest output at which marginal revenue equals marginal cost, this means that it is profit-maximizing (or loss-minimizing)—it is making the highest profit that it could make given the demand and cost conditions. To calculate the profit (or loss) actually made, managers can measure the profit per unit, by calculating:

Average revenue (the price) – Average cost

When this profit per unit is multiplied by the sales, the total profit is obtained. Therefore the marginal condition shows where to produce, and the average condition shows how much profit is being made.

Business analysis 5.3

In the first half of 2012 losses at at Euro Disney were up 22 per cent because of higher wages and the cost of refurbishments made to prepare for its twentieth anniversary later in the year. The company lost nearly €121 million (£97.4m; $157.4m) in the first half of the financial year compared with a net loss of €99.5 million in the same period a year earlier. The number of visitors to Disneyland fell, but those going spent more on average, which meant that revenues actually increased by 1 per cent. UK visitors were noticeably down. Euro Disney said that the 'challenging economic environment' had affected attendance, but that its twentieth-year celebrations presented a very important growth opportunity.

To what extent should Disney be worried about its fall in profits?

Source: http://www.bbc.co.uk/news/business-17981798

Producing in the short run—the shutdown point

In the short run, a business will be committed to pay fixed costs whether or not it produces. Even if output is zero and there are no sales, fixed costs still have to be paid (so a loss equal to the fixed costs of the business is made at zero output). Once the organization starts to produce, variable costs will be incurred. Provided that the revenue generated from the sales at least covers the variable costs, the business should produce in the short run, even if a loss is made.

For example, assume that the variable costs at a given level of output are £10,000, the fixed costs are £20,000, and the revenue is £11,000. Overall, if the business decides to produce, it will make a loss of £19,000, because the revenue of £11,000 does not cover the costs of £30,000. But the firm should still produce in these circumstances, because the revenue covers the variable costs and generates an excess of £1,000; this £1,000 is called a 'contribution' because it contributes to the fixed costs of £20,000 (see Figure 5.16). This means that the loss is only £19,000 if the firm produces, whereas if it were to shut down, it would still have to pay all of the fixed costs and make a loss of £20,000. By producing, the loss is smaller than the loss it would have made were it not to produce.

Therefore a manager should keep producing in the short run provided that revenue is greater than the variable costs. If he/she can reduce the variable costs (for example, through cost cutting), this can make it more feasible to keep going with a lower revenue.

If this situation is analysed in terms of individual units, a business should continue producing provided that the revenue per unit (the price) is greater than the average variable costs (that is, the variable cost per unit). This means that there is a contribution per unit, which can be put towards fixed costs.

The point at which there is no difference in terms of losses whether or not the firm produces is called the **shutdown point** (see Figure 5.17). This occurs when the total reve-

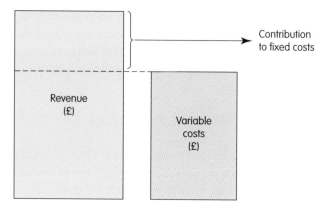

Figure 5.16 A contribution to fixed costs

nue equals the variable cost (which is the same as the price being equal to the average variable cost). In Figure 5.17, the units are all sold at the same price, so the revenue per unit can be calculated as:

$$\text{Average revenue} = \text{Price} = \text{Marginal revenue}$$

If the price is less than the average variable cost, the firm not only has to pay its fixed costs, but is also unable to pay its variable costs and so would be better shutting down.

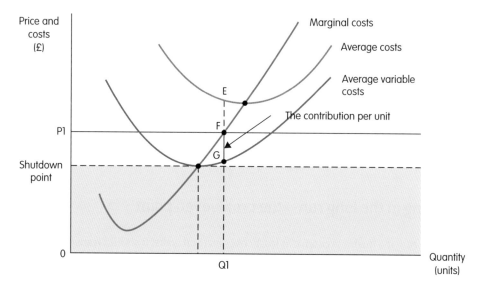

Figure 5.17 Shutdown point. The best output (i.e. profit-maximizing or loss-minimizing) at which to produce is where MR = MC, i.e. Q1. At this output the price (P1) more than covers the average variable costs and makes a contribution of FG towards the fixed costs. Overall a loss is made because the price does not cover the average costs, but the loss is smaller than if the business had shut down.

Assume that the price is £10, the average variable costs are £12, the fixed costs are £10,000, and the output is 1,000 units. If the firm decides to produce, the revenue fails to cover the variable costs by £2 a unit; given that 1,000 units are produced, this means there is a £2,000 difference between the revenue and the variable costs. The fixed costs also have to be paid, so the overall loss is:

$$£10,000 + £2,000 = £12,000$$

If the business were shut down, the losses would be only £10,000 (fixed costs).

Overall, therefore, a firm should produce in the short run provided that the price is greater than or equal to the average variable cost, but not if it is less. This highlights how important it is for managers to distinguish between the variable and fixed costs. If they were to scale right back in the short run, they would need to know the costs to which they would still be committed.

Contribution

The importance of understanding the concept of contribution can be seen in many business situations in which managers may be seeking to minimize their losses. Assume that a hotel is half empty and you ring up late in the day wanting to book a room. The price for the room is normally £100 a night, but you offer £60. Should the manager accept this offer? The answer is that he/she might, provided that the £60 covers the variable costs (such as the food provided at breakfast). In this case, what you are offering contributes to the fixed costs that have to be paid anyway. The hotel may still make a loss, but it will be less of a loss than if the offer was not accepted.

However, if a business regularly accepts prices below its published price, customers will all start to ask for the lower price and this may drive the price ever further downwards, removing any profits being made. Also, if the fixed costs are not fully covered, the business would not be able to sustain this sort of approach in the long run and would have to shut down.

Producing in the long run—the break-even point

In the long run, if a business cannot at least cover its total costs, it should transfer resources out of this sector and into another or simply stop producing, because it is making a loss. Therefore in the long run the total revenue must cover the total costs for a business to stay in this industry. This means that the price per unit (the average revenue) must equal the average cost (see Figure 5.18). If the price falls below the average cost, the business will have to shut down in the long run. (e.g. if the price is P2 a loss of EF is made on each unit.)

If a business is making a loss in the short run, the manager will need to try to change this position to stay in the industry by using one of the following strategies.

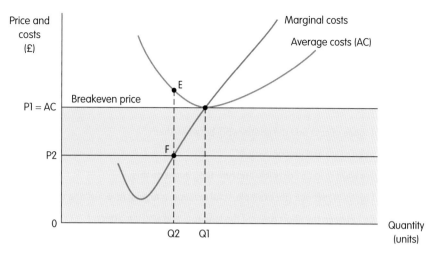

Figure 5.18 Break-even point

- *Trying to increase revenue* For example, managers might launch a marketing campaign to try to increase demand. This will, of course, increase costs as well, but the aim would be to boost revenue by more than the costs.

- *Trying to reduce costs* For example, the manager might try to reduce the amount of resources used in the production process. The danger of this approach is that the quality of the offering may suffer and therefore demand may fall and the overall financial position may be worsened.

}{ *People in economics: William Baumol*

William Baumol (born 1922), an American economist at New York University, argued that managers may maximize revenues rather than profits because their earnings may be linked to sales. This is examined in more detail in Chapter 10. Baumol has written numerous books and the focus of his work has highlighted the importance of entrepreneurship in promoting economic growth. Baumol has always tried to take economic theory and analyse how it works in real life business.

Summary

Managers must make decisions regarding the output that they want to produce and the prices that they want to charge. In some cases, they must make decisions about whether to produce at all. To make such decisions, they need to know what happens to costs and revenues at different output levels. In the short run, they can produce provided that the price at least equals the average variable costs. In the long run, the price must at least equal the average cost—that is, normal profits must be made. A profit-maximizing business will produce where marginal revenue equals marginal cost.

Checklist

Having read this chapter, you should now understand:

☐ the different types of cost and the relationship between them;

☐ the link between costs and productivity;

☐ why managers want to keep costs low and how they might do this;

☐ the different types of revenue (for example, total revenue, marginal revenue, and average revenue);

☐ the difference between the short run and the long run, and why it matters;

☐ the marginal condition for profit maximization.

Short answer questions

1. Define profit. Explain why an accountant's understanding of profit is different from that of an economist.

2. Is it true or false that fixed costs never change? Explain your answer.

3. Is it true or false that the shutdown point for a business in the short run occurs when the price equals the average variable cost? Explain your answer.

4. Explain three types of internal economy of scale.

5. Explain two reasons why internal diseconomies of scale might occur.

6. If marginal costs are below average costs, what will happen to average costs?

7. Distinguish between horizontal and forward vertical integration.

8. Explain one reason why a business might undertake a conglomerate merger.

9. What is meant by contribution?

10. Explain why the supply curve is derived from the marginal cost curve.

Discussion questions

1. To what extent do economies of scale matter?

2. Discuss the potential cost advantages and disadvantages to a business of expanding.

3. Why do marginal costs matter?

One step further

🌐 Visit our Online Resource Centre at **www.oxfordtextbooks.co.uk/orc/gillespiebusiness2e/** to test your understanding, watch video walk-throughs, and access further information on topics covered in this chapter.

Supply

6

Learning objectives

At the centre of the free market system are the elements of supply and demand. In Chapter 4, we examined the factors influencing demand. In this chapter, we examine the determinants of supply.

By the end of this chapter, you should:

☑ understand the influences on supply;

☑ understand the difference between a movement along, and a shift in, supply;

☑ understand the price elasticity of supply and factors influencing the price elasticity of supply;

☑ be able to explain the effect of an indirect tax on supply;

☑ be able to explain the effect of a subsidy to producers on supply.

Business economics

Case study

Ross had run a number of music shops and so knew quite a lot about the retail side of the music industry. Five years ago he decided to start his own business producing plectrums—these are small plastic items used by guitarists to strike the strings on guitars. There were a couple of major producers of plectrums that Ross knew about, but these were American. Ross decided to produce his plectrums in the UK, and as a special feature his plectrums would feature very British symbols on them and he would make them in red, white, and blue plastic. Imprinted on the plectrums were references to the Queen, London, the 1966 World Cup, red postboxes, and a range of other British icons.

Ross found a UK-based manufacturer who used plastic injection moulding to make a plectrum from recycled plastic (another selling point) for about 0.6 pence. The plectrums were sold in packs to music retailers. However, the shops proved reluctant to switch suppliers to an unknown brand and wanted a big incentive to take the risk of stocking his products. Although Ross managed to sell a few hundred early on, he needed to get unit costs down to be able to make a profit. He searched around and found new suppliers in China. Ross had wanted his plectrums to be produced in the UK, but he could produce them abroad for about 0.06 pence per item—significantly cheaper.

Although there was some growth in his business over the next few months, technology was improving fast and companies and even individuals were starting to buy 3D printers. These gave them the ability to design and build their own plectrums with their own designs. They do not need to buy from anyone else any more. The total number of plectrums being produced was increasing rapidly, but the market for Ross's plectrums was disappearing fast.

Questions

1. What do you think determines the total number of plectrums that can be supplied in the UK?

2. What is the effect on the quantity producers might want to supply at a given price if they find cheaper sources of production?

3. Ross reduced costs by finding suppliers in China. Can you think of other examples of manufacturers switching production abroad to benefit from lower costs? What factors apart from costs might businesses think of when deciding whether to relocate production abroad?

4. What is the impact of technological change on the amount firms can supply at each and every price? Can you think of industries where technology has had a significant impact on supply?

5. If the price of plectrums increased significantly, do you think Ross would find it easy or difficult to increase production? Explain your answer. Think of one industry where it would be difficult to increase output quickly, and one other industry where you think it would be relatively easy.

Introduction

Markets are important for managers to understand because that is where they buy their resources and sell their products. One aspect of a market is demand, which reflects what people are willing and able to buy at each price in a given period, all other things unchanged. The other element of a market is supply; this reflects what producers are willing and able to produce at each and every price. This chapter focuses on the determinants of, and influences on, supply.

The supply curve

A **supply curve** shows how much of a product producers are willing and able to produce at any price in a given time period, all other factors unchanged. To produce, suppliers will have to transform resources into the finished product.

Notice the key elements of the definition of a supply curve, as follows.

■ It shows the amount that producers not only want to produce, but also are able to produce—that is, simply wanting to produce something is not enough; suppliers must have the capacity and skills to deliver it.

■ It highlights changes in quantity supplied in relation only to price changes; it assumes that all other factors are constant. This is because if these 'other factors' change, such as the number of firms in the industry, a new supply curve will have to be constructed, because more or less will be supplied at each price.

In Figure 6.1, the quantity supplied at P1 is Q1; at a higher price of P2, the quantity supplied is Q2—this is known as an 'extension of supply'. The supply curve is generally upward-sloping, which means that more is supplied at a higher price, all other factors unchanged. At higher prices the quantity supplied increases as firms can now cover the higher extra costs involved in producing more units.

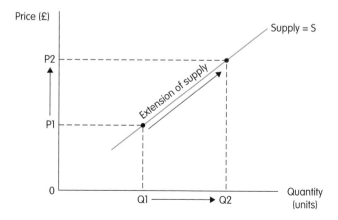

Figure 6.1 A movement along the supply curve—an extension of supply

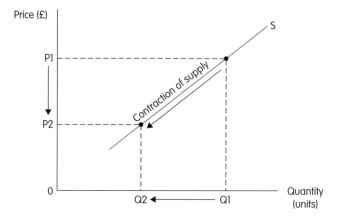

Figure 6.2 A movement along the supply curve—a contraction of supply

In Figure 6.2, as the price falls from P1 to P2, less is supplied; this is known as a 'contraction of supply'. With a lower price the business cannot afford to cover all the extra costs that it could before and this means that firms will reduce the output it produces.

Therefore a change in price leads to a movement along the supply curve and a change in the quantity supplied.

Producer surplus

As demonstrated in Figure 6.3, the supply curve shows how much a producer will supply at each price, all other factors unchanged. To supply Q1, for example, the supplier needs a price of P1. But to supply more output, such as Q2, the supplier needs a higher price P2 to cover the higher marginal costs. If this price is paid on all units, then the supplier has gained an 'excess' on all units up to Q2, known as **producer surplus**.

A producer surplus occurs when the price paid for items is higher than the price for which suppliers would be willing and able to sell them. The customer is paying the price needed to cover the marginal costs of the last unit; this means that he/she is paying more than is needed for the units before creating this surplus for producers.

? *Think about it ...*   6.1

Assume that you do not pay the same price for all units of the product, but insist on paying a different price for each one. You bargain hard and pay the price for each unit that the supplier needs to supply it, but no more (that is, you pay the price for each one shown by the supply curve).

A powerful buyer such as this in a market is known as a 'monopsonist'.

What is the producer surplus equal to in this case?

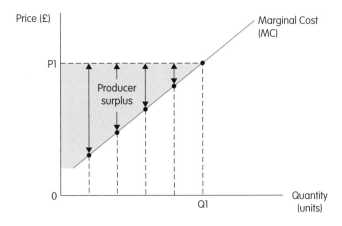

Figure 6.3 Producer surplus

The derivation of the supply curve

The supply curve in an industry shows how much businesses are willing and able to supply at each and every price, all other factors unchanged. We assume that businesses want to profit-maximize and so will want to produce where marginal revenue equals marginal costs.

If we assume that the products in a market are all sold at the same price, then the price (which is the average revenue) will equal the marginal revenue. If every unit is sold for £10, the extra revenue gained from a sale is £10. The marginal cost curve is usually a 'tick' shape as it is the inverse of the marginal product curve. When the marginal product of the variable factors starts to fall, due to the Law of Diminishing Returns, the extra cost of producing increases.

Figure 6.4 shows the derivation of the supply curve. At price P1 a business will profit-maximize at Q1 because this is where MR = MC and no more profit can be made. There is no extra profit to be gained and so profits are maximized. If the price increases to P2, more units are now profitable and businesses will produce at Q2. Therefore the marginal cost curve shows the quantity that is produced at each and every price and is the supply curve for a business.

Obviously it needs to be worthwhile supplying, and so:

■ In the long run the price must be above the break-even point, which means that the supply curve is the marginal cost curve above the minimum of the average costs. At prices below P1 the business would make a loss and therefore could not supply in the long run;

■ In the short run the price must be above the shutdown point, i.e. the supply curve is the marginal costs curve above the minimum of the average variable cost. At prices below P2 the business would not be covering its variable costs and would be better off shutting down;

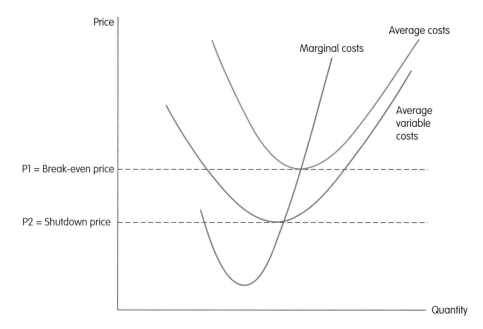

Figure 6.4 Derivation of a supply curve

■ To summarize, the supply curve of a business is the marginal cost curve above the minimum average costs in the long run and above the minimum of the average variable costs in the short run.

As cost conditions change this will affect the marginal cost and supply curve. A reduction in costs reducing the extra cost of producing would shift the marginal cost to the right, leading to more being supplied at any price.

To find the industry supply curve, the supply curves for all the individual firms are horizontally summated. The quantity supplied by each business is added up to give the total quantity supplied in the industry (see Figure 6.5).

 You and economics

It does not seem that long ago that Apple brought out the iPad. You remember how amazed you were when one of your friends got one—brilliant design, fairly intuitive to use, and a product that seemed to change the way we accessed information. Life would never be the same again. And now there are lots of different tablet computers to choose from—Apple has created a whole new category of product that has been so successful and profitable that others have followed them and supply has increased. The question now is where they will head next to try and capture more profits before others catch them up. Supply shifts as businesses move from one segment to another.

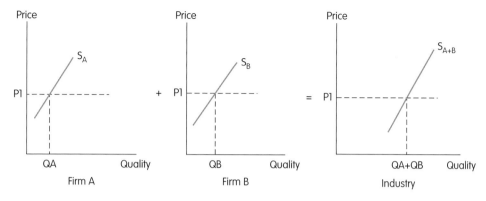

Figure 6.5 Deviation of the industry supply curve

Data analysis 6.1

An additional employee produces 200 units. The next additional employee produces 100 units due to the law of diminishing returns. They are both paid £600 a week.

Calculate the extra cost per unit in terms of labour as each of these employees is hired.

Shifts in supply versus movements along the supply curve

A change in price leads to a movement along the supply curve. It leads to a change in the quantity supplied. However, if there is a change in 'other factors', apart from price, this will shift the supply curve (see Figure 6.6). This is because it will change the amount supplied at each and every price.

An increase in the amount supplied at each price (that is, an outward shift in supply) might occur in any of the following situations.

■ If there are more producers in the industry—that is, if more firms enter an industry—this increases the total capacity and shifts the supply to the right. This may occur when profits are high in an industry, attracting firms from other sectors. For example, the success of organic food has led to more farmers switching to offer this type of product. The opening up of many international markets because of fewer restrictions on trade has also increased the supply in many markets. Just look at the products on your supermarket shelf to see how firms from all over the world now compete with each other.

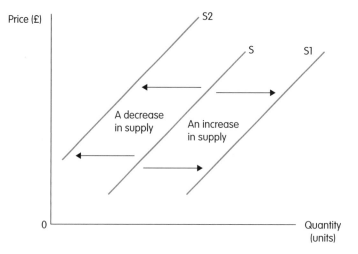

Figure 6.6 Shifts in the supply curve

- If technology improves, more products can be produced at each price, shifting the supply curve to the right. This can be seen in industries such as car production and the computer industry, in which investment in technology over the years and improved production methods have increased the industry's capacity significantly. Similarly, better farming methods in many economies have meant that more can be produced from the same amount of land.

- If the costs of producing and delivering the product fall, more can be supplied at any price, which again shifts the supply curve to the right. This could be due to a fall in energy costs, materials costs, components, or labour, or even a fall in the cost of borrowing money.

Go online to access a video walk-through of shifts versus movements along the supply and demand curves.

? *Think about it...*   6.2

In 2012 the Government's Chief Scientific Adviser said that genetically modified (GM) crops were required to meet increased demand for food over the next 15 years. The comments were made as testing of GM wheat began in Hertfordshire and protestors gathered to try and disrupt the testing. The Adviser said that it was essential to think about the future which he described as 'frightening'. He said that there are going to be significant increases in demand for food, and when prices go up it is the poor who will suffer. That is why he regarded GM testing as important to provide a greater supply of food and crops less vulnerable to disease. The Adviser said that a combination of climate change, water shortages, changing land use as crops are increasingly used for biofuels, and a growing population are creating what he described as a 'perfect storm'. He said that this 'storm' could threaten the health and welfare of hundreds of millions of people in coming years, but that scientific and technological advances such as GM crops could help avoid a catastrophe.

Opponents of GM argue that genes from one modified strain could spread into neighbouring fields and lead to unintended consequences. They claim that there has been no evaluation of whether foods made from the GM variety would be safe to eat.

What effect does GM have on the supply of food?

Do you think tests with GM crops should be allowed to continue?

Sources: http://www.telegraph.co.uk/foodanddrink/foodanddrinknews/8278014/GM-food-needed-to-avert-global-crisis-says-Government-adviser.html; http://www.organicconsumers.org/articles/article_24932.cfm; http://www.bbc.co.uk/news/science-environment-18215022

 Business analysis   6.1

Moore's Law

'Intel co-founder Gordon Moore is a visionary. His bold prediction, popularly known as Moore's Law, states that the number of transistors on a chip will double approximately every two years. Intel, which has maintained this pace for decades, uses this golden rule as both a guiding principle and a springboard for technological advancement, driving the expansion of functions on a chip at a lower cost per function and lower power per transistor by introducing and using new materials and transistor structures.'

Discuss the possible implications of Moore's Law for businesses in this sector.

Source: http://www.intel.com

An inward shift in supply

Managers need to consider the supply conditions in the markets in which they operate (both the markets in which they acquire factors of production and those in which they sell) and think about how these conditions might change in the future. For example, a major increase in supply due to the entry of many producers from abroad would significantly change the nature of the market, and managers must prepare for this. The specific factors affecting supply will vary from market to market. For example, the primary sector is very dependent on the weather and natural conditions. Supply in these markets is extremely vulnerable to change: a disease can wipe out a crop and shift the supply curve to the left very significantly and very rapidly. If you are relying on such inputs for your production, you may need to have contingency plans in case one supplier, or even a group of suppliers in one region, cannot supply you.

? **Think about it...**   6.3

Which of the following statements are true and which are false?

A: A supply curve shows how much producers would like to produce at each price.

B: A supply curve shows how much customers want to buy.

C: A reduction in costs should shift supply outwards.

D: A change in price causes a shift in supply.

The importance of labour productivity to supply

A key influence on a firm's costs, and therefore its supply, is the output per worker (i.e. labour productivity). Managers are always eager to find ways of increasing the productivity of their workforce because it can increase the amount that producers might want, and be able, to produce at a given price. This would shift the supply curve outwards. Improving productivity is a key operational objective in many organizations.

Methods of increasing labour productivity include:

- better training of employees so that they know exactly what they have to do and have the skills to do it more effectively;

- developing an open business culture within the business, so that employees feel able to contribute and suggest ideas that might lead to productivity gains;

- finding ways of motivating employees so that they try harder—motivation is likely to depend on factors such as the management style, how jobs are designed, whether employees get feedback, and whether employees are given enough feedback on their efforts;

- greater investment in capital, such as new machinery and technology, which can provide employees with better tools to do the job, and can lead to faster and better quality production—the amount of investment that managers undertake will depend on their ability to raise finance and their expectations of future profits, which in turn will depend on their view of the business climate.

Economics and employability

What is your name?
Claire Watt Smith.

What made you set up your own business?
My passion for business has always been apparent from a young age, but it was really cultivated when studying at university. I am incredibly determined, driven, and passionate about my label, BoBelle London, and thought if I didn't set up now, when would I? Taking the plunge is the hardest step, but my job is incredibly diverse, challenging, and rewarding.

What is BoBelle London?
BoBelle London is the luxury accessories brand with its heart and soul in London. Established in 2008, BoBelle London was conceived with the aim of creating sumptuous and elegant lifestyle accessories with a definitive British flair. Our luxurious accessories are hand-crafted in Britain using only the finest leathers and materials. The BoBelle London brand mixes elements of fun and sophistication with elegance that is based on a foundation of never-dating British style.

I am very passionate about style and longevity of fashion—this is what the label is about. BoBelle bridges the gap between classic elegance and luxury.

How are you affected by economic issues?
Every business is affected by economic issues. The recession has proved incredibly tough for many businesses, even fatal, but BoBelle has experienced a strong period of growth, and at the moment we are adapting in order to weather the storm and take advantage of growing markets. Being small and nimble allows this transition to be smoother and as our brand has been heading towards the luxury end, this is the best time to pursue the move.

What kinds of supply issues have affected the business?
We sold the last of our old season's lines a while ago and for the last six months we have been preparing for the new launch. This has included working with UK suppliers, rather than overseas as previously. This in itself has been a huge change and not as smooth as first thought. We are having to work with different deadlines and more suppliers than we did for our initial collections. This has proved to be a big learning curve, and aligning the different stakeholders, ensuring all deliveries are made at the same time, has been crucial. We work with only the highest quality suppliers and manufacturers so quality control has been highly focused. We have had to do a lot of research into the best quality for the brand and this takes time. We have also had to work around delays, which multiply the more suppliers you use, and learn more on the job than before. It has been an incredibly exciting transition and the new site is set to launch in August.

Did you study economics at all before starting up? If so, has it helped you?
I studied Business Studies at college and then consequently achieved my BSc (Hons) in Management and French and then an MSc in European Business with Spanish. Although the degrees I studied were more suited to working for a multinational organization and not necessarily

a start-up business, I feel that the university experience and studies helped to develop key skills that I wouldn't have learnt elsewhere. University opened my eyes to corporate social responsibility and business ethics. This has been a core element in BoBelle's culture right from the start. I also learnt in depth about supply and demand, budgeting, USPs and being flexible in business, as well as countless other subjects. University allows you to focus on yourself and setting personal goals. I found the experience invaluable in helping me to network with people and to have the courage to self-promote. Applying these elements to BoBelle has been fundamental in its success thus far.

How do you see BoBelle London developing next?

We have major plans for the brand; BoBelle London has a new business partner, so we expect huge growth over the next few years. Our repositioning as a luxury British brand allows us to tap into new markets and pursue our goals of overseas growth, as well as focusing on our home market here in the UK.

website: http://www.bobellelondon.com

Data analysis   6.2

Labour productivity measures the output per employee. It can be calculated as:

$$\frac{\text{Output}}{\text{Number of employees}}$$

1. If you employ 200 employees and your output is 8,000 units a week, what is the labour productivity per week?
2. If the weekly wage is £400, what is the labour cost per unit?
3. If productivity increases by 20 per cent what will be:
   A: the total output?
   B: the labour cost per unit?
4. What does this show us about the relationship between productivity and the labour cost per unit?

You and economics

You have been working at the local supermarket for the past few weeks. You thought that working on the tills and serving customers would be relatively stress free—how difficult could that be? But after your first few days your supervisor called you in and said that you were taking too long to scan the items. Apparently they monitor how long you take to process each order and monitor this very closely. Your supervisor has said that you are on probation and they will be reviewing your progress—you need to talk less and scan more to keep their costs down, they tell you!

The impact of lean production on supply

As well as increasing productivity, managers will also try to reduce costs in other ways. By reducing costs, they are able to supply more at a given price. Primark, the low-cost clothes retailer, can only offer such low prices and still make a profit by keeping its costs very low. The same is true of organizations such as Superdrug, EasyJet, Asda, and Poundstretcher, which use their low costs as a competitive weapon.

A major movement in operations management in recent years aimed at reducing costs is known as **lean production**. This involves efforts to reduce waste in all its forms throughout the production process.

Waste can occur in many different ways such as:

- when you are waiting for work to be delivered to you;
- when you have to rework items because they are faulty;
- when you make too many items and therefore they have to be thrown away;
- when stock is produced and is waiting to be sold.

If these forms of waste can be reduced, costs fall for any level of output and the business is more efficient. Therefore the supply curve can shift to the right.

Lean production aims to reduce costs and increase the efficiency of businesses. The lean approach is one reason why Japanese companies have achieved large market shares in many markets, such as cameras, televisions, and consumer electronics. They have been able to offer products with many benefits for relatively low prices, out-competing many of their competitors.

}{ *People and economics: Taichi Ohno (1912–1990)*

Taichi Ohno is considered to be the founder of the Toyota Production System which involves lean production techniques. He highlighted the need to remove waste from the production process and wrote several books about this such as *Toyota Production System: Beyond Large Scale Production*.

A particular element of waste focused on by Ohno was the level of stock held by a business; this was seen as a waste, because it represented materials sitting idle. This led to Ohno developing **just in time (JIT) production** at Toyota. JIT involves producing to order and holding as little stock as possible.

Holding stock can be expensive because:

- it involves storage and warehousing costs;
- it involves opportunity costs, because money is tied up in the stock rather than earning interest in a bank;
- stock that has been produced may deteriorate or may not sell if demand is not there.

Business analysis 6.2

In 2011 an earthquake in Japan affected businesses around the world. This was because so many manufacturers depend on Japanese suppliers. These days, many businesses try to hold relatively few stocks as part of their lean production approach, because stocks represent money sitting idle. The result is that they are very vulnerable if there are problems at suppliers. For example, the flash memories for Apple iPads are only produced in Japan, so when the factory was damaged by the earthquake there was a knock-on effect on iPad production. Sony had to close five of its six factories in Japan, which affected its production globally. Car companies were also affected. For example, the area in Japan affected by the earthquake produced 12 per cent of Honda's engines.

What effect would the Japanese earthquake have on the supply curves of consumer electronics and car manufacturing plants in Europe? Explain your answer.

Lean production is also linked to *kaizen*. This is a Japanese word meaning 'continuous improvement' and involves working with employees to find ways of continuously improving the way in which things are being done. This approach believes that gradual incremental change will, if undertaken continuously, add up to major improvements in performance through better quality and also cost reduction. It requires a positive working relationship between employers and employees, with a sense of them working towards the same goals.

 Business analysis 6.3

The Japanese car company, Toyota, is famous for the Toyota production system. This is an approach that is 'steeped in the philosophy of the complete elimination of all waste imbuing all aspects of production with this philosophy in pursuit of the most efficient production method'. The objective is 'making the vehicles ordered by customers in the quickest and most efficient way, in order to deliver the vehicles as quickly as possible'. It is based on the following:

● *Jidoka*—an approach that aims to highlight and make any problems visible as and where they occur, so that they can be prevented in future. If a defective part or equipment malfunction is discovered, the machine concerned automatically stops, and operators stop work and correct the problem;
● JIT production—that is, making only 'what is needed, when it is needed, and in the amount needed'.

1. Why might employees resist the introduction of a system like that of Toyota?
2. Why do many businesses have high levels of waste?

Table 6.1 Summary

An outward shift in supply	An inward shift in supply
An increase in the numbers of producers	A decrease in the numbers of producers
A decrease in costs (e.g. lower material costs)	An increase in costs (e.g. wages)
Reduction in indirect tax	Increase in indirect tax
Increase in productivity	Reduction in productivity

The price elasticity of supply

The extent to which the quantity supplied will change in response to a price change, all other factors constant, is measured by the **price elasticity of supply**. It is shown by the slope of the supply curve (Figure 6.7).

The price elasticity of supply measures the percentage change in the quantity supplied, given a percentage change in price. It can be calculated as:

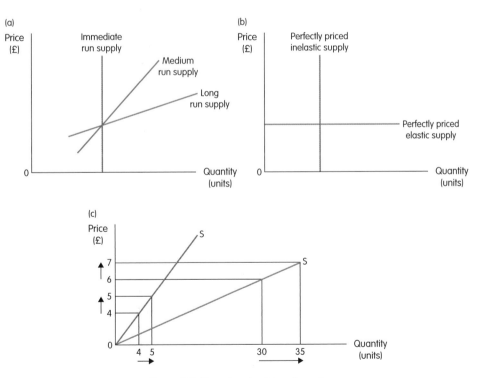

Figure 6.7 The price elasticity of supply

$$\frac{\text{The percentage change in quntity supplied}}{\text{The percentage change in price}}$$

If supply is 'price elastic', the percentage change in quantity supplied is greater than the percentage change in price—that is, the value of the answer will be >1. For example, if the quantity supplied increases by 20 per cent following a 10 per cent increase in price, this means that the price elasticity of supply is:

$$\frac{+20\%}{+10\%} = +2$$

The value of the price elasticity of supply here is +2, which means that the quantity supplied changes twice as much as the price has changed.

The sign of the price elasticity of supply is usually positive; this is because an increase in the price usually leads to an increase in the quantity supplied, so they have both moved in the same direction, which results in a positive answer. A negative answer would imply a downward-sloping supply curve (for example, less was supplied at a higher price), which would be unusual.

If supply is price inelastic, the percentage change in quantity supplied is less than the percentage change in price. For example, if quantity supplied increases by 2 per cent following a 10 per cent increase in price, this means that the price elasticity of supply is:

$$\frac{+2\%}{+10\%} = +0.2$$

Whenever the value of the price elasticity of supply is <1, the percentage change in the quantity supplied is less than the percentage of price—that is, that supply is price inelastic.

 ## Data analysis   6.3

1. Assume that you are a small producer of bracelets and necklaces selling to a big retailer. At an average price of £10, the quantity supplied is 4,000 units a week. If the price increases to £12 and this leads to an increase in the quantity to 4,400 units, calculate the price elasticity of supply.

2. Assume that you are the producer of homemade cakes to local stores. At a price of £3, you produce 500 a week. The price elasticity of supply is +0.8. How many will be produced if the price offered increases to £4?

Any straight-line supply curve that cuts through the origin has a unit price elasticity—any given change in price (in percentages) leads to the same percentage change in the quantity supplied. Any straight-line supply curve that cuts the X axis is price elastic, and any straight-line supply curve that cuts the Y axis is price inelastic.

? *Think about it...* 6.4

1. What will the value for the price elasticity of supply be if the curve is perfectly inelastic?
2. What will it be if it is perfectly elastic?

Determinants of the price elasticity of supply

The price elasticity of supply measures the ability of a business (or of all businesses in a market if we are looking at the industry as a whole) to respond to changes in price in a given time period, with all other factors unchanged. This depends on how easy it is to increase resources in the industry to increase output and how much the price has to increase to cover additional costs. If specialist skills and equipment are needed, or if it is a large-scale project, it may take time to increase the quantity supplied when the price goes up (think nuclear power stations, football stadia, or motorways). This would make supply relatively price inelastic in the short term compared with something such as the supply of cafés which can be set up relatively quickly. Within months, the supply could increase if the rewards were there. Over time, the supply of most products will become more price elastic as more resources are brought in.

If managers face a price inelastic supply in the markets for their resources, increasing the quantity supplied of these inputs may require significant increases in the price paid for them; this would increase the buyer's costs and either squeeze profit margins or lead to an increase in the price of the final product. If specific resources can become available only at much higher prices, managers may look for alternative ways of producing them.

 You and economics

When the tickets for the next Lady Gaga tour went on sale you immediately went online to buy them. The website went down within minutes because of the demand, and by the time you logged on again the tickets had all gone. You were devastated. The only option was to try and buy a ticket from someone else, but this proved more difficult than you thought. You hadn't realized other Gaga fans were just as devoted as you were. In the end you were almost embarrassed by the amount you had to pay—supply for these tickets proved very price inelastic.

6.5

? Think about it...

Organic food is grown without pesticides. It takes about two years for a farm to adjust from farming methods that use chemicals to be completely clear of pesticides; this makes the supply price inelastic.

1. What do you think will happen to the supply of organic foods when the economy recovers?
2. Do you think that the supply of organic food is price elastic or inelastic? Why?
3. Do you think that the supply of tickets to Wembley Stadium is price elastic or inelastic? Why?
4. Do you think that the supply of a song on iTunes is price elastic or inelastic. Why?

If the price elasticity of supply has a value of 0, this means that supply is perfectly inelastic; there is a given amount of supply and this is not affected at all by price changes. This may be the case in the very short run in many industries; businesses cannot suddenly increase output and so supply is fixed. Cinemas, restaurants, and even schools have a limited supply of places at any moment. This can lead to queues and shortages if demand increases, because supply is fixed; over time, more resources can be put into these areas and supply can become more price elastic.

How can managers make their supply more price elastic?

Managers may want to ensure that they can respond to price changes effectively—that is, they may want to make supply more flexible. Supermarkets would like to be able to handle more or fewer customers according to the number of people visiting the store; airlines need to cope with more passengers at particular times of the year; and car producers have to be able to increase or decrease production according to levels of demand.

Attempts to increase the flexibility of production include the following.

- Using temporary and part-time staff when demand is high—something that is common in sectors such as hotels, leisure, and fruit picking. It enables the labour input to be adjusted more easily to changes in requirements: when less has to be supplied, these staff can be laid off.

- Having flexible contracts in which staff can easily be moved from one job to another as demand changes from one product to another. These include annualized-hours agreements under which employees' contracts determine the total number of hours that they will work in a year, while how many hours they work in any given week or month can be varied according to demand, as long as it stays within the total agreed.

- Investing in new technology that is flexible enough to switch from producing one product to another easily and so has little 'downtime'.

Companies such as Zara have pioneered 'fast fashion'; this involves responding to changes in taste by producing new fashion lines and getting them into the shops within weeks. By using its own designers, controlling its own production, and having flexible production equipment, it can turn out new designs and clothes very quickly. Each store orders small quantities, which are made just in time; every week, a new order is placed. This means that the company does not get left with stock and does not have to discount to get rid of **surplus** items. Some of Zara's competitors buy months of stock in large quantities, which may enable bulk discounts, but runs the risk of the stock going out of fashion and being hard to sell. The responsive production system of Zara gives it a competitive advantage. Companies such as Domino's Pizza and Vision Express have also used the speed of their supply systems to gain market share.

The industry supply curve

The supply curve for an industry is the horizontal summation of the supply curves of each of the individual businesses (Figure 6.8). This simply means that it is the sum of all the amounts that each firm can supply at each and every price. For example, when more businesses enter the market, more is supplied at each price and the industry supply curve shifts to the right.

More firms are likely to come into an industry if:

■ barriers to entry are reduced or removed—for example, a government may remove restrictions on foreign goods coming into its country, or developments in technology might make it easier to provide services (e.g. online holidays);

■ they are attracted by high rewards (or potential high rewards)—for example, the success of Facebook as a social networking site may bring in more providers of this type of service, such as LinkedIn.

Figure 6.8 highlights the difference between the supply of one firm and the total supply in an industry. Actions by managers to shift their own supply to the right (perhaps through

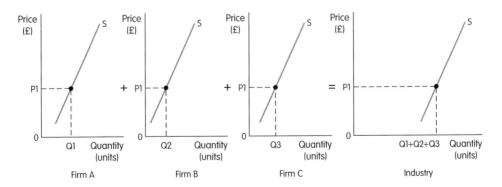

Figure 6.8 The industry supply curve

investment in capital or more training) may have little effect on the overall supply in the industry if the business is relatively small.

? ## Think about it ...   6.6

Which of the following statements are true and which are false?

A: If a supply curve is upward-sloping, the price elasticity of supply is positive.

B: If the price elasticity of supply is +0.5, a 4 per cent increase in price leads to a 2 per cent increase in the quantity supplied.

C: An increase in labour productivity should shift the supply curve to the left.

D: The introduction of lean production should shift the supply curve to the right.

Joint supply

Some products will be provided together and this is known as 'joint supply'. If you produce more beef, more hides will also be produced. An increase in the supply of one increases the supply of the other. This highlights that markets are interrelated, but these links may not always be desirable. For example, greater production of some products may also lead to an increased supply of pollution.

Government influences on supply conditions

A government can influence supply conditions by introducing indirect taxes and/or subsidies.

Indirect taxes

An **indirect tax** is a charge tax placed on the producer, who is legally responsible to pay it to the government. This form of tax is used by a government to raise revenue for its spending projects and, in some cases, to discourage consumption (for example, of alcohol or cigarettes). Indirect taxes increase the costs of producing and shift the supply curve, as shown in Figure 6.9. For any given quantity, a higher price now has to be charged to cover the higher costs.

Some indirect taxes are a fixed amount per unit, in which case the supply curve shifts in parallel (see Figure 6.9a). Other indirect taxes are a percentage of the price (see Figure 6.9b), in which case the supply curve will diverge (because 20 per cent of a high price is more than 20 per cent of a low price).

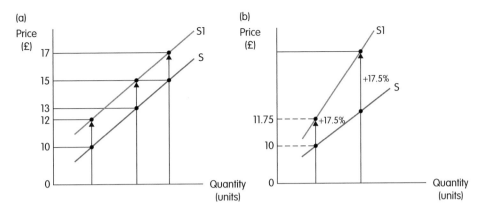

Figure 6.9 The effects of indirect taxes

Subsidies

A government may offer subsidies to producers to help an industry to produce more cheaply. For example, it may want to encourage the consumption of particular products that it thinks are desirable (such as local bus services) and, to achieve this, it reduces the costs of producers via subsidies. For example, in recent years the European Union has subsidized dairy farmers to help keep these producers in business.

A subsidy shifts the supply curve downwards (see Figure 6.10): any given quantity can be supplied at a lower price.

? Think about it...   6.7

1. If a government is going to subsidize a business, where will it get the money from? What problems might raising the finance to subsidize an industry create?
2. Do you think that subsidizing an industry is a good way of increasing consumption?

>> You decide ...

If you were a government minister, what would make you decide to subsidize one industry rather than another?

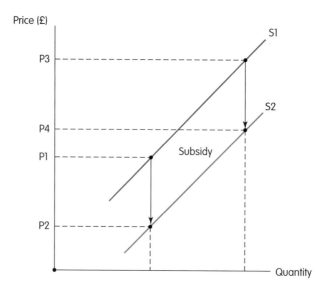

Figure 6.10 The effect of a subsidy

Summary

A supply curve shows the quantity supplied at each and every price, all other factors held constant. A change in price leads to a movement along the supply curve and a change in the quantity supplied; a change in the other factors, such as technology or the number of producers, leads to a shift in the supply curve. The sensitivity of the quantity supplied to a change in price is measured by the price elasticity of supply. An increase in indirect taxes adds to the costs of a supplier; a subsidy reduces the costs of a supplier.

Managers need to understand the determinants of supply, because an increase in supply might make the market much more competitive. Managers may also try to increase their ability to respond to price changes by making supply more price elastic.

Checklist

Having read this chapter, you should now understand:

- ☐ what is shown by a supply curve;
- ☐ the difference between a movement along, and a shift of, a supply curve;
- ☐ why a supply curve may slope upwards;
- ☐ why a supply curve might shift to the right;
- ☐ the effect of lean production and changes in productivity on supply;
- ☐ the meaning of the price elasticity of supply and an understanding of how to calculate it;
- ☐ how to derive the industry supply curve;
- ☐ the effect of an indirect tax on a supply curve;
- ☐ the effect of a subsidy on a supply curve.

Short answer questions

1. Explain what is shown by a supply curve.

2. Explain three factors that influence the supply of a product.

3. Distinguish between a movement along, and a shift of, supply.

4. Explain how an increase in costs might affect the supply curve.

5. What is meant by the price elasticity of supply?

6. Explain what determines the price elasticity of supply.

7. Explain what is meant by a price elasticity of supply of +0.5.

8. Do improvements in technology lead to a movement along, or a shift of, the supply curve?

9. What is meant by producer surplus?

10. How is the supply curve for the industry derived?

Discussion questions

1. Discuss the factors influencing the supply of a product.

2. Discuss the main determinants of the price elasticity of supply.

3. Discuss the ways in which managers can seek to shift supply to the right.

One step further

Visit our Online Resource Centre at **www.oxfordtextbooks.co.uk/orc/gillespiebusiness2e/** to test your understanding, watch video walk-throughs, and access further information on topics covered in this chapter.

Markets

7

Learning objectives

Much of economic analysis focuses on markets. There are markets throughout economies, such as the markets for products, currencies, money, and factors of production. In this chapter, we examine how demand and supply interact in a market, and how the price mechanism adjusts to bring about equilibrium.

By the end of this chapter, you should:

- ✓ understand how the price mechanism works;
- ✓ understand the meaning of equilibrium;
- ✓ understand the meaning of excess demand and excess supply;
- ✓ understand how the price mechanism adjusts to equate supply and demand;
- ✓ be able to explain the effect of a change in demand or supply conditions on the equilibrium price and output in a market;
- ✓ be able to explain the effect of the introduction of an indirect tax or subsidy on the equilibrium price and output in a market;
- ✓ understand the meaning and importance of community surplus and allocative efficiency.

ⓒ *Case study*

You were not sure if you could really afford to run a car whilst at university, but your parents said that they would help out a bit and it was certainly useful having one in terms of getting to and from the campus.

You just about managed to juggle the money in the first year; you were helped by friends giving you donations when you helped drive them around. However, you have had a couple of bumps that you had to claim for and when your insurance renewal came through the rates nearly made your eyes water. Your parents' insurance is quite reasonable, but they are reluctant to put you on their policy as they have had no claims for twenty years. Your insurance rates are nearly as much as the car cost you in the first place!

What is also worrying is that filling up the car with petrol is now a major investment decision—you cannot believe the price of petrol these days. It seems to be more expensive every time you go to the garage. Whatever happens, the price of petrol always seems to go up. Why does it never seem to go down? Part of the problem is the high level of indirect taxes placed on petrol by the government, but is that all there is to it?

You heard on the news yesterday that more oil companies are trying to get oil from shale rock—technically quite difficult but if they can do it efficiently it could increase the supply of oil considerably. You hope it will, but it probably won't happen soon enough to enable you to keep your car!

Questions

1. What do you think determines the price of car insurance?
2. Using supply and demand diagrams explain why the price of oil has been rising in recent years.
3. What do you think is the impact of rising petrol prices on:

   A: consumers

   B: businesses
4. Using supply and demand show the possible effect on oil prices if extracting oil from shale rock becomes more possible. What will determine whether companies invest in the technology to extract oil from shale rock? What is the impact of an indirect tax on supply and the equilibrium price and output?

Introduction

Managers oversee a transformation process within their organizations, creating an output to sell to customers. Resources such as labour, capital, and enterprise are transformed into final goods and services: take some food, some knives, whisks, pans, and an oven, add in a famous chef, and you may end up with a meal worth a lot of money. To produce this meal a restaurant is operating in markets for inputs where it buys supplies and the market for the final product which is sold to their customers. A market occurs when buyers and sellers come together to trade over a given period. If you have something to sell and you can find someone who wants to buy it, you have a market. Just think of eBay—millions of potential buyers and sellers trading in an online market.

Understanding how markets work is clearly important to managers. Why are rents higher in some areas than others? What are they likely to be in the future? Do some employees need to be paid higher wages than others to keep them? Why can energy prices vary so much? These changes in input prices can all be explained by changes in supply and demand conditions in their markets, and an understanding of these elements should enable managers to analyse and anticipate the effects of changes in market conditions on the costs of the business.

Similarly, the price at which a business can sell its products will also be affected by market forces. An increase in demand for a product or a change in supply conditions will affect the market price. A surge in demand for Lady Gaga merchandise, antibacterial handwash during a flu pandemic, or sun cream in a heat wave may all lead to more sales and pull up prices. Markets also affect many other factors that determine business success, such as the value of a country's currency. In previous chapters, we have examined demand and supply conditions separately. In this chapter, we analyse how supply and demand interact when buyers and sellers come together, and the significance of this for business decision-making. An economy comprises trillions of markets—local, national, global—with transactions occurring in many different ways: online, via market stalls, via email. An understanding of how these markets work and what the implications of changes in supply and demand might be is essential for managers.

Reaching the equilibrium price and quantity in a market

A market consists of buyers and sellers who come together to trade. The demand curve shows what customers are willing and able to purchase at each and every price, all other things unchanged, in a given period. The supply curve shows what producers are willing and able to produce at each and every price, all other things unchanged, in a given period. The price acts as a signal, incentive, and rationing device to bring about equilibrium in the market. It will adjust to bring the different independently made decisions of buyers and sellers in line with each other. Equilibrium occurs when there is no incentive to change; the market position is stable.

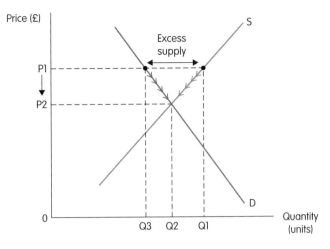

Figure 7.1 Excess supply

For example, if the price in a market is at P1, given the supply and demand conditions, the quantity demanded is less than the quantity supplied at this price (see Figure 7.1). This means that there is excess supply (equal to Q1,Q3), known as a 'surplus'. In this case, there will be downward pressure on the market price.

As the price falls, this reduces the quantity supplied (because there is less incentive for producers to produce if the price is lower) and increases the quantity demanded (because there are now more units that are affordable for customers and which provide benefits that are worth this price).

This process of the price falling will continue until P2 is reached, at which point the quantity demanded equals the quantity supplied at Q2 and there is market equilibrium—that is, at this price, there is no incentive for price and quantity to change.

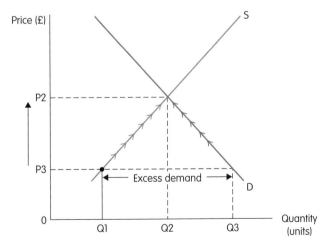

Figure 7.2 Excess demand

However, if the price in the market was originally at a price of P3, the quantity supplied is less than the quantity demanded. This means that there is a shortage—that is, excess demand (see Figure 7.2). When there is a shortage, there will be upward pressure on prices. As the price increases, it rations demand, reducing the quantity demanded because the item is more expensive, while also acting as an incentive for producers to produce more because the price at which they can sell their products has risen, increasing the quantity supplied.

In a free market, the price reconciles the aims of buyers and sellers, and finds the combination of price and output where their interests overlap. Just look at the value of the pound in the currency market during any day, and you will see it constantly changing as supply and demand conditions change. Alternatively, look at the share price of any major business over a few hours or weeks and, again, you will see it constantly moving as market conditions change. These are both examples of the price mechanism in action. In markets across the world every moment of every day, prices are adjusting to equate supply and demand, and to determine what is produced, how it is produced, and for whom. The workings of specific markets are examined in more detail in Chapter 8. Of course, the price mechanism may not always move fast enough to bring about equilibrium instantaneously. It may take time to realize that conditions have changed or to change the prices in a brochure. Prices may have been agreed and publicized for some time into the future, and so the price mechanism may not work as fast in all markets as it does in the currency or share markets. Even so, left to themselves in the free market, profit-maximizing firms and utility-maximizing consumers make independent decisions that bring about equilibrium via price changes; this is why the price mechanism was called the 'invisible hand' by Adam Smith in 1776. Individuals focusing on their individual needs make their own decisions, but this is all pulled together and coordinated by the price mechanism. If you want something and are prepared to pay for it, there is likely to be a market for it.

? Think about it...   7.1

The prices of most goods in the shops do not change every day. Does this mean that the price mechanism does not work in reality?

@ You and economics

You were on holiday in Morocco recently and visited the market stalls in the souk. You saw some fantastic gifts for your family back home. The trader asked for a price, but you knew that this was just to get the bargaining going so you offered much lower. You haggled for about fifteen minutes until you finally agreed a price. You were fairly sure that he would have gone a bit lower but you thought that the goods were well worth the price you paid for them and you were pleased to have pushed him down a bit. The souk is an example of markets in action.

Of course, market conditions are not static, and as there are changes in demand and supply this leads to changes in the market equilibrium. Businesses are continually improving their product markets; customers often change their purchasing patterns; new products are being developed; new technology develops; and input costs are increasing or decreasing. All these factors shift demand and supply curves, and change the equilibrium price and output.

Data analysis   7.1

Table 7.1 Equilibrium price and quantity

Price (£)	Quantity demanded (units)	Quantity supplied (units)
10	50	150
9	70	140
8	100	100
7	140	90
6	180	70
5	230	60

1. What is the equilibrium price in the market shown in Table 7.1?
2. What is the difference between the quantity demanded and the quantity supplied at a price of £6? What will happen to the price in this case to bring about equilibrium? Explain how this brings about equilibrium.
3. What is the difference between the quantity demanded and the quantity supplied at a price of £10? What will happen to the price in this case to bring about equilibrium? Explain how this brings about equilibrium.

? Think about it...   7.2

1. Can you think of anything that would prevent the price from moving up or down to achieve equilibrium in any market instantaneously?
2. Can you think of any market in which the price does not move up or down? Why not?

Markets are continually changing: for example, new products are being developed, changing supply and demand conditions.

When do you think the following occurred?

A: Google was launched.

B: The first iPod was sold.

C: The first Playstation was sold.

D: Apple was set up.

E: Facebook was set up.

F: Twitter was set up.

What happens if demand conditions change?

Assume that a market is in equilibrium at P1,Q1 in Figure 7.3. Given the demand and supply conditions in this market, there is no incentive to change at the moment at this price because the quantity supplied equals the quantity demanded. But these conditions can change: incomes change; businesses change their marketing; competitors change their prices; and new substitutes emerge. Look at your lifestyle compared with those of your parents or grandparents and you will see how much consumption patterns have altered. How many products do you buy that simply did not exist when your grandparents were your age? How many brands would your great-grandparents recognize? How similar is your shopping basket to theirs?

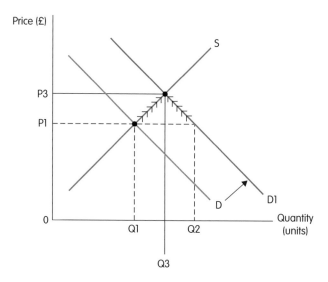

Figure 7.3 Impact of an outward shift in demand

If demand for a product increases, perhaps because of an increase in the number of buyers, this means that there is now excess demand at the given price P1; the quantity demanded Q2 is greater than the quantity supplied Q1. This will put upward pressure on prices which, in turn, will reduce the quantity demanded and increase the quantity supplied. The new equilibrium occurs with a higher price in the market and a greater quantity demanded at Q3 (see Figure 7.3).

However, if demand falls, meaning that at each and every price less is demanded, this should lead to a fall in the equilibrium price and a lower equilibrium quantity (see Figure 7.4). With lower demand conditions, businesses face lower prices and output. This is because at the original price of P1 there is excess supply (the quantity demanded is less than the quantity supplied); this excess supply leads to a fall in the price. As this happens, the quantity demanded increases and the quantity supplied falls, and this continues until a new equilibrium is reached.

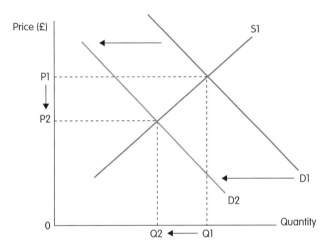

Figure 7.4 A decrease in demand

? Think about it... 7.3

Which of the following might explain an increase in demand?

A: An increase in the price of a substitute.

B: An increase in the price of a complement.

C: An increase in income for an inferior good.

D: A decrease in the costs of production.

Business analysis   7.1

In 2012 Rio de Janeiro hotel owners agreed to cut prices during a major United Nations meeting, amid concerns that rising prices were putting off visitors. The Brazilian government said room rates should now be at least 25 per cent lower.

About 50,000 visitors were expected in Rio for the UN Conference on Sustainable Development and with demand outstripping supply, average prices increased to $818 (£514) a night. The move to cut prices came after talks between the government, Rio de Janeiro's mayor, and local hoteliers and tourism operators. Some delegates, including non-governmental organizations and the European Parliament, had decided not to attend, citing costs. Rio de Janeiro has a hotel capacity of some 30,000 rooms. To ease the pressure, the mayor's office urged residents to rent their flats.

Do you think that the government should interfere with market forces?

? Think about it...   7.4

The Office of National Statistics (ONS) measures the price of a typical basket of goods to monitor the cost of living. As consumer buying patterns change, the items included in the basket change as well. In 2012 the ONS added tablet computers and teenage fiction such as the *Twilight* books. Cans of stout, such as Guinness, were also added to widen the coverage of beers in the basket, along with pineapples, hot oat cereals, and takeaway chicken and chips. In the same year it dropped casserole dishes, step-ladders, and charges for developing film. Walking and hiking boots were replaced by outdoor adventure boots.

What items do you think should be added next to the basket of goods?

Managers need to understand the consequences of reduced demand in their businesses, because it will reduce the quantity sold; this will affect decisions within many other areas of the business, including cash-flow forecasts, workforce plans, and the ordering of supplies (see Figure 7.5). A general fall in demand in an economy may make businesses more wary when it comes to expansion and more focused on ensuring that they have the cash that they need to survive. This means that managers may be concerned about when they are going to be paid and therefore may delay payments to their own suppliers. They may also reduce the labour force and hold back on any expansion plans.

The extent to which demand shifts will depend on how much the relevant factor has changed and how sensitive demand is to that factor. If demand is income elastic, for example, a change in income would shift the demand curve more than if demand was income inelastic (see Figure 7.6).

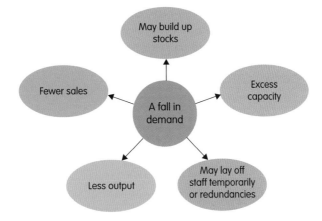

Figure 7.5 The effect of a fall in demand

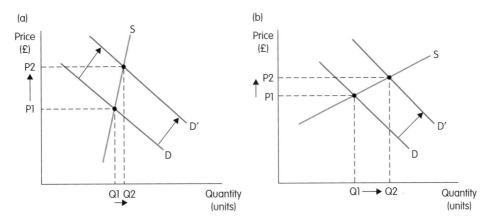

Figure 7.6 (a) An increase in demand when supply is price inelastic affects the equilibrium price more than quantity. (b) An increase in demand when supply is price elastic affects the equilibrium quantity more than price.

The impact of a shift in demand on price relative to output also depends on the price elasticity of supply. If supply is price inelastic, the impact will be mainly on price rather than output. If supply is price elastic, the impact will be mainly on output not price.

Data analysis   7.2

1. Would the effect of an increase in demand on the equilibrium price relative to the equilibrium quantity be greater if the price elasticity of supply were +1.2 or +0.2? Explain your answer.
2. Given an increase in income of 10 per cent, would the shift in demand be greater or smaller if the income elasticity were +2 or +0.2? Explain your answer.

Note that it is important to distinguish between a change in demand, which shifts the demand curve, and a change in quantity demanded, which refers to a movement along the demand curve. A change in demand shifts the demand curve, leading to a new equilibrium with a new quantity demanded and a new quantity supplied.

Economics and employability

Tell us your name and a bit about your role at RM Education.
My name is Andrew Iles and I'm a Senior Product Manager at RM Education. My role involves working with software development teams to design and develop web-based software for schools and, with our sales and marketing teams, to ensure that it is successfully released into the market.

In what ways is an understanding of economics useful in your work?
Macroeconomic knowledge is useful in understanding how the wider economy could influence our market. However, in my role as a Product Manager microeconomic knowledge is far more important; it helps with decisions such as whether to enter new markets, pricing, and resource allocation.

How does economic change affect your work?
Because we work in the education sector, the economic crisis and resulting cuts in government spending have had a significant impact on our market.

In what ways does economic change affect your clients?
The cuts to government budgets have changed the way information and communications technology in education is funded, with proportionately more of the available funding being held by schools rather than local authorities. Schools are now also more focused on using technologies which provide cost savings, such as reducing printing costs, or using cloud software instead of running servers in their schools.

Did you study economics at university as part of your studies and, if so, how has it helped you in your work? If not, do you wish you had and why?
I studied economics at university as part of my business and management degree. I've found a knowledge of economics to be valuable in my role as it helps support my decision-making and provides a deeper understanding of the factors influencing the market I compete in.

What skills are important in your role? (This could include functional skills, interpersonal skills, etc.)
Product management requires a wide range of skills. However, the key attributes needed are communications skills when working with customers or teams within the business, strong presentation skills, a good understanding of finance to help when writing business plans, and problem-solving skills.

Changes in supply conditions

Just as changes in demand conditions will alter the equilibrium price and quantity in a market, so changes in supply will also affect the equilibrium price and output. Assume that a market is in equilibrium at P1,Q1 (see Figure 7.7). If there is an increase in supply, meaning an increase in the quantity supplied at each and every price, the supply curve will shift to the right. This increase in supply will lead to a surplus at the existing price—the quantity supplied is greater than the quantity demanded. In a free market, this will lead to a fall in the price. This, in turn, will lead to a fall in the quantity supplied (because there is less incentive to produce at the lower prices) and an increase in quantity demanded (because products are cheaper to buy) until a new equilibrium is reached at P2,Q2. Therefore an increase in supply usually leads to a greater quantity being supplied at a lower price (assuming a downward-sloping demand curve and an upward-sloping supply curve).

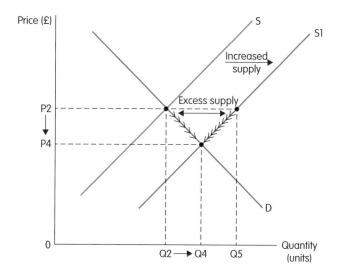

Figure 7.7 Effect of an outward shift in supply

Managers need to be aware of changes in the industry, such as new technology being adopted by other producers, because this can drive the overall market price down by increasing the supply. Managers need to be able to adapt to these new conditions to produce at this lower price. Think of markets for consumer electronics, such as televisions, cameras, and DVDs, and you will appreciate how the price of these products has been driven down over the years because of major shifts in supply.

By comparison, if supply in a market falls (i.e. less is supplied at each and every price so that the supply shifts to the left), there will be excess demand at the existing price (the quantity demanded exceeds the quantity supplied). This will lead to an upward pressure on prices, increasing the quantity supplied and reducing the quantity demanded, until a new equilibrium is reached with a lower quantity and a higher price. The lower quantity supplied will have implications for staffing and the amount of capacity needed.

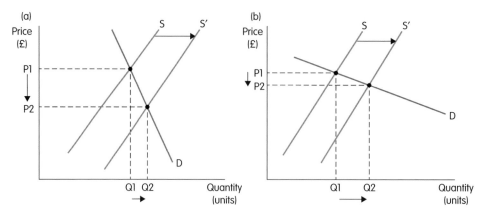

Figure 7.8 (a) An increase in supply when demand is price inelastic affects the equilibrium price more than quantity. (b) An increase in supply when demand is price elastic affects the equilibrium quantity more than price.

The effect of a shift in supply depends on the price elasticity of demand. If demand is price inelastic, the effect of a shift in supply will affect the equilibrium price more than quantity. If the demand is price elastic, a shift in supply will affect the equilibrium quantity more than the equilibrium price.

 ## Business analysis   7.2

In January 2012 the price of orange juice being traded on global markets hit a record high. According to traders, the main reason was safety concerns about juice from Brazil, the world's biggest producer of orange juice, and cold weather in Florida, another major supplier.

The US Food and Drug Administration said that carbendazim, a fungicide, had been found in shipments from Brazil. This fungicide is banned in the US but is used legally in Brazil to treat black spot, a type of mould that grows on trees. The FDA warned that any juice that might present a risk to the public would be taken off the shelves.

According to figures from the US Department of Agriculture Foreign Agricultural Service, in 2010–11 Brazil produced more than half the world's orange juice:

- Brazil: 1,440,000 tonnes
- USA: 645,000 tonnes
- Mexico: 85,000 tonnes
- EU: 73,000 tonnes

Using a supply and demand diagram, explain why the price of orange juice has increased.

? Think about it ...   7.5

1. Which of the following will increase supply?

   A: An increase in income.

   B: An improvement in technology.

   C: An increase in production costs.

   D: An increase in the price of a complement.

2. What will happen to the price of wheat in a year during which crops are poor?

3. Why might farmers welcome a poor year?

4. Would a shift in supply have a greater effect on equilibrium price than on quantity if the price elasticity of demand were −0.1 or −1.1? Explain your answer using a supply and demand diagram.

Movements along versus shifts in supply and demand curves

If demand for a product increases, at each and every price more is demanded and the demand curve shifts to the right This means that, at the original equilibrium price, there is now excess demand and the price is pulled upwards. The result is a new equilibrium and a new quantity supplied, because of the higher price (see Figure 7.9). The shift in demand has led to a movement along the supply curve. The supply curve itself has not moved because supply conditions have not changed.

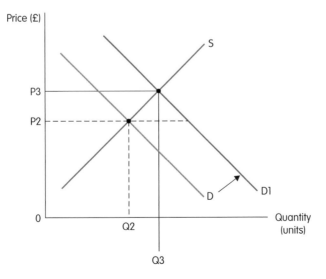

Figure 7.9 Effect of an outward shift in demand

If supply shifts, the supply curve moves to the right or left. This leads to a new equilibrium quantity demanded and supplied; there has been a movement along the demand curve but the demand curve has not shifted because demand conditions have not changed.

Possible causes of shifts in demand and supply are shown in Table 7.2.

Table 7.2 Causes of shifts in demand and supply

Causes of shifts in demand	Causes of shifts in supply
Changes in incomes	Changes in costs
Changes in the price of substitutes	Changes in technology
Changes in the price of complements	Changes in the number of producers
Changes in marketing activities	Changes in indirect taxes or subsidies
Changes in population size	Changes in productivity

? Think about it...   7.6

1. As a result of changes in demand or supply conditions, the equilibrium price and quantity have increased in your market. What change in market conditions might have caused this? Illustrate your answer with a supply and demand diagram.
2. As a result of changes in demand or supply conditions, the equilibrium price has increased and the quantity has decreased in your market. What change in market conditions might have caused this? Illustrate your answer with a supply and demand diagram.
3. As a result of changes in demand or supply conditions, the equilibrium price and the quantity have decreased in your market. What change in market conditions might have caused this? Illustrate your answer with a supply and demand diagram.

? Think about it...   7.7

In April 2012 house prices in the UK fell sharply after a change in tax regulations meant that first-time buyers had to pay stamp duty (a tax) when buying a house. Awareness of the ending of stamp duty meant that buyers brought forward their purchases so that demand was higher earlier in the year. House prices had been flat or falling all year because of fears that the UK would not grow in the short term, continuing difficulty in getting credit, and a worry that the cost of borrowing was going to increase.

1. Identify four influences on the demand for housing.
2. Explain two reasons why demand for housing may have fallen between 2011 and 2012.

3. What do you think determines the supply of housing?
4. Do you think that the supply of housing is price elastic or price inelastic. Why? Does this mean that price or quantity is affected more by a fall in demand?
5. Why do you think changes in the price of housing are so significant in the UK?

 Go online to access a video walk-through of how markets adjust to restore equilibrium.

The speed of market adjustment

The speed with which the price changes to restore equilibrium following a change in supply or demand will vary from market to market. Share prices and currency prices, for example, change very quickly according to market conditions. This is because millions of transactions occur regularly in these markets, so that any change in demand or supply is quickly reflected in the equilibrium price and quantity. Similarly, commodities, such as gold, wheat, and silver, are traded on a worldwide market with prices fluctuating all the time. This, in itself, creates a 'futures' market in which people are speculating by agreeing to buy and sell these products at a future date—that is, they are trading in something that has not even been produced yet.

However, the price may be slower to adjust in other markets. In the labour market, for example, salaries are often negotiated for a year or even more, and so cannot instantaneously adjust to a change in demand and supply—wages are relatively 'sticky'. In other markets, prices may be agreed as part of a contract set for at least several months in advance. This means that prices will not change immediately, and this can prevent markets from reaching equilibrium in the short run. Similarly, the costs and effort required to reprint brochures and alter price lists may mean that prices of some businesses move occasionally, rather than instantaneously, to bring about equilibrium. Also, businesses often buy supplies every few weeks, or even every few months, and so any price changes caused by input costs may take time to work through the transformation process.

This means that the effect on price and quantity in the short run may be different from the long-run impact (see Figure 7.10).

In Figure 7.11, the effect in the short run of an increase in demand is mainly an increase in price, because supply is price inelastic. Initially, the price rises to P2 and the new equilibrium quantity is Q2. Over time, supply becomes more price elastic, and the price falls to P3 and the quantity increases to Q3.

There may be other barriers that prevent the price adjusting to equate supply and demand. In the labour market, for example, employees may be reluctant to accept a reduction in their wages even if there is a fall in demand for labour. They might simply refuse a pay cut and threaten industrial action. The result is that those in work maintain a relatively high wage, but fewer people are employed than would be the case if the market were to 'clear'.

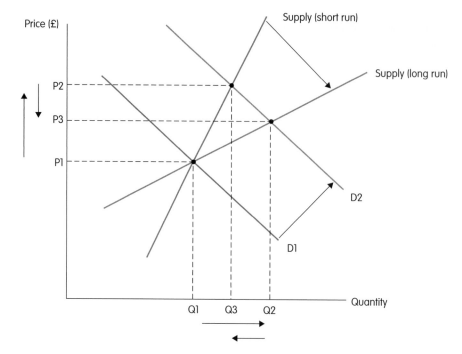

Figure 7.10 The effect of price and quantity in the short and long run

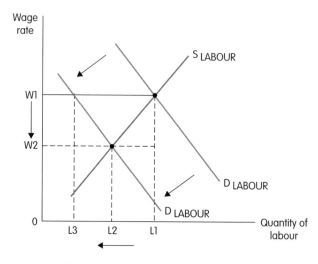

Figure 7.11 A fall in the demand for labour

In Figure 7.11, there is a fall in demand for labour, perhaps because of a fall in demand for products in the economy. If market forces worked efficiently, the wage should fall to W2 and the equilibrium number of people employed would then be L2. However, if employees insist on still receiving W1, the quantity demanded of labour would be L3 and there would be excess supply of labour equal to L3, L1. Those employed retain their earnings at the original wage W1, but, because the wage is kept higher than equilibrium, the number employed falls to L1.

? *Think about it...*   7.8

Which of the following statements are true and which are false?

A: If there is excess demand in a market, the price is likely to increase.

B: An increase in demand will usually lead to a higher equilibrium price and lower quantity.

C: An increase in supply will usually lead to a lower equilibrium price and lower equilibrium quantity.

D: If there is excess supply in a market, the equilibrium price is likely to rise.

Different market conditions

Prices will differ in markets because of differences in supply and demand conditions (see Figure 7.12). If the demand for an item is high and supply is limited, the market price will be relatively high (think of the price of Ferraris). If demand for an item is low and/or supply is higher, the price is likely to be relatively low (think of the price of milk).

In theory, producers of milk might be attracted into production of Ferraris because of the higher price—but the particular skills, expertise, and experience required for the production of Ferraris limits the numbers of firms that can compete in this market niche.

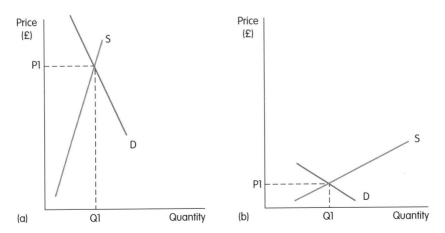

Figure 7.12 Demand and price: (a) limited supply and high demand; (b) low demand and price elastic supply.

Think about it...   7.9

Using supply and demand analysis, explain why a painting by Rembrandt is expensive, whereas the price of a newspaper is relatively cheap. Illustrate your answer with diagrams.

£ Business analysis   7.3

Several major companies, such as Samsung, LG Display, Sharo, and Panasonic, are producing flat panel screens at the moment but none of them are making profits. It is estimated that between 2004 and 2010 the industry had total losses of $13 billion. This is not because of a lack of sales—in 2011 over 220 million TV screens were sold at a value of $115 billion. Another 2.7 billion screens went into products such as smartphones and tablets. The problem facing producers is that they cannot differentiate their screens from each other, and so buyers have plenty of choice. Secondly, there has been major increase in capacity which means that there is excess supply, bringing the price down. The price of LCD panels fell by 80 per cent between 2004 and 2008, reducing profit margins to about nothing!

What do you think will happen in this industry in the long term?

Even within a 'market', conditions can vary considerably because there can be very different segments, each with their own supply and demand conditions. The market for housing will be very different across the country depending on a range of factors, such as the availability of jobs, the facilities, the crime rates, and the ease of building. Even within one region, the demand will vary between types of housing, such as small flats and family homes, because demand and supply will differ so much. Similarly, consider the market for confectionery in the UK; this is growing as a whole, but, within it, the demand for bubble gum is falling (partly due to restrictions on advertising to young children that are now in place) and the demand for boiled sweets is falling (due to a lack of innovation), while the demand for chewing gum is booming (due to heavy investment in new product development). The different segments are performing very differently within one overall 'market'. Marketing managers are, of course, well aware of the difference between segments (for example, chocolate bought to eat yourself is different from chocolate bought to share watching a film, which is different from chocolate bought to give as a gift) and adapt their marketing mix accordingly.

You and economics

You have just got your first job and are due to start in a month. You have been studying in the North but your job is based in London. The salary looked good compared with some of the other offers you had which were based elsewhere, but you have now started to look at house prices and have realized how expensive property is in London. Not only that, but when you spent a weekend looking at possible flats you noticed how expensive things were in general.

The markets for property in London and the North are different in terms of both supply and demand, which accounts for the differences in prices.

The effect of an indirect tax on equilibrium

An indirect tax is a tax placed on producers when they sell products. For example, VAT is an indirect tax. It is charged when you buy a product, and the producers have to hand over the tax to the government. An indirect tax places an additional cost on producers, and this affects the supply curve. The introduction of an indirect tax leads to an upward shift of supply: to supply any given quantity, a higher price is required by producers to try and cover the additional costs. This leads to a high price and a lower equilibrium quantity. The impact of an indirect tax on the equilibrium price and quantity will depend on the price elasticity of demand. The more price inelastic demand is, the greater the effect on price.

Although producers are responsible for paying the tax, they will want to pass on as much of it as they can to customers. The incidence of the tax on consumers depends on how much the price has increased as a result of the tax; the incidence of the tax on producers depends on how much they have to absorb because they have been unable to pass it on in the form of higher prices (see Figure 7.13).

The ability of a business to pass on an indirect tax to customers depends on the relative price elasticity of demand and supply. If demand is more price inelastic than supply, the consumer will bear the greater proportion of the tax; this is because demand is not especially sensitive to price and therefore the consumers will absorb a high proportion of the tax. If demand is more price elastic than supply, the producer will pay the greater proportion of tax (see Figure 7.14). This is because demand is relatively sensitive to price and so less of the tax can be passed on.

The importance of the relative price elasticities highlights why managers are often eager to make demand more price inelastic (that is, less sensitive to price), so that they can pass on indirect tax increases to the consumer. To do this they will try and differentiate their products.

The government will use indirect taxes partly to raise revenue to finance its spending; in this case it would want demand to be price inelastic. Also, it will impose indirect taxes

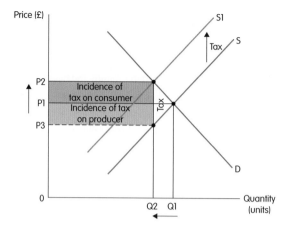

Figure 7.13 The imposition of an indirect tax

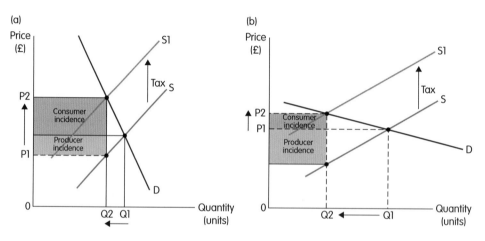

Figure 7.14 The incidence of an indirect tax on consumers and producers

to discourage consumption (e.g. the consumption of cigarettes and alcohol). In this case the biggest impact on quantity would come if demand was price elastic, but in the case of products such as alcohol and cigarettes, which are price inelastic, a large rate of tax is required to have a noticeable impact on consumption.

 Business analysis   7.4

In 2012 hundreds of bakers in the UK protested against plans to tax hot take-away foods such as pasties. The Treasury had recently announced that it was going to charge VAT of 20 per cent on pies and pasties to close a 'loophole' because most hot food was already subject to VAT.

A director of the Association of Master Bakers said that customers would be squeezed. He said that it would be impossible for businesses to absorb all of these costs and so they would have to be passed on to the customer. An alternative would be to let the pasties cool down because then they would not be liable for VAT.

In the end the government made a U-turn and withdrew the pasty tax proposal.

Discuss the factors that determine how much of the tax bakers would have been able to pass on to consumers if the pasty tax had been introduced.

The effect of a subsidy on equilibrium

As we saw in Chapter 6, a subsidy to producers reduces their costs and leads to a downward shift in the supply curve. Each quantity can be supplied at a lower price. The effect of a subsidy is to reduce the equilibrium price and increase the equilibrium quantity (see Figure 7.15). The effect on price relative to quantity will be greater the more price inelastic demand is. Subsidies will be used by a government to encourage production or consumption of products.

 Data analysis 7.3

Table 7.3 The effect of lower costs on the equilibrium price and quantity

Price	Quantity demanded	Quantity supplied
£1.50	200	200
£1.40	210	180
£1.30	240	160
£1.20	250	120

1. What is the original equilibrium price and quantity in the market shown in Table 7.3?
2. As a result of a fall in production costs, supply rises by 50 per cent at all prices. What would be the new equilibrium price and quantity?
3. What would the government want to subsidise? Why would it need to?

Markets and managers

Managers are operating in hundreds, if not thousands, of markets. For example, they trade in the different markets for factors of production, the markets for their different

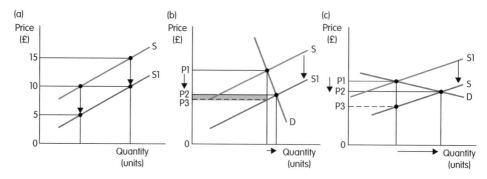

Figure 7.15 The effect of a subsidy on equilibrium

products in different regions, the money market in which they may raise money, and the currency market if they trade overseas. By understanding market conditions and the effects of changes in supply and demand, managers can anticipate possible changes in areas such as the price of land, the price of labour, the cost of borrowing money, and the price of inputs bought abroad. This should aid planning and lead to better decision-making.

Equilibrium, social welfare, and community surplus

One of the significant benefits of the free market system is that the independent decisions of buyers and sellers in a market automatically bring about equilibrium and this equilibrium maximizes the welfare of society.

A demand curve shows the marginal benefits (also called satisfaction or utility) of consuming a product; this shows how much customers are willing to pay for an additional unit, which therefore reflects its extra benefit to society. This means that it can also be labelled a social marginal benefit (SMB) curve. The supply curve reflects the marginal costs of producing another unit, because these need to be covered by the price. Therefore it can be called a social marginal costs (SMC) curve (see Figure 7.16).

In the free market, equilibrium occurs at P1,Q1. This means that all the units in relation to which the extra benefit to society is greater than the extra cost to society are produced, up to the point at which the SMB equals the SMC. In other words, all the units that represent a net gain to society (because the extra benefit exceeds the extra costs) are produced up to the point at which society would not gain overall from another unit; as a result, the welfare of society must be maximized and the economy is said to have achieved **allocative efficiency.**

This can also be shown by the fact that the area of the consumer surplus plus the producer surplus—which is known as the **community surplus,** i.e. the combined welfare to producers and consumers that is not paid for—is maximized at this point. Any other combination of price and output would lead to less community surplus overall. For example, if the price was set higher than P1, this would reduce the quantity demanded.

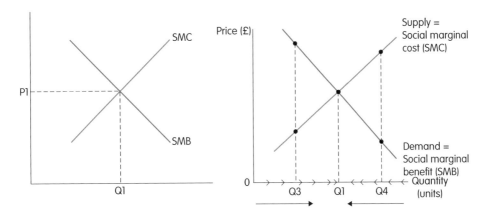

Figure 7.16 The social marginal benefit and social marginal costs curves

This situation might occur if one business dominated the market and used its power to push up prices. As can be seen in Figure 7.17, this would increase the producer surplus (which is why the dominant producer pushes up prices in the first place) but, at the same time, reduce consumer surplus and the overall community surplus.

Producer surplus is now shown by the area P2abc, consumer surplus is shown by the area P2ae, and community surplus overall is reduced by the area abf, which is known as a 'welfare loss (or deadweight) social burden area'. On units Q1,Q2, the social marginal benefit is greater than the social marginal cost, so society would benefit if these

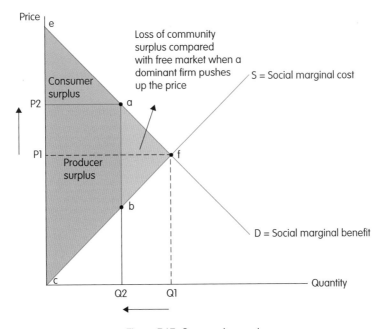

Figure 7.17 Community surplus

units were produced. This means that the business is not allocatively efficient, because the community surplus is not maximized and a deadweight social burden (welfare) loss area exists.

Therefore the appeal of the free market, when it works perfectly, is that it brings about a price and quantity equilibrium outcome that maximizes society's welfare. This is why market forces are encouraged in many countries; no other combination of price and output could achieve the same level of community surplus. But to maximize community surplus, market failures (such as a dominant firm) may need to be avoided—and this may require government intervention.

}{ People and economics: Vilfredo Pareto (1843–1923)

Vilfredo Pareto developed the concept of Pareto efficiency, which occurs when nobody can be made better off without making somebody else worse off. If an economy's resources are being used inefficiently, it should be possible to make somebody better off without anybody else becoming worse off.

Summary

Equilibrium occurs at the price and quantity at which demand equals supply, and at which there is no incentive to change. In a free market, the price mechanism should adjust to bring about equilibrium. At this point, the extra benefit to society of a unit equals the extra cost to society; this maximizes the welfare of society and is allocatively efficient. The speed at which a market moves from one equilibrium to another following a change in demand or supply depends on the flexibility of price and will vary from market to market.

However, governments may intervene in several ways to influence the market system, and this affects the equilibrium price and quantity.

Checklist

Having read this chapter, you should now understand:

- [ ] how equilibrium is reached in a market economy;
- [ ] the meaning of shortage and surplus;
- [ ] the effects of shifts in supply and demand on the equilibrium price and quantity;
- [ ] the significance of the price elasticity of supply and demand following a shift in supply or demand;
- [ ] the effect of an indirect tax on the equilibrium price and quantity;
- [ ] the effect of a subsidy on the equilibrium price and quantity;

- the meaning of producer surplus;
- the meaning of consumer surplus;
- the meaning of community surplus;
- the meaning of allocative efficiency and welfare loss.

Short answer questions

1. What is the difference between a movement along, and a shift of, the demand curve?
2. Identify three factors that might influence demand for a product.
3. Identify three factors that might affect the supply of a product.
4. Explain how the price mechanism adjusts to bring about equilibrium.
5. What is the likely effect of an increase in demand on the equilibrium price and output?
6. What is the likely effect of a decrease in supply on the equilibrium price and output?
7. What determines how much the price of a product falls if there is a fall in demand for the product?
8. What is meant by consumer surplus?
9. What is meant by community surplus?
10. Explain what is meant by a deadweight social burden loss?

Discussion questions

1. Discuss the factors that influence the impact of a new indirect tax on the market price.
2. Discuss the case for and against the free market system as a way of analysing resources.
3. Discuss the factors that would determine how effectively the price mechanism could adjust to bring equilibrium if there was a change in supply or demand conditions.

One step further

Visit our Online Resource Centre at **www.oxfordtextbooks.co.uk/orc/gillespiebusiness2e/** to test your understanding, watch video walk-throughs, and access further information on topics covered in this chapter.

Market analysis: shares, currency, and labour markets

8

Learning objectives

In this chapter, we illustrate the workings of the market mechanism by examining the determinants of supply and demand, and the effects of changes in demand and supply in some particularly important markets. This analysis will highlight the importance of the market mechanism to managers. The principles explored can be applied to other markets.

By the end of this chapter, you should:

- ✓ understand the key factors influencing supply and demand in the labour, share, capital goods, and currency markets;

- ✓ understand the consequences of changes in supply and demand conditions in these markets;

- ✓ be able to explain the effects of changes in these variables.

ⓒ *Case study*

'I've worked for twenty-five years and in that time I've tried to put a bit of money in the bank, to put money into my pension, and to pay off the mortgage on my house. It now turns out that the rate of interest my savings earns does not even keep pace with the rate that prices are increasing. Then I see that my pension, which has been invested in shares, shrunk last year and so I am going to have to work far longer than I thought—so that's my time in the sun gone!

And now to make things even worse I have seen that my next door neighbour's house, which is just like mine, is on the market for £200,000—that's £20,000 less than I paid for mine. When I asked my boss for a pay increase, she almost laughed, so I suggested that it might be time for me to leave; I thought this would make her rethink. Instead she just said that there were plenty more fish in the sea—you can imagine how good that made me feel! All in all it makes me think I should just have spent it all when I had it rather than try and prepare for later on in life. Enjoy it while you can—that's my motto now. Except even that's difficult—I was going to book a long holiday to Spain this summer but when I worked out the prices and cost of living in pounds it was going to be too expensive given the value of the pound these days.'

Questions

1. What do you think determines share prices? Why might the price of a share fall? Why does this matter?

2. What do you think determines house prices? Why might they fall? Why does this matter?

3. What do you think determines someone's pay? Does it matter if people earn different amounts of money? Do you think that this is desirable?

4. What do you think determines an exchange rate? Is it better if the pound is worth more or less in terms of foreign currencies?

5. Do you think it is better to spend money whilst you have it or save it for the future?

Introduction

There are many different types of markets in an economy; for example, there can be markets for goods, services, people, land, currency, shares, and money. These markets are all driven by the same fundamental forces of supply and demand, but they can differ significantly for the following reasons.

- *The relative importance of different factors affecting demand or supply will vary* For example, the demand for education and nappies is strongly related to demographic factors; the demand for ice cream depends more on the weather. The supply of PCs will depend strongly on technology; the supply of ballet performances often depends more on government subsidies and the supply of carrots on the weather.

- *Markets vary in terms of how much demand and supply shift over time* Demand for clothing may be vulnerable to sudden changes in fashion; demand for salt may be more stable. The supply of gold can depend on the ability to find new sources; the supply of Mars bars may depend more on investment in production facilities.

- *Markets vary in terms of the price sensitivity of demand and supply* The demand for Ferraris may not be particularly sensitive to the price; the demand for washing machines may be more price elastic. The supply of power stations may be more price inelastic, whereas the supply of newspapers may be more price elastic.

- *The extent of intervention by the government may vary from market to market* In the UK, the National Lottery is a **monopoly** with the sole rights to supply this service granted by the government; similarly, the government grants franchises to run railway services. But the market for cafés has millions of suppliers, many of which are located close to each other with very similar offerings and which are not regulated particularly strongly by the government.

As a result of these differences in market conditions, the extent and frequency to which the equilibrium price and quantities change in markets can vary considerably. For example, the prices of shares of public limited companies which are quoted on the Stock Exchange change every few seconds because of constant changes in demand, whereas the price of a postage stamp does not change as often and needs approval by OfCom, the government regulator.

In this chapter, we examine the nature of several important markets in an economy, and the causes and effects of changes within them, to highlight the importance of supply and demand analysis.

? *Think about it...*   8.1

Can you think of two markets in your economy in which supply is likely to be price elastic and two markets in which demand is likely to be price inelastic?

The foreign exchange market

The foreign exchange market ('forex') is where the exchange rate is determined. An exchange rate is the price of one currency in terms of another. The value of one currency in terms of other currencies is determined by market forces of supply and demand in the currency markets (unless the government intervenes to fix a price). If the value of a currency is high in relation to other currencies, it is called a 'strong' currency; this could be because of a high level of demand or a fall in supply. If the value of the currency is low, it is called 'weak'; this could be because of low levels of demand for it. When a currency increases in value, it 'appreciates'; when it falls in value, it 'depreciates'.

The value of a currency affects the price of a firm's products abroad, which will affect sales abroad (i.e. exports). If the value of £1 changes from €1.4 to €1.1, then a £100 product would sell for €110 not €140, all other things unchanged. This change in the price abroad in terms of foreign currency can have a significant impact on UK firms exporting abroad. Changes in the value of a currency will also affect the cost of buying supplies from abroad (i.e. imports). The stronger the value of the pound, the more euros are received in return for a pound, and so fewer pounds have to be spent buying something from abroad; this reduces import prices in pounds. Changes in the value of a currency are particularly significant now that so many businesses operate globally and economies are increasingly 'open', meaning they are trading more with other countries. There are, in fact, many different markets for currency—for example, the value of the pound sterling compared with the US dollar, the yen, the renminbi, or the rouble. In each of these markets, supply and demand interact to determine the value of one currency against another. This means that it is possible for the pound to increase in value against one currency while decreasing in value against another. When analysing currency changes, managers will focus on the changes in markets in which they sell their products and those from which they buy materials or resources.

 ## Data analysis   8.1

1. If the equilibrium value of £1 changes from US$1.5 to US$1.1, is the pound getting weaker or stronger?

2. What would happen to the price of a £200 product in dollars if the exchange rate were to change in this way?

3. What would happen to the price in pounds of a US product that was priced at $200?

4. If the pound gets weaker would exporters prefer the demand for exports to be price elastic or price inelastic? Why?

5. What is the value of your currency? Do you know how much it has changed in value against another currency in the last year? Two years? Do you know if it has got stronger or weaker?

You and economics

You would love to surprise your partner with a few days holiday in Paris. You have looked at prices online and can just about afford the flight and hotel, but you are worried about how much spending money you will need. Everyone has told you that Paris is an expensive city, and you have just checked the exchange rate and the pound has fallen again against the euro. By the time you have added in the costs of getting around Paris, eating, and generally enjoying the city, it's going to be too much with such a weak pound. You decide to settle on cooking her a meal at home and a bottle of French wine instead!

Demand for pounds from abroad

The external demand for UK currency comes from foreign individuals and organizations who want to change their currency into pounds to buy UK goods and services. The more expensive the price of a pound, the more foreign currency has to be changed to buy it (that is, the more expensive UK products will be in terms of foreign currency). Assuming that all else remains constant, this will reduce the quantity demanded of pounds. Therefore the demand for pounds will be a downward-sloping curve: the more expensive the pound is, the lower the quantity demanded of pounds.

The slope of the demand curve for pounds will depend on the price elasticity of demand for UK products in foreign currencies. If demand for UK exports is very price sensitive, a given increase in the price of UK products abroad following an increase in the value of the pound will lead to a relatively large fall in the quantity demanded of products and therefore the quantity demanded of pounds. In other words, the more price elastic is the demand for the products, the more price elastic is the demand for pounds (see Figure 8.1). This is because

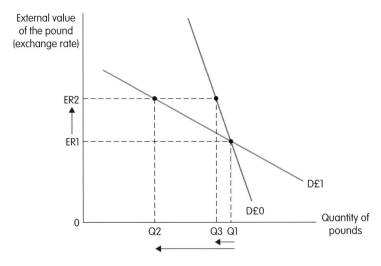

Figure 8.1 The demand for pounds in the currency market: if demand of UK exports is price elastic the effect of an increase in the value of the pound will be greater, i.e. D£1 rather than D£0.

the demand for pounds is derived from the demand for UK products. The price elasticity of demand for UK products will depend on factors such as the uniqueness of these products the power of the brand, the quality, and the reliability. If UK engineering is admired world-wide, UK firms have patented their technology or if the UK is hosting an unmissable event such as the Olympics, demand for British products will be relatively price inelastic.

Data analysis 8.2

Your handmade designer furniture sells for around £3,000 per piece in the UK. Your main export market is the USA, where you sell 500 units a week.

1. If the value of the UK currency were to change from US$1.2 to US$1.4, what would happen to the price of your products in the USA, all other things unchanged?
2. What actions could you take to prevent your sales from falling in this situation?
3. If the price elasticity of demand for your products in the USA is −1.5, what would happen to your sales and your revenue following the increase in the exchange rate?
4. If your business were to keep the same price in dollars following the exchange rate change, how much would it earn in pounds for each item?

Supply of pounds to the foreign currency market

The supply of pounds to the foreign currency market depends on the desire of individuals and organizations to change their pounds into foreign currency (for example, if they plan to visit countries abroad or buy goods and services from abroad). If the value of the pound increases in terms of foreign currency, this means that the pound has more purchasing power abroad. This makes foreign goods and services cheaper, because fewer pounds are required for any given amount of foreign currency. For example, if you want to buy a €600 suit and the exchange rate is €1 : £1, the suit costs £600; if the pound appreciates to €1.2 : £1, it will cost £500.

This means that an increase in the value of the pound should lead to an increase in the quantity demanded of foreign products. If demand for foreign products is price elastic, the total spending on imports increases—although the price is lower in pounds, a signifi-cant increase in the quantity demanded increases the overall amount spent. Instead of buying 40 suits at £600, spending £24,000, you might buy 60 at £500, spending £30,000 overall. In this case, the supply of pounds to the foreign currency market is upward-slop-ing—a higher value of the pound increases the quantity supplied.

However, if the demand for imports is price inelastic, the lower price of imports will lead to a relatively smaller increase in the quantity demanded of products from abroad and the total spending on imports will fall. If you were only to buy 42 suits at £500, spending would have fallen to £21,000. In this case, the supply of pounds is downward-sloping because an increase in the price of pounds leads to fewer being supplied (see Figure 8.2).

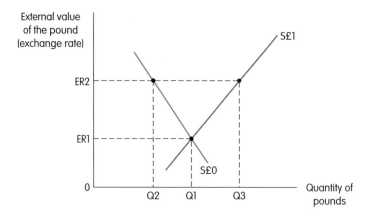

Figure 8.2 The supply of pounds in the currency market: if demand for imports is price elastic the supply of pounds is upward-sloping (S£1) but if demand for imports is price inelastic the supply of pounds is downward-sloping (S£0).

 ## Data analysis   8.3

The price of a bottle of Italian olive oil is €12. The exchange rate is £1 : €1 and you import 30,000 bottles a month.

1. What is the price of the product in pounds?
2. How much do you spend in pounds a year on this product?
3. The exchange rate rises to £1 : €1.2 and you import 40,000 bottles a month.
4. What is the price in pounds of the product now?
5. How much do you spend in pounds a year on this product now?
6. Calculate the price elasticity of supply for this product. Given an increase in the exchange rate, has the supply of pounds risen or fallen?

Reaching equilibrium in the currency markets

In a free market, the price of the currency will adjust until the quantity supplied equals the quantity demanded. The price mechanism adjusts to bring about equilibrium. As illustrated in Figure 8.3, if the exchange rate is ER3, for example, there is an excess supply of the currency. In this case, the value of the pound falls, reducing the quantity supplied (if the supply curve is upward-sloping) and the quantity demanded falls. This process continues until equilibrium at ER1. At ER2, there is excess demand (a shortage) of Q3,Q2 and the price of the currency will rise. This increases the quantity supplied and reduces the quantity demanded until the equilibrium is reached at ER1. Currencies are being bought and sold all the time, with many buyers and sellers and billions of pounds being traded, and the price changes rapidly, reacting to any changes in conditions to bring about equilibrium rapidly.

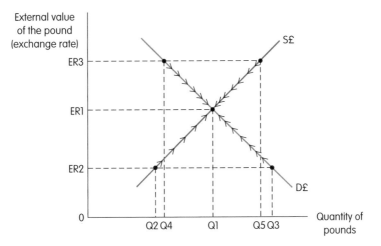

Figure 8.3 Reaching equilibrium in the currency market

Shifts in demand for a currency

An increase in the demand for a currency will shift the demand curve outwards and will usually lead to a higher exchange rate. The demand for pounds in the foreign currency markets may increase because of the following.

■ An increase in incomes overseas, leading to more demand for UK products (assuming that they are normal products)—the more income elastic demand is the greater the shift will be.

■ An increase in UK interest rates relative to the returns available elsewhere, which attracts foreign investors searching for high returns in UK banks and other financial institutions, and wanting to save pounds in the UK.

■ A belief by speculators that the pound will increase in value against other currencies in the future, which means that these speculators will buy pounds now in the hope of selling later at a higher price. Speculation can be a major factor that can change the value of a currency rapidly. News of possible government policy changes, rumours about economic indicators about to be published, and gossip about trade deals can all change a currency's value.

Shifts in supply of the currency to the foreign currency market

An increase in the supply of pounds to the foreign currency market may be due to the following.

■ An increase in UK incomes, leading to more demand for imports, so that more pounds will have to be supplied to change into foreign currency to buy the products from abroad.

- An increase in overseas interest rates, leading to money flowing out of the UK in search of higher returns abroad.
- Speculators selling pounds in the belief that the pound is going to fall in value in the future. The danger here is that speculators bring about what they expect; they worry that the pound will fall and so sell the currency, thereby putting pressure on the pound to fall and so it does lose value. Speculators may do this deliberately by selling at a relatively higher price, pushing the price down if others start to sell as well; they can then buy the currency back at the lower price.

Changes in supply of and demand for a currency

An increase in demand for a currency will lead to an increase in price and an increase in the equilibrium, assuming that supply is upward-sloping (see Figure 8.4a). A decrease in supply of a currency will lead to an increase in the price, but a fall in the equilibrium quantity (see Figure 8.4b).

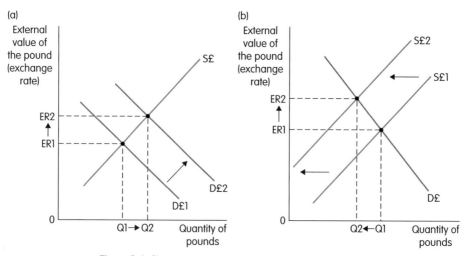

Figure 8.4 Changes in supply of and demand for a currency

 Data analysis 8.4

1. Assume that the exchange rate changes from £1 : US$1.5 to £1 : US$2 and that a UK product sold in the USA sells for £100 in the UK. What is the price in dollars before and after the change in the value of the pound?
2. Originally, 500 units were sold. If the price elasticity of demand for this product is −2, what will the new level of sales be? What was the original spending in pounds on the product? What would it be after the change in the exchange rate?

3. The exchange rate changes from £1 : US$1.5 to £1 : US$2 and a UK business buys a US$300 product from the USA. What is the price in pounds before and after the change in the value of the pound?

4. Originally, 200 units were bought.

  A: How much was originally spent in pounds buying these products?

  B: If the price elasticity of demand for the product is −2, what will be the new sales and the new level of spending in pounds? Has the spending increased or decreased, and what does this mean in terms of the supply curve for pounds? Will it be upward- or downward-sloping?

  C: If the price elasticity of demand for the product is −0.2, what will be the new sales and the new level of spending in pounds? Has the spending increased or decreased, and what does this mean in terms of the supply curve for pounds? Will it be upward- or downward-sloping?

5. Illustrate the effect of an inward shift in the demands for a currency and an outward shift of the supply of a currency on the equilibrium price and quantity in a currency market.

 Business analysis   8.1

Using supply and demand explain how:

1. the equilibrium price and quantity of a currency traded might both increase;

2. the equilibrium price and quantity of a currency traded might both decrease;

3. the equilibrium price might increase but quantity decrease;

4. the equilibrium price might decrease but quantity increase.

Why do changes in exchange rates matter?

If the pound falls in value on the foreign currency markets, this means that it is cheaper relative to the relevant foreign currency. If a UK business keeps its prices the same in pounds, the prices in overseas currencies will be less. This should increase the quantity of products demanded from abroad. This means that a UK business needs to be ready and able to export more. This can help stimulate economic growth within the UK and help employment.

Alternatively, managers of UK businesses may decide to maintain the same price in terms of the foreign currency (perhaps because contracts have been negotiated or price lists printed already), which leads to a higher profit margin. This may lead to higher returns for investors.

In contrast, if the pound increases in value and the price in pounds is kept the same, the price in foreign currency is now higher than it was, which is likely to reduce sales. Alternatively, the business might keep the overseas price the same, which would reduce its profit margins.

Changes in the value of the pound will also affect import prices. Many of the products we buy are imported or contain imported elements, so changes in the price of these affect UK firms' costs and therefore their profits. If a UK business buys in supplies and the pound strengthens, this will reduce its import costs. This may lead to higher profit margins or enable the firm to reduce its prices. But the strong pound also means that customers can buy products from overseas competitors more cheaply, which might reduce the UK firm's domestic sales as customers switch to overseas producers. The scale of this effect depends on how easy it is to switch and how similar overseas products are to UK ones.

Given the large amount of international trade today, especially by UK firms, managers are almost certainly buying products from abroad and/or selling products abroad. Therefore an understanding of the exchange rate is crucial to modern-day business. It is particularly important to monitor and try to anticipate changes because the exchange rate is out of the control of any one business: the price is determined by millions of transactions happening all the time and a single manager cannot influence this.

The demand and supply conditions in currency markets can change suddenly, and this can lead to major movements in the value of a currency. In particular, the markets can be strongly influenced by speculators, which can make it hard to predict what a currency will be worth in the future. This makes financial planning difficult and can quickly change the competitive position of a business.

 ## Data analysis   8.5

1. Briefly summarize the changes in the value of the pound against the US dollar in the period 2008–12 shown in Figure 8.5.
2. Explain, using supply and demand diagrams, what might have caused the changes in the value of the pound.
3. Discuss the possible effects of such changes for UK businesses.

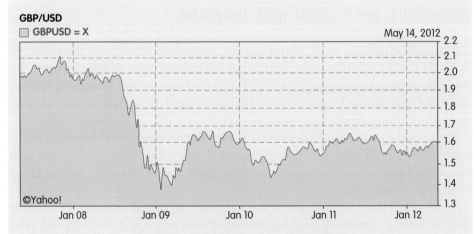

Figure 8.5 The value of the pound against the dollar
Source: Reprinted with kind permission of Yahoo!

The McBurger index

Sometimes currencies may be over- or undervalued compared with the long-term value that would be reached with the underlying demand and supply conditions. Pressure from speculators or government policy may push the value high or low in the short term. To identify the long-term underlying value of a currency, *The Economist* magazine uses the 'McBurger index'; this helps it to decide whether a currency is over- or undervalued. The McBurger index compares the actual exchange rate with what it would need to be to keep the prices of burgers in different countries comparable. A McDonald's burger is chosen because it is a fairly standardized product in different countries.

The exchange rate that would give each currency the same purchasing power in both currencies, and so the McBurger index, is a crude measure of what is known as 'purchasing power parity' (PPP). PPP is usually calculated by comparing the costs of similar baskets of goods; for example, if the basket were to cost £150 in the UK and US$300 in the USA, the PPP rate would be £1 : US$2. But, given the very different spending patterns between countries, agreeing on what is included in the baskets can be difficult, which is why *The Economist* uses this much simpler McBurger index.

 You and economics

The thing about a McDonald's is that you know what you are going to get. There might be some slight changes to the recipe or menu from one country to another, but the model does not change very much. Even though you do not eat them very much in the UK, you often do when you go abroad because it's an easy reference point, and if you are in a rush in a city you don't know it makes life simple for you. It also gives you a very quick insight into prices in the country so you get an idea of whether this is going to be an expensive trip or not.

Overcoming exchange rate problems

Possible exchange rate changes clearly make planning difficult and can change the cost position of a business or its competitiveness abroad very quickly. The exchange rate is an example of a PESTEL factor that is outside the direct control of a business but is a very significant influence on its success. There are also administration costs of changing currency which reduce the profits that can be made from overseas trade. While managers cannot themselves directly influence the exchange rate, they can take steps to reduce the impact.

To overcome some of the problems of fluctuating exchanges rates, managers may decide to:

- target markets that use the same currency (for example, a US producer may find that there is enough demand within that country to meet its targets; a French producer may decide to concentrate on countries such as Germany and Italy which use the euro as their currency), but a decision to do this may reduce export opportunities and the ability to buy the best inputs at the best prices;
- operate in several overseas markets, so that unfavourable changes in the currency of one market may be offset by more favourable changes in the currency of another country;
- buy currency in advance at a set price, so that they know what their exchange rate will be (this is known as a 'futures market');
- speculate in currencies to try to offset any movements;
- set contracts in their own currency.

Again, it must be remembered that one currency may be moving in different directions against others, so it is important to analyse with which markets a particular business is trading (that is, buying from and/or selling to) and the relevant currency movements in these markets.

The impact of an exchange rate change

The impact of a change in the exchange rate on a business depends on:

- what proportion of its sales are exported;
- what proportion of its inputs are imported;
- the degree of competition in the market from overseas businesses;
- how much the value of the currency has changed (and in what direction) against the currencies in its export and import markets;
- the price elasticity of demand for exports and imports;
- the availability of alternative markets to export to or other suppliers to switch to.

Of course, the exchange rate is only one factor that affects the competitiveness of a business. A strong pound may make it more difficult to export, but not impossible. Sales depend on the overall value for money which, in turn, depends on factors such as the design, the quality, the effectiveness of the marketing, and the speed of delivery. Therefore managers can take steps to overcome adverse exchange rate changes or to protect themselves against them. Adopting leaner production techniques to drive down costs, for example, may enable businesses to remain price competitive abroad even if the currency is strong. Alternatively, they may try to develop features that differentiate their products, so that demand becomes price inelastic.

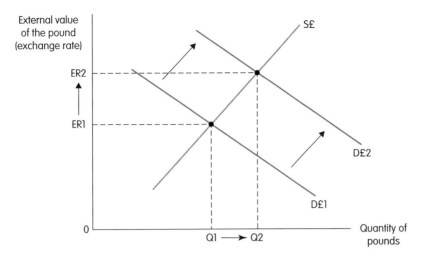

Figure 8.6 Government intervention to increase demand for a currency and increase its external value

Government intervention in the foreign currency markets

If the value of a currency is determined entirely by market forces of supply and demand, this is known as a 'floating exchange rate'. However, given the significant impact of currency changes on businesses and households, a government may want to influence the value of its currency. It may even want to stabilize the value of its currency and fix its value. This is known as a 'fixed (or pegged) exchange rate', and can be achieved by buying and selling currency and/or using interest rates.

To increase the value of its currency, a government can undertake the following.

■ *Buy its own currency using foreign currency reserves that it will have acquired in other periods*—that is, when selling its currency to bring the value down. By buying its own currency, the government shifts the demand for it to the right, increasing the equilibrium price (see Figure 8.6). The limit to such intervention is the amount of foreign currency that the government holds or is willing to borrow from foreign banks or governments.

■ *Increase interest rates* The interest rate is the return given to savers in a country's banks and can be influenced by the government (see Chapter 13). A high interest rate will attract investors into the country in search of high returns (although it is likely to reduce demand domestically because of the higher costs of borrowing).

? *Think about it...* 8.1

1. What do you think the effects on the domestic economy of an increase in interest rates might be?
2. How could a government reduce the value of its currency? Illustrate your answer using supply and demand diagrams.

Business analysis   8.2

The European Exchange Rate Mechanism (ERM) was an exchange rate system in which member currencies were fixed against each other. The ERM gave national currencies an upper and lower limit on either side of a central rate within which they could fluctuate (6 per cent, in the case of the UK). The UK joined the ERM in 1990, but in 1992 struggled to keep within the set boundaries. Speculators kept selling pounds, forcing the UK government to buy its own currency (using around £27,000 million to do so) and increase interest rates.

On 16 September 1992, the crisis became clear and despite billions of pounds worth of foreign currency reserves being used by the UK government to buy its currency, and interest rates being increased from 10 per cent to 12 per cent and then to 15 per cent in one day, the downward pressure was too great and the UK withdrew from the ERM. The pound fell immediately and this day became known as 'Black Wednesday'. The Italian lira also left the ERM and the Spanish peseta was devalued.

During this period, some speculators made fortunes. George Soros, for example, is believed to have made over US$1,000 million by speculating. He sold huge quantities of pounds at the relatively high price at which the government was trying to keep it. When the pound did eventually fall in price, Soros was able to buy them all back again at much lower prices.

How do you think being a member of the ERM might have helped UK businesses?
Was the collapse inevitable, do you think?

The euro

The euro is the official currency of sixteen of the twenty-seven countries in the European Union (EU); euro notes and coins first started being used on 1 January 2002. It is managed and administered by the European Central Bank (ECB) in Frankfurt. These countries have given up their own currencies, such as the German mark and French franc, to adopt the euro. The benefits of belonging to the 'Eurozone' include the following.

- There are no transaction costs for converting one currency to another.

- Managers do not have to worry about the effects of currency fluctuations with other Eurozone countries, which provides greater stability and makes planning easier.

- It is easier to compare prices of suppliers, which may allow a manager to find a better deal and force suppliers to be price competitive.

However, joining the Eurozone does involve the following.

- Giving up your own currency, which can be politically unpopular.

- Accepting a Eurozone interest rate set by the ECB, which may be changed to alter the value of the euro relative to other currencies. A particular government may find that the

ECB increases the interest rate to increase demand for the euro even though, within its own country, it would want to reduce the interest rate to stimulate demand. Therefore governments must be prepared to give up control over their domestic interest rates.

■ Accepting a value of the currency that may be determined by the behaviour of different countries rather than your own. In 2012, countries such as Greece and Spain were struggling with debt levels in their countries; this put downward pressure on the euro which worried stronger economies such as Germany. These countries were bailed out by the ECB to try and support them whilst they made the necessary changes to their spending plans.

The UK is not a member of the Eurozone, although there has been interest in joining at various points in the past. The position of the UK government was that five tests must be passed before the UK would join the euro. These focused on whether the UK's economic structure and the state of the economy were compatible with European interest rates, whether joining would create better conditions for long-term investment in the UK, and the impact on UK financial markets, growth, stability, and jobs. These issues would still be considered if the UK was to join, but the instability in the Eurozone in recent years has made membership in the near future most unlikely.

? *Think about it …* **8.3**

Which of the following statements are true and which are false?

A: An increase in the demand for a currency is likely to increase its value.

B: Higher interest rates in an economy are likely to reduce its value.

C: An appreciation of the currency occurs when it decreases in value.

D: A stronger currency is usually beneficial for importers, rather than exporters.

The market for shares

A company is a business organization which has its own legal identity in law and is owned by shareholders. Each share represents part-ownership of the business. There are different types of share, but 'ordinary shares' are the most common.

Holders of ordinary shares:

■ have one vote per share, so that the more shares they have, the more votes they have;

■ can vote on what happens to any profits that are made—that is, they can decide how much is retained for investment and how much is paid out as dividends each year;

■ can benefit (or suffer) from changes in the share price between when they buy them and when they sell them;

- have limited liability, which means that investors are liable for the amount that they have invested and can lose this, but their personal possessions are safe.

The shares of public limited companies (plcs) can be traded on the stock exchange. A stock exchange provides a huge market for buyers and sellers of shares. Shares of private limited (ltd) companies can be traded, but not on the stock exchange; they must be sold privately.

The price of shares in both private and public companies is determined by demand and supply conditions.

The demand for shares in a company is determined by the following factors.

- **The extent to which individuals or organizations want a vote to influence the company's policy** Generally, there is one vote per share, so the more shares you accumulate, the more control you have over the company's activities. For example, when a business is taking over another it will want to gain control of enough shares to influence decisions.

- **The expected dividend** Each year, the shareholders vote on what they want to happen to the profits of a business. They need to decide how much profit is retained within the business to finance future growth and how much is paid out to the investors as dividends. The 'dividend per share' shows the amount of money paid out to investors. The 'dividend yield' shows the dividend as a percentage of the market price of a share.

- **The expected change in the price of the shares** If potential investors believe that the share price will increase in value (for example, if they think that, in future, other investors will want to buy the shares), the demand will increase now, which is likely to bring about the increase in the share price that was originally anticipated. This increase in the value of a share is known as a 'capital gain'.

 You and economics

You have a few hundred shares that you inherited when your grandmother died. They are in a couple of different companies. Twice a year you get a dividend cheque from each of them. Most recently, one was for £3.07 and the other was for £2.11, so you are not going to become a millionaire from this! However, you are going to hold on to them for as long as you can and hope that their price continues to rise. You never know—it might be a nice little nest egg when you are in your retirement.

The supply of shares in a company at any given moment is fixed. All companies have an agreed number of shares that can be issued; more may be sold in the future, but this requires the permission of the existing shareholders. When new shares are issued, they are usually offered to existing owners who have the right to buy them; this is known as a 'rights issue'. However, in the market for existing shares, the number that people are willing to sell is likely to be upward-sloping up to the maximum number; as the price increases, so does the amount supplied to the market.

Data analysis   8.6

The dividend yield is calculated by:

$$\frac{\text{(dividend per share)}}{\text{(current market price of the share)}} \times 100$$

For example, if the dividend is 5 pence and the share price is £2.00, the yield is

$$(5/200) \times 100 = 2.5\%$$

1. What happens to the dividend yield if the share price increases, all other things being equal?
2. Why might an investor hold on to a share even if the dividend yield is low?
3. Why will the dividend yield change many times daily?

? Think about it...   8.4

1. If the supply of shares is fixed at any moment, what is the price elasticity of supply? Explain your answer.
2. What would make you decide to invest in one company rather than another?
3. What determines the price that you should be willing to pay for a share?
4. Draw a diagram showing the effect of an increase in demand on the price of a share.

The price of a share will determine the overall value of the company. The total value of all the shares in the company (that is, the price that would have to be paid to buy all the shares) is known as the **market capitalization** of the business and can be calculated as follows:

Market capitalization = Current share price × Number of shares available

If the market capitalization of a business is perceived to be low relative to what an investor believes is the true potential value of the company, some investors may want to buy shares or even try to take over and gain control of the company.

People and economics: Warren Buffet

Warren Buffett (born 1930) is an American businessman who is often regarded as the most successful investor of this century. He is the main shareholder and Chief Executive of Berkshire Hathaway. Consistently rated as one of the wealthiest people in the world and sometimes called the 'Wizard of Omaha' or the 'Sage of Omaha', Buffet has pledged to give away 99 per cent of his fortune to philanthropic causes.

£ Business analysis   8.3

In 2012 the world's largest social networking site, Facebook, announced plans for a stock market flotation. The company said that it was seeking to raise $5 billion (£3.16bn, €3.8bn). This first selling of shares on a stock exchange (an initial public offering (IPO)) was the largest sale of shares by an internet company. Facebook, which was started by Harvard University students, was just eight years old; it had 845 million users and in 2011 made a profit of $1 billion from revenues of $3.7 billion. The founder Mark Zuckerberg owns 28.4 per cent of Facebook and has more than 50 per cent of voting rights.

Other major flotations are:

- Google—raised $1.67 billion for 7 per cent of the company in 2004;
- Rosneft—raised $10.4 billion for 15 per cent of the company in 2006;
- Visa: raised $19.1 billion for 50 per cent of the company in 2008;
- Agricultural Bank of China—raised $22.1 billion in 2010, making it the world's largest IPO to date.

Why do you think that Facebook was valued so highly despite being such a new business?

Why do changes in share prices matter?

Changes in share prices are significant in the UK because:

- they represent part of the assets that households own, meaning that a fall in the value of shares reduces their wealth and, as a result, they may cut back on their spending, reducing demand in the economy;

- a significant proportion of shares are owned by pension funds, meaning that a fall in share prices reduces individuals' pensions and so is likely to reduce spending now, as individuals worry about their future;

■ they reflect the confidence that investors have in a company and an economy, meaning that if share prices generally fall, this may suggest that investors are concerned about growth in the economy.

The company's share price is important to senior managers because it reflects how much investors value the business. An increase in the share price increases the wealth of the investors, and this should mean that they are happy with the managers' performance. Of course, managers may also hold shares in the business.

The share price will also influence the amount of money that can be raised if the investors agree to sell more shares. Therefore this influences a company's access to finance through shares as opposed to loans.

You and economics

When you started your first job, the company had a private pension scheme which you were encouraged to join. You could save up to 10 per cent of your salary; for up to 5 per cent the company would match the money you paid in and this would add to the contributions put into the fund. The money collected would be invested by a fund manager for you to grow so that you would have a good pension when you retired. The fund manager asked what sort of approach to investment you wanted and you decided on high risk. This means that he/she would take relatively high risks with your money to earn higher returns. You understood the implications of this, or at least you thought you did until you saw your first annual pension statement and discovered that what was left was smaller than the amount you had put in because of a collapse in share prices. No early retirement for you then!

The market for capital goods

Capital goods are products, such as new equipment, that are used to help produce in the future; they represent an investment. Businesses invest in capital goods to help them to produce more efficiently and to enable them to produce more products in the future. For example, managers buy factories, machinery, and new IT systems. Look at the impact that investment in technology can have on a Formula One racing team and you can appreciate the benefits of investment in terms of improving a firm's competitiveness. It is said that the team that wins the first race of the Formula One season would come last by the end of the season if it failed to innovate at the same rate as the other teams during this period; this highlights the rate of technological change in this industry.

Gross investment is the total investment in capital goods in an economy. Some of this investment will be used to replace and update capital equipment that has worn out (called 'depreciation'). Net investment can be calculated as follows:

$$\text{Net investment} = \text{Gross investment} - \text{Depreciation}$$

An economy that has high gross investment, but low net investment, is simply replacing capital rather than increasing its capital resources.

When considering whether to invest in more capital goods, managers will consider the extra returns generated by an investment. This is known as the **marginal efficiency of capital (MEC)** (see Figure 8.7). The MEC represents the rate of return from each additional unit of investment; for example, the expected profit from a project could be 10 per cent a year, meaning that an investment of £200,000 would be expected to generate a profit of £20,000 a year. This return depends on managers' expectations of future levels of demand and costs. Projects can be ranked according to their returns, from the most to the least profitable.

Managers will compare the expected marginal benefits (the MEC) with the marginal costs of investing (which is generally the interest rate paid to borrow money). If the MEC is greater than the marginal cost, an additional project generates a higher return than the cost of undertaking it and a profit is made. For example, if the cost of borrowing money from a bank were 10 per cent, every investment project that was expected to earn more than 10 per cent would be desirable up to the point at which a project earned 10 per cent itself (that is, the same as the cost of borrowing), at which point no extra profit could be made. Therefore the profit-maximizing level of investment occurs when the MEC equals the marginal cost. Again, we can see the marginal condition in action; if the marginal benefit exceeds the marginal cost, then going ahead with this means a net gain for the individual or business. Where the marginal benefit equals the marginal cost, the net gains are maximized. For more on investment decisions, see Chapter 12.

If the marginal cost falls (for example, if the extra cost of borrowing money falls), more projects have a higher return than the marginal cost and therefore the quantity of investment should increase. A change in interest rates is shown by a movement along the MEC schedule (see Figure 8.8).

A shift in the MEC schedule occurs when there is a change in expectations: if managers expect that sales are likely to be higher in the future than first thought, the expected return

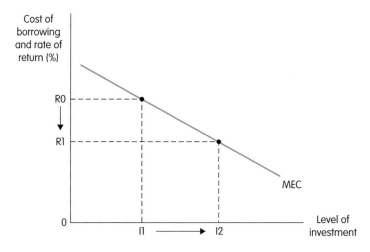

Figure 8.7 The marginal efficiency of capital

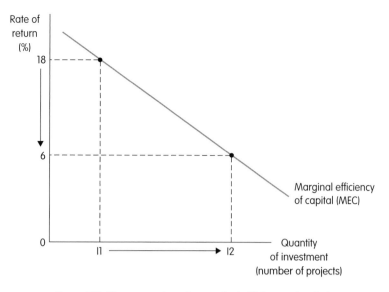

Figure 8.8 Movement along the marginal efficiency of capital

on projects increases and the MEC shifts outwards. This means that, at any given interest rate, there are now more projects that generate a higher return than the cost of borrowing, and investment should increase. The MEC may be highly volatile, and constantly shifting inwards and outwards, because of changes in expectations. Greater optimism shifts the MEC outwards, increasing investment for any given interest rate, whereas less optimism shifts the MEC inwards, reducing investment for any given interest rate (see Figure 8.9).

Therefore the level of investment for any given interest rate largely depends on expectations of the future and companies' forecasts of expected profits. The importance of expectations can be seen in the number of surveys of business confidence that appear in the media.

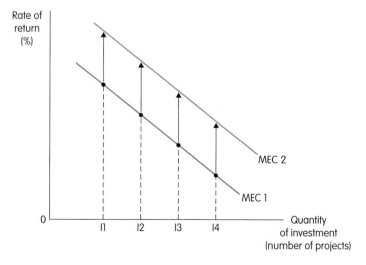

Figure 8.9 A shift in the marginal efficiency of capital

Business analysis   8.4

In 2012 the Governor of the Bank of England cut the forecast growth of the UK economy from 1.2 to 0.8 per cent. He also said that problems amongst members of the Eurozone currency area was a great worry and that there was a 'risk of a storm heading our way from the continent . . . We have been through a big global financial crisis, the biggest downturn in world output since the 1930s, the biggest banking crisis in this country's history, the biggest fiscal deficit in our peacetime history, and our biggest trading partner, the euro area, is tearing itself apart without any obvious solution.'

Given the Governor's statement, what do you think is likely to happen to investment? Why?

Source: BBC

You and economics

You go and look at a new car. You have always said that there was no point buying a new car because it lost value so quickly, but you have reached a point in your life where you think you deserve one! The prices are extremely high and there is no way that you can buy one outright—you need to do a deal. In the end you agree to make repayments for the next five years at the end of which you can either buy it or trade it in for another new one. Even so, you need to borrow the money and so there are some sums to do. Is it really worth the extra costs? You look again at the car, smell the new leather, hear the purr of the engine, and look at your reflection in the polished bonnet, and you know that it's worth every penny!

Why is investment important?

Spending on capital goods is an injection of spending into an economy, and therefore affects the total level of demand. Falls in the level of investment reduce demand in certain industries, and can lead to lower employment and less growth in the economy.

Investment is also important on the supply side of the economy because it enables firms to produce more; an increase in investment shifts the production possibility frontier (PPF) outwards and leads to an increase in supply over time.

Therefore the level of investment is important because of its impact on current spending and future growth. Governments will want to influence investment because it can be so volatile due to expectations; sudden falls in the level of optimism in the economy can shift the MEC inwards and reduce investment. This volatility means that governments will keep a close watch on the total level of investment in an economy because of its impact on total demand.

Think about it...   8.5

1. How do you think a government could influence the level of investment in an economy?
2. Governments are often keen to talk about the investment that they are putting into areas such as education and health. Is all investment desirable?

Economics and employability

What is your name?
Ben Andersen-Tuffnell.

Tell us about your role.
The British Bankers' Association (BBA) is the leading association for UK banking and financial services representing members on the full range of UK and international banking issues. It represents over 200 banking members active in the UK, which are headquartered in 50 countries and have operations in 180 countries worldwide. I am responsible for developing and implementing the BBA's government affairs strategy.

In what ways is an understanding of economics useful in your work?
Given the nature of financial markets and the wide variety of issues covered by the BBA, an understanding of economics is critical to understanding the impact of political and economic developments.

In what ways does economic change affect your clients?
Being financial services institutions, the BBA's members, and their personal and business customers, are notably affected by economic change. For example, the ongoing uncertainty in the Eurozone and lack of business confidence in the UK affects investment decisions undertaken by consumers and businesses.

Did you study economics at university as part of your studies, and, if so, how has it helped you in your work?
I did not study economics during my time at university, though I did take a few modules in political economy. They were particularly helpful in providing a historical context to some of the issues that arise today.

What skills are important in your role?
In no particular order—communication, judgement, stakeholder engagement, knowledge of political institutions and policy-making processes, and, of course, a sense of humour!

The labour market

One of the key resources of a business is its employees. Indeed, many companies, such as Intel, state that their 'employees are [their] greatest asset'. Like any other asset, employees have to be acquired and retained. How this is done is part of the human resources (HR) function of a business. Employees need to be managed effectively because they are a cost; they have to be paid for and this will affect the profits of the business. This is particularly important in labour-intensive organizations, such as hairdressers, football clubs, and insurance companies. In the UK, which is predominantly a service economy, labour costs as a whole are a very significant part of the total costs of a business.

Of course, employees also generate revenue; both directly and indirectly, their actions determine the nature and quantity of the product provided, as well as the quality of customer service and the degree of innovation that occurs. Therefore, when deciding how many employees to hire, managers will be trying to compare the likely gains from employing an extra employee with the potential costs of doing so. A business would want to hire any employee where the extra benefit of employment exceeds the extra cost up to the point at which the marginal benefit to the business equals the extra cost. Again, economic analysis focuses on what happens at the margin in order to maximize returns.

What determines the price of labour?

The price of labour is known as the 'wage' (if paid weekly) or the 'salary' (if paid monthly). Wages and salaries are often (but not always) determined by market forces—that is, the demand for labour and the supply of labour.

The demand for labour

The demand for labour depends on the benefits that employees generate for a given business. The demand for labour is a derived demand; this means that it is derived from the demand for the final product. Employees help to add value for the business by developing new features, improving customer service, coming up with new approaches, and actually producing the product and providing the services.

The value of an extra employee to a business will depend on:

- the extra output that he/she helps to produce, which is the 'marginal product';
- the revenue generated by selling this extra output, which is the **marginal revenue**.

The **marginal revenue product (MRP)** shows the revenue earned by the extra output produced by an employee and can be calculated as:

$$MRP = \text{Marginal product} \times \text{Marginal revenue}$$

This determines the additional financial benefit that an additional employee brings to the business.

The MRP curve will usually be downward-sloping because:

■ the revenue earned by selling extra employees' output is likely to fall as more employees are hired—to sell more, the price is likely to have to be lowered and so less is earned by selling additional units;

■ the marginal product of labour is likely to fall in the short run because of the law of diminishing returns.

The demand for labour will shift if:

■ demand for the product changes—for example, if demand for the product increases, this will increase the value of the output produced and therefore increase the MRP of employees, which shifts demand for labour to the right;

■ productivity increases—that is, if employees produce more units, they are adding more value to the business and this again shifts the MRP to the right (see Figure 8.10).

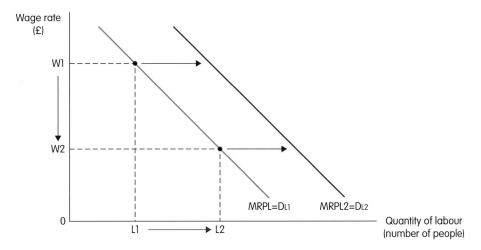

Figure 8.10 A movement along versus a shift in demand for labour

 Business analysis 8.5

In an interview in 2012, at a time of high unemployment in the UK, Foreign Secretary William Hague said: 'There's only one growth strategy: work hard.' The Communities Secretary, Eric Pickles, agreed: 'Government can't create growth, it can create the conditions for growth but we're only going to be able to do this if we all work harder. The world has changed and our competition has changed, and I think the only way we can pull out of this is by us all working harder.'

Hague also said that businesses needed to 'do more with less—that's the twenty-first century. We're trying to rescue the work ethic just in the nick of time.' He said that changes to benefits, such as a limit to the benefits that can be paid to someone, 'will be seen in the 2020s as being as important to this country as the trade union reforms and privatizations were of the 1980s'.

Do you think that to increase productivity employees need to work harder? What else might help?

Why might trade union reforms have helped reduce unemployment?

Why might a cap on benefits help reduce unemployment?

Source: http://www.bbc.co.uk/news/uk-politics-18048963

The wage elasticity of demand

The wage elasticity of demand for labour shows how sensitive demand for labour is to changes in the wage level. This depends on the following factors.

■ *How easy it is to substitute other factors of production for labour* If it is relatively easy to replace employees with computer systems or to automate their jobs, for example, the demand for labour will be wage elastic. Copywriters in an advertising agency, designers in a computer games company, or star basketball players may be more difficult to replace with machines, so demand would be wage inelastic.

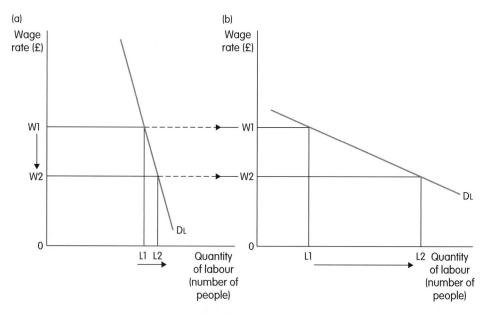

Figure 8.11 The impact of a change in wages: (a) demand for labour is wage inelastic; (b) demand for labour is wage elastic.

■ *How sensitive the demand for the final product is relative to changes in price (that is, the price elasticity of demand for the final product)* An increase in wages will increase costs and push up the price of the final product. If demand for the final product is price elastic, this will lead to a relatively large fall in the quantity demanded of it and therefore the quantity demanded of labour. If demand for the final product is insensitive to price changes, the demand for labour is also likely to be insensitive to wage increases (see Figure 8.11).

■ *Labour costs as a percentage of the total costs* If a wage increase for employees has a significant impact on the firm's total costs (for example, in an accountancy firm) and therefore on the price of the product, the fall in the quantity demanded of the product is likely to be relatively high and this will lead to a relatively significant fall in the quantity demanded of labour. However, if labour costs are only a small percentage of the total costs of the business (for example, in an aircraft manufacturing business), an increase in wages is not likely to have significant impact on the final price and therefore the quantity demanded of labour is not likely to fall significantly.

The supply of labour

The supply of labour to an industry shows the number of people who are willing and able to work at the given wage, all other factors held constant. Generally, the higher the wage, the more people will want to work, because of the higher rewards and the higher opportunity cost of staying at home. This means that the supply of labour is usually upward-sloping in relation to wages (see Figure 8.12a).

The supply of labour to an industry depends on the following.

■ The number of people in the working population, which determines the maximum number of people who could work in an industry. The size of the working population will be affected by factors such as school-leaving age and retirement age.

■ The appeal of the jobs in the industry, which might relate to the working conditions, the status of the jobs, and the nature of the tasks involved. For example, there may be more people willing and able to be shop assistants than surgeons.

■ The degree of training and experience required—that is, what skills, qualifications, and previous achievements are required. For example, there may be many people wanting to be professional footballers, but they may lack the necessary skills, while a job such as learning to fly a plane takes time to master, which would limit the supply of labour at any moment.

■ The availability of information about jobs in the industry, so that people know that they exist (if you don't know what opportunities there are, you can't supply your labour).

■ The cost and ease of people moving to the area to take the jobs, which is known as 'geographical immobility'—that is, the cost of living can be higher in some areas than others, which can act as a barrier to movement, as can large differences in costs such as house prices.

■ The incentives to accept these jobs relative to the incentives to not work—for example, a high rate of income tax may deter people from working, whereas low levels of unemployment benefits may increase the desire to work. The 'unemployment trap' occurs when people are worse off working than they are on benefits, and so do not make an effort to work.

A shift in the supply of labour (see Figure 8.12b) might result if the following occurs.

■ *The working population increases, perhaps because of an increase in net immigration* In 2004, the expansion of the EU led to an inflow of over half a million workers to the UK from Eastern Europe, providing an increase in the labour supply in sectors such as construction, leisure, and retail.

■ *The tax rates on income are reduced, so that employees keep more of their earnings* Lower tax rates provide an incentive to work at each wage rate, whereas higher income tax rates might shift the supply of labour to the left. In 2009, when the UK government announced a 50 per cent income tax rate for earnings over £150,000, several footballers announced that they would have to leave the country to earn enough. Some clubs decided to pay their players in the form of interest-free loans rather than salaries because this avoided the extra tax. In 2012 this tax was removed— the government argued that it had not brought in much revenue as so many people had avoided it and that it was a disincentive for business people to stay in the UK and generate high earnings.

■ *Education and training improves* Improvements in education and training may mean that more people have the skills to accept the jobs. This shifts the supply curve to the right.

■ *Fewer benefits for those who are unemployed*, encouraging people to take jobs.

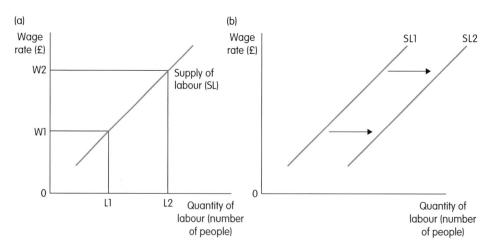

Figure 8.12 The supply of labour to an industry

Data analysis 8.7

When an individual is considering how many hours to work in relation to the wage rate, there are two effects to consider:

- the substitution effect;
- the income effect.

With a higher wage, it is more expensive not to work, so the 'substitution effect' encourages the individual to work more hours. Individuals substitute work because leisure is so expensive, but with higher wages, an individual can work fewer hours and still earn the same amount of money (known as the 'income effect'). This would tend to lead to less hours worked.

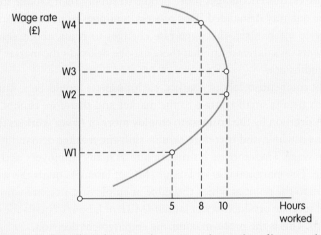

Figure 8.13 The effect of a change in wages on the number of hours worked

Look at Figure 8.13. What can you deduce about the relative size of the income and substitution effects when the following wage rate changes occur?

A: From W1 to W2.

B: From W2 to W3.

C: From W3 to W4.

@ You and economics

You have been working at a local gym for £7 an hour and have enjoyed the work. However, you have found it hard to juggle studies and work. You recently went to an interview at a new health club that was starting up and they offered you a supervisory position at £10 an hour. They would like you to work more hours than you are doing at the moment, but you are reluctant to commit to that; in fact, with the extra earnings you are wondering whether you can cut back a bit more.

Equilibrium in the labour market

Equilibrium in a labour market occurs at the wage at which the quantity supplied of labour equals the quantity demanded (see Figure 8.14). At W2, for example, the wage is above equilibrium and there is excess supply of labour—the number of people wanting to work at this high wage is greater than the number of people whom businesses want to employ. This surplus of labour would lead to downward pressure on wages. As the wage falls, this reduces the number of people willing and able to accept a job, and increases the quantity demanded. This process continues until the equilibrium wage is reached.

At W3, by comparison, there is an excess demand of labour—the quantity demanded of labour is greater than the quantity supplied of labour at this wage. This shortage will put upward pressure on the wage rate, because there is more demand than supply. As the wage rate increases, this encourages more people to supply their labour to this industry and reduces the quantity demanded. This process continues until equilibrium is reached. Just like the price mechanism, the wage rate changes to bring about equilibrium. But annual agreements on salaries mean that there may be delays in the market's adjusting to reach a new equilibrium.

In a perfectly competitive labour market, each business would be a wage-taker. This means that each firm is small relative to the market and therefore cannot influence the market wage. A decision by the business to employ more or fewer workers is insignificant to the market as a whole and therefore cannot shift the market demand for labour and the equilibrium wage. Therefore each firm can hire as many employees as it wishes at the given wage rate. The marginal cost of labour (MC of labour) equals the wage. The firm employs staff up to the point at which the value of employing an extra employee, known as the marginal revenue productivity of labour (MRP of labour), equals the marginal cost (see Figure 8.15). This is the profit-maximizing employment decision.

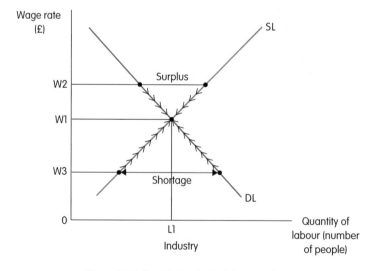

Figure 8.14 Equilibrium in the labour market

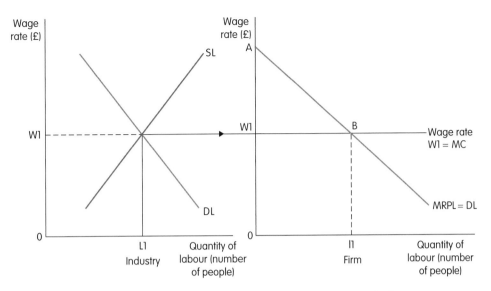

Figure 8.15 Equilibrium in the labour market for the industry and a firm

Of course, this is an extreme model in which labour markets are assumed to be competitive and businesses are wage-takers. In reality, labour markets may be uncompetitive, with employees trying to restrict supply (perhaps through a **trade union**) to push up the wage and managers trying to use their power as a major employer to push down wages.

? *Think about it...* 8.6

Illustrate the effect of an increase in the supply of labour, and show its effect on the equilibrium wage and quantity employed.

Wage differences

Wage differences will occur in labour markets if supply and demand conditions vary. For example, in Figure 8.16a the demand for labour is high because of the amount of money that football players earn for their clubs via merchandising and attendance fees. Supply is limited because of the high levels of natural ability required to compete at this level. In the case of cleaners (see Figure 8.16b), the supply of labour is much higher because the job is relatively unskilled and easy to do, and demand is low because cleaners do not directly earn a business much money. The result is that some football players are paid much more than cleaners.

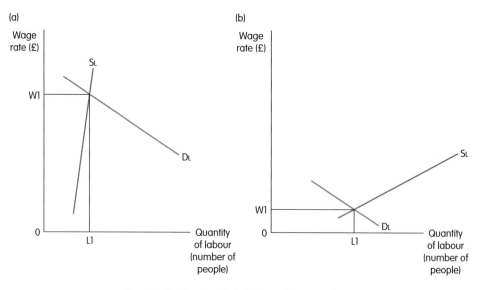

Figure 8.16 Wage levels in different labour markets

 Business analysis   8.6

Bosses of the UK's biggest companies earn millions in 'excess remuneration' according to a recent report by the research company Obermatt . Pay packages that were intended to provide an incentive to FTSE 100* chief executives actually had little effect on company performance. The researchers compared profit growth and total return to shareholders against the total realized pay earned by bosses between 2008 and 2010.

The findings showed that former Reckitt Benckiser boss Bart Becht earned £138.6m more than the performance of his company justified—a 1,199 per cent overpayment.

The researchers said that there was absolutely no pay-for-performance link in the UK for the period covered. They felt that the committees responsible for setting pay were more concerned about retaining employees than rewarding performance. Shareholders of several companies, including Aviva, Trinity Mirror, Barclays, and Pendragon, have recently shown their unhappiness at excessive pay and bonus packages.

How would you decide on the reward to give to senior managers?

Can the very high levels of pay of some senior managers, such as the chief executives of the major banks, be justified?

*The FTSE100 is an index of the share prices of the UK's 100 largest companies (by market capitalization).

Changes in labour market conditions

If the demand for labour increases in a market, perhaps because of an increase in demand for the product, this means that, at the old wage W1, there is an excess demand of labour. This puts upward pressure on wages. As wages increase, this leads to an increase in the number of people wanting to work and a reduction in the quantity demanded. This process continues until the new equilibrium at W2, L2 (see Figure 8.17). The increase in demand has led to more people being employed at a higher wage.

The effect of any shift in the demand of labour on the equilibrium wage and quantity depends on the extent of the shift and the wage elasticity of labour supply. The sensitivity of the supply of labour to wage changes depends on how easy it is to recruit employees into this industry which, in turn, depends on the mobility of labour. The more inelastic supply is, the greater the effect of a shift in demand on wages rather than the quantity of labour (see Figure 8.18).

If the supply of labour increases, perhaps due to immigration, this means that there is excess supply at the previous equilibrium wage. This puts downward pressure on wages. As wages fall, this reduces the number of people willing to work and increases the quantity demanded. This process continues until a new equilibrium is reached at W2, L2 (see Figure 8.19). The increase in the supply of labour leads to more people being employed at a lower wage.

The effect of any shift in the supply of labour on the equilibrium wage and quantity of people employed depends on the extent of the shift and the wage elasticity of labour demand. The more inelastic demand for labour is, the greater the impact on the wage rather than the quantity of labour employed.

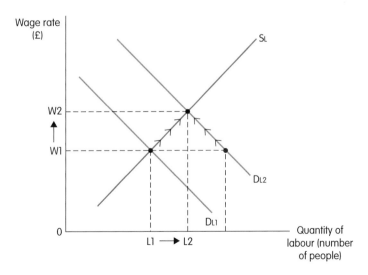

Figure 8.17 A shift in the demand for labour

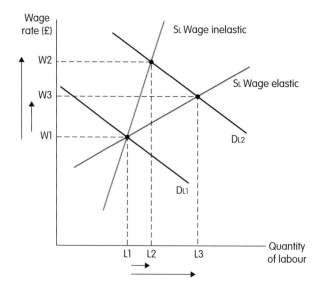

Figure 8.18 The effect of a shift in demand for labour on equilibrium wage and quantity

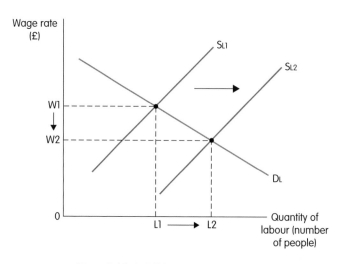

Figure 8.19 A shift in the supply of labour

? *Think about it...*   8.7

1. In which of the following industries is the supply of labour likely to be most wage inelastic? Explain your reasoning.
   A: Doctors
   B: Plumbers

     C: Stockbrokers

     D: University lecturers

     E: Airline pilots

     F: Cleaners

2. **Using supply and demand analysis what could lead to:**

     A: higher equilibrium wages and quantity of labour employed;

     B: lower equilibrium wages and quantity of labour employed;

     C: higher equilibrium wages and lower quantity of labour employed;

     D: lower equilibrium wages and higher quantity of labour employed.

 ## Business analysis 8.7

Whilst we can analyse the local labour market, it is also interesting to consider what is happening in labour markets globally. The most significant development to watch for in the future is the growth in the education of the workforce in China and India. At present approximately 25 per cent of Chinese and 70 per cent of Indians do not have even a primary education, but this is changing quickly. The two countries combined are likely to add nearly 200 million college graduates to the labour market. Furthermore, the fact that they are now better educated and working in industry with large investments in capital means that they are much more productive than those before them. Meanwhile more developed economies are facing an ageing population and fewer graduates. This means that there is likely to be a shift towards the emerging markets to target the skilled workforce and fill the skills gaps elsewhere.

How might these changes in the global labour market affect a firm's human resources function?

Trade unions

The wage level in a business or industry may also be affected by trade unions. A trade union is an organization that represents and bargains for employees' rights. The aims of unions are to protect employees' interests and to ensure that they are properly rewarded. This may involve restricting the supply of labour to an industry so that only union members can gain employment; this would lead to higher wages and less employment. Unions may also push wages above the equilibrium level, leading to an excess supply of labour. For example, they could try to insist on L1 employees being employed at a wage of W2, which forces the employer off his/her demand curve (see Figure 8.20).

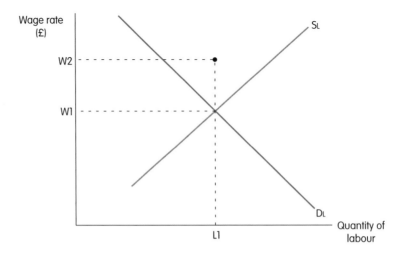

Figure 8.20 Effect of trade unions

Other factors influencing wages

While market forces of supply and demand are undoubtedly important influences on many labour markets, not all labour markets are competitive and not all earnings are directly determined by market forces.

For example, in the public sector employees do not always produce output that is sold (for example, in the health service and education), and therefore the monetary value of what they produce is difficult to estimate and the demand curve cannot be the MRP. In such situations, employers may try to match the jobs with those in the private sector and therefore arrive at the appropriate level of earnings. However, there will inevitably be financial pressures in the public sector because these jobs do not produce saleable output and this may limit the amount that may be awarded to employees.

Government may also intervene to influence wages. For example, the UK's Minimum Wage Act prevents the wage level from falling below a certain level. This is because it is felt that in some jobs, such as unskilled factory workers, wages might be so low in the free market that they will be perceived as unfair (even if they are economically efficient). To prevent this from occurring, a government may ensure that everyone is paid what it regards as a 'fair' wage. The result of this is that those in work earn at least the minimum wage. However, fewer people will be employed compared with a free market, because wages have been pushed above equilibrium (see Figure 8.21).

}{ People and economics: Dubner and Levitt

Steven Levitt and Stephen Dubner are the authors of *Freakonomics*, a book which uses economic theory to explain cheating teachers, unusual baby names, and the activities of estate agents. The book has sold more than four million copies in thirty-five languages. In their book they studied the

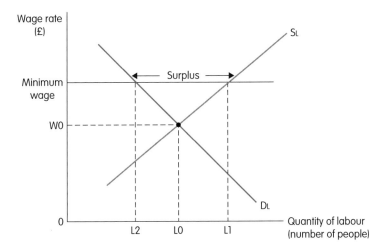

Figure 8.21 The effect of a minimum wage in the labour market

finances of a drugs gang to understand how much the members earned. By studying four years of the gangs' accounts they found that the organization included many levels of hierarchy with many different 'officers' and 'footsoldiers'. Although those at the very top might have high earnings, the foot soldiers were on $3.30 an hour in what is an extremely dangerous profession. Perhaps surprisingly, Dubner and Levitt managed to explain why most drugs dealers still live with their mothers!

Source: http://www.freakonomics.com/

When examining wage levels, it is important to realize that there are many different labour markets. Supply and demand conditions may vary considerably between regions, for example. There are also differences between different jobs in an industry and even between the same jobs; for example, there may be many sales managers in the tourism industry, but within this there may be markets for managers at different levels of seniority and focusing on different types of tourism. This means that while the principles of market forces are very important, each market being analysed must be carefully defined.

The equi-marginal condition

Labour is only one input into the transformation process, and managers must consider the right combinations of resources to use. As you would expect, this will be influenced by the productivity and costs of these factors of production relative to each other.

If the price of labour increases (perhaps because of a decrease in supply), this is likely to make managers reconsider the mix of resources that they use in their transformation process. With all other things unchanged, managers will want to switch away from labour towards other relatively cheaper factors of production. Whether this is possible will depend on factors such as the price and productivity of the other factors.

A profit-maximizing producer will employ different factors of production up to the point at which:

$$\frac{\text{Marginal product of factor A}}{\text{Price of factor A}} = \frac{\text{Marginal product of factor B}}{\text{Price of factor B}}$$
$$= \dots \frac{\text{Marginal product of factor X}}{\text{Price of factor X}}$$

This is known as the 'equi-marginal condition'. If the marginal product per pound spent of factor A were higher than other factors, this would mean that it would be better value for money. The manager would switch to this factor and away from the other options. As this happens, the marginal product is likely to fall due to the law of diminishing returns and the price of the factor may increase with more demand. This process of switching resources should continue until each one offers the same extra productivity per pound. At this point, the manager is employing resources efficiently.

The effect of an increase in the price of labour, by comparison, will reduce the marginal product per pound spent on labour, which should therefore lead managers to switch away towards other factors, such as capital, until the equi-marginal condition is fulfilled.

? Think about it...   8.8

Which of the following statements are true and which are false?

A: An increase in labour productivity shifts the supply of labour outwards.

B: An increase in demand for the final product shifts the demand for labour outwards.

C: An increase in the supply of labour should increase the equilibrium wage and quantity of people employed.

Summary

Markets can differ considerably in terms of their demand and supply conditions, and the price elasticity of demand and supply. A change in demand or supply can have very different effects in terms of the equilibrium price and quantity. In this chapter, we have examined a number of important markets to highlight the importance of the market mechanism and to show how it varies from market to market.

Checklist

Having read this chapter, you should now understand:

☐ the meaning of an exchange rate;

☐ the determinants of the supply of and demand for a currency;

☐ the impact of an increase or decrease in the value of a currency;

☐ the meaning and significance of market capitalization;

☐ why the demand for labour is a derived demand;

☐ the meaning of the marginal revenue product (MRP);

☐ causes of shifts in the demand and supply of labour;

☐ the possible impact of a trade union on the market wage;

☐ the factors affecting the share price of a company;

☐ the meaning and significance of the equi-marginal condition.

Organizations and economics

The London Stock Exchange (LSE)

'The London Stock Exchange is at the heart of the global financial market and is home to some of the largest, most successful, and most dynamic companies in the world.

The Exchange is the most international of all the world's stock exchanges, with around 3,000 companies from over seventy countries admitted to trading on its markets.

From conducting its business in the coffee houses of seventeenth century London, the Exchange is one of the world's oldest stock exchanges and can trace its history back more than 300 years.

Live financial broadcasts are transmitted throughout the day from the Exchange's own TV studios.

Over 400 firms, mainly investment banks and stockbrokers, are members of the London Stock Exchange.'

By having their shares quoted on a stock exchange, companies can gain access to millions of investors to raise finance.

Source: http://www.londonstockexchange.com

Trades Union Congress (TUC)

Trade unions are organizations set up to represent and protect employees. The TUC represents 58 trade unions in the UK which in turn represent 6.2 million working people. The TUC is a campaigning and lobbying body that seeks to ensure a fair deal at work for employees and social justice

Source: http://www.tuc.org.uk.

Short answer questions

1. What determines demand for a currency?

2. What determines the supply of a currency?

3. What is meant by a 'strong' pound?

4. How might a government intervene to increase the value of its currency?

5. Why do investors buy shares?

6. What is meant by market capitalization?

7. What is meant by marginal revenue product?

8. What factors determine the supply of labour to an industry?

9. What determines the wage elasticity of demand for labour?

10. Why is demand for labour a derived demand?

Discussion questions

1. Discuss the main reasons why exchange rates are often so unstable.

2. Discuss the main factors influencing the level of investment in an economy.

3. To what extent does a change in share price of a company matter?

One step further

Visit our Online Resource Centre at **www.oxfordtextbooks.co.uk/orc/gillespiebusiness2e/** to test your understanding, watch video walk-throughs, and access further information on topics covered in this chapter.

Perfect competition, monopoly, and price discrimination

9

Learning objectives

In this chapter, we consider some of the different forms of market structure that exist and the implications of these structures for managers. We examine the two extremes of perfect competition where there are many small firms producing similar products and have to accept the market price, and a monopoly situation where one firm dominates the market and sets the price. We also consider how a business with power over the market may charge different prices in different segments of the market, which is known as price discrimination.

By the end of this chapter, you should:

- ✓ understand different market conditions and the impact on price and output decisions;

- ✓ understand the meaning and significance of barriers to entry;

- ✓ understand the price and output decisions in a perfectly competitive market in the short and long runs;

- ✓ understand the price and output decisions in a monopoly market in the short and long runs;

- ✓ understand the conditions and impact of price discrimination.

ⓒ Case study

Seth inherited his farm from his father when he was just 24. Working outdoors was not an easy existence and his father's health had declined in recent years. Seth had always been interested in farming but had not expected to be running the family business at such a young age. At 24 he had a tough decision to make, but he decided that this business had been in his family for several generations and he was going to keep it going. However, he had not realized what he was taking on. The

business grew potatoes which were sold to one of the big supermarkets. When they had first won this contract ten years ago the family had been delighted because it was for such huge quantities and they thought that it gave them some stability—prior to this they seemed to be rushing around trying to win orders all the time. However, the supermarket knew its power and was not slow to use it. Seth soon found out that the supermarket's buyers were very eager to remind him that he needed them more than they needed him. 'We have lots of other farmers who would be only too pleased for our business,' they said. 'After all, a potato is a potato is a potato—if you try and push your prices up we'll just switch to someone else who will be delighted to supply us. We get farmers approaching us all the time so there is no shortage of choice as far as we concerned and there's very little to choose between you.'

Seth knows they are right—he needs them but the profit margins on the potatoes are so small that he is keen to find a way out of this situation. He cannot see much future in the potato market; after all the supermarkets have all the power. But what if he started to make premium crisps with his own potatoes or what about vodka? Perhaps in these markets he could create a brand and make some proper money. Time to start planning!

Questions

1. Why do the supermarkets have power over Seth's business?
2. What might the effect of this be on the price he receives?
3. What ethical issues do you think might occur in this situation?
4. Do you think a government should regulate the prices paid to farmers?
5. Why is Seth unable to push prices up to increase his profits?
6. Do you think moving into crisp or vodka production might give Seth more opportunity for profits? Why?

Introduction

There are many different types of market in the business world. Some are local, such as the supply and demand for taxis within a city; others are global, such as the market for oil or wheat. The structure of these markets can vary considerably in terms of the number and size of firms competing. In some markets, such as hairdressing and newsagents, there are hundreds of thousands of small providers of very similar products. In other markets, such as insurance, banking, and pharmaceuticals, there are relatively few large producers. In this and the following chapter we examine the different market conditions and the implications of this for managers.

The concentration ratio

One key element of the structure of a market is the number of firms operating within it and their relative size. A market with many small firms of roughly equal size may be more competitive than one dominated by one or two firms. The **concentration ratio** measures the market share of the largest firms in a market. For example, the 'four-firm concentration ratio' measures the market share of the largest four firms in the market. This ratio varies significantly between markets in the UK. In the case of sugar, oil, and cars, for example, it is very high; in the case of hairdressing, web design, and plumbing, it is low, highlighting that there are many small firms in these industries. The higher the concentration ratio, the more a market is dominated by a few firms. This influences the degree of competition and rivalry.

If one firm dominates a market (that is, if it has a high market share), it is called a 'monopoly'. If a few firms dominate it, is an **oligopoly** (which is analysed in the next chapter). If there are many thousands of firms and none of them are particularly large, it is known as a 'competitive market'. In **monopolistic competition** there are many firms but they differentiate their products in some way (such as branding) to gain some market power. In a **perfect competition** there are many firms offering very similar products and buyers can easily switch from one to the other so that firms cannot charge more than their rivals (see Figure 9.1). Of course, when analysing the competition, managers must be clear what they mean by the 'market'. A retailer may be interested in the competition within a twenty-minute drive, because this is where their shoppers come from; a shampoo producer may be interested in competition nationally or even globally.

Figure 9.1 Market structures

Data analysis   9.1

The product sales of the top five businesses as a percentage of the total market sales in the UK are summarized in Table 9.1.

Table 9.1 Market share

Product	Percentage sales of top five businesses
Tobacco	99%
Sugar	99%
Confectionery	81%
Coal extraction	79%
Soft drinks and bottled water	75%
Telecommunications	61%
Pharmaceuticals	57%
Alcoholic beverages	51%
Soap and toilet preparations	40%
Accountancy services	36%
Jewellery and related products	20%
Fishing	16%
Hotels, catering, and pubs	13%
Advertising	10%
Market research, management consultancy	10%
Wood and wood products	9%
Legal activities	9%

Source: adapted from *Economic Trends*, 2006

1. Why do you think concentration ratios differ so much from one industry to another?
2. What do you think are the possible effects of a high concentration ratio on:
   A: customers?
   B: investors?
3. Do you think that these ratios would be the same in other countries?
4. Why might they change over time?

? Think about it...   9.1

Can you think of any markets in your economy in which the concentration ratio has changed in recent years? Why and how has it changed?

Managers will be interested in the market share of their business and the market share of other businesses because this will influence their power relative to that of their competitors. For example, Microsoft dominates the software market, which offers it various advantages, such as:

■ it may be able to negotiate better prices with suppliers;

■ some programmers will be keen to work for it because of its leading status;

■ it may have a brand loyalty and recognition that makes launching a new product easier than for an unknown business;

■ it has huge resources which can be used to deter anyone else entering the market and it can therefore protect its position.

% Worked example

Market share = (Sales of your product or business/Total market sales) × 100

For example, if your sales are £40,000 and the total market size is £200,000:

Market share = (£40,000/£200,000) × 100 = 20%

If your market share is 25 per cent and the market is worth £400,000:

Your sales = (25/100) × £400,000 = £100,000

A smaller producer may be in a much weaker position and be trading on less favourable terms, making it more difficult for it to survive and grow. In some markets, two firms (think Coca Cola and Pepsi, McDonald's and Burger King, Google and Microsoft) fight it out to win orders—that is, two giant companies fight for dominance, mainly through product development. In other markets, such as advertising agencies and hairdressers, there are many small businesses, but no single firm has a significant share of the market.

The conditions within a market will affect a manager's ability to control the price, the likely level of output that a business will be producing, and how it competes. These decisions will, in turn, affect many other aspects of the business, such as:

■ its workforce planning (for example, whether it needs to recruit or make redundancies);

■ the likely profits of the business (for example, whether it needs to warn shareholders of a likely fall in their rewards in the future);

■ the desired level of capacity (for example, whether it is time to expand);

■ the level of investment in marketing and in research and development.

Therefore understanding market conditions is very important for a manager. This means not only understanding the implications of the current concentration ratio, but also considering how easy it is for other firms to enter the market and the impact of this on future levels of competition.

The threat of entry may influence a firm's behaviour as much as its existing rivals; for example, it may force a business to ensure that it remains competitive in what it offers and the level of service provided for fear that otherwise it may fall behind.

?   Think about it ...   9.2

Why do you think there are so many taxi businesses and hairdressers in the UK, but relatively few electricity or train companies?

@   You and economics

You have always been keen to support small businesses and local businesses. If you can, you find a local butcher, a local coffee shop, a local pub that does not belong to a big chain, and an independent book shop, you would prefer to use these businesses. All well and good in theory, but in practice you find that there is a limit to what you can do. When it comes to food shopping there are so few independent retailers nearby that you have to use the big supermarkets. And there are very few options for electrical products. It seems that we live in a world, much of which is dominated by big global businesses.

Barriers to entry

The number of businesses competing in a market will depend, in part, on how easy or difficult it is to enter. The more difficult it is to enter, the greater the power of established firms and the less likely it is that it will be a competitive market.

Barriers to entry are factors that make it difficult for new firms to enter the market and include the following.

- *Access to suppliers and distributors* New businesses need to be able to access the required materials or components; without them, they cannot produce or sell. If most of the land that can be farmed in the Champagne region of France is already growing grapes, then starting up as a champagne producer could be difficult. Similarly, if a business cannot get its products on the shelves of stores because the retailers prefer to stick with brands that they know or are worried about upsetting the bigger producers, newcomers will find it difficult to gain any market share. Several years ago Wall's ice cream was prosecuted for giving chilled cabinets to independent retailers and, in return, insisting that they stock Wall's products. Given the physical size of these stores, if they accepted Wall's gift, they did not have space for another freezer cabinet and so, in effect, Wall's was preventing competitors from accessing the market. Vertical integration by existing firms is another way of creating barriers to entry by controlling elements of supply and distribution and not allowing newcomers access to suppliers to distribution channels. For example, in India, foreign companies cannot invest in retail outlets except for single-brand stores in which they can own 51 per cent. This means that a business such as Reebok can open a store, but a supermarket such as the French chain Carrefour cannot. Trading is made more difficult by numerous taxes charged if you move goods between states and even within some states. Small family-owned retail outlets dominate this market and big Western retailers cannot get to the customers.

- *The costs of entering a market* The set-up costs for some industries can be so high that it will deter entrants. For example, imagine trying to compete in the aircraft manufacturing business: the design costs and costs needed to set up a production system would be huge. This market is dominated by Boeing and Airbus, and it is difficult for other firms to enter. Even consumer markets, such as perfume, are very difficult to enter because of the marketing costs. The cost of simply promoting a new perfume in the UK is estimated to be £1 million if you want any chance of success; this is too much for small producers, thereby blocking their entry. Chanel spends over £7 million a year on promoting its products.

- *Legal requirements* In some markets, the existing firms are legally protected and entry by other businesses is prevented. For example, some countries use protectionist measures to protect their domestic industries against foreign competition. Quotas or tariffs are often used. Quotas limit the amount of units that foreign producers can sell in a country; a tariff places a tax on foreign goods, making them relatively expensive compared with domestic products. This makes it difficult for overseas firms to enter these markets.

- *Fear of retaliation* Firms may be wary of entering a market if they are afraid of what existing firms might do—for example, if they were worried that they would start a price war. If the existing firms react aggressively whenever anyone enters, this may act as deterrent over time and stop more from coming in. The way in which firms react will depend in part on the size of the market and whether or not it is growing. In a shrinking market, any further competition would be strongly resisted because it would take away even more sales at a time when winning and maintaining sales is difficult (whereas in a growing market it is possible that all of them can sell more). Also, the extent to which established firms have money invested in an industry that cannot easily be transferred will affect how fiercely they resist entry. A 'sunk cost' represents spending that cannot be recovered if a business leaves the market—for example, investment in specialized equipment that cannot be transferred to another industry. If there are high sunk costs, existing firms will fight harder to protect their market share.

- *The learning curve* As a firm gains experience in a market, it is likely to become better at producing—it will learn by doing. If you start a job at a new business, it will take time for you to get up to speed—that is, to work out how things are done, to find out who you ask for various things, to find out where you buy supplies from, and so on. Those people who have been there a while should know the answers to many of these questions because they will have learnt along the way. A new person has much to learn and therefore will be less efficient at first. The same is true for businesses—if managers have been in an industry for a while and have expanded, they will have more experience than newcomers, should make fewer mistakes, and should make better decisions. As a result of the learning curve, entering a market can be difficult and therefore this acts as a barrier to entry.

£ Business analysis   9.1

The 22,000 London 'black cab' taxis are amongst some of the most expensive in the world. They compete to some extent with minicabs, which tend to be cheaper. However, minicabs are not allowed to pick up customers off the street, they have to be booked in advance, and their drivers do not have to memorize a London street map. Minicabs operate in a more competitive market and require less of the drivers. Black cab (i.e licensed) cab drivers must pass a background check and medical tests, and pay a fee of over £200. This may help to ensure that passengers are safe and drivers are accountable, but it also means that they have a monopoly on picking up people on the streets.

What does the item above suggest about what happens in markets that are difficult to enter? Why doesn't the UK government let anyone set up a taxi cab business?

Barriers to entry can change over time and make it more or less difficult to enter a market. For example, additional investment in advertising by existing firms can raise the costs for new entrants, making it more difficult to enter. By comparison, the internet has reduced the costs for businesses of entering many markets; this is because a physical presence is no longer required (think of travel agents, insurance, and banking). Similarly, to enter the 'book' market, you used to have to print the books physically; books are now increasingly being stored electronically and more digital book readers are being launched on the market, which reduces the costs of entry.

? Think about it ...   9.3

Can you think of markets other than those mentioned above in which the barriers to entry have been reduced by the internet?

The effectiveness of barriers to entry depends, in part, on who wants to enter. Wrigley's dominated the chewing gum market in the UK for many years, with a market share of over 90 per cent. Many firms considered entering this market, but rejected the idea on the basis that:

- it would be expensive to develop a chewing gum product;
- marketing costs would be too high to try to gain any market share from Wrigley's;
- Wrigley's would be likely to fight back and had considerable resources and power in the market, which would make survival difficult.

However, in 2007 Cadbury's entered the UK chewing gum market with Trident gum. Cadbury's already had links with retailers and had considerable power over them because of its chocolate products. It also had the financial resources to sustain a battle against Wrigley's and had experience in chewing gum from companies that it owned elsewhere in the world. What had been barriers to entry for many were not enough to discourage Cadbury's in the long run.

Barriers to entry may also be avoided or made obsolete over time by technology. For many years, Kodak dominated the camera and film industry, only to be bypassed by digital camera makers, such as Canon and Sony, which were big in completely different industries. Technology revolutionized the industry, making the existing businesses the laggards, and firms from other sectors created a new market. The producers of pianos used to be traditional musical instrument makers until the development of the electronic keyboard revolutionized this sector.

The extent to which barriers to entry exist will influence the level of profits that a business can make. If you are making high profits, this will attract other firms into the industry. If they are able to enter easily, they will compete away the abnormal profits. Porter (1985) talked of a 'pool of profits' being available in any industry—with more firms competing, these profits have to be shared out. But if there are barriers to entry, this means that an established business should be able to earn high profits for longer; although other firms may be attracted by the higher returns and want to switch resources into this market, they will not be able to enter.

 You and economics

Your parents still remember the days when UK telephones were all provided by British Telecom. If you wanted a phone you could choose between about two models, three colours, and two different ring tones. That was before mobile phones! Just think how different life is now—how many different models there are to choose from, how you can choose between phoning, texting, and emailing—this market has changed beyond recognition.

Can you think of other markets that are radically different than thirty years ago?

Business analysis   9.2

Sixty-five per cent of the world's cymbal market is controlled by a family business called Zildjian which was founded nearly 400 years ago. The company was established in Istanbul, but fourteen generations later it is now based in the USA. Its cymbals are used by the best drummers all over the world. One reason for its success seems to be the special mix of copper, silver, and tin it uses which gives the cymbals a unique sound. Only a very few family members know what that mix is.

Apart from its special mix of metals why else do you think Zildjian has been able to dominate the world cymbal market for so long?

Types of market

There are many different types of market structure. In some, there are relatively few businesses and it is difficult to enter; in others, there are many firms and it is easy to start up. Each market structure leads to different price and quantity outcomes. In the next section, we examine the short-run and long-run outcomes in different market structures, and the impact of these in terms of efficiency.

Perfect competition

One type of market structure is known as 'perfect competition'. In perfect competition, we imagine a market in which there are hundreds of thousands of providers of similar products. You manage one business, which offers goods or services that are exactly the same as the others. For example, it may be the wheat or milk market, in which there are thousands of farmers producing similar outputs, or it could be the market for shares or currencies markets, in which there are many organizations or individuals buying and selling exactly the same thing. This means that the product is a 'commodity'—that is, it is not differentiated from other products. There is no difference in what each producer is offering.

The assumptions of a perfectly competitive market are that:

- there are many producers offering similar products (also called 'homogenous products'), each of which is a small part of the market—that is, its supply is insignificant relative to the total supply in the market;

- customers have perfect information, which means that they know what is on offer from all the producers and what prices are being offered;

- there are no switching costs so customers can move from one product to another easily;

- there is freedom of movement of other providers into and out of this market.

The last assumption is important, because it means that there are no barriers to entry. This means that if existing businesses are making abnormal profit (that is, if revenue is greater than costs), this will attract firms in from other industries. Managers operating elsewhere will want to make the high returns available in this sector, and will look to reallocate resources and enter this market. We can see in the UK how, over the years, resources have moved out of industries such as coal and manufacturing, and into sectors such as leisure, hospitality, finance, and the media, which have been growing and offering higher returns.

By examining the outcomes of perfect competition, you can see the effects of an extremely high level of competition. Although very few markets come close to anything like perfectly competitive, analysis of this form of market structure provides a benchmark against which to assess the effects of competition and a point of comparison when considering less competitive markets. Therefore it is a model, as described in Chapter 2—that is, it has a set of assumptions that lead to particular outcomes. These may not exactly reflect reality, because no market is fully perfectly competitive, but it shows what happens as markets move towards this structure, and therefore policy-makers can decide whether this is desirable or not.

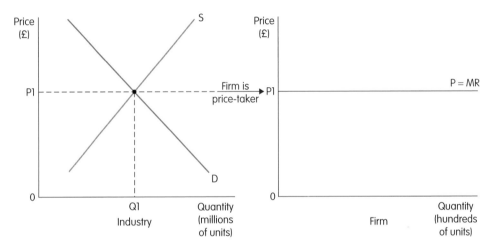

Figure 9.2 The firm in perfect competition is a price-taker

In Figure 9.2, market supply and demand are shown in the left-hand diagram. In the right-hand diagram, we see the position of one individual firm. Each firm is very small in relation to the industry as a whole, so it is producing, say, hundreds of units, while the market produces millions. Each firm is a price-taker; this means that it can sell as much as it wants at the given market price. A firm is a price-taker because it is so small relative to the industry as a whole that changes in its output do not shift the total supply in the industry to any significant extent and so its output decisions do not change the market equilibrium price.

If every unit can be sold at the same price, this means that the price is equal to the marginal revenue. If every unit can be sold at £10, then the extra revenue from selling a unit is £10. The price (which is the average revenue) equals the marginal revenue.

Each business will profit-maximize at the output at which the marginal revenue equals the marginal costs (see Chapter 5). At this point, there is no extra profit to be made. In perfect competition, the price equals the marginal revenue, and so a business profit maximizes where:

Price = Marginal revenue = Marginal cost

In Figure 9.3, the firm is making abnormal profit at P, Q1. This is because the price is greater than the average cost, so abnormal profit is higher per unit. This sends a signal to businesses in other industries that they should reallocate their resources and move into this industry because of the high returns available. They can do this because there are no barriers to entry.

The entry of new firms into the industry means that existing managers will face more competition and customers will have more choice. With more firms providing the products, the market price is driven down. Whereas changes in output by one firm on its own cannot shift the industry supply curve enough to move the equilibrium price, if many firms enter the market producing more output, this will shift the industry supply curve to the right. This increase in supply in the industry will lead to a fall in the price. As an existing business, what you are experiencing is more firms entering your market and competing away your profits; unfortunately, with similar products, ease of entry, and perfect knowledge on behalf of the customers, there is nothing that you can do about this.

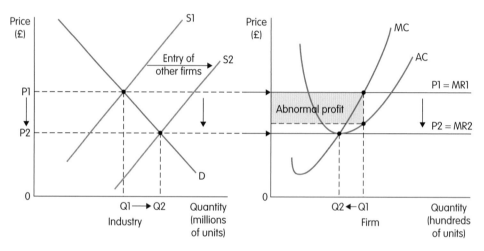

Figure 9.3 The adjustment process from short-run abnormal profit to long-run equilibrium in a perfectly competitive market

 You and economics

A few months ago you went to the horse races for a day out. You sat in the stadium near the track and near the bookmakers who set the odds you can bet at for different horses. There were five or six to choose from. In each case there was a bookmaker with a helper and computer and an electronic board showing the prices. There seemed to be nothing to choose between them except their names; the odds they quoted were exactly the same. Very occasionally one of the bookmakers would change its odds; within seconds the others copied this and they all came back in line again. This was clearly a competitive market.

The long-run equilibrium in perfect competition

Freedom of entry into a market is good for customers, but competes away the abnormal profits of the existing businesses. Firms will keep entering this market until normal profits are earned (when the price or average revenue equals the average costs, which means that total revenue equals total costs). Once this level of profit is achieved, firms are earning the level of rewards that they would expect to make, given the risk and resources involved; there is no further incentive for businesses to move into this industry. The industry will be in long-run equilibrium.

However, if businesses were making a loss in this industry, firms would leave (because they were not covering the opportunity cost of being in it). As they leave the industry, this reduces the total number of suppliers. Again, whereas one firm cannot shift the supply curve, if many firms leave the market, the effect is significant enough to shift the industry supply to the left (see Figure 9.4). With less being supplied in the industry, the market price increases (as the product becomes scarcer); this process continues until the price has risen sufficiently to enable those firms that are left to make normal profits.

Therefore in long-run equilibrium in perfect competition, firms make normal profits. This means that they are making sufficient rewards to keep their resources in this industry without there being an incentive to leave or for others to enter. They are also efficient, which is why this market structure appeals to many analysts. There are two main types of efficiency: allocative and productive. In long-run equilibrium in perfect competition, businesses are both allocatively efficient and productively efficient.

■ **Allocative efficiency** occurs when the number of units being produced maximizes the welfare of society. To see where this occurs, we consider the extra benefit to society of a unit being produced (shown by how much consumers are willing to pay for it—that is, the price) and the extra cost to society of producing it. If the extra benefit is greater than the extra cost, society will benefit from the unit being made. So, for allocative efficiency, every unit for which the extra benefit (price) is greater than the extra cost

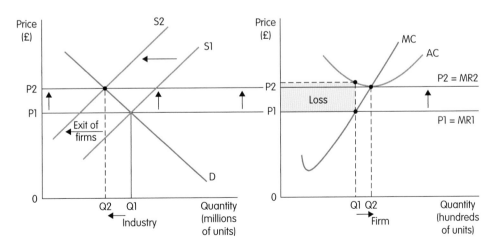

Figure 9.4 The adjustment process from short-run losses to long-run equilibrium in a perfectly competitive market

should be made up to the output at which the extra benefit equals the extra cost—that is, a firm should produce at the output where price equals marginal cost. As we shall see later, this does not happen in many markets, but in perfect competition the profit-maximizing output is also the output for which social welfare is maximized.

■ **Productive efficiency** occurs when firms produce at the minimum of the average cost curve—that is, at the lowest possible cost per unit.

The fact that perfect competition leads to an efficient solution without government intervention highlights why society might like competitive markets. Businesses make normal profits, production is productively efficient, and the welfare of society is maximized (see Figure 9.5). However, a business may not necessarily want this situation: you are more likely to want to differentiate your products and gain some control over the market so that your business gains, even if society as a whole suffers.

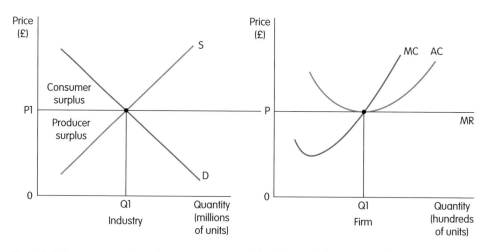

Figure 9.5 Long-run equilibrium in a perfectly competitive industry. In long-run equilibrium we have P = MR = MC = AC.

 Think about it...   9.4

Which of the following statements are true and which are false?

A: In perfect competition, businesses must make normal profits in the short run.

B: In perfect competition, the marginal revenue curve for a business equals the price.

C: In perfect competition, an individual firm is small relative to the industry as a whole.

D: In perfect competition, a business is a price-taker.

E: In perfect competition in the long run, the price equals the marginal revenue equals the marginal costs equals the average cost.

ⓦ Go online to access a video walk-through of analysing perfect competition.

Monopoly

A very different type of market structure from perfect competition is a monopoly. This occurs when one firm dominates the industry. Under UK competition law, a monopoly is defined as a business that has a market share of over 25 per cent, but in its most extreme version a monopolist would have a 100 per cent market share. This could happen if, for example, the government were to insist that there was only one provider of a service, such as water, gas, or electricity; for example, in the UK only Camelot is allowed to provide the National Lottery. While a single-firm monopoly is not common, the model is useful for showing the effects of a dominant firm, which can be compared with the outcome in perfect competition.

In a monopoly market structure, it is assumed that:

- there are barriers to entry—that is, the existing firm is protected from competition by mechanisms such as legal protection, the need for specialist skills, or high costs of entry;
- the firm's product is differentiated from the competition—that is, there are no providers of a similar product, which means that the business is in a much more powerful position than in perfect competition, when the business is just one of many.

In a monopoly, it is possible for a business to earn abnormal profit in the long run as well as the short run. Although other firms will be attracted by these high rewards (as in perfect competition), they will not be able to enter the market because of the barriers to entry. This means that the monopolist business can continue to enjoy high rewards even in the long run.

Not surprisingly, many managers will be looking for ways in which to create a monopoly position for their business—for example, by trying to stress the brand differences between their product and others, and by developing brand loyalty. Coca Cola, for example, stresses that it is the 'real thing' and promotes its heritage to try to differentiate it from other cola drinks. Innocent stresses that its drinks do not include any artificial additives. The desire for a dominant position is why firms are continually fighting for market share. Virgin and British Airways, for example, have competed vigorously to have dominance on transatlantic routes. Microsoft is fighting hard to catch up in the search engine market and to gain market share from Google. Google, meanwhile, is attacking Microsoft's dominance of the software market.

 You and economics

You pull off the motorway because you need a break; it's stupid to drive when you are tired. You park the car and decide to go and get a cup of coffee. When you get to the coffee shop you cannot believe the prices—significantly higher than you are used to. You are tempted to turn around and walk out, but you are desperate. You don't really have much choice and so decide to pay up. That's what market power can do to you!

In a monopoly, the business is a price-maker; it does not have to charge what everyone else is charging (that is, it does not have to be a price-taker) because it has a monopoly position. This generally leads to higher prices and lower outputs than in a perfectly competitive industry. The lack of competition means that the business can drive up price by restricting what is on offer.

In Figure 9.6, the monopolist is profit-maximizing (that is, producing when marginal revenue equals marginal cost). This means that it charges price P1 and sells quantity Q1.

The lack of competition in a monopoly market may lead to poor-quality service for the customer. If customers do not have much choice, managers may decide that it does not matter how they are treated. This is why governments worry about monopolies: they are concerned that monopolies may exploit customers and not act in the interests of the general public.

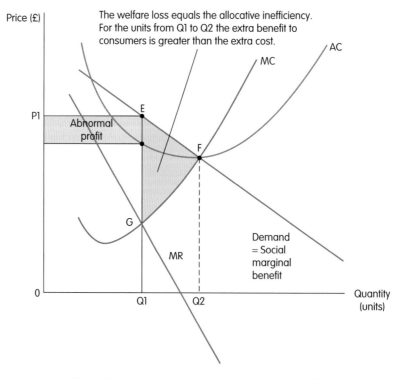

Figure 9.6 The price and output outcome in a monopoly

Therefore most governments have regulations in place to oversee the behaviour of monopolies. In the UK, competition policy does not assume that a monopoly is always acting against the public interest, but it reserves the right to check on its behaviour or possible behaviour.

The possible need to investigate monopolies is reinforced by the fact that monopolies are allocatively inefficient; this is because, at output Q1, the price paid by the customer is greater than the marginal cost of providing it. The price represents the extra benefit to the customer of consuming this unit; this is greater than the extra cost of providing it, and so the welfare of society could increase if this unit were produced. In fact, on all the units Q1,Q2, the extra benefit is greater than the extra cost and so society's welfare would be increased if these were produced. The socially optimal (or allocatively efficient) output is Q2; the shaded area EFG represents a deadweight social burden area, which is allocatively inefficient.

The reason that a monopolist does not provide these additional units (Q1,Q2) is because the impact of lowering the price on these and on all the preceding units would be reduced profit. Profits are maximized where marginal revenue equals marginal cost, so that is where the monopolist wants to be, regardless of social welfare.

As well as being allocatively inefficient, a monopolist is productively inefficient because it is not producing at the minimum of the average cost curve. Although it could produce at a lower average cost, selling these units would involve lowering prices and it would end up with lower profits; as a result, the business restricts output and pushes up the price to compensate for the higher costs.

 Think about it... 9.6

1. As a manager, would you prefer your business to be in a monopoly position or a perfectly competitive market? Why?
2. In what ways do you think a monopolist might exploit its customers?

Go online to access a video walk-through of analysing a monopoly.

 Business analysis 9.3

In 2012 Apple and major book publishers were sued by the US Department of Justice over the pricing of e-books. Apple and Hachette, HarperCollins, Macmillan, Simon & Schuster, and Penguin have all been accused of colluding over the prices of the e-books that they sell.

The lawsuit was over the firms' move to a business model where publishers set the prices. Hachette, HarperCollins, and Simon & Schuster have already settled, but the case is being brought against Apple, Macmillan, and Penguin 'for conspiring to end e-book retailers' freedom to compete on price', the Justice Department said. 'As a result of this alleged conspiracy, we believe that consumers paid millions of dollars more for some of the most popular titles', said the US Attorney General.

The European Commission has also been probing e-book price fixing.

Under an agency model, publishers set the price of a book and the agent selling it gets a 30 per cent cut. The agency model was adopted by publishers largely at the prompting of the late Steve Jobs.

For most physical books, publishers set a wholesale price, often about half the cover price, and then let a retailer decide how much they actually want to charge for the title. The shift to agency pricing was also seen as a protective measure to head off attempts by Amazon to corner the market in e-books. It had been aggressively cutting prices to win customers over to its Kindle e-book reader. But publishers were not happy with this pricing model because they felt that the cost of e-books was getting too low. Books were in danger, they argued, of becoming like music had become under iTunes—worth very little.

Apple entered the market in 2010 with its iBooks platform and agreed to the terms of publishers, taking the same cut of 30 per cent as it takes from apps and music.

Amazon, faced with the prospect of losing sellers to Apple, soon agreed to adopt the agency model.

The Justice Department has been investigating whether Apple's decision to side with the publishers is anti-competitive, as has the European Commission on the other side of the pond.

Do you think that Apple's behaviour is anti-competitive?

Some commentators argue that monopolies need to be prevented from being inefficient and therefore government intervention is vital. Other economists, such as Schumpeter (1942), argue that monopolies may actually lead to lower prices and higher outputs than more competitive markets. The one firm in a monopoly may produce on a much larger scale than any one firm in perfect competition; this may mean that it benefits from internal economies of scale and therefore that the average costs are lower than they would be in a competitive market, which can bring the price down.

It is also worth considering that the higher profits of monopolies may provide the finance needed for expensive investment in research and development. In industries such as cars, pharmaceuticals, and computers, developing new products is a hugely expensive business requiring major investment. GlaxoSmithKline, the pharmaceutical business, claims that developing a new medicine costs over US$500 million and takes over twelve years because of the amount of testing required. It is possible that abnormal profits help to finance this, and that this can bring about innovations that improve the choice available to customers, reduce costs, and bring down prices. This is Microsoft's defence of its actions when it is accused of abusing its monopoly power; it would argue that it has pushed technology forward and that this is why it is so successful.

Its profits are either reinvested into the business, funding further research, or are paid out to the investors, many of whom are likely to be pension funds and banks. Smaller businesses and customers may take a different view of the desirability of monopolies making high profits.

Schumpeter's argument in defence of monopolies also highlights that their profits are often generated by offering a better service or product than those of their rivals; in many cases, they sustain this profit only by continuing to be better than the competition. If this view is correct, the profits of monopolies are the sign of excellent customer service; if they were to fail to provide this level of service, others would enter and take away customers. Schumpeter calls this 'creative destruction'—that is, a monopoly position may be created by innovation, but will be swept away by further innovation unless the original firm keeps developing and improving its offering to stay ahead of the competition. Many markets that are dominated by large firms clearly experience a high level of innovation—for example, razor blades and toothpaste. Research into British manufacturing firms by Blundell, Griffith, and Van Reenen, of the Institute for Fiscal Studies, found that higher market shares were associated with higher investment in research and development, and in innovation. However, few firms are ever safe; Schumpeter argued that as one firm establishes a lead, others would follow.

}{ *People and economics: Schumpeter*

The Austrian American economist Joseph Schumpeter introduced the phrase 'the gale of creative destruction'. In his book *Capitalism, Socialism and Democracy* (1942), Schumpeter argued that the creative–destructive forces unleashed by capitalism lead to invention and innovation. Capitalism is associated with change and movement that revolutionizes the economic structure from within. In 2009 *The Economist* started a column on business and management named 'Schumpeter'. The introduction to this column praised Schumpeter as a 'champion of innovation and entrepreneurship' whose writing showed an understanding of the benefits and dangers of business that proved far ahead of its time.

Therefore more market power may be used in such a way that the public gains. While it is true that many brands have dominated their markets for years (think of Kellogg's, Marlboro, Heinz, and Colgate), it is also true that new products are being developed each year, that many products die each year, and that companies also die as they fail to keep up with the competition. Kwik Save supermarkets, Woolworth's the retailer, and Zavvi all suffered and disappeared because they could not keep up and were removed by competition or substitutes. In recent years Thornton's, Habitat, Agent Provocateur, and JJB Sports have all struggled in their markets. Gaining market share may give firms power in the short run, but in the long term this may spur on more competition, and in this situation, to keep alive, you have to keep looking for ways of staying ahead of rivals.

Therefore there is considerable debate over the desirability of monopolies and the extent to which they are good for customers or not. From the perspective of a manager, however, the advantage of creating a monopoly position is that it enables him/her to earn abnormal profits to reward investors (and presumably him/herself). The manager of a perfectly competitive firm is subject to market forces and has to accept the market price. However, a monopolist can influence demand through its operations and marketing activities; it can try to shape the demand and make it less sensitive to price—it can be a price-maker—to try to boost its profits.

How can a business create a monopoly position?

To build a monopoly position, you must differentiate your product significantly from the competition and protect your market from others entering. You might differentiate your product by:

- developing new technology which can then be patented, providing legal protection;
- developing a unique selling proposition (USP), such as 'one-hour delivery' or '24-hour opening', but the problem with this type of offering is that, over time, it can be imitated by others and so maintaining a monopoly position may be a continuous process of continually raising the barrier;
- building brand loyalty so that customers perceive your product as different from the rest—this is likely to require heavy investment;
- gaining government protection—for example, you may lobby government to prevent other businesses from competing in your market, arguing that your monopoly is important to keep jobs in the country or that it is such a vital industry that it cannot be open to foreign competition (such as the defence or energy industries);
- forcing competitors out of business via a price war or through a takeover and making it clear that further entry will be responded to aggressively, but the competition authorities will probably prevent this behaviour.

? Think about it...   9.7

Which of the following statements about a monopoly are true and which are false?

A: The marginal revenue curve equals the average revenue.
B: The monopolist profit maximizes when marginal revenue equals marginal cost.
C: A monopolist can make abnormal profits in the long run as well as in the short run.
D: A monopolist is allocatively efficient in the long run.

Price discrimination

So far, the analysis has focused on the behaviour of businesses in relation to a single market and has assumed that only one price is charged for all units of output. In reality, businesses operate in many market segments. A 'segment' is a group of similar needs within an overall market.

Managers can segment a market in many different ways, including the following.

- Age: for example, developing different toys for different age groups (such as Lego for younger children and the Playstation for older children).

- Region: for example, producing different versions of a newspaper for different regions to reflect the local news.

- Reason for purchase: for example, some people buy chocolate to reward themselves, some people buy it because they feel that they need cheering up, and some buy it to give to others; therefore chocolate companies develop different products to target these different needs and promote them in different ways (a Mars bar is a snack product, After Eights are a gift, and Celebrations are for sharing).

- Income: for example, some products clearly target higher income earners than others and the promotional channels are chosen accordingly (for example, a Ferrari is unlikely to be promoted in a local newspaper).

? Think about it...   9.8

Can you think of three different brands of chocolate and the particular reason for purchase that they are targeting?

Each of these segments may face its own demand and conditions: the demand may be higher or lower, and more or less price elastic. In some of these cases, different products will be developed for the different segments, and therefore the cost conditions will also differ; in this case, with different costs and revenue conditions, the profit-maximizing price and output will clearly vary.

However, in some cases the same product may be being sold, but demand may still differ between different segments. For example, the demand for sandwiches at a railway station is different from the demand for sandwiches once you are on the train, even though the sandwiches themselves are the same product. If demand conditions do vary (for example, demand for taxis in the city centre at 2 a.m. compared with 2 p.m.), managers will be able to increase profits by charging different prices in the different segments rather than having one price fits all. Charging a different price for the same product is known as 'price discrimination'. (Note that this is different from producing different products for the different segments.) The ability to price discriminate occurs if a business has some mono-poly power and therefore the ability to set price in these different market segments.

Economics and employability

What is your name and role?
My name is Dr Peter Colman and I am Senior Director at Simon–Kucher & Partners.

Tell us about your role at Simon–Kucher & Partners.
My business card says Dr Peter Colman, Senior Director at Simon–Kucher & Partners Strategy & Marketing Consultants. Our company mission is to provide 'smart profit growth' for our clients through profitable and practical commercial programmes. For me specifically, I manage a team

working with industrial sector clients (manufacturing and engineering companies producing cars, smartphones, robots, etc.) to help their sales and marketing teams improve pricing management and therefore improve profit margins.

In what ways is an understanding of economics useful in your work?
Both macro- and microeconomics are very important for pricing work. It's important to stress that our clients aren't looking for wonderful academic theories; they're very pragmatic and concerned with the practical implications of economics because it directly affects both company performance and personal success in their particular job. Therefore our solutions must deliver measurable financial benefits, i.e. more money to that company.

Let's take an example of a manufacturing company making products that could be sold worldwide. The company has a limited amount of resources (people, money, etc.) and needs to prioritize the markets in which they'll operate. Macroeconomics helps our team at Simon–Kucher to select countries presenting the best opportunities for the manufacturer. So we look at a country's growth prospects, exchange rates, inflation, financial stability, etc.

Our team would then need to apply principles of microeconomics to financial models to determine the price that the manufacturer should charge for particular products in particular countries (we travel a lot!).

How does economic change affect your work?
Economic changes have a huge effect on our clients, the types of challenges they face, and therefore the nature of the work we conduct for them. Let's take inflation, for example, and continue the case of the manufacturer.

When the manufacturer's raw material costs (steel, fuel, etc.) increase significantly, the company must make important decisions. First, is the company/product strong enough (in terms of brand, innovation, uniqueness, etc.) to pass on a price increase to customers, thereby protecting profit margins? If so, what proportion of the cost increase will they pass on (some, all, etc.)? Will all customers carry the increase equally, or will some carry more? What happens if customers threaten to look for alternative suppliers? The answers will fundamentally affect the profit outlook within the company and so will need careful assessment to ensure that the correct decisions are made.

How can organizations maximise profits?

The profit equation has three levers—cost, volume (i.e. number of units sold), and price. Many clients tell us that they have exhausted the cost option by constant cost-cutting. The next lever, volume, is affected by price; simply put, in order to make a profit, companies hope to sell lots of units at a lower price, or fewer units at a higher price. Price is the company's biggest profit lever, yet few companies invest the same effort in professional price management as they do in cost management. Therefore pricing represents a significant profit improvement opportunity for most companies. We advise clients that to maximize profits, they should create a pricing programme to systematically improve all aspects of their price management process.

Did you study economics at university as part of your studies, and, if so, how has it helped you in your work? If not, do you wish you had and why?

An economics background is probably the most common degree amongst my colleagues as it's highly relevant to our work. However, my academic background was focused on science/engineering, and because I now look after clients in related sectors and the mathematical nature of my work, that has also been pretty useful. If I were starting university now, I would probably make similar choices overall, but this time I would choose some economic/business-related modules within the course, as I think this would have broadened my outlook faster.

What skills are important in your role? (this could include functional skills, interpersonal skills etc.)

Ultimately, consulting is a people business, so interpersonal skills are critical. You have to generate an instant rapport with senior executives of international corporate companies and have them trust your experience, knowledge, and skills.

To create this trust, you need to keep up to date with the current global economic situation and the trends within your chosen industries. The type of work conducted at Simon–Kucher can be very analytical, so strong mathematical ability is required for consultants. However, the insights uncovered need to be developed into a powerful story to convince clients that they may need to change business behaviour in various areas. This should all be combined with excellent written and verbal communication. We need to be able to tell our clients clearly and convincingly why they should follow our recommendations, which are often based on the economic environment.

 ## Business analysis   9.4

JSTOR, a non-profit organization that makes back copies of scholarly journals available online, analyses the electronic data to charge libraries and academic institutions different fees, depending on their use and circumstances.

As a customer, do you think that you benefit or suffer from price discrimination?

When demand conditions vary in different markets, the profit-maximizing price and output occur when the overall marginal revenue equals marginal cost *and* when the marginal revenue in each market is equal. For example, if the marginal revenue of selling another unit were higher in market segment A than in market segment B, then the business would be better reallocating its products and selling more in A and fewer in B. The extra revenue gained in A outweighs the revenue lost in B, so the business gains overall (see Figure 9.7).

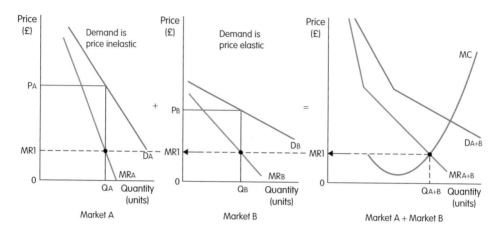

Figure 9.7 Profit-maximizing by setting different prices in markets with different demand conditions

The combined marginal revenue in the two market segments is calculated by horizontally adding the marginal revenue in each of the markets. The profit-maximizing output is found where the combined marginal revenue equals the marginal cost. This determines the level of marginal revenue in each market. From this, the relevant price can be identified. The higher price occurs in the market in which demand is more price inelastic.

This form of price discrimination (that is, charging different prices in different markets for the same product) is called 'third-degree discrimination'.

For third-degree price discrimination to work, markets must be kept separate—that is, you need to avoid someone buying at the low price and then reselling at the higher price in the other segment. The separation of markets may be based on factors such as time, status (for example, whether the customer is a loyalty-card holder or not), region, or age.

Price discrimination boosts the profits of the business by reducing consumer surplus. Ideally, managers would like to charge each customer exactly what they are willing to pay. This would mean that they completely remove all the consumer surplus, but charge a different price for every unit sold. This is called 'first-degree price discrimination'. Think of street traders haggling with you to find out exactly what you are willing to pay. In what is known as a 'Dutch auction', the price starts high and is gradually reduced until someone bids; the price paid should be close to the maximum that they are willing to pay and therefore there would be no consumer surplus.

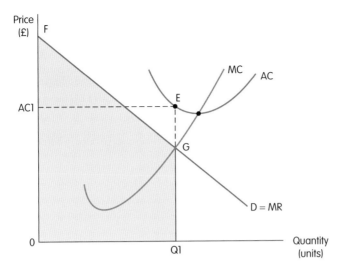

Figure 9.8 Perfect price discrimination

In Figure 9.8, a firm charges a different price for every unit sold; to sell more, the price is lowered on the last unit, but not on the preceding ones. Therefore the extra revenue from the sale is the same as the price, and in this case the demand curve is the same as the marginal revenue curve. A business will profit-maximize where marginal revenue equals marginal cost (that is, Q1). At this output, the cost per unit is AC1 and therefore the total cost is shown by the area 0AC1EQ1. Given that the cost per unit is higher than any price, a business charging one price for all its units would make a loss and would not provide this product in the long run. But by perfectly price discriminating, the revenue is all the shaded area under the demand curve (0FGQ1). This revenue is greater than the total costs and therefore the perfect price discriminator can provide products that would not be provided otherwise. By removing all consumer surplus, the business makes more profits than a single-price producer, which may mean that it can cover high costs.

With first-degree price discrimination, the business maximizes its own producer surplus and completely removes all consumer surplus.

There is also another form of price discrimination called 'second-degree discrimination'. This occurs when a business is trying to use up any excess capacity that it has, such as last-minute deals in the airline and hotel industries, or in end-of-season sales. In these sectors, fixed costs are high, but the marginal cost of serving a customer or passenger is very low, so the price can fall a lot and the business can still make a contribution to its fixed costs.

By price discriminating, a business can make more profits, but consumer surplus is reduced. However, one possible benefit for the consumer is that businesses may cross-subsidize using profits made in one segment to finance losses in other segments. In theory, for example, higher prices in developed markets could subsidize lower prices for drugs in developing economies. It may also mean that some products are provided that would not otherwise be because a profit could not be made if only one price were charged.

Business analysis 9.5

A recent study showed that some currency exchange providers offered different rates at different branches across the UK. The study found differences of up to €30 (£24) being offered by the same provider in different cities in exchange for £500.

How do you think companies are able to offer different exchange rates in different cities?

Summary

There are several different types of market structure, ranging from a monopoly to a perfectly competitive industry. The structure depends on the number of firms in a market, the relative size of these, and the ease of entry and exit. The structure of a market will affect the behaviour and performance of businesses, and the price and quantity outcomes that a manager chooses. For example, if managers can create a monopoly position, their business can earn abnormal profits even in the long run.

Checklist

Having read this chapter, you should now understand:

- [ ] the assumptions behind the different market structures;
- [ ] the short- and long-run outcomes in perfect competition;
- [ ] allocative and productive efficiency;
- [ ] the arguments against and for monopoly;
- [ ] why the government allows firms to protect their intellectual property;
- [ ] the importance of barriers to entry;
- [ ] why the price and quantity outcomes depend on the assumptions that a manager makes about his/her competitors;
- [ ] what happens to the price and quantity outcomes of different market structures in the short and long run.

Organizations and economics

Competition Commission (CC)

The Competition Commission undertakes investigations if it thinks that companies' actions are against the public interest. For example, under the Enterprise Act 2002 the Office of Fair Trading or Secretary of State can refer a merger to the Competition Commission if there is a danger that it will substantially reduce competition in the market.

The Competition Comission has several powers, such as preventing the merger going ahead or insisting that some of the merged business is sold off.

Source: http://www.competition-commission.org.uk

Office of Fair Trading (OFT)

The aim of the OFT is to make markets work effectively for consumers. To do this they aim to make business open and fair and ensure that there is vigorous competition. Its job is to make sure that consumers have as much choice as possible in the market.

Source: http://oft.gov.uk/

Short answer questions

1. What is the profit-maximizing condition?
2. What is meant by abnormal profit? Does normal profit mean that the company makes no profits in accounting terms?
3. What is meant by allocative efficiency?
4. Explain, with examples, what is meant by barriers to entry.
5. How does a profit-maximizing manager know how much to produce?
6. State three assumptions of perfect competition.
7. Does a firm in perfect competition make abnormal or normal profits? Explain your answer.
8. Does a monopolist make abnormal or normal profits? Explain your answer.
9. What is meant by price discrimination?
10. What conditions are necessary for effective price discrimination?

Discussion questions

1. Are monopolies undesirable?
2. To what extent do you think managers can prevent entry into their market?
3. To what extent do you think that price discrimination is desirable?

One step further

Visit our Online Resource Centre at **www.oxfordtextbooks.co.uk/orc/gillespiebusiness2e/** to test your understanding, watch video walk-throughs, and access further information on topics covered in this chapter.

Imperfect competition and alternative theories of the firm

10

Learning objectives

In the last chapter we considered two extremes in relation to market conditions: the highly competitive conditions of perfect competition with many firms and identical products compared with a single-seller price-setting monopoly which enjoyed barriers to entry. In this chapter we consider two other market forms that lie between perfect competition and monopoly: monopolistic competition and oligopoly. We examine the likely price and output decisions in these market structures in the short and long run and the impact of this on efficiency. We then go on to consider alternative theories of the firm apart from profit maximization. What if managers actually aimed to maximize revenue or growth, for example?

By the end of this chapter, you should:

- ☑ understand the price and output decisions in the short and long run in monopolistic competition;

- ☑ understand the meaning of oligopoly;

- ☑ understand game theory;

- ☑ understand the price and output decisions in an oligopoly market in the short and long run;

- ☑ understand Porter's five forces;

- ✓ understand different objectives managers and owners may have.

Case study

Samantha had started her career working as a dinner lady at a local primary school. After a few years doing this she was keen to set up her own business with the help of a few friends. She noticed that many schools were now outsourcing the provision of their food, and Samantha decided that she and the others should bid for one of these contracts. After a few failed bids they finally won the right to supply a small local school and from then on never looked back.

Since then Samantha has built up her business over the years and now is one of the biggest suppliers in the country. There are two other main competitors, and Samantha is increasingly going head to head with them when bidding for contracts. To win the deals she is having to guess what they are going to bid and try to undercut them; this process is eating into all their profits. At a recent meeting of the UK Catering Society the bosses of Samantha's biggest rivals asked for a chat. They suggested to Samantha that life could be a lot better for all of them if they took it in turns to bid for contracts. That way they would avoid competing against each other. Samantha liked the sound of this but asked for a few days to think about it.

Questions

1. Discuss the possible consequences of these firms competing against each other.
2. Should Samantha accept the proposal to take it in turns to bid for contracts?
3. Should the government allow firms to make agreements on which contracts to bid for?
4. If the government decided not to allow such agreements, what would be an appropriate penalty for businesses that continued to make them?
5. Do you think that competition is a good thing?

Introduction

In the last chapter we considered the two extreme market structures of perfect competition and monopoly. In perfect competition there are many firms selling similar products; in monopoly one business dominates and sets the price. However there are a number of market structures that lie between these extremes—that is, they are not as competitive as perfect competition but have more competition than monopoly. These structures are called imperfect competition, and in this chapter we examine oligopoly, which occurs when a few firms dominate, and monopolistic competition, which occurs when there are many firms but they offer differentiated products. We consider the different price and output outcomes in these markets.

Monopolistic competition

Monopolistic competition is another market structure in which managers have some control over their markets, but, unlike monopoly, there is freedom of entry and exit into and out of the market. Examples of monopolistic competitive markets are hairdressers, shoe shops, and coffee shops. Each business is different in some way from its rivals, and so the demand curve for each one is downward-sloping. A price increase will lead to a loss of some customers, who switch to competitors, but will not lead to the loss of all customers; some will stay because of the particular features of this business. Similarly, a price decrease will attract some customers from competitors, but not all of them, because each business is different in some way.

? Think about it... 10.1

You are running a shoe shop in a city centre. How could you differentiate your business from the other shoe shops nearby? What about a taxi business?

In the short run, a firm operating in monopolistic competition can make abnormal profits or losses. But, unlike a monopoly market, there can be entry and exit into and out of the market in the long run. This means that it is not difficult for other businesses to set up in these markets, perhaps because the start-up costs are not that high and there are limited specialized skills required; also, closing down is not that difficult (for example, the premises can easily be reused for something else and so should be fairly easy to sell). This means that if existing firms are making abnormal profits, other businesses will be attracted into the market. These new businesses will attract some customers, taking these away from the existing firm; this will shift demand inwards for the established firms, thereby reducing their profits. Entry will stop when the profits being made are only normal profits and so there is no further incentive for firms to enter.

Think about what happens when a new feature is offered on mobile phones by one provider—it is not long before others follow. Manufacturers then seek new ways of differentiating themselves to push their demand outwards again.

However, if the established firms were making losses (perhaps because of a fall in demand), some of them would leave; this would increase demand for the ones left and this process will continue until those left make normal profits.

In Figure 10.1a, the established firm is profit-maximizing at P1,Q1. It is making abnormal profits (because the price is greater than the average cost). More firms enter the market, which reduces the demand for the established business and shifts its demand curve inwards until only normal profits are made. In Figure 10.1b, a loss is being made; firms leave and demand for those left increases, shifting demand to the right until only normal profits are made.

In a monopolistically competitive market, managers will try to differentiate their products and gain even more monopoly power. In the short run, it is possible to earn abnormal profits, but this will lead to more entry into the market; to regain abnormal profits, the manager will want to try to shift demand for his/her own business outwards again and regain more control over the market or develop barriers to entry to stop others entering.

? Think about it... 10.2

1. What do you think determines the slope of the demand curve in a monopolistically competitive market?

2. What makes you choose one restaurant rather than another? How loyal are you?

From society's viewpoint, monopolistic competition is inefficient, like monopoly. In the long-run equilibrium, the price is above the marginal costs, so the business is allocatively inefficient. The shaded area of Figure 10.1 is a deadweight social burden triangle representing allocative inefficiency; in these units, the extra benefit to society is greater than marginal cost.

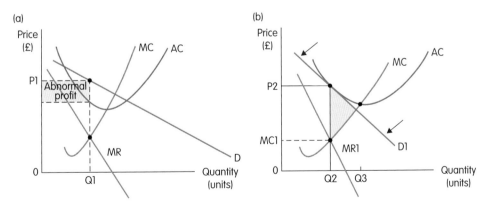

Figure 10.1 Profits in monopolistic competition. Short-run abnormal profits (a) are competed away by the entry of other firms so normal profits are earned in the long run (b)

The business is also productively inefficient because it is not producing the output for which the average cost is minimized. As with monopoly, the firm is more interested in profit-maximizing than serving society's interests, and this means pushing the price up by restricting output to the point at which marginal revenue equals marginal cost.

Economics and employability

What is your name?
My name is Edmund Cohen.

Tell us about your role at Landed Houses.
I started the company Landed Houses (www.landedhouses.co.uk) and now run it on a part-time basis. There are others who manage some of the company's day-to-day dealings but ultimately I remain responsible. The site's aim is to help landlords fill wonderful houses with guests through events like balls, birthdays, weddings, etc.

In what ways is an understanding of economics useful in your work?
Rather than alter the way I work, economics explains some of my decisions more quickly and easily than I could otherwise. For example, every year I try to work out what my customers are prepared to pay. The higher the price, the fewer the customers. Economics can explain the precise relationship (elasticity of demand), but in real life it comes down to gut-feeling and testing different price points. I also try to ensure that the company does everything more efficiently than its competitors, and part of this involves running a better website. In economics these are known as product differentiation and non-price competition.

In what ways does economic change affect your clients?
Thankfully our industry has not been buffeted too much by economic cycles. Even though the spending is discretionary (not absolutely necessary), people seem prepared to pay to host a memorable party or wedding. In a similar vein, spending on fashion goods and luxury brands has also held up well over recent years. However, other matters, like tax, do have a significant impact. The threshold level of VAT makes some houses more competitive than others. Capital gains tax also alters the attractiveness of buy-to-let properties and the numbers of houses that we can offer.

Did you study economics at university as part of your studies, and, if so, how has it helped you in your work?
Yes I did. My most useful memories are around competition and pricing. I frequently ask myself what my competitors do better, how can I differentiate Landed Houses, how much do competitors charge, what other products might my houses want and at what price? All of those feature in competition economics.

What skills are important in your role?
Business leadership, decision-making, negotiation skills, influencing, and old-fashioned customer service are all absolutely essential attributes.

Oligopoly

An oligopoly is a market that is dominated by a few large firms. This type of market structure is quite common: for example, the banking sector, travel business, and petrol market in the UK are all oligopolistic markets. In these sectors, the firms are interdependent; this means that managers realize that the actions of one business affect the others, and therefore that they must take into account each other's possible actions and reactions when making decisions. Therefore price and quantity outcomes in oligopoly depend on the assumptions that managers make about their rivals and how they will behave.

Possible outcomes are shown by different models such as the following.

 Business analysis 10.1

Table 10.1 gives examples of markets dominated by a few firms in the UK.

Table 10.1 UK market domination

Market	Companies
Accountancy	Deloitte, Ernst & Young, KPMG, PricewaterhouseCoopers
Brewers	Allied Domecq, Carlsberg Tetley, Diageo, Interbrew, Scottish & Newcastle
Electrical retail	Currys, Dixons, Kesa (Comet)
Fast food	Burger King, KFC, McDonald's
Food retail	Asda/Walmart, Morrison's, Sainsbury's, Tesco
Food and personal care products	Procter & Gamble, Unilever
Home DIY	B&Q, Focus, Homebase
Mobile phone networks	O2, Orange, T-Mobile, Vodafone
Motorway service operators	Macquarie (Moto), Roadchef, Welcome Break
Oil and gas extraction	British Gas, BP, ConocoPhillips, ExxonMobil, Shell
Pharmaceuticals	Astra-Zeneca, Eli Lilly, GlaxoSmithKline, Pfizer
Soft drinks	Cadbury Schweppes, Coca Cola
Sugar	British Sugar, Tate & Lyle
Tobacco	BAT, Gallaher Group, Imperial Tobacco Group

1. Can you think of any other oligopoly markets in your economy?

2. Why do you think these markets are oligopolistic rather than more competitive?

The kinked demand curve model

The kinked demand curve model was developed by Sweezy in 1939. It assumes that managers are pessimistic about how their rivals might act and believe that their competitors will not collaborate with them. Managers assume that if they cut their prices, their rivals will follow because they will be worried about losing sales. Therefore they assume that demand will be price inelastic if they cut price (the increase in quantity demanded will be less than the increase in price in percentage terms).

However, they assume that if they push the price up, their rivals will be happy for them to be the only ones doing so and will *not* follow. This means that demand will be price elastic if they put the price up, because the fall in quantity demanded will be larger than the rise in price (in percentage terms).

These assumptions mean that the demand curve is kinked around the existing prices and that there is no incentive to change price (see Figure 10.2). A price cut leads to a relatively small increase in quantity demanded, so revenue would fall; the increase in sales would not be enough to compensate for the lower price. A price increase leads to a relatively large decrease in quantity demanded, so revenue would fall because although the price is higher, sales have fallen significantly. Therefore it is better to keep the price where it is.

This model helps to explain why prices of producers in oligopoly are often similar and do not change much (this is called 'price stickiness'). Rather than start price cutting, firms often compete in ways other than price. For example, investing in technology to add features or investing in marketing to build the brand is common in oligopolies, as firms try to avoid price wars and reducing all of their margins.

? ## Think about it...   10.3

Assume that you are managing a chain of juice bars stores across the UK. You are reluctant to cut price in case it simply leads to everyone cutting price and sales do not increase significantly. How else could you compete?

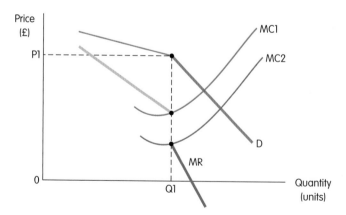

Figure 10.2 The kinked demand curve in an oligopoly. The kinked demand curve model also highlights that costs can change from MC1 to MC2 and the profit-maximizing price and output are still P1Q1.

Business analysis 10.2

In 2011 cement production in the UK fell to 9 million tonnes, 30 per cent down from its peak in 2007 before the economic crisis which hit investment and construction projects. Unfortunately, foreign exports were also hit. Until the early 1980s Britain exported over 1 million tonnes of cement a year. Manufacturers in cheaper countries have taken that business, as costs have increased significantly within the UK.

About 40 per cent of the industry's costs are on energy, and much of this energy comes from coal which has become very expensive in recent years. Additional costs have been imposed by increasing European emissions regulations on an industry that generates huge amounts of carbon dioxide.

The UK market is now dominated by five large foreign firms that account for 90 per cent of the trade: France's Lafarge; Tarmac, owned by Anglo American; Mexico's Cemex; Hanson, part of Germany's HeidelbergCement; and Holcim, a Swiss company. The industry has consolidated with numerous takeovers and mergers.

However, regulators are increasingly worried that high barriers to entry (a new cement plant might cost £200 million, or $315 million), vertical integration of aggregates and cement, and the dominant position of the big five firms are damaging competition. The Office of Fair Trading asked the Competition Commission to scrutinize the entire industry.

What might be the consequences of these changes in the construction industry?

How should the government react to such changes?

The cartel

The **cartel** model of oligopoly assumes that firms will collude and work together. They will try to maximize the profits available to them by restricting output and pushing up price. It is exactly this type of behaviour that governments worry about and usually try to prevent for fear that the customers will lose out due to monopoly power. Under a cartel arrangement, the member firms may decide how much output each one will make (called a 'quota') and at what price this will be sold. In effect, the individual businesses are joining together to act like a single monopolist. Customers may end up paying more for less compared with a competitive market. The result is that a cartel can maximize the total profits of the members.

Cartels will differ in terms of the nature of the agreements, but typically include deals involving the choice of area in which members will sell, to which customers different members will sell, prices, terms and conditions, and even who will gain which contract.

In a cartel, the combined membership maximizes profits at the point at which the marginal revenue in the industry equals the marginal cost (that is, P1,Q1 in Figure 10.3a).

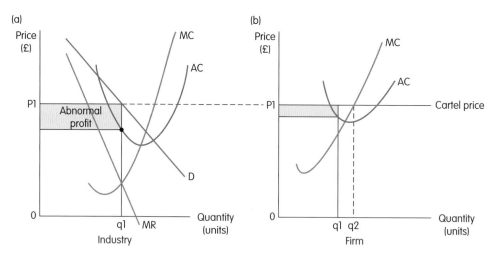

Figure 10.3 The cartel model

This determines the profit-maximizing price (P1). The total quantity (Q1) will be divided among members, who will be given a quota each.

For example, a firm might be told to produce at q1 and sell at price P1. Under these circumstances, it makes a profit equal to the shaded area in Figure 10.3a.

Given that the product is all being sold at price P1, this means the marginal revenue also equals P1; as a result the firm would profit maximize by producing at q2 where marginal revenue equals marginal cost. This would increase its own profits, but would lead to more output in the industry as a whole and move the industry away from the profit-maximizing position. This firm would gain at the expense of others. Therefore there is a real temptation for individual firms to break the cartel and ignore the quota. The more firms that do this, the more that will be produced, driving down the industry price and reducing the total profits of the industry; this is likely to lead to the end of the cartel unless it can be effectively policed by other members to prevent this from happening. Those cheating need to face a significant threat if they pursue their own interests to the detriment of the cartel as a whole.

? **Think about it...** 10.4

At the start of 2012 two Japanese businesses, the Yazaki Corporation and the Denso Corporation, pleaded guilty and paid fines for fixing the prices of parts supplied to US manufacturers. According to the BBC, Yazaki paid $470 million (£300m), the second-largest fine for anti-competitive behaviour in US history, while Denso paid $78 million. The two companies were accused of fixing prices for ten years. Four Yazaki executives were also committed to a US prison for up to two years.

Yazaki and Denso are among the world's largest auto part suppliers. Any fixing of prices affects all the major car producers, increasing their costs and therefore the selling price of the vehicles.

Why do you think car manufacturers continued to work with Yazaki and Denso rather than other parts producers?

Source: http://www.bbc.co.uk/news/business-16803876

Cartels have been found in many sectors, such as the cement industry, private schools, and airlines. The factors that make collusion more likely include:

■ relatively few businesses which can monitor each others' actions easily;

■ significant barriers to entry, providing existing firms strong control over the market;

■ similar costs, so that they will gain similar rewards and disputes are less likely;

■ stable market conditions so that any agreements will remain valid.

However, cartel agreements are often unstable. This is because individual members of the agreement might try to increase their own rewards at the expense of others in the cartel. If they have agreed a price and quotas, for example, individual members may start to overproduce and try to sell their additional output. By doing this, they increase the total amount of products on the market and this starts to drive the price down. The cheating firms may benefit and increase their own rewards because of their extra output, but the other members and the industry overall will make fewer profits if they have stuck to their original quota because the price has now fallen. Some members might also object to the set price and quantities if they think that they are unfair. For example, if one producer has higher costs than the others, its profits will be less per unit than the others if they all charge the same price. Therefore cartels have to be closely monitored by their members to make sure that cheating is not happening and/or to find those responsible.

Governments are naturally eager to find out when cartels are occurring because of the potential exploitation of customers. In the UK, anti-competitive agreements are prohibited by the Cartels and Competition Act 1998 and Articles 81 and 82 of the EC Treaty. Many governments have now adopted a policy that encourages members to inform on any other cartel members. For example, in the USA the first member to inform on its partners automatically gets full immunity from criminal prosecution.

 You and economics

You have just been reading the paper and saw that several supermarkets had been fined by the Office of Fair Trading (OFT) for alleged price fixing of dairy products. In total, nine firms (Arla, Asda,

Dairy Crest, McLelland, Safeway, Sainsbury's, The Cheese Company, Wiseman, and Tesco) were fined a total of nearly £50 million for allegedly colluding over the price of milk and cheese in 2002 and 2003 (see Table 10.2). The OFT estimated that the collusion saw shoppers pay 2 pence extra for a litre of milk and 2 pence extra for 100 grams of cheese. The OFT found that they infringed the Competition Act by coordinating rises in the prices consumers paid for certain dairy products in 2002 and/or 2003.

Table 10.2 Penalties in total

Arla	£0
Asda	£9.39m
Dairy Crest	£7.14m
McLelland	£1.66m
Safeway	£5.69m
Sainsbury's	£11.04m
Tesco	£10.43m
The Cheese Company	£1.26m
Wiseman	£3.2m

Source: Office of Fair Trading

Although a couple of pence does not sound like a lot, it does add up when you are buying these products every day, and if you think how many people are buying them it probably runs into hundreds of millions of pounds. That kind of behaviour makes you cross—it's the big firms using their power to exploit you.

Game theory

The interdependence of firms within an oligopolistic market and the importance of considering the reactions of other firms is highlighted in **game theory**. This highlights how the strategy of one business is likely to depend on its assumptions about the behaviour of other firms. Game theory examines various strategies based on different assumptions about the actions and reactions of other firms. Different assumptions will lead to a number of outcomes in the market. A 'game' involves two or more individuals or organizations.

An example of game theory is known as the 'prisoners' dilemma', in which two individuals have both been arrested for a crime. The question is whether they should confess to the crime or not, and that, in turn, depends on what they think the other person will do. Unfortunately, they are locked up in separate rooms and cannot communicate, so they have to make assumptions about the other person's behaviour. It is assumed that if they both confess, they will be imprisoned for a long time; if they both refuse to confess, the police cannot prove anything and they will be released. The problem comes if one person refuses to confess and the other one confesses; the latter gets a light sentence and the one who refused to talk gets a very long sentence for non-cooperation. The ideal solution, from the prisoners' point of view, is not to confess and then they would both get off. But if you do not trust your fellow prisoner and think that he/she will confess, it is better for you to confess as well. On this basis, they will both confess because they do not trust each other.

The prisoners' dilemma highlights how your decisions about what to do depend on your relationship with other prisoners (or businesses in an oligopoly) and your view of whether you think you can trust them or not. You can imagine the manager of one business thinking carefully about what a major competitor might be about to do and trying to work out the best action in different situations. The prisoners' dilemma shows the dangers of oligopoly from a manager's view: a lack of trust may lead to an outcome in which firms are worse off than if they trusted each other.

The prisoners' dilemma in a business context is highlighted in Figure 10.4. Two businesses are considering what level of output to produce—high or low. If they both produce low outputs, this will push the price up and both will win. But if one produces relatively little and its competitor produces a lot, this will increase supply and drive the price down; the first producer will do badly because its rival wins the market and is selling more. As a result, both producers might flood the market, fearing that the other will do this anyway; the total output in the market ends up very high and the market price is low, meaning that both are worse off compared with a situation in which both had restricted their output.

Figure 10.4 shows the financial results of each possible outcome: if both firms produce high levels of output, they will gain £1 million each; if both restrict output, they will earn £2 million each.

This model shows the importance of managers' assumptions about what other businesses will do. The past behaviour of businesses becomes very important here—how they have behaved in the past may influence assumptions about what they will do in the future.

Game theory can become much more complex depending on the assumptions that are made. Assume that, in relation to Figure 10.5, you are the manager of Firm A thinking about your pricing options. Assume that you are pessimistic and look at the worst possible outcome of any decision. If you choose a price of £2, the worst that can happen is that B will charge £1 and you will make profits of £5,000. If you were to charge £1, the worst

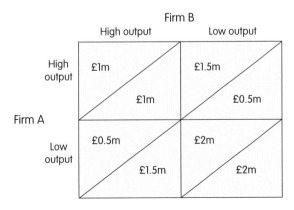

Figure 10.4 The prisoners' dilemma in a business context (the top area of each quadrant shows the pay-off for A; the bottom area shows the pay-off for B).

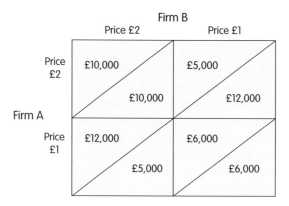

Figure 10.5 Pricing options (the top area of each of the quadrants shows the pay-off for A; the bottom area shows the pay-off for B).

that could happen is that B would do the same and you would end up with £6,000. If you decide to choose the 'best of the worst', then you choose a £1 price. This is called a 'maximin' strategy because you are maximizing the minimum outcomes. If Firm B were to do the same, it would choose £1 as well and you would both end up with £6,000, when you could have had £10,000 had you agreed to charge £2 and believed each other.

A 'maximax' strategy occurs when a manager is optimistic and bases decisions on the 'best of the best' outcomes. The best outcome if you choose a price of £1 is that your rival will choose £2 and you end up with £12,000. The best outcome if you choose a price of £2 is that your rival chooses £2 and you end up with £10,000.

In this case the best strategy whether you adopt a minimax or a maximin approach is the same—the business should set the price at £1. Because both assumptions give the same solution, this is known as the **dominant strategy**.

Now let us look at the game shown in Figure 10.6 which considers whether a business should increase its promotional spending or not.

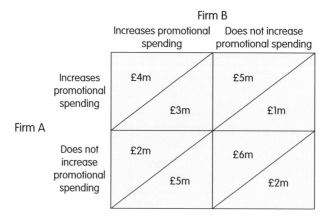

Figure 10.6 Choosing a promotional strategy

If A is pessimistic and looks at the worst possible outcomes then these are £4 million if it increases promotional spending and £2 million if it does not. Therefore to maximize the minimum outcomes it would choose to promote. (This is the maximin outcome.)

If A is optimistic the best outcomes are £5 million if it promotes and £6 million if it does not. The maximax strategy would therefore be to not promote. This means that the maximin and maximax outcomes differ and that there is no dominant strategy.

This means that the best strategy for B is to increase its promotional spending regardless of what A does. If A realizes this, it will also increase its promotional spending so that both will end up increasing their spending. This is known as the 'Nash equilibrium'. A Nash equilibrium occurs in a game involving two or more players, in which each player is assumed to know the equilibrium strategies of the other players. If each player has chosen a strategy and no player would benefit by changing his/her strategy while the other players keep theirs unchanged, the current set of strategy choices and the corresponding pay-offs represent a Nash equilibrium.

 Business analysis   10.3

Assume that a business (business A) is deciding whether or not to increase its promotional expenditure. It is concerned about how its main rival B will react. The expected outcomes are shown in Figure 10.7.

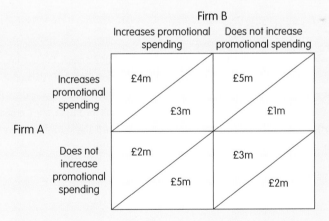

Figure 10.7 Deciding whether to increase promotional spending

What is the best strategy for firm A if B increases promotional spending?

What is the best strategy for firm A if B does not increase promotional spending?

What is the best strategy for firm B if A increases promotional spending?

What is the best strategy for firm B if A does not increase promotional spending?

3{ ## People and economics

John Nash (born 1928) is a US mathematician who was the subject of the film *A Beautiful Mind*. His work in game theory forms an important part of oligopoly analysis. He was a Senior Research Mathematician at Princeton University and in 1994 shared the Nobel Prize in Economic Sciences with Reinhard Selten and John Harsanyi. Throughout his adult life Nash has struggled with schizophrenia.

Therefore decision-making in business can be like a chess game in which you are anticipating what your opponents will do next. Interestingly, world chess champion Gary Kasparov has written a book on business strategy called *How Life Imitates Chess*, in which he argues the importance of planning but also the need, at times, to trust your instincts when making business decisions. Game theory has many possible applications—for example, thinking about whether to lower price, increase advertising, enter a market, or launch a product. In each of these cases it is worth considering the possible reactions of competitors. Of course, game theory can become far more complex if it includes multiple stages considering how A might react once B has acted in a certain way in response to an initial move by A and so on!

You and economics

You have agreed with your partner to meet at the coffee shop at 2 o'clock, but you know that she is always at least ten minutes late so there is no point getting there until 2.10. Of course, after five years she knows you well, so she won't really aim to be there until 2.10 anyway because she knows that's when you'll get there. So if she sets herself 2.10 as the target, she'll probably be there at 2.20ish so there's no point getting there until then. Of course if she knows you have worked that out, she might decide not to get there until 2.20 in which case …

So will you ever meet up?

Think about it ...   10.5

Which of the following statements about oligopoly are true and which are false?

A: The kinked demand curve is a model in which firms cooperate.

B: In a cartel, the industry produces at the point at which marginal revenue equals marginal costs.

C: In game theory, businesses base their decisions about what to do on assumptions about what others are doing.

D: In oligopoly, a few firms dominate the market.

How to protect your success

While governments are wary of the possible abuse of power by businesses that gain a monopoly position, they also recognize that individuals and firms should be able to protect their ideas. This is why legislation exists to protect intellectual property (IP) rights. Intellectual property refers to the ownership of a brand, invention, design, or other kind of creation.

The protection that managers can gain for their IP includes the following.

- *Patents* A patent protects new inventions and covers how things work, what they do, how they do it, what they are made of, and how they are made. It gives the owner the right to prevent others from making, using, importing, or selling the invention without permission. To gain a patent, an invention must be new, have an inventive step that is not obvious to someone with knowledge and experience of the subject, and be capable of being made and used.

- *Trademarks* A trademark is a sign that can distinguish your goods and services from those of your competitors. For example, it can be words, logos, or a combination of both. To be registered, a trademark must be distinctive (that is, it must differentiate your goods and services from those of competitors).

- *Copyright* Copyrights protect literary works (including novels, instruction manuals, computer programs, song lyrics, newspaper articles, and some types of database), dramatic works, musical works, artistic works, recordings, and broadcasts. The originator of these works automatically has a copyright on it; he/she does not need to register it.

- *Registering a design* This is a legal right that protects the overall visual appearance of a product in the geographical area in which you register it. The visual features that form the design include such things as the lines, contours, colours, shape, texture, materials, and ornamentation of the product which, when applied, give it a unique appearance.

Business analysis   10.4

In 2012, Microsoft bought the majority of AOL's patents in a deal worth $1.06 billion (£668m). The deal gave Microsoft the rights to over 800 innovations, providing it with new technology and protecting it against being sued by AOL for infringing its patents. Many companies, such as Intel, Google, and Facebook, are buying up patents from other technology companies to protect themselves in a similar way.

The deal was announced just before Microsoft's appearance in a court in Germany on 17 April 2012 when it faced claims that it infringed Motorola Mobility's H.264 video compression technologies.

Analyse the potential benefits of owning a patent.

How would you value a patent?

? Think about it...　　　　　　　　　　　　　　　10.6

What do you think are the long-term consequences for the industry of illegally downloading music?

Contestability

When making decisions about price and output, managers will consider not only how many firms are in the market already, but also the likelihood of entry and exit in the future. This affects the contestability of a market. For example, there is an obvious difference between operating exclusively in a market and knowing that the government prevents any other entrants at all, and having a short-term monopoly position but suspecting that other firms might and could enter at any moment.

The importance of possible future entry is highlighted in the theory of contestable markets. If markets are heavily contestable, i.e. if entry is relatively easy, this puts more pressure on the existing firm (or firms) to be competitive, whereas if the market is very protected, managers are able to be more inefficient and survive. What matters when managers are considering how to set price and output is not only the present situation, but also how likely it is that others could enter in the future, i.e. what barriers to entry exist. For example, with low barriers to entry abnormal profits will be competed away.

Market structures are summarized in Table 10.3.

Market structure and profits

Table 10.3 Summary of market structures

	Perfect competition	Monopolistic competition	Oligopoly	Monopoly
Differentiated products	No	Yes	Yes	Yes
Number of firms	Many	Many	Few	One
Entry and exist in the long run	Yes	Yes	No	No

The importance of the structure of an industry was analysed by Michael Porter (1985) in his 'five forces' model (see Figure 10.8). This highlighted the importance of five factors in determining how the profits of an industry are shared between firms, their suppliers, their distributors, their competitors, and their customers.

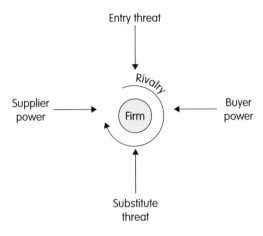

Figure 10.8 Porter's 'five forces'

The five forces are as follows.

- *Rivalry* This describes the extent to which firms are competing with each other. The greater the rivalry, the fewer profits any one firm is likely to make. The degree of rivalry will depend on factors such as the number of firms in the industry and their relative size, market growth (because if a market is shrinking, firms are likely to be very competitive as they struggle to survive), and how they compete (for example, is it by cutting price or trying to differentiate themselves?).

- *The entry threat* If there is a high entry threat, competitors are able to enter the market and take away profits. As we have seen, the entry threat depends on factors such as the entry costs and likely retaliation from the existing firms, and refers to the contestability of a market.

- *Substitutes* These are alternative goods and services that perform a similar function in the eyes of the customer. For example, you may buy wine or flowers as a thank you gift; you may buy a card or an e-card; you may buy a new sofa or a holiday. Although these are very different products, customers choose between them and so they are substitutes. The more substitutes that are available, the more pressure on a business to keep prices down or risk losing customers.

- *Buyer power* If you are heavily reliant on one or two buyers (for example, you sell healthcare products to the National Health Service), the buyer is likely to push down the price and negotiate very favourable terms, giving it more of the profit available.

■ *Supplier power* If you are heavily reliant on suppliers (for example, airlines are reliant on the oil companies), they have the power to push up prices and 'take away' your profit. The greater the supplier power, the lower your profits are likely to be.

Porter highlighted that the average return on investment (ROI) was much higher in some industries than in others, and had been for many years. His analysis suggested that this was because of unfavourable forces acting on firms in the industry: for example, high rivalry, a low entry threat, high buyer and supplier power, and a high substitute threat.

This does not mean that a business must accept the forces acting upon it; rather, it could try to change the forces to make them more favourable. For example, it could change its strategy as follows:

■ join with others in the industry to have more power when negotiating with suppliers;

■ take over others in the market to reduce the degree of rivalry;

■ differentiate the product to make it different from anything else and reduce the degree of substitution.

Data analysis   10.1

Between 1992 and 2006, the average rate of return in various US industries was as shown in Table 10.4.

Table 10.4 Average rate of return in different US industries 1992–2006

Industry	Average rate of return
Soft drinks	37.6%
Pre-packaged software	37.6%
Pharmaceuticals	31.7%
Perfume, cosmetics, and toiletries	28.6%
Tyres	19.5%
Household appliances	19.2%
Book publishing	13.4%
Laboratory equipment	13.4%
Hotels	10.4%
Airlines	5.9%

Source: Adapted from Porter (1985)

With reference to Porter's five forces model, why do you think the rates of return might have differed so much between these industries?

Regulation of markets

Managers wanting to grow or considering working with other businesses need to consider competition legislation. Competition laws are established to protect consumers and to ensure that they are not exploited.

In the UK, competition laws are overseen by the OFT. The OFT declares itself:

> ... responsible for making markets work well for consumers. We achieve this by promoting and protecting consumer interests throughout the UK, while ensuring that businesses are fair and competitive.

It aims to make sure that consumers have as much choice as possible, believing that 'When consumers have choice they have genuine and enduring power.'

The OFT implements many pieces of legislation and has a range of enforcement options. At one level, it provides advice and guidance; at another level, it prosecutes and can levy fines of up to 10 per cent of a firm's turnover.

Business analysis   10.5

Consumer protection legislation includes:

- the Consumer Credit Act 1974, as amended by the Consumer Credit Act 2006;
- the Estate Agents Act 1979, as amended by the Consumers, Estate Agents and Redress Act 2007;
- the Unfair Terms in Consumer Contracts Regulations 1999;
- the Consumer Protection (Distance Selling) Regulations 2000;
- the Consumer Protection from Unfair Trading Regulations 2008;
- the Business Protection from Misleading Marketing Regulations 2008;
- the Enterprise Act 2002.

Are there any areas in which you think consumers still need protection?

Business objectives

In economics, it is often assumed that managers will behave rationally and be aiming to maximize profits for their owners. But while there are many good reasons why managers will want to maximize profits (or at least why their investors want profits maximized), they may also have other objectives, for the following reasons.

■ We often assess the performance of a business in terms of its size or revenue, rather than its profits. We may be impressed by a business with many stores or with a very visible brand even if we do not know much about its profitability. Therefore a manager may want to be running a bigger business with more output or more sales revenue in order to be seen as being successful by the general public and the media, even if this growth reduces profit because of diseconomies of scale or the spending necessary in the short run to expand the business.

■ Managers' rewards are often linked to targets set for them that are not necessarily directly linked to profits; for example, they may have sales-based bonuses or bonuses linked to the successful growth of the business. Again, this would make managers focus on objectives other than profits. According to Williamson (1964), managers will try to maximize their own utility, not their investors' rewards. Their own utility, he argues, is linked to their salary, their job security, their power, and their professional status. Therefore they may pursue their own interests rather than those of investors. For example, many takeovers and mergers do not lead to the cost savings that were promised because they are actually driven by the desire of the managers to achieve something for themselves rather than profits. The relationship between investors and managers is an interesting one, and has been studied a great deal. This is because there is a 'divorce between ownership and control' (Berle and Means 1933). The investors who own the business appoint the managers to control and run it in their best interests. However, on a day-to-day basis managers know far more about what is happening in the business than the investors; there is an asymmetry of information. The investors are known as the 'principals' in this relationship and the managers are their 'agents'.

In reality, managers are likely to have their own challenges, their own values, and their own agenda, and may not always be working towards the same goals as those of the investors.

To try to bring shareholders and managers closer together, many managers have been given shares in the business or profit-related bonuses. To monitor managers' behaviour, shareholders elect directors to review the plans and work of managers, and are provided with an annual report at the annual general meeting (AGM). Shareholders have also insisted on more outside directors being appointed (rather than the directors also being managers, which can lead to a conflict of interest). But the effectiveness of directors is sometimes called into question, and in some cases the shareholders have had to organize themselves to force the directors to resign. The ways in which shareholders try to monitor managers' behaviour and actions is known as 'corporate governance'.

Therefore possible objectives of managers, apart from profit maximization, may include the following.

■ *Sales revenue maximization* (Baumol 1956) This occurs when a firm produces at an output level when the total revenue cannot increase any more. This happens when marginal revenue is zero (that is, there is no extra revenue to be made). Such an approach does not focus on costs; managers are simply interested in the value of sales. But to keep shareholders satisfied, in reality a certain level of profits might need to be made and therefore managers might seek to maximize revenue subject to making a given level of profit.

■ *Growth maximization* (Marris 1964) This occurs at the highest level of output at which a firm can produce without making a loss. This occurs when the average revenue (price) is equal to the average cost.

A business will maximize profits at the point at which the marginal revenue equals the marginal cost (that is, Q2 in Figure 10.9); at this output, there is the biggest positive difference between revenue and costs.

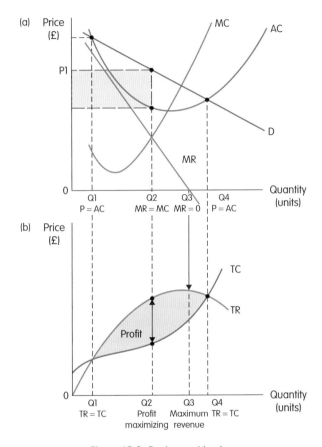

Figure 10.9 Business objectives

A business will maximize revenue when marginal revenue equals zero (that is, at Q3); this is the highest level on the total revenue curve.

A business will produce the highest output possible without making a loss (that is, maximize its growth) by producing at Q4. At this output, the total revenue equals the total costs (that is, the price per unit equals the average cost per unit).

In reality, in both the revenue and growth maximization models, managers may have to achieve a minimum level of profit to satisfy their investors. In this case, they may aim for the output for which marginal revenue equals zero or for which average revenue equals average cost, but they have to be as close to this as they can while making a given level of profit. For example, to achieve a given level of abnormal profit to satisfy investors, managers pursuing growth may have to produce slightly below Q4. Similarly, for managers trying to maximize revenue, if the profit is not high enough for investors at Q3, they may have to produce slightly nearer to Q2.

Forms of growth

Managers may want their business to grow because of the potential gains from internal economies of scale. This growth may be organic (internal) or external. Internal growth is achieved by generating more sales from the existing business. This type of growth is usually relatively slow and therefore may be relatively easy to manage. External growth occurs when one business joins together with another (this is called a 'merger') or one business takes over another one (called a 'takeover' or 'acquisition'). External growth can lead to a sudden change in the scale of a business. This can be difficult to manage because it involves two different enterprises coming together and rapid transitions in size. This can cause cultural clashes, because employees have different ways of doing things, different priorities, and different procedures. Studies suggest that most mergers and acquisitions actually end up performing worse than the companies would have done had they remained separate. This is due to the problems of diseconomies of scale and cultural clashes.

When undertaking a merger or takeover, managers may seek to join with one of the following.

- *A supplier* This is known as 'backward vertical integration', because the business is joining with another organization at an earlier stage of the same production process. By joining with a supplier, you can remove or reduce its profit margin, and may be able to guarantee the volume and quality of supplies you want. For example, Tyrrell's, the crisp manufacturer, highlights the fact that it uses its own potatoes and turns this into a marketing point because it can rely on the quality of home-grown inputs.

- *A distributor or a retailer of their products* This is known as 'forward vertical integration' and occurs when one business joins with another at a later stage of the same process (that is, at a stage nearer to the final customer). A business may undertake this form of integration to guarantee access to the market. Music equipment producers Bose and Bang & Olufsen sell through their own outlets to ensure that the buying experience fits with the overall brand values. In 2009, Pepsi bought its top two bottlers for US$7,800 million (£4,600m) in an effort to save money and get its products to market more rapidly. In the oil industry, companies such as Shell and BP have undertaken forward and backward integration so that they control every aspect of the supply chain, from exploration, refining, and transport, through to retail. This gives these businesses complete control over the production and marketing processes, but requires heavy investment and many different skills to understand and operate in these different markets. This is why many businesses prefer to specialize in a particular stage of the process rather than to control the whole process.

- *A business at the same stage of the same type of production process* This is known as 'horizontal integration', and is often undertaken to achieve greater market power and economies of scale. For example, the businesses may share research and development facilities, IT resources, HR departments, or marketing teams. Horizontal integration can enable a business to increase its market share rapidly. It may also help a business to expand into different regional markets quickly. For example, in 2012 the wholesaler Booker bought another wholesaler Makro for nearly £140 million. These companies were able to share their expertise and systems. However, these takeovers are not guaranteed to be successful—just look at the Royal Bank of Scotland's disastrous £49 billion takeover of Dutch bank ABN Amro in 2007.

- *A business that operates in a different market* This is known as 'conglomerate integration' and may be undertaken because a business wants to operate in different markets. This may reduce the risk if demand falls or slows in one market. For example, in 2008 Mars paid US$23,000 million for Wrigley's; the company wanted to diversify out of chocolate, which is slowing in growth, and move into the faster-growing chewing gum market. In 2012 Facebook paid $1 billion for Instagram. However, managing a conglomerate may be difficult, because it means bringing together very different types of business.

? *Think about it ...*   *10.7*

If the majority of mergers and takeovers have led to poor performance, why do so many still occur?

What can prevent a business from growing?

While many managers may want to expand their business, they may not be able to raise the money to finance the desired growth. Both external growth (for example, taking over another business) and internal growth (for example, opening new stores) will require money. If you do not want to sell shares or use loans to raise the funds externally, or if you do not have the profits that you need to finance this growth internally, it may not be possible to expand even if you feel that it is desirable.

There may also be restrictions on your growth. Governments are often concerned about the power that large firms can have and therefore enact legislation to control monopolies. In the UK, the Competition Commission has the right to investigate any business that has a market share of more than 25 per cent. The Competition Commission may prevent a merger or takeover on the grounds that it will lead to one organization holding a market share of more than 25 per cent if it fears that this power may be abused and may not work in the public interest. (The role of the Competition Commission is examined in Chapter 9.) Companies found to be abusing their dominant position can be fined up to 10 per cent of their turnover, and takeovers or mergers that might lead to a market share of more than 25 per cent may be prevented or conditions may be imposed upon them.

Limitations of models that assume maximization

In reality, managers may not actually maximize anything. This is partly because they will not necessarily know exactly what costs and demand conditions are, or what they will be in the future. Gathering information in itself is expensive and time-consuming, and even if you undertake market research, it cannot be guaranteed to be 100 per cent accurate. Therefore Simon (1955) claims that managers have 'bounded rationality' and make decisions by 'satisficing' rather than maximizing. They reach a decision that is 'good enough' and with which they are happy, given the uncertainties that exist, even though this may not be the optimal decision. It is the best decision that can be made in the circumstances and with the information available, but may not maximize anything.

Managers also face many different interest groups within the business, all of whom may want different things. They will need to balance the different needs of these stakeholders rather than maximizing anything. The sales department may be desperate to hit its sales targets, the finance department may be worried about cash flow and financing expansion, and the local community may be worried about congestion if the business expands and has more deliveries. The final price and quantity outcome may be the results of different targets from different stakeholders. Therefore managers will have different forces acting on them and may end with a form of compromise.

Managers may also avoid maximizing profits because they want a certain degree of 'organizational slack' within their business. If managers allow costs to be higher than they could be in 'good' years, it means that they can make cut-backs relatively quickly and easily when demand conditions are less favourable. Having slack, such as excess labour and stocks, also allows them to meet changes in demand easily. Another phenomenon that may prevent maximization is that managers may set targets that are relatively easy to achieve, rather than ones that maximize results but which may be difficult to achieve. Setting conservative targets may enable them to look better when reporting to investors on what they have achieved.

A further problem with the maximization model is that decisions to maximize, say, profit will vary depending on the time period involved. For example, if a manager were aiming to maximize profits in the immediate run, he/she might cut back on training and investing in new products. This would be unnecessary expenditure because he/she is looking for quick rewards. But to achieve longer-term profits, a manager might invest heavily in research and development to build a portfolio for the future. He/she might also reduce price to gain market share to develop a strong market position for the future. Short-term profits may suffer in the search for higher long-term profits. When deciding whether to maximize profits, a real problem is to know over what period to try to achieve this.

In defence of the concept of maximization, however, is the idea that, whether managers know it or not, if they finally end up with the biggest sales or the highest possible profits, then, by definition, they are maximizing these. A manager may not know cost and revenue conditions precisely, and may not compare marginal costs and revenues, but if he/she continually adjusts his/her decisions to boost profits, then he/she is moving towards the output at which marginal revenue equals marginal costs even if he/she does not know it. Managers may well experiment with prices and outputs, and gradually move towards the maximization position.

}{ People and economics: Herbert Simon

Herbert Simon (1916–2001) was an American political scientist and economist, a psychologist, and a sociologist. His research covered areas such as psychology, computer science, economics, management, and sociology. In 1978 Simon won the Nobel Prize in Economics 'for his pioneering research into the decision-making process within economic organizations'. He received an honorary degree from Harvard University in 1990.

? Think about it... 10.8

Which of the following statements are true and which are false?

A: A business maximizes its revenue when marginal costs are zero.

B: A business maximizes profits when marginal revenue equals marginal costs.

C: A business produces the highest level of output without making a loss when the average revenue equals the average variable cost.

D: A normal profit is made when average revenue is greater than average costs.

Profits and risk

In 2008, the global banking system hit major problems. Banks all over the world had been lending excessively and making high-risk loans. Once the dangers of this were exposed, it became clear that their loans lacked the collateral that it had been assumed that they had and that banks were dangerously exposed. When this combined with a global **recession**, which drove down asset prices, it became clear that banks had overextended themselves and, in some cases, their loans were worthless because the individual or organization could not repay. To protect the banking system, governments had to intervene and provide more finance. In the UK, the government bought control of the Royal Bank of Scotland (RBS) and Lloyds Bank, and provided billions of pounds of extra support.

What had gone wrong? Directors and managers had been pursuing profit to such an extent that they had taken excessive risks in search of more rewards. The banking system had not been regulated enough, allowing behaviour that proved to be dangerous to investors and customers. As a result of lending excessively, banks responded by cutting back lending to such an extent that this halted growth in many economies. Many analysts who had previously argued that governments should leave markets to work for themselves now wanted the state to take greater control. Alan Greenspan, who had been the head of the US Federal Reserve (the US central bank) for eighteen years, wrote, in his book *The Age of Turbulence* in 2007: 'Why would we wish to control the pollinating behaviour of Wall Street bees?' At that stage, he was in favour of the actions that banks were taking to make more profits. In 2008, in front of a US Congressional Committee, he said:

> I made a mistake in presuming that the self-interests of organizations, specifically banks and others, were such as that they were best capable of protecting their own shareholders and their equity in the firms ... [T]he reason I was shocked [was] because I have been going for forty years or more with very considerable evidence that it was working exceptionally well.

Therefore profit-maximizing behaviour may lead to firms taking too many risks; the lessons of the recent crisis may curb the desire of some managers to pursue profit so aggressively.

The precise price and output decision will depend on the objectives of managers. We tend to assume that managers profit-maximize, meaning that they will produce when marginal revenue is equal to marginal costs. But it is possible that, because of a lack of information, they do not actually maximize profits; rather, they end up aiming to make what they and their owners regard as a satisfactory level. Also, given the nature of the way in which managers are often rewarded, and the divorce between the ownership and control of many businesses, managers may end up pursing other aims such as growth and revenue targets.

Summary

In an oligopoly, the decisions facing a manager are particularly complex because there are other large firms in the market and he/she needs to think about what they will do. Oligopoly highlights the complexity of business strategic planning.

Checklist

Having read this chapter, you should now understand:

- [ ] the meaning of oligopoly;
- [ ] cooperative and competitive models of oligopoly;

- [ ] cartels;
- [ ] game theory;
- [ ] price discrimination;
- [ ] different business objectives;
- [ ] satisficing;
- [ ] how Porter's five forces model helps to analyse market structure and influences business strategy.

Organizations and economics

Oil Petroleum Exporting Countries (OPEC)

The mission of OPEC is to coordinate and unify the petroleum policies of its member countries and ensure the stabilization of oil markets in order to secure an efficient, economic, and regular supply of petroleum to consumers, a steady income to producers, and a fair return on capital for those investing in the petroleum industry.

OPEC was founded in Baghdad, Iraq, with the signing of an agreement in September 1960 by five countries, namely the Islamic Republic of Iran, Iraq, Kuwait, Saudi Arabia, and Venezuela. They were to become the founder members of OPEC. Currently, OPEC has a total of twelve member countries.

Source: http://www.opec.org?

Intellectual Property Office (IPO)

The IPO is the government organization responsible for intellectual property (IP) rights in the UK. These rights include patents, designs, trademarks, and copyright.

The aim of the IPO is to promote innovation by providing a system of intellectual property rights that is clear, accessible, and widely understood. This enables the economy and society to benefit from ideas.

Source: http://www.ipo.gov.uk?

Short answer questions

1. State two differences between a monopoly and monopolistic competition.
2. If a business is making abnormal profits in monopolistic competition, what will happen in the industry?
3. What is an oligopoly?
4. What is meant by the prisoners' dilemma?
5. Why are prices 'sticky' in the kinked demand curve model of oligopoly?
6. Why might cartels be unstable?

7. What is the condition for sales revenue maximization?

8. What is satisficing?

9. State Porter's five forces.

10. Distinguish between horizontal and vertical integration.

Discussion questions

1. Is monopolistic competition efficient?

2. What determines the price and output outcomes in an oligopoly?

3. Is profit-maximizing behaviour likely?

One step further

Visit our Online Resource Centre at **www.oxfordtextbooks.co.uk/orc/gillespiebusiness2e/** to test your understanding, watch video walk-throughs, and access further information on topics covered in this chapter.

Market failures and imperfections

11

Learning objectives

In Chapter 7 we examined the free market system and highlighted the benefits of leaving market forces to solve the fundamental economic problems. In this chapter, we examine some of the failures and imperfections in a free market that prevent an optimal allocation of resources.

By the end of this chapter, you should:

- ☑ understand different types of market failure and imperfection;

- ☑ be able to explain the effect of failures and imperfections on the allocation of resources;

- ☑ understand the ways in which a government might intervene in the economy to remedy market failures and imperfections.

© Case study

'I'll tell you what I think,' said Olivia. 'The government is getting it all wrong.' This was a common theme of Olivia's—she had very strong views about the government—any government—and was not reluctant to voice them! 'Let me give you some examples. Last week there was a proposal in front of the council for a massive casino to open up in the city centre. Why are they even considering this? Given the high levels of unemployment in the

area, I hardly think a casino is what we want; it will only lead to people losing whatever money they once had. And then there's my neighbours—they seem to spend most of their time having barbecues and fires in their garden with no consideration at all for the effect of the smoke on my washing. I've called the council but they say that there's not much they can do—they're probably too busy talking to casino owners. What really gets me is that there's lots the government should be doing but they spend most of their time interfering in areas where they are not needed. I've heard they are about to introduce a minimum price for alcohol—I doubt that will have any effect, so why waste time on it? And then all the protection that exists these days to protect employees—anti-discrimination, redundancy rights, dismissal rights, maternity and paternity rights—all they do is make it more expensive and more difficult to employ people. They'd be better keeping out of it.'

Questions

1. Do you think that the government should be involved in determining where new casinos are opened?

2. Do you think that a minimum legal price for alcohol is a good idea?

3. Do you think that the government needs to protect employees? Is there more the government should be doing to protect employees?

4. What aspects of business behaviour do you think the government should regulate more?

Introduction

In a free market, the equilibrium price and output are determined by the market forces of supply and demand. In Figure 11.1, this is shown by P1,Q1. This price and quantity combination maximizes the welfare of society—that is, the consumer surplus plus the producer surplus (which combined are called community surplus). In this case, the free market is allocating resources efficiently because the area of community surplus is maximized by this price and quantity combination.

Of course this equilibrium will change as market conditions change. Assume that a market is originally in equilibrium but then there is an increase in demand for the

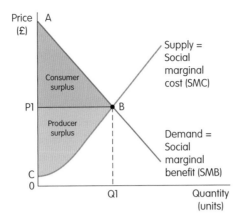

Figure 11.1 The community surplus is maximized at price P1 and quantity Q1

product. This will lead to a higher price and output, assuming that the supply curve is upward sloping. The increase in demand raises the potential rewards in this industry, and resources should switch into this sector and out of another attracted by the higher prices. In the new equilibrium, community surplus will once again be maximized. Therefore the free market works to allocate and reallocate resources efficiently, and so letting market forces operate can lead to an optimal outcome; this is why some economists believe that the government should not get too involved in an economy. If an item is demanded, then customers will pay for it and it will be produced if a profit can be made. If an item is not wanted, demand will fall and resources will move out of this industry because the rewards are no longer appealing. Millions of independent decisions are made by rational decision-makers pursuing their own interests and these determine what is produced, how it is produced, and who gets what.

However, there are various problems in the free market that prevent it from working effectively and efficiently. These are known as market 'imperfections' and 'failures'. In this chapter, we examine these failings of the free market and consider what governments might do to intervene to overcome these.

Monopoly power

The free market system can achieve an efficient allocation of resources when markets work effectively. In reality, however, some firms may come to dominate their markets, reducing the degree of competition; this means that they have a high share of the market relative to that of their rivals. In the extreme case of a pure monopoly, there is only one firm in the market, so it has a market share of 100 per cent. More generally, the term 'monopoly' is used when a business, such as Microsoft or Wrigley's, has a large market share (in UK law, a monopoly is a business with a market share of more than 25 per cent). From a manager's perspective becoming a monopoly may allow you to dominate suppliers, distributors, and the media, and have enormous buying power; this can lead to economies of scale. Having a monopoly position also reinforces your brand as the leader in the market and this may create brand loyalty. However, what is good for one business may not necessarily be good for the consumer or other businesses.

A monopoly dominates the market in which it operates and is able to set the price in this market because of the lack of competition. In a competitive market, if one firm were to increase its price, customers would simply switch to cheaper alternatives—the buyers have access to good information and can easily switch to a substitute. However, if there is a dominant firm, it may be able to charge significantly higher prices than would be possible in a competitive market because its product is differentiated and customers have fewer alternatives. In a competitive market with many thousands of small firms, each firm has to follow the market price or it will lose business and make a loss. This means that market forces bring equilibrium at P1,Q1. This is where the market is in equilibrium. As we saw in perfect competition in Chapter 9, each firm is a price-taker selling as much as it can at the market price of P1. Each individual firm profit-maximizes where the price equals marginal revenue equals marginal cost; the firm is allocatively and productively efficient in the long run.

A monopolist is a single firm and a price-maker. It faces a downward-sloping demand curve, and if it lowers the price on one unit this reduces the price on all the others before leading the marginal revenue curve below the demand and then diverging. The monopolist will profit-maximize at the output where marginal revenue equals marginal costs (which was the supply curve in a competitive industry).

As we can see, faced with the same demand and cost conditions, a monopolist has a higher price and lower quantity than a perfectly competitive industry (P2Q2 versus P1Q1). Overall, the producer is better off (because the producer surplus has increased to P2, BCF, which is why the firm used its power to push up prices), while consumer surplus falls to ABP2 (see Figure 11.2). The result is that society, as a whole, is worse off due to the deadweight social burden loss triangle BEC. This occurs because, on units Q2,Q1, the

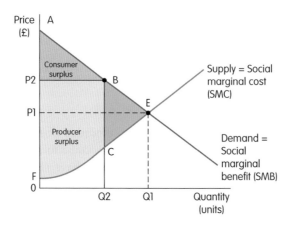

Figure 11.2 Monopoly power reduces the community surplus

extra benefit to society is greater than the extra cost and so society would benefit from having these produced. If the output Q2,Q1 could be produced, the extra benefit of these units would be greater than the extra cost and so society's welfare would increase. The socially optimal position is where the marginal condition is met at P1Q1 but the business itself is better off at P2Q2. The monopolist does not want to sell more because it has to lower the price on all the previous units and so the marginal revenue (MR) is below the marginal cost and would reduce profits. At P2Q2 the business is allocatively inefficient (because the price is greater than the marginal cost) and productively inefficient because the business is not operating at the minimum of the average cost.

The allocative and productive inefficiency created by monopoly is why governments regulate firms that dominate their markets to consider the extent to which they are abusing their power and exploiting consumers. The rules regulating monopolies form what is known as 'competition policy'. For example, competition policy may prevent companies from expanding or joining together if they are going to become too large, or may involve fining companies that are already dominant if they are charging 'excessive' prices to their customers. Managers who want to grow their businesses (to increase the firm's producer surplus so that they can reward their owners) or who already have monopoly power need to be aware that there may be government restrictions on their behaviour.

The price and output decisions in monopoly and the underlying cost and revenues curves relative to competitive markets are examined in more detail in Chapter 9.

? Think about it ...   11.1

1. Can you think of any stakeholder group that might benefit if one firm were to dominate a market?

2. What percentage share of a market do you think that it is acceptable for one firm to have? Explain your choice.

£ Business analysis   11.1

In 2012 James Heneage, the founder of Ottakar's book chain, described Amazon as a force that needed watching because it is damaging high street book sellers and threatened the ability of publishers to find and develop new writers. Heneage argued that many good writers were not immediately successful and it took time for them to develop their readership. Publishers had to work with them and invest in them for a number of years. These comments came shortly after Amazon was reported to have paid no corporation tax on the profits made from its sales of £3.3 billion in the

UK. The main threat to book shops is the growth of e-books; these now account for over 20 per cent of the UK book market. Critics claim that Amazon does not have much loyalty to authors because books are just one of many products that it sells. If book shops do continue to close, this might lead to less choice for readers as e-book providers focus mainly on best sellers and so the range of books on sale is relatively small. Some also think that the continued growth of Amazon will remove an important element of the high street which helps bind communities together.

Do you think that Amazon should be controlled and prevented from growing?

Externalities

In a free market, managers will take account of the extra benefits that any action brings to the business (for example, the extent to which it helps increase revenue) and the extra costs to the business (for example, the cost of resources used to produce the output). However, they are naturally selfish and so consider only what is relevant to the business; they will not take account of extra costs and benefits that might affect society as a whole, but which do not directly affect them as private organizations. If their actions happen to pollute the environment, why should they care unless they are made to? Would a fast food outlet willingly take responsibility for the litter its customers leave around the city? What about a chewing gum business—would it take responsibility for the gum left by its customers on the streets? Similarly, if their business happens to help the local economy grow, this, in itself, would not necessarily matter to them. As profit-maximizers, it is assumed that managers focus on the extra private benefits and costs to the business to pursue private profits, but will not want to take account of any other benefits and costs unless they are made to do so.

Therefore in a free market managers are assumed to ignore the external effects of what they do (which are called 'externalities'). This means that the factors considered by managers when making decisions about prices, output, and investment are not the same as the decisions that would be made if we were looking at them from the perspective of society as a whole, because they are based on different views of the relative costs and benefits (private rather than social). The result is that the free market does not lead to the same allocation of resources that society as a whole would want. This is highlighted by an analysis of negative and positive externalities.

Negative externalities

Figure 11.3 shows the supply curve for a product and reflects the private marginal costs to the business of producing more units. In this case, the demand curve is assumed to reflect the marginal social benefits to the customer of consuming an additional unit. As we saw earlier, the equilibrium at P1,Q1 maximizes the community surplus (which is consumer surplus and producer surplus combined). However, if the business is generating external costs, such as noise and air pollution, P1,Q1 is no longer going to be the

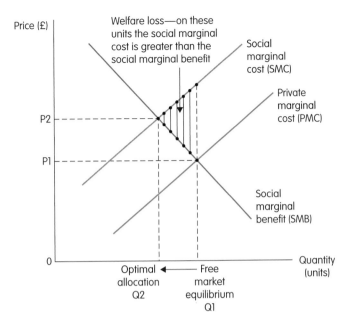

Figure 11.3 A negative externality

socially optimal price and output. Assume that businesses in this industry generate large amounts of pollution contributing to climate change, that their vans are causing congestion and creating traffic jams, that their staff drop litter in the local community on the way to work, and that their production processes are destroying the local wild-life. These actions are all imposing costs on others that are not included in the private costs of production—costs which society would like the business to take account of, but which managers will not consider unless made to do so. If we add the external costs to the private costs, we can see a new supply curve reflecting the social marginal costs (SMC) and the socially optimal equilibrium (at Q2). On all the units between Q1 and Q2, the extra cost of the unit to society exceeds the extra benefit and so overall society is worse off at Q1 than at Q2. The shaded area represents a deadweight social burden triangle and a loss of welfare (allocative inefficiency) due to overproduction.

When the social costs of production are greater than the private costs, this is called a 'negative production **externality**'. In this situation, we might want government to inter-vene to reduce production to Q2, which is the socially optimal level. A government may do this in various ways, including the following.

■ *Introducing indirect taxes to raise the private costs of the producer so that they match the social costs* The precise monetary cost of external effects, such as pollution, can be difficult to quantify in reality, but, in theory, if costs were increased to the social level, the market could settle naturally in equilibrium at P2,Q2. Congestion charges and taxes on alcohol, betting, air travel, petrol, landfill, and vehicles are all examples of the government trying to reduce the effects of negative externalities.

- *Legislating to control production to the level of Q2* Again, it is difficult for a government to estimate social costs accurately and so limit the production to exactly the right level, but the aim of such legislation would be to place restrictions on production to Q2. For example, legislation on clean air or pollution emissions are designed to combat negative externalities. Since 2009, only energy-efficient light bulbs can be sold in the UK; energy-inefficient bulbs are prohibited.

- *Highlighting the importance of issues, such as climate change, to try to encourage business to take into account the effects of its actions on society as a whole* There have been an increasing number of businesses that have tried to adopt a more socially responsible approach rather than only to focus on profits. **Corporate social responsibility (CSR)** refers to an approach in which the needs and interests of different groups, such as the community, employees, society in general, and even future generations, are taken into account when making decisions, rather than only those of the shareholders. With more managers and owners seeing the long-term benefits for society as a whole of behaving as a corporate citizen and not just a profit-maximizing organization, some businesses are trying to take into account the external costs of their actions and are attempting to reduce them even without government intervention.

- *Subsidizing other options* By subsidizing the purchase of fuel-efficient vehicles, for example, the government could bring about a fall in demand for 'gas guzzlers' and increase the purchase of energy-efficient cars. Subsidies of substitutes reduces their prices, making them a more affordable and attractive option, and therefore reduces demand for the less environmentally friendly alternative.

- *Taking control of production and providing the product itself* When a government takes over a business, this is known as 'nationalization'. By nationalizing, a government can control what is produced, how it is produced, and how it is allocated. In the past, the UK government nationalized many industries, such as coal, trains, airlines, water, and gas. The political belief at the time was that these 'commanding heights' of the economy were best run by government, which could ensure that the provision of them was fair and available to all who needed it at a reasonable price. The private sector, it was felt, pursues profit and not social objectives, and would ignore the social benefits of the consumption of these products. A counter-argument is that the pressure of market forces and shareholders will force managers to be more efficient and push costs down.

? Think about it...   11.2

Technology should enable governments to tax motorists for every mile they travel. Do you think that this would be a good way of taxing car drivers for the external costs that they generate?

Positive externalities

As well as external marginal costs that managers do not take account of in the free market, there may be external marginal benefits arising from the activities of a business. These are gains that do not directly earn income for the business, but which benefit society as a whole. They are called 'positive externalities' (see Figure 11.4). For example, setting up a business in a deprived low-income area helps to create jobs and increase earnings in the region which might improve the quality of life for those living there. Because these external marginal benefits do not directly generate revenue, they are not taken into account by profit-maximizing managers who focus purely on private costs and revenues. As a result, the free market produces at P1,Q1, whereas if the full benefits of the business's activities to society were taken into account, the socially optimal level of output is Q2. On units Q1,Q2, the extra benefit to society is greater than the extra costs and so society would benefit from production of these units. There is a potential welfare gain from producing Q1,Q2; society is losing out by underproducing because the benefit of units is undervalued.

To encourage the production of products with a positive externality, a government might:

- subsidize production, which would lower costs and therefore increase the profit-maximizing output—for example, the government might subsidize the arts, opera, sports provision, and museums;

- regulate—for example, in the UK there are private train, bus, and telecommunications operators, but they are regulated by the government (e.g. train prices are only allowed to increase by 1 per cent more than any increase in the general price level);

- take over supply to increase output and consumption—for example, the government may provide education and healthcare.

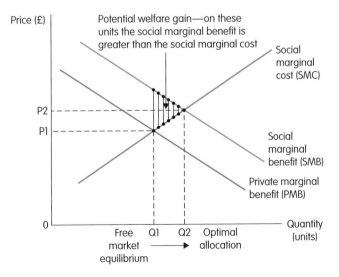

Figure 11.4 A positive externality

Business analysis 11.2

Football clubs only pay for the cost of policing inside the stadium and in the area immediately outside the ground. However, in 2012, it was suggested by a member of the Association of Chief Police Officers (ACPO) that football clubs should incur all the costs of security involved when a game was on.

Whenever a match is being played, crime in the area can increase significantly and ACPO suggested that the clubs should take responsibility for these costs. However, the Football League defended the present position, claiming that football already contributes more than £1 billion a year in taxation.

1. What are the negative externalities that might be generated by a football match?
2. What about positive externalities?
3. Should clubs pay for extra policing?

 Go online to access a video walk-through of analysing externalities.

 ## You and economics

Your generally get on well with your next-door neighbours, but in recent weeks their late night parties have been stopping you studying. At first you didn't mind and even went to a couple, but they seem to be getting more frequent and you have some important exams coming up. You have talked to your neighbours but they don't seem to see the problem and increasingly seem to see it as your problem not theirs.

Your neighbours are imposing an external cost on you, can you think of other external costs that affect you?

Cost–benefit analysis

When undertaking investments, such as building a new school or motorway, a government will take account of any external costs and benefits, as well as the private costs and benefits, to achieve the socially optimal level. This is known as **cost–benefit analysis** and involves putting a monetary value on externalities. This means that the government has to try to value, in pounds, the external costs and benefits of any investment; for example, it would place a monetary value on the impact of a road-building project on wildlife, the environment, the quality of life, noise, and the well-being of those using the road and living nearby.

Cost–benefit analysis often has to be used to make difficult decisions and involves the use of scientific techniques; however, it does require a manager to make estimates of factors that are, in reality, very difficult to quantify. For example, in the area of healthcare, limited budgets are available because any money used in healthcare is not being used somewhere else in the economy, and the costs and benefits of any investment must be weighed up. Healthcare administrators must decide on how to use the money available, which means deciding which treatments and which patients justify the use of funds. This involves numerous calculations regarding, for example, the impact of spending on life expectancy and the likelihood of improvement in someone's quality of life. Inevitably, a price has to be put on health, injury, and illness, and while more people could be saved with more investment, it is not always economic to do so.

? Think about it... 11.3

Do you think that it is right to try to put a monetary value on quality of life?

Business analysis 11.3

In 1970, Ford discovered that its Pinto car had a major design flaw, which meant that it might burst into flames if another car hit it from behind. Rather than immediately recall the cars, Ford's managers allegedly undertook a cost–benefit analysis taking into account:

- the number of cars that it had sold at that point;
- the likelihood of an accident occurring;
- the likely number of deaths if the cars that had been sold were left on the road.

The amount that Ford might have had to pay in damages if it did not recall its cars was calculated to be around US$49 million; this was less than the likely cost of recalling the cars, which was estimated to be US$137 million.

When this cost–benefit analysis was discovered by the media, there was considerable outrage, which led to the cars being recalled and serious damage to the company's image.

Do you think that Ford was right to undertake a cost–benefit analysis in these circumstances?

Business analysis 11.4

For many years there has been a debate over the need for and benefits of a third runway at Heathrow. The entrepreneur Sir Richard Branson is a great believer in the gains to the UK of the runway. He argues that greater capacity is needed. The government did consider a third runway, but in 2010 scrapped these plans and started to consider an airport in the Thames Estuary.

Branson claims that Virgin Atlantic's plans for growth had come to a halt when it could be creating thousands of jobs. He highlighted that the lack of capacity was limiting business traffic to Africa, China, South America, and the USA. The opposition to the runway focuses on the environmental damage this would cause.

Discuss the possible case for and against creating a third runway at Heathrow.

Property rights

According to the economist Ronald Coase, the problem of externalities arises because the external costs and benefits are not traded in a market; this is because of a lack of clearly defined 'property' rights (that is, it is not clear who has the right to do what). For example, if you were to have a legal right to silence, then those wanting to make a noise (which generates an external cost) would have to pay you to allow them to do this. They would consider the extra benefit of making more noise and the extra cost of paying for your agreement to allow them to do this, and this would lead to the optimal level of noise output (at which the marginal benefit equals the marginal cost). Therefore noise would be traded.

Alternatively, if the people making a noise were to have the right to do so, you would consider the cost of paying them to be quiet relative to the impact of their noise on your well-being.

? *Think about it...* 11.4

Why is the socially optimal level of noise not zero?

Similarly, if you have a legal right to no pollution, then any firm wanting to pollute more must consider the extra benefits of doing so (for example, the benefits from the extra production) and the extra costs of gaining the acceptance of others to be allowed to do so. Therefore it will consider the extra costs and benefits of more pollution, and keep producing up to the output level at which the extra benefits equal the extra costs. Alternatively, if it has a right to pollute, you would consider how much you were willing to pay to reduce its emissions. By clearly establishing property rights, this enables externalities to be traded and valued in a market economy, and a value is placed on the external effects.

? *Think about it...* 11.5

Which of the following statements are true and which are false?

A: Negative externalities occur when the social benefit is greater than the private benefit.

B: Some products are overproduced in the free market because of negative externalities.

C: Governments may want to subsidize products with positive externalities to encourage their consumption.

D: A deadweight social burden area occurs when the social marginal cost is greater than the marginal benefit.

E: If production generates a negative externality, it should be stopped.

Merit and demerit goods

A **merit good** is a product that the government thinks provides a benefit to society that is greater than the individual appreciates. Examples of merit goods include education and healthcare. By being educated, you can increase your earnings, you can contribute to the success of businesses, and thereby help others, and you are likely to have a better standard of living. You may not fully appreciate these benefits when you are younger and so are likely to underconsume merit goods if left to yourself. This is why the government provides merit goods directly or subsidizes them to encourage consumption or production.

A 'demerit good' is one that is more harmful to you than you might realize. An example of this is drugs; you may not appreciate the long-term damaging effects of these to you and others, and so overconsume them. This is why the government regulates, restricts, and discourages the consumption of demerit goods. Obesity has become a significant issue in the UK and so the government is trying to educate us about the dangers of a poor diet.

In the free market, merit goods would be underprovided, because the individual undervalues them, and demerit goods would be overprovided, because the individual does not realize how bad they are. Therefore, to achieve a socially optimal output, a government will provide or subsidize merit goods, and tax or discourage demerit goods. In the UK, for example, students must stay in some form of education until they are 18, and this is provided free of charge by the state because they are merit goods; however, drugs such as heroin and cocaine are illegal because they are demerit goods.

Public goods

Public goods are products which, once provided, offer a benefit to everyone. For example, if you build a lighthouse, every ship that passes will benefit from it; you cannot prevent any ship from benefiting from the light, because consumption is non-excludable.

Another significant aspect of public goods is that they are non-diminishable. With most products, if one person consumes them, there is less for everyone else; for example, if you buy one of the bottles of water on the shelf of the supermarket, there is one bottle fewer for someone else to buy. The consumption of the product by one person reduces the amount left for others. In the case of a public good, no matter how many people consume it, it does not reduce how much is available; there could be thousands of ships passing the lighthouse and there is still the same amount of light available.

Public goods would not be provided in a free market, because the producer would not be able to make a profit from doing so; this is because it could not prevent people from consuming the product and therefore they would be able to get it free (known as the 'free-rider problem'). As a result, no one would volunteer to pay for a public good, because consumers would ride for free on the back of anyone who paid for it. If these products are to be provided, a government needs to step in and provide them itself.

You and economics

You live in a cul-de-sac which is a private road, and so the maintenance of the road is the responsibility of the residents not local government. The road is in a bad state with many pot-holes which make it difficult to drive down. You are worried that you will burst a tyre or even break the suspension of your car. You have visited most of your neighbours to try and see if you could get repairs done, but you cannot agree about who would pay what. Some people are not interested at all and think it is fine as it is; some people think that they should pay less than others because they do not drive very often.

You are clearly facing the free-rider problem!

Factor immobility

In theory, resources can reallocate from one market to another very easily in the free market. As demand for computer games increases and demand for printed books declines, producers move out of the latter sector and into the former. As they do so, they shift labour, land, and capital equipment from one industry to the next, in which the potential rewards are higher. This reallocation of resources can be shown on a production possibility frontier (PPF) as the economy moves from X to Y due to changes in demand (see Figure 11.5).

In reality, resources may not be perfectly mobile; they may struggle to reallocate, which means that the economy ends up at point Z (see Figure 11.6), at which resources are under-utilized and the resource allocation is inefficient. Resources have come out of printed books, but have not been able to shift into computer games development.

The immobility of capital resources may arise because they are specialized and suitable for one type of production, but cannot easily be reset, reprogrammed, or moved to

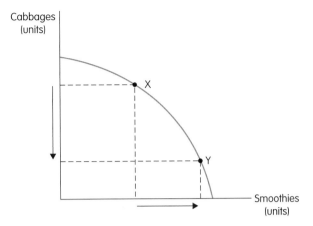

Figure 11.5 The reallocation of resources

produce something else. The immobility of some land resources is also clear—demand for pineapples may be high, but land in the UK cannot easily be adapted to grow these.

In the case of the labour market, immobility may occur because:

- employees lack the necessary training and skills to transfer from one industry to another, meaning that there may be a delay (possibly a very long delay) before they can move into new jobs—this is called 'occupational immobility';

- employees may be located in one area and find it difficult to move because of family ties, friends, or school arrangements with their children, or it may simply be very expensive to move, perhaps because of the differences in house prices, which acts as a barrier—this is called 'geographical immobility';

- employees may also lack information about what vacancies exist—that is, if they do not know what jobs there are, they will not be able to transfer.

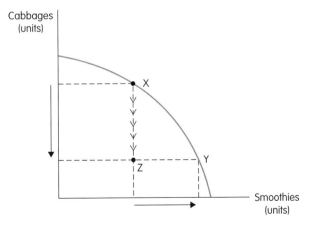

Figure 11.6 The inefficient reallocation of resources

To reduce labour immobility, a government might:

- try to promote better information about vacancies that exist (e.g. via job centres);
- offer training schemes and subsidize or encourage training within business, so that employees have the skills that they need;
- offer subsidies to help people to relocate.

Price instability

Another problem with the free market is that, with changes in demand and supply, there can be major movements in the prices of some products and resources. This instability can make planning difficult for managers. The prices of commodities, for example, are particularly vulnerable to shifts in supply (for example, due to changes in the weather). These shifts can have significant effects on the price because both supply and demand are so price inelastic; this is highlighted by the 'cobweb' model.

Assume an agricultural market in which supply is totally price inelastic at any point in time. This is because, no matter what the price is, only a certain amount of the crop is available at any given time. Over time, more crop can be planted and more land can be allocated to this crop, so supply will become more price elastic, but in the immediate run, there is a fixed amount available regardless of price.

Assume that the market is originally in equilibrium at P0,Q0 and then there is a shock to supply that reduces the quantity available to Q1. Given the fall in quantity available, this leads to a higher equilibrium price of P1. This high price sends a signal to farmers to produce more because of the higher rewards that they think they can now earn. When this larger crop is eventually harvested, the increased supply will lower the equilibrium price. The low supply price will then send a signal to farmers to reduce the quantity supplied; when this low quantity is produced and harvested, it will lead to a high price to clear the market.

If demand is more price inelastic than supply, the changes in price in each session are moving the market away from equilibrium. This is known as an 'exploding cobweb' (see Figure 11.8).

? *Think about it ...* 11.6

1. The cobweb model assumes that farmers continually base next year's planting decision on this year's prices. Do you think that this is a realistic assumption? On what else might they base their decisions?

2. If demand is more price elastic than supply, the cobweb is imploding—that is, the price changes each year, moving back towards equilibrium. Can you illustrate this using supply and demand diagrams?

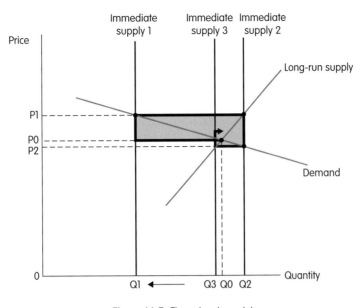

Figure 11.7 The cobweb model

In markets such as agriculture, in which prices can change a great deal, the government may intervene to stabilize prices. To do this, they might adopt a buffer stock scheme (see Figure 11.9). In this system, when there is an increase in supply (perhaps due to good weather), the government can buy up the excess to prevent the price from falling. In periods when supply is low, the government can release the stocks that it has built up from the good periods. This can help to keep the price at the same level.

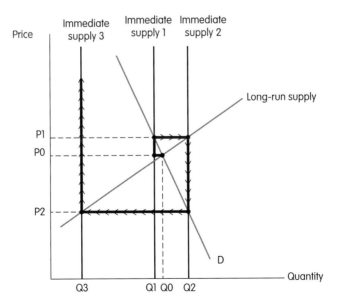

Figure 11.8 The exploding cobweb

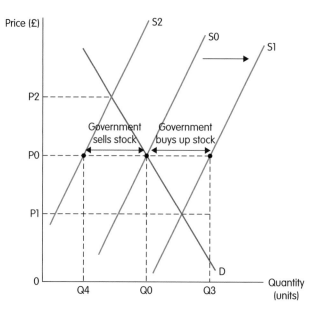

Figure 11.9 A buffer stock scheme

However, there are problems with the buffer stock system, including the following:

■ it incurs stockholding costs to store the products in 'good' years;

■ there may be more good periods than bad periods, in which case the government is left holding stocks for long periods, or there may be more bad periods than good periods, in which case the surplus does not meet the shortages;

■ there are administration costs to running the scheme.

Instability means that producers are uncertain of the revenue that they will generate. It also creates problems further down the production chain. For example, a cereal manufacturer, such as Kellogg's, will have to make plans based on forecasts of grain prices. Unexpected falls in supply can increase the price of its materials significantly, which can reduce profit margins and/or force it to pass on increased costs, which may damage sales. The same problems face airlines uncertain about petrol prices, manufacturers uncertain about energy prices, and chocolate companies uncertain about cocoa prices.

? Think about it... 11.7

Do you think that the government should intervene to stabilize the prices of agricultural products?

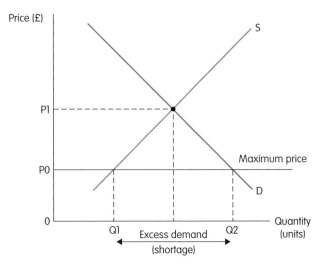

Figure 11.10 A maximum price below the equilibrium level leads to excess demand

As well as using buffer stock a government might intervene in the market system by using price controls; these can stabilize price by limiting the maximum and/or minimum prices allowed in a market. For example, if a government thinks that the price in a market is too low or too high, perhaps because of its effect on society as a whole, it may decide to intervene and fix the price or limit its movement in some way. A government may intervene in a market to control the price at which some products are sold. For example, a government may set a maximum price to prevent prices from going too high. This may occur if the government feels that a high price would be unfair; for example, a government might want to make sure that certain medicines are affordable for the vast majority of people and so it might decide to keep prescription prices down below the equilibrium market price. The effect of such intervention is to create excess demand (see Figure 11.10). This is when queues and waiting lists can develop, and it acts as a rationing device because the price mechanism is not being allowed to work properly.

If a government decides to set a maximum price below equilibrium, a black market may develop. In a black market products are traded illegally at a price that is higher than the set price. Given the high levels of demand, people are willing to pay more than the 'official' price to buy the item; those who bought it at the set price can resell at a higher one and make a profit on the black market.

Alternatively, a government might set a minimum price to prevent prices from falling too far. For example, in the labour market, the government may feel that employees are exploited if wages are too low. As a result, the government may set a minimum wage above equilibrium that all employers must pay. The result of this is that there is excess supply (see Figure 11.11).

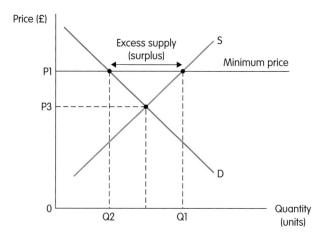

Figure 11.11 A minimum price above the equilibrium level leads to excess supply

 ## Business analysis   11.5

The Common Agricultural Policy (CAP) is an example of a buffer stock scheme and accounts for over half of the European Union's budget. It began in 1962 and was seen as a way of protecting famers and reducing Europe's reliance on imported food. However, it soon led to overproduction, and food mountains and wine lakes. Reforms to the CAP to make it less expensive began in the 1990s, although in 2010 the direct payments to farmers still amounted to €43 billion.

France is the biggest beneficiary of the CAP followed by Spain and then Germany.

What do you think the consequences of removing the CAP might be?

Imperfect information

In a perfect free market, each of the different groups involved in transactions, such as firms, employees, and customers, make rational decisions to maximize their returns and have perfect information about the options open to them. For example, if demand were to increase, firms would immediately realize that there was excess demand at the old price and begin to increase the price until a new equilibrium was reached. In reality, information is far from perfect: customers do not always know their options when it comes to suppliers, employees do not always know their work and leisure options, and suppliers do not always know the relevant demand conditions. For example, a manager of a restaurant business would like to be able to change the prices of its food according to the likely levels of demand; if he/she was sure of a busy lunch period, he/she might push up its prices because he/she cannot fit in everyone who would want to eat at the old price. But anticipating exactly what demand will be is difficult and therefore managers will tend to set prices based on 'average' levels of demand. The result is that sometimes a restaurant has empty tables because the price is too high for the demand, while at other times there are queues because the price is too low given the levels of demand.

Asymmetric information

Asymmetric information in markets occurs when one party has more information than another; for example, a garage may recommend that certain parts are changed without the customer knowing whether this is actually necessary. In the private healthcare market, doctors know more than patients about healthcare, and so could be tempted to diagnose treatments that are not needed.

Asymmetric information can lead to two situations.

- *Adverse selection* This problem occurs when the ignorant party lacks information when negotiating an agreement. This means, for example, that people with higher risks may want to buy insurance because the insurance company cannot tell the difference between applicants. Of course, sometimes it is the seller who knows more than the buyer—think about estate agents! The problem of a lack of information encourages opportunism, whereby the informed people try to benefit at the expense of those with less information. The problems of imperfect information were examined by George Akerlof in his analysis of the second-hand car market. A 'lemon' is the name given to a poor-quality second-hand car. Akerlof highlighted that buyers of second-hand cars are never sure if they will be buying a lemon or not, and so are only willing to offer average prices for what might actually be better-than-average second-hand cars. This means that people with better-than-average second-hand cars decide not to sell them; therefore the average price becomes too high for what is actually on the market and the price falls. This could potentially lead to the collapse of the market entirely.

- *Moral hazard* This occurs when the ignorant party lacks information about the performance of the other party following a transaction (i.e. moral hazard is about hidden actions). For example, once insured there may be less incentive to drive carefully. In the case of companies the shareholders may not have perfect information about the exact position of the business or the actions of the managers. There is the danger that managers will not act in the interests of the owners (this is known as the principal–agent problem, where the owners are the principal and the managers are their agents). In recent years moral hazard has been a big issue in relation to the banks. There is the danger that the banks have become 'too big to fail'; they know that if they struggle governments will rescue them because of their significance in the economy, as the UK government did with Northern Rock, RBS, and Lloyds in 2008. This may lead to high risk lending because the banks believe that they will never collapse. In the UK the government has set out to increase the amount of competition in the banking sector to ensure that no single bank becomes too big—it wants it to be clear to bankers that they will be allowed to fail in future. The government also separated the different parts of banks so that the relatively low risk retail side was divorced from high risk investment banking. As George Osborne, the Chancellor, said: 'Our objective is clear. We want to separate high street banking from investment banking, to protect the British economy, protect British taxpayers and make sure that nothing is too big to fail.'

Ways of overcoming these information asymmetries include the following.

- *Screening* This is action taken by an uninformed person to find out the information held by the informed people. For example, you might test drive a second-hand car and not just take the seller's word for it; similarly you would insist on an independent survey of a house before buying it.
- *Signalling* This refers to action taken by an informed person to send information to a less informed person. For example, dentists and lawyers may have certificates on their walls to show their qualifications. Companies may have their claims independently verified.

? Think about it...   11.8

The costs of car insurance in the UK are significantly increased because of the large number of whiplash injury claims. In 2012 the House of Commons Transport Select Committee said that claimants should provide much greater proof that they have suffered a whiplash injury. The problem with whiplash claims is that it is difficult to know whether the claimant is telling the truth or not, and it is up to the insurance company to prove that the claim is invalid if they have suspicions. Some insurance companies have encouraged anyone involved in an accident to claim for whiplash, which has increased insurance costs for all motorists. According to the Committee there has been a 70 per cent increase in injury claims resulting from an accident, and whiplash was the major reason for such claims. At present there is one whiplash claim every minute of every day.

Do you think that claims for whiplash should be banned?

Do you think that people claiming should have to prove that they have suffered from whiplash?

People and economics: Michael Spence

Michael Spence proposed the idea of signalling to resolve the problem of asymmetric information. This was originally examined in the case of someone looking for a job. If an employer wanted someone 'skilled in learning', all applicants would claim to be this and it would be difficult to know if this was true, so there is asymmetry of information. Spence highlighted that finishing university acts as a credible signal that the individual is skilled in learning.

Economics and employability

What is your name and role?

My name is Andrew Gillespie and I am a lecturer and author in business and economics.

Did you study economics at university?

I read modern history and economics at university, and when starting at university considered myself a historian. I had not studied economics before, but I was interested in the impact that economic conditions could have on historical events and thought that an understanding of economics would give me greater insight into why events had occurred (or not occurred) in the past. My degree course involved a great deal of mathematical analysis; without any background in the subject I had little idea of what we were actually trying to prove at first, so it made it more difficult to get to grips and become engaged with the topics. The mathematical analysis seemed a bit abstract and I had few points of reference in terms of linking it to what was happening around me. We were solving equations, but I could not see how it related to my everyday life. My own initial experience of studying the subject is one reason why I have tried to write books that make economics more accessible to students and help them become confident in the essentials, so that they can then move on to more complex analysis with a solid foundation and an understanding of what they are studying and why it is useful.

How has studying economics been useful?

One of the key aspects of economic analysis at the micro-level is the marginal condition. To maximize profits, for example, businesses should produce up to the point where marginal revenue equals marginal cost; at this point there is no further profit to be made. Similarly, to maximize social welfare the government should aim for production up to the level of output where the social marginal benefit equals the social marginal cost; at this point society's welfare cannot be increased and therefore is maximized. An understanding of this marginal principle made me think differently about issues. Perhaps most significantly it made me realize that decision-making was far more complex than simply deciding whether or not something should be allowed to occur. Take pollution—we may not like this but it is the result of the production of goods and services; more production may bring an extra cost in the form of pollution, but it also brings an extra benefit in the form of additional products. The solution is not to stop pollution completely but to get production to the point where the extra benefit equals the extra cost. Therefore studying economics has made me think more carefully about the benefits and costs involved in any decision, and the importance of considering the additional gains and costs of any additional activity. Not that this is necessarily easy to do—just look at the difficulties involved in measuring the benefits and costs of the proposed high speed rail link. Does less time commuting lead to more time and work and therefore more business being done? If so, how is this valued? And what, in fact, is the increase in productivity given that people can now work on the train? And how do we value the impact on the environment? All these are interesting issues which highlight how difficult it can be to apply these fundamental principles in practice.

What interests you most in economics?
My interest seems to change according to the current issues being debated in the news. Obviously the recession and the Eurozone crisis have been high on the agenda recently, which is why I have included a number of case studies on them in this edition. However, at the moment I am fascinated by the whole question of how much we can trust markets. Whilst the potential benefits of market forces are appealing in many ways, the danger of leaving organizations to themselves seems to be increasingly evident with the scandals around the behaviour of bankers and journalists, the protests at the power of buyers pushing the price of milk paid to suppliers down, and various price-fixing allegations all making you question how much markets do need to be regulated. As new stories emerge, it makes me continually evaluate how much markets can or should be trusted.

Inequality

In a free market, your earnings are determined by the supply and demand for your labour. If you are highly able and talented, and work in an industry that generates high returns, you are likely to be paid a lot. However, if you lack training and there are many others with a similar level of skills, your earnings will be low. If you are unemployed, you will earn nothing. Therefore in the free market there are likely to be great differences between the incomes of different individuals. This means that there will be income inequality. Whether this is regarded as fair or not, and whether the government should make it a priority to intervene to change the distribution of income, are questions of normative economics, rather than positive economics. An efficient allocation of resources in the free market may mean that there is inequality. It is up to society to decide whether this is acceptable.

The level of incomes earned and the distribution of incomes in an economy can be considered by looking at the following factors.

- *Absolute and relative poverty* 'Absolute poverty' measures the number of people living below a given income level. 'Relative poverty' measures the extent to which a household's income falls below the average income for the economy.
- *The income distribution in an economy* This is shown by the **Lorenz curve** and the **Gini coefficient**.

The Lorenz curve plots the cumulative income share on the vertical axis against the distribution of the population on the horizontal axis. In Figure 11.12, 40 per cent of the population earns around 10 per cent of the total income. If each individual were to have the same income (that is, if there were total equality in the economy), the income distribution curve would be the straight line in the graph—the line of total equality. To measure

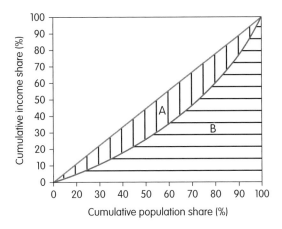

Figure 11.12 Lorenz curve of income distribution

how far away an economy is from total equality—that is, how unequal the income distribution is within an economy—you can use the Gini coefficient. This coefficient is calculated as:

$$(\text{Area A})/(\text{Area A} + \text{Area B})$$

If income is distributed completely equally, the Lorenz curve and the line of total equality are the same, and the Gini coefficient is 0. If 1 per cent of the population receive all the income, the Lorenz curve would pass through the points (0, 0), (99, 0), and (100, 100), and the surfaces A and B would be nearly equal, leading to a value of nearly 1 for the Gini coefficient. Therefore the Gini coefficient lies between 0 and 1, sometimes expressed as a percentage (that is, between 0 per cent and 100 per cent)—the higher its value, the more unequal is the income distribution within the economy.

 Business analysis   11.6

In 2011 the US Congressional Budget Office published data on a study it had undertaken on changes in income in that country over the last 28 years. The findings showed that, on average, the income of Americans had grown by over 60 per cent during that period. However, the growth in incomes was uneven; for example, the income of the lowest paid Americans only grew by 18 per cent, whilst the income of the top 1 per cent grew by 275 per cent! Therefore inequality has been growing in the USA, as it also has in Britain (see Figure 11.13 below). A study published by the BBC suggests that the income share of the top 1 per cent of earners is returning to where it was in 1918.

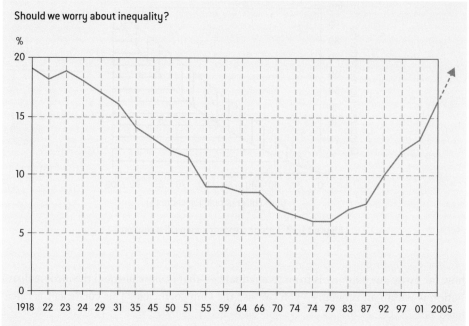

Figure 11.13 Share of all income received by the richest 1 per cent in Britain
Source: Danny Dorling, *Fair Play*, Policy Press, 2012

To change the distribution of income in an economy, a government can use:

■ the tax system—for example, a progressive tax system is one in which the marginal (extra) rate of tax increases as income increases, which reduces the difference between the highest earners and the lower income earners;

■ the benefit system—for example, higher benefits could be given to low income earners and those who are unemployed to reduce the differences between high and low income earners.

}{ *People and economics: Karl Marx*

Karl Marx (1818–1883) was a German economist who wrote the *Communist Manifesto* with Friedrich Engels in 1848, and *Das Kapital* published in stages between 1867 and 1910. Marx argued that the free market was ultimately doomed. Economic power and wealth would be concentrated in relatively few hands creating a proletariat that would rise up creating a 'dictatorship of the proletariat'.

Government intervention

In the previous sections we have discussed a number of possible failures that can occur in the market system such as monopoly power, price instability, asymmetric information, and price instability. We have also considered some of the ways a government might intervene to remedy these, such as a buffer stock scheme, the use of regulators, and taxes. The problems and possible ways of intervening are summarized in Table 11.1.

However, it is possible that government intervention may not actually solve some of these problems very effectively or efficiently, and could in fact generate new ones. We shall examine this next.

Table 11.1 Summary of market failures and possible government actions

Issue	Consequence	Possible government action
Monopoly	Welfare loss	Competition policy
Negative externality	Overproduction	Legislate/taxation
Positive externality	Underproduction	Subsidize/legislate
Public goods	Not provided	State provision
Imperfect information	Over- or underprovision	Regulate
Price instability	Problems in planning	Buffer stock scheme/price controls
Inequality	Perceived unfairness	Redistribute income via taxes and benefits

Government failure

'Government failure' occurs when intervention to reduce some market failures actually creates more inefficiencies in the market. The term was introduced by Roland McKean in 1965 and highlighted that even if markets were not perfectly competitive it may still be better not to intervene. Government failure can occur for the following reasons.

- *Politicians may intervene for political reasons (e.g. to win votes) rather than to remedy a market failure* This may lead to inappropriate decisions being made; for example, inefficient businesses may be subsidized in an area to keep jobs and win votes.

- *Regulatory capture* This occurs when a government organization set up to monitor an industry or business begins to work in its interests rather than those of society as a whole. Years of working with managers in a declining industry, for example, may lead ministers to start sympathizing with their interests—especially if managers and employees in this industry are well organized in terms of lobbying support.

- *Imperfect information* Just as managers and households lack perfect information, so does the government. This may mean that intervention is mistimed or inappropriate because the government has misunderstood the nature of the problem. Intervention may make the situation worse—for example, by overtaxing a negative externality, resulting in less than the socially optimal output being produced.

Problems with financing intervention

If a government wants to intervene in a market, it may need funds to do so. For example, it may need funds to:

- take over and nationalize an industry;
- subsidize merit goods and positive externalities;
- fund organizations to regulate markets, such as competition policy.

These funds may be generated through different types of taxation. For example, direct taxes, such as income tax and corporation tax, are taken directly from the earnings of individuals and companies. Indirect taxes, such as value added tax (VAT), are paid to the government by producers when products are purchased. By introducing such taxes, the government will affect the behaviour of consumers and business, and this may reduce some of the initial benefits of intervention. For example, higher income taxes may reduce the incentive to work; higher corporation taxes may reduce the incentive to invest; and VAT may deter consumption of some products. All these consequences of taxation may create unwelcome side effects of intervention.

Governments can also borrow money by selling bonds (effectively, IOUs). The government agrees to pay a return each year and repay the initial sum on a given date. Selling such bonds may affect markets because, if large sums of money are spent buying bonds, they cannot be used for anything else. A large sale of government bonds may 'crowd out' private investment projects because the money that would have been used for these is now with the government. Again, the intervention may lead to an undesirable consequence.

The theory of the second best

As we have seen, there are many potential failures and imperfections in a free market system; this is why governments intervene in economies to rectify these problems. But governments must be careful not to create more failures by trying to solve the ones that already exist. In raising finance to subsidize merit goods, for example, the government may create distortions elsewhere, such as higher income taxes, leading to less incentive to work.

In fact, the 'theory of the second best' argues that it may be better to leave some failures, because this may lead to a better outcome for society. For example, a monopolist may restrict output, but in the case of a negative externality this may be desirable because, otherwise, there would be overproduction in a free market.

Failures, imperfection, and managers

The existence of failures and imperfections all influence managers' behaviour. A lack of perfect knowledge means that, sometimes, there may be shortages or surpluses in a market. The existence of monopolies may mean that a business buying from such a seller pays a higher price than it would in a free market. Instability makes planning difficult. At the same time, it is useful to understand and anticipate possible government intervention because of its potential impact on costs, regulations, and even market structure.

Summary

A perfect free market would maximize the welfare of society. In reality, however, there are numerous imperfections and market failures which move the economy away from the socially optimal position. In these situations, the government may intervene. Intervention can occur via taxation, subsidies, legislation, or direct provision.

The extent to which a government intervenes will depend on its political philosophy and the extent to which it believes that the free market can work unaided. The recent collapse of many banks across the world because of high risk lending, and the consequent downturn in many economies, has led many governments to reconsider the extent to which they leave markets unregulated.

Checklist

Having read this chapter, you should now understand:

- [ ] what is meant by market failure;
- [ ] what is meant by monopoly power;
- [ ] what is meant by a negative externality;
- [ ] what is meant by the deadweight social burden triangle;
- [ ] what is meant by a positive externality;
- [ ] what is meant by a merit good and a demerit good;
- [ ] what is meant by the immobility of labour;
- [ ] what is meant by public goods;
- [ ] what is meant by regulatory capture;
- [ ] what is meant by asymmetric information;
- [ ] what is meant by crowding out;
- [ ] the possible effects of a maximum or minimum price.

Short answer questions

1. Explain what is meant by a negative externality.
2. How might the government intervene in an economy to rectify the problems of negative externalities?
3. Explain using a diagram what is meant by a welfare loss.

4. What are the key features of a public good?

5. What is meant by a merit good?

6. Explain two causes of labour immobility.

7. Explain two actions that the government might take to reduce labour immobility.

8. What is meant by a buffer stock scheme?

9. Why do queues occur at cinemas?

10. What is meant by monopoly power?

Discussion questions

1. Discuss the reasons why governments need to intervene in the free market.

2. Discuss the ways in which the government may intervene in the free market.

3. Can the free market be trusted?

One step further

Visit our Online Resource Centre at **www.oxfordtextbooks.co.uk/orc/gillespiebusiness2e/** to test your understanding, watch video walk-throughs, and access further information on topics covered in this chapter.

Macroeconomics 12

Learning objectives

In this chapter, we examine the macroeconomy, and the workings of aggregate demand and aggregate supply.

By the end of this chapter, you should:

- ☑ understand the meaning of macroeconomics;
- ☑ understand the circular flow of income;
- ☑ understand different measures of national income;
- ☑ understand what is meant by the standard of living;
- ☑ understand the meaning of aggregate demand and influences on it;
- ☑ understand the meaning of aggregate supply and influences on it;
- ☑ understand equilibrium in the economy;
- ☑ understand the difference between gross domestic product and gross national product;
- ☑ understand the circular flow of income;
- ☑ understand the multiplier;
- ☑ be able to explain the effect of a shift in aggregate demand or aggregate supply on equilibrium in the economy.

© **case study**

My grandmother always tells me that things aren't like they used to be: 'You may have more money these days but are you happier? So much has changed in terms of technology—communications, transport, even the jobs people do now are alien to me,' she said recently. 'Just think about travel—going abroad these days seems as easy as catching a bus to town. I never left the UK until I was forty-five! But at the end of it all, with this so-called progress, are you really better off than we were?' She took a sip of coffee and continued.

'Young people these days,' she said, 'seem to have so many things to worry about—getting a job, getting a house, and then saving enough to pay to bring up children. It all seems so much more difficult than it used to be and you all have to live life at full speed. Even the weekends have disappeared—your bosses email you at home, on the way to work, on the way back from work, and these days you may even be expected to work on Sundays—now that used to be a day of rest when I was a girl. And if you don't keep up there's always someone else they will get to do it instead either in this country or even someone based abroad from what I've heard on the news—so much seems to be produced overseas these days. And to add to it all you have to wait to see a doctor, you probably have to pay to see a dentist, and now you have to pay to go to university. It's a funny sort of progress if you ask me.'

I sat and wondered if grandmother knew more than I thought.

Questions

1. How would you measure the success of an economy?
2. How would you measure the standard of living in a country?
3. Do you think people are better off today than they were 50 years ago?
4. Do you think that the government should focus on getting the economy to grow faster?
5. Do you think that medical care and education should be provided free of charge?

Introduction

So far, we have focused on what happens in specific markets. For example, we have ana-lysed the influences on the demand and supply of labour, shares, and foreign currency. We have examined issues such as the impact of a change in demand or supply conditions in these individual markets, and we have considered the potential differences in the price and output decisions of firms operating in different market structures, such as monopoly and oligopoly. However, each individual market is a part of the whole economy, which is examined in the following chapters.

In this chapter, we analyse factors in the overall economy and consider their significance for business decision-making. This is known as 'macroeconomic analysis' (looking at the big picture) as opposed to 'microeconomic analysis' (looking at a small part of the picture). Variables such as interest rates, exchange rates, inflation, and national income affect businesses throughout the economy, and therefore are macroeconomic factors. The global economic environment is always changing—just look at the debt crisis of many governments in recent years, the concern over the future of the euro currency, and the slowdown in the growth of the Chinese economy; these are examples of macro-factors which could be very important to a business.

Understanding macroeconomics is vital to managers because of the impact of changes in factors such as exchange rates and interest rates on both supply and demand conditions. A fall in the value of the currency and higher prices, for example, will affect a firm's costs and possible levels of demand. In the last few years in the UK economy, interest rates have fallen to their lowest level ever, the economy has shrunk in size, the currency has been weak in value, unemployment has increased significantly, and house prices have been static or fallen. Managers need to understand what determines changes in macro-conditions and how they might change in the future, so that they can plan for these. They need to understand the causes of change and the effects of it. Whereas managers have some control over micro-conditions (for example, their costs, their marketing, and their strategy in relation to their competitors), they have little influence over the macroeconomic climate. Although the collection of decisions by millions of businesses will affect the economy, the decisions of any one firm will have limited effect, so it is especially important for managers to prepare for macroeconomic change because they cannot easily influence it once it happens. The need to understand the economic environment is vital given the dynamic nature of economics. On a day-to-day level, this can be seen by the constant movement in the value of most currencies; on a bigger scale, it can be seen in major changes such as the rise of the Chinese, Indian, and other emerging economies in recent years which have had major implications for the strategies of many businesses, in terms of both possible sales and where they produce.

 ## You and economics

Watch the news, listen to the radio, follow the news feeds, and you will see and hear constant updates on the euro crisis, unemployment rates, government spending cuts, exchange rate changes and inflation rates. The prices of goods in the shops, how much your holiday costs, how easy it is to get a job, and whether you get a pay increase are all linked to macroeconomic issues. Macroeconomics directly affects you, and therefore understanding why these changes have happened and what might happen next are important to you in your personal life and in your career, not least because you can plan accordingly. If you are in an export business or buy in products from abroad, you need an understanding of exchange rates and trade. If you are working in finance, you need to budget for inflation. Macroeconomics will inevitably impact on your job in some way, and so it makes sense to try and get ahead of the wave and not get washed away by it!

When analysing the macroeconomic environment, it is essential to understand **aggregate demand** and **aggregate supply**, and the impact of changes in these on factors such as:

- the growth in the income of the economy, because this might affect demand;
- the rate at which prices in general are increasing (this is called inflation);
- the exchange rate—this is the cost of one currency in terms of another, and changes in it can affect the price of UK products abroad and the cost of imports;
- the labour market—for example, if there is low unemployment it might make it difficult to recruit.

The starting point to understanding aggregate demand and supply is the circular flow of income model.

The circular flow of income

This model highlights how money and goods and services flow around an economy over a given period.

Let us start with a very simple economy comprising two sectors: businesses who provide products in return for revenue, and households who provide their labour to the businesses (see Figure 12.1). Households receive income for working and then spend this on the businesses' goods and services so that the money they earn flows back round (hence the term 'circular flow'). In this very basic model the household spends all its earnings on the output of the businesses and money flows back in return for the output produced. We can see here that the economy is in equilibrium, with the value of what is being produced (output) equalling the value of spending equalling the value of income earned. Therefore the income of an economy over a given period can be measured using the output, the income, or the expenditure:

National income = National output = National expenditure

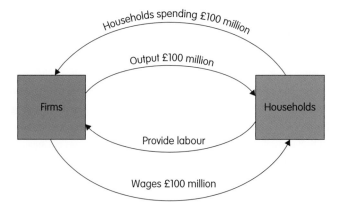

Figure 12.1 Simple circular flow model

Obviously, an economy is more complex than this so we can now add in other features such as government and foreign trade. This is now a four-sector economy with households, firms, government, and trade. In this model we see the following

1. Out of its income a household may save some of its earnings—these savings are known as a withdrawal (or leakage) from the economy and reduce the level of demand because it is money not being spent.

2. Out of its income a household may spend some money abroad on foreign products (imports)—again, this is a withdrawal from the economy because the earnings are not being spent on domestic final goods and services, but are leaking abroad.

3. A government will take some of its citizens' incomes in tax—again, this is not being spent and is a withdrawal.

Out of the income earned by households, savings (S), taxes (T), and import spending (M) are all withdrawals (or leakages) and do not feed back into demand for the output produced domestically. Withdrawals reduce the level of demand in the economy.

However, there are also injections into the economy; these represent other sources of demand for goods and services, apart from household spending. Injections comprise investment spending by the businesses (for example, on new machinery), government spending on final goods and services, and export earnings which represent demand from abroad. If these injections compensate for the withdrawals, the economy is in equilibrium, with what is being produced equalling what is being bought. This means that if the level of planned injections (investment (I) plus government spending (G) plus exports (X)) equals the planned withdrawals (savings (S) plus taxation (T) plus imports (M)), the economy is in equilibrium. For equilibrium in an economy:

$$\text{planned } (I + G + X) = \text{planned } (S + T + M)$$

At this point the total demand for final goods and services equals the amount supplied, i.e. aggregate demand equals aggregate supply. In the example in Figure 12.2, households withdraw £40 million of their earnings and spend £60 million. Injections equal £40 million and precisely compensate for the withdrawals.

If the planned injections do not compensate for the withdrawals, firms will not sell everything that is produced and this will lead to unplanned increases in stocks. In the example shown in Figure 12.3, the planned injections do not compensate for the withdrawals. Demand comprises £60 million from households and £30 million from firms, i.e. £90 million in total. This is not enough to buy the £100 million produced by firms, so businesses will end up with £10 million of unsold stock. The economy is not in equilibrium and businesses will reduce output in the next period as demand is too low.

If the planned injections are greater than the withdrawals there will be too much demand and firms will expand over time. In the example shown in Figure 12.4, the planned injections are greater than the withdrawals so demand is too high. Demand comprises £60 million by households and £50 million by injections. This means that demand is £110 million but output is only £100 million. Firms will have to run down their stocks. The economy is not in equilibrium because demand is too high. Businesses will increase output in the next period.

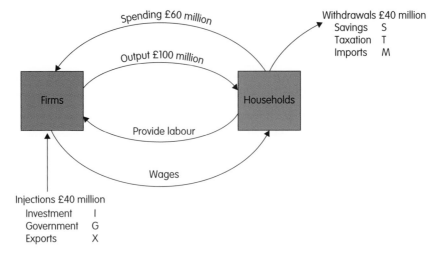

Figure 12.2 Four-sector circular flow model: equilibrium

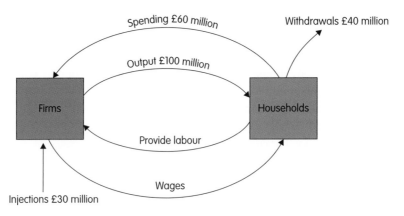

Figure 12.3 Four-sector circular flow model: aggregate demand is too low because planned injections are less than withdrawals

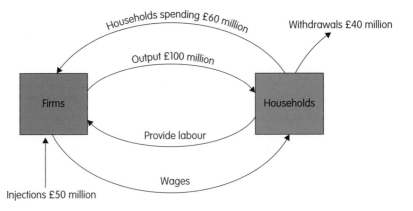

Figure 12.4 Four-sector circular flow model: aggregate demand is too high because planned injections are greater than withdrawals

This more complex circular flow model demonstrates the importance of household spending, the level of withdrawals from the economy, and injections to boost demand. These relationships can be studied in further detail by examining aggregate demand and supply.

 You and economics

To help pay for your studies you work part-time. You are part of the labour input into the economy, helping businesses to produce output which is then sold. The money you earn is spent on items such as food, rent, and travel—you are a consumer in the economy. Each week you are putting a few pounds away in your holiday fund; these are your only savings at the moment. Some tax and national insurance is deducted from your earnings, and some of the money spent on products goes to overseas providers; these are withdrawals from the circular flow because the money spent is not staying with UK producers.

Measures of national income: gross domestic product versus gross national product

The circular flow of income illustrates how income is created in an economy and also shows that this can be measured by considering the value of the output, the income, or expenditure over a given period. In fact, there are several different measures of the income of an economy (see Figure 12.5).

Gross domestic product (GDP) measures the value of the income produced within an economy over a given time period regardless of who owns the factors of production. For example, the GDP of the UK measures the income produced within this country, including the earnings of overseas companies and citizens based here, over a given time period (usually a year).

Gross national product (GNP), by comparison, measures the income of a country's citizens regardless of where they are based in the world. It is calculated by taking GDP, adding on the income earned by UK citizens abroad, and deducting earnings within the UK by non-UK citizens.

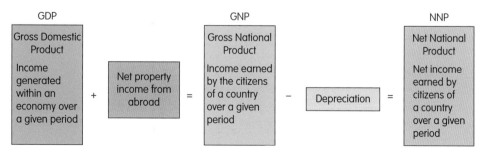

Figure 12.5 Measures of national income

The GDP and GNP figures show the total earnings of an economy or of a country's citizens, respectively. Economists and managers will also be interested in the income per person (that is, GDP per capita or GNP per capita) and in the rate of growth of income. This will be likely to influence factors such as spending patterns and wage rates. For example, if national income is growing at 3 per cent but the population is growing at 5 per cent, the income per person is falling.

You will also see data on 'real' GDP per capita. This considers the income per person but also takes account of inflation—if the income per head doubles but prices double over the same period, then in real terms nothing has changed. Simply measuring income changes is not enough; you need to see what this can buy which means that it is important to take price increases into account as well and calculate real national income or real national income per person. Real GDP per person is the most common measure of the standard of living within a country and is a popular indicator of how well an economy is performing.

 Business analysis   12.1

The GDP of a number of countries (in US dollars) in 2010 was as follows:

Brazil	2,087,889,553,822
USA	14,586,736,313,339
UK	2,261,713,093,830
China	5,926,612,009,750
Netherlands	779,356,291,391
Germany	3,280,529,801,32

What do you think will determine the level of national income in a country?

Source: World Bank: http://www.worldbank.org

 Data analysis   12.1

1. China's GDP per person has been growing at 10 per cent a year at various points in the last few years. If someone were to be earning £10,000 a year now, how much would they earn in five years' time at this growth rate?
2. In the USA, the growth rate is nearer 2 per cent a year. If someone were to earn £10,000 a year now, how much would they earn in five years' time at this growth rate?
3. If GDP growth is 5 per cent and population growth is 7 per cent, is GDP per person rising or falling?
4. If GDP growth is 3 per cent and inflation is 4 per cent, is real GDP growing or not? Explain your reasoning.

Limitations of real GDP per person as a measure of the standard of living

Real GDP per person gives an idea of the purchasing power of an average citizen in a country. However, it has a number of limitations as an indicator of the standard of living.

■ It does not show how income is distributed. This is shown by measuring the Gini coefficient (see p. 324). The bigger this coefficient, the more unequal the distribution of income (e.g. there may be a few very high income earners in the country which is pulling up the average). For example, the distribution of income in Sweden is far more equal than it is in Namibia.

■ It does not take into account how the income is earned. You may end up working 60 hours a week with little or no leisure time; this increases the income of the economy but you may feel worse off. To measure the quality of life you may want to think about factors such as working hours, holidays, stress levels, access to medical care, and health issues.

■ It does not measure the value of non-marketed items. If you had an economy in which there was a high level of barter, goods and services would be exchanged but no income would be calculated. GDP also fails to record sales that are not officially declared; in some economies there is a great deal of activity that is not recorded as people want to avoid tax.

■ It does not reflect the quality of the goods and services. Over time the prices of computers have fallen even though they are much more powerful than they used to be. The quality of the products has risen even though the price, and therefore the national income, has fallen.

People and economics: Corrado Gini

Corrado Gini (1884–1965) was an Italian statistician and sociologist who developed the Gini coefficient. He was a professor at the University of Rome and his statistical work began with using probability when analysing population data. He developed the theory of the Gini coefficient in his 1912 paper 'Variability and mutability'.

Business analysis   12.2

When David Cameron became leader of the Conservative Party, he said 'It's time we admitted that there's more to life than money, and it's time we focused not just on GDP, but on "GWB"—general well-being.'

The Labour Party, which was in government at the time, was also increasingly interested in the concept of well-being. Local authorities were given an obligation to maximize their citizens' well-being, and John Prescott, the deputy prime minister, started to publish a range of quality-of-life indicators, admitting that GDP alone gave little insight into what's really happening in society. Meanwhile, the secretary general of the Paris-based Organization for Economic Co-operation and Development (OECD) highlighted the gulf between what statistics show and how ordinary citizens feel. The OECD stressed that economic factors are not all that matter in people's lives.

The weakness of GDP as an indicator of well-being can be seen by the debt-fuelled crises of the US and UK economies in recent years. Jospeh Stiglitz highlighted that by looking at GDP figures you had no idea whether growth was sustainable or not—in the case of recent growth it obviously wasn't. Then there is the problem that GDP takes the price as being equal to the value of something. So if there is boom which means that assets such as property and shares are valued too highly, GDP figures will be very misleading. Although the US financial sector generated huge profits between 2003 and 2007, the massive losses in 2008 quickly wiped them out. Therefore monitoring GDP figures could send misleading signals to policy-makers.

Therefore the debate concerns what would be a better measure of economic success: equality? health? happiness? Recent attempts include the 'happy planet index' from the New Economics Foundation, a British thinktank, bringing together measures of environmental damage, health, and happiness with raw economic data.

In 2012 the first World Happiness Report was published. This report was commissioned for a United Nations Conference on Happiness, and was edited by Jeffrey Sachs and two happiness experts, Richard Layard of the London School of Economics and John Helliwell of the University of British Columbia. The report finds that the world's happiest countries are in northern Europe (Denmark, Finland, Norway and The Netherlands), and the most miserable are in Africa (Benin, Central African Republic, Sierra Leone, and Togo).

How would you measure the standard of living in a country?

If you were in power what would you do to increase your country's happiness levels?

Aggregate demand and aggregate supply

When examining a particular market, managers have to consider the demand for, and supply of, that product. The same type of analysis can be used for the whole economy, except that this time we are interested in the following.

- Aggregate demand—that is, the total demand in a given period for all final goods and services in an economy. Final goods and services are the products at the end of the transformation process, such as a newly completed house or laptop; the demand for final goods and services includes the demand for all of the intermediate products and components, the raw materials, and other resources that are used in the process.

By measuring demand for final goods and services the demand for all other products used along the way is also captured.

■ Aggregate supply—that is, the total supply of all final goods and services in an economy in a given period with given resources.

In an individual market, equilibrium occurs at the price at which demand equals supply; in the economy as a whole, equilibrium occurs when aggregate demand equals aggregate supply (this is where the planned injection equals the planned withdrawal). The interrelationship between aggregate demand and supply determines the output and income of the economy as a whole.

Aggregate demand

Aggregate demand shows the quantity of final goods and services in an economy that customers are willing and able to buy at each and every price in a given period, when everything other than the price level is held constant (see Figure 12.6). When the price falls, households, firms, and governments can buy more, all other factors unchanged, and this leads to an increase in quantity demanded. A fall in price increases your real income so more can be demanded.

The total planned demand in the economy is made up of the desired spending of four different sectors—that is, households, businesses, the government, and overseas trade (see Figure 12.7).

Aggregate demand is made up of the following.

■ Consumption demand (C)—that is, the demand from households for final goods and services, and the largest element of aggregate demand. It includes spending on items such as food, clothing, and holidays.

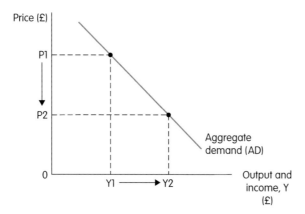

Figure 12.6 The aggregate demand curve

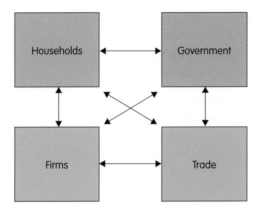

Figure 12.7 The four sectors of the economy

- Investment demand (I)—that is, the demand from businesses for final goods and services. This may be for capital goods such as equipment and machinery or investment in stock.

- Government spending (G)—that is, the demand from the government for final goods and services, such as its spending on education, the military, roads, and health. The spending may be by central or local government.

- Exports (X)—that is, the demand from abroad for final goods and services in the economy, such as sales of British-made Jaguar cars that are sold in the USA but generate income for the UK.

- Imports (M)—that is, spending by domestic households, businesses, and government on foreign goods and services. This is part of the spending of households, firms, or the government that leaves the domestic economy and so has to be deducted from overall spending to show the demand for domestic goods and services. For example, if a household spends £10,000 in total, but £3,000 is on foreign goods, the spending domestically can be calculated as:

$$£10,000 - £3,000 = £7,000$$

Therefore the equation for aggregate demand (AD) can be calculated as:

$$AD = C + I + G + X - M$$

This is a key equation in macroeconomics. For example, the impact of changes in government economic policy can be tracked through the effect on these different elements of aggregate demand. For example, a change in policy may increase consumer spending, boosting aggregate demand, or it may dampen spending by businesses, thus reducing investment. In the next part of this chapter we will examine the different elements of aggregate demand in more detail.

}{ *People and economics: Arthur Pigou*

Arthur Pigou (1827–1959) was a British economist who worked in welfare economics and whose work includes *Wealth and Welfare* in 1912 and *The Economics of Welfare* in 1932. He analysed externalities, and proposed the taxation of negative externalities and subsidies for positive externalities. Amongst his other work Pigou analysed the wealth effect (known as the Pigou effect) that occurs if prices fall. Lower prices lead to a higher real value of savings; this makes people feel wealthier and able to spend more. This leads to an increase in demand.

? *Think about it…* 12.1

How might a significant increase in aggregate demand affect a business's workforce and operational planning?

£ *Business analysis* 12.3

After a long period of stagnation the Japanese economy picked up in 2012. Aggregate demand was increased by government spending that helped fuel a gradual recovery from the 2011 earthquake and tsunami. A recovery in private consumption has also helped boost the economy. However, analysts were still cautious about the future, as growth slowed in Europe, China, and the US. Analysts said that whilst consumer spending was improving, the key to sustainability for the economic recovery was exports.

Discuss what might determine the level of exports from Japan.

Why might export growth be more desirable than government led growth?

Consumption (C)

The level of consumption spending in an economy is likely to depend strongly on the level of households' current income. With more income, consumption is likely to increase (see Figure 12.8). The importance of current income as a determinant of consumption was highlighted by the economist Keynes. According to Keynes:

$$C = a + bYd$$

where:

- 'a' represents an autonomous level of consumption spending—even if income were zero, consumers spend a certain amount of money to survive; this is known as dis-saving;

- 'b' represents the marginal propensity to consume (that is, the amount spent out of each extra pound) which determines the slope of the consumption function; the marginal propensity consumer (MPC) is given by the equation:

$$MPC = (\text{Change in consumption})/(\text{Change in income})$$

For example, if the MPC is 0.6, this means that for every extra pound a consumer earns 60 pence is spent on consumption.

- 'Yd' represents disposable current income—that is, the income after tax that consumers have available to spend. For example if $C = 10 + 0.6 \, Yd$, this means that if disposable income is £900 billion the consumption spending in the economy would be:

$$C = 10 + (0.6 \times 900) = 10 + 540 = £550bn$$

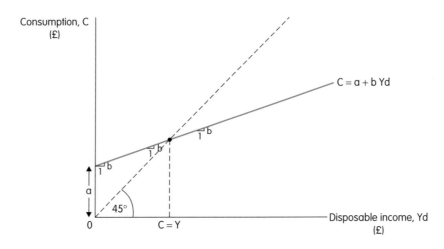

Figure 12.8 The consumption function

Data analysis 12.2

$$C = 10 + 0.8Yd$$

$$Yd = £500m$$

1. What is the level of consumption in this economy?
2. What is the level of saving (given that household income is used for either consumption or saving)?
3. How much is saved out of each extra pound? (This is called the 'marginal propensity to save'.)
4. How much would be spent if income were zero? (This is called 'dis-saving'.)
5. What do you think the equation would be for the savings function?

As well as disposable current income, the level of consumption spending in an economy may be affected by other factors.

- *Expectations of future income* What households spend may be influenced by what they think they are going to earn over the long term, and not only their present income. Imagine that an individual loses his/her job, but expects to find a new one fairly soon: his/her present level of consumption would not necessarily drop significantly, even though his/her current income has, because of his/her long-term projected earnings. This highlights the importance of expectations in influencing household spending decisions. The economist Milton Friedman argued that households' consumption is related more to their 'permanent income'—that is, their expected average income over their lifespan—rather than what they are actually earning at any given moment. This means that changes in the level of current income in the economy may not lead to significant changes in consumption if households expect the economy to return to its long-term path soon. This suggests that consumption would be less vulnerable to changes in current income than Keynes suggested.

- *Interest rate* Interest rates reflect the cost of borrowing money from a bank and the possible returns you might gain with your savings. With higher interest rates there are higher returns on money saved, so there is more incentive for households to save and less desire to borrow. This means that the marginal propensity to save increases and the marginal propensity to consume rises, so that the level of consumption is likely to fall.

- *The prices of assets* If assets (such as houses and shares) increase in value, this will influence households' views of their wealth and therefore their confidence when it comes to spending. With greater wealth, more spending is likely.

- *Confidence.* The amount consumers are likely to spend will depend on how confident they are about the future. If they are worried about their jobs and uncertain whether they will get a pay increase, this may lead to more savings and less consumption.

? *Think about it ...*   12.2

Which of the following might increase the level of consumption in the economy?

A: A rise in house prices.

B: A decrease in interest rates.

C: A rise in taxes on expenditure.

D: A rise in taxes on income.

Investment (I)

Investment represents spending on capital goods, such as machinery and equipment, as well as investment into stocks. This capital expenditure is spending by businesses for future production; for example, it might involve the purchase of a new IT system, a new logistics system, or a new office block, all of which are intended to help production. As we saw in Chapter 8, investment is likely to be strongly influenced by interest rates and estimates of future returns. Lower interest rates reduce the cost of borrowing and make more projects look financially attractive. This is shown by a movement along the marginal efficiency of capital (MEC) schedule as the price of investment has changed (see Figures 12.9 and 12.10).

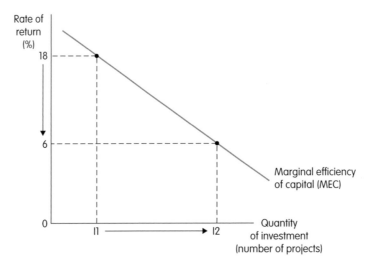

Figure 12.9 The marginal efficiency of capital

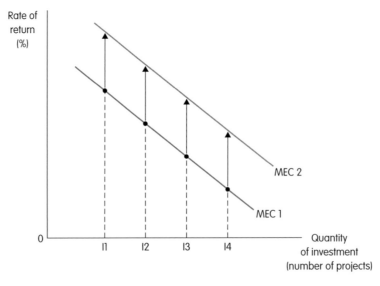

Figure 12.10 A shift in the marginal efficiency of capital

When the interest rate is at 18 per cent there are I1 projects that are worth investing in. Up until I0 the expected return on a project (the MEC) is greater than the cost of borrowing. The business is investing up until the point where the marginal benefit equals the marginal cost and therefore is maximizing profits. If the interest rate falls to 6 per cent, more projects now have a higher return than the cost of borrowing and so the level of investment increase to I2. However, the MEC schedule may shift if there is a change in the expected profits of projects. For example, if expectations change and managers become more pessimistic about likely levels of demand, the MEC would shift down; lower returns would be expected on projects and, for any given interest rate, the number of profitable projects would fall.

To assess the expected profits of projects, managers must consider future costs and revenues. Naturally, this includes a great deal of forecasting and relies on assumptions and presumptions about the economy. News about changes in government policy or how the economy is doing can shift the MEC curve and influence investment. Therefore investment is potentially quite unstable, and yet can have a large effect on aggregate demand.

In the UK in 2012 there was great concern over the recovery of the economy, which had started to shrink in 2008. Many individuals and businesses feared that growth was likely to be slow for many years to come. There were also worries about how other European countries were doing; if they were struggling, it would make it difficult to sell to them. The combined effect of this was a fall in corporate investment and a significant increase in corporate saving. Businesses held on to their profits in case they would need them in the future; they did not invest as much because they were worried that it would be money wasted.

 ## Business analysis 12.4

In 2012 steelmaking returned to Teesside with the relighting of the blast furnace at the former Corus plant in Redcar. Its new owner, SSI, had invested millions getting the huge furnace ready, which had shut down when the plant was closed by its previous owner, Tata Steel, in 2010.

Many of the 1,600 work-force who had lost their jobs two years previously have been re-employed by Thai-based SSI.

Win Viriyaprapaikit, president of SSI, said that he believed that the investment made at Teesside would result in a very successful business which will benefit all the stakeholders involved, including the local community and employees for generations to come. Initially, all the steel produced in Redcar will be shipped to Thailand, but it was hoped some could be used in the UK to support the wind turbine manufacturing industry.

Discuss the factors that SSI would have considered before investing in the Redcar plant.

Government spending (G)

This represents spending by central and local government on final goods and services, such as public services, including education, health care, and the armed forces, in a given period. The level of this spending will be strongly influenced by government policy and the perceived position of the economy at any given time. An interventionist government is likely to spend more than a government that is more laissez-faire and wants to leave the market system to function.

The amount of spending by a government will also depend on how much it thinks it can afford to intervene. To spend more, it must borrow more and/or increase taxes; the consequence of this may have negative effects on the economy. For example, raising more finance by selling bonds (IOUs) may require higher interest rates, which may reduce household borrowing and spending. Raising revenue through higher income taxes may reduce the incentive of employees to work. The government must weigh up the costs and benefits of more spending in any situation. In the years after the global economic crisis, in which many governments had struggled to pay their debts, there was a push in many countries to reduce government spending as part of an 'austerity' programme. This in itself reduces aggregate demand and led to several protests about the dangers of this approach.

£ *Business analysis*   12.5

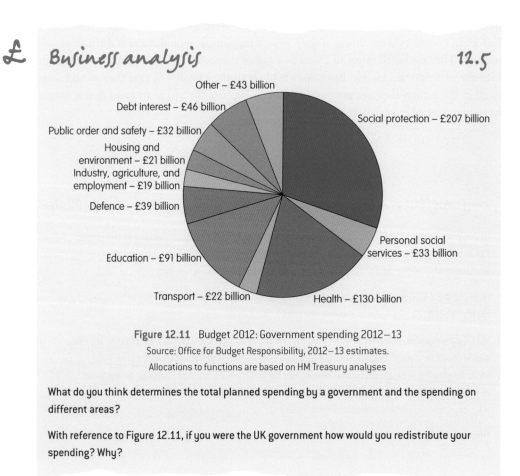

Figure 12.11   Budget 2012: Government spending 2012–13
Source: Office for Budget Responsibility, 2012–13 estimates.
Allocations to functions are based on HM Treasury analyses

What do you think determines the total planned spending by a government and the spending on different areas?

With reference to Figure 12.11, if you were the UK government how would you redistribute your spending? Why?

Export spending (X)

This represents spending on domestic products from abroad. This spending will be determined by the consumption patterns abroad. The levels of income overseas, the cost of borrowing, and the expectations of their future income levels by foreign businesses and households will all be important determinants of demand for UK exports. Other key factors affecting a country's exports include the extent to which its firms are allowed to trade abroad (sometimes other governments put barriers on this) and the cost of one currency in terms of another (that is, the exchange rate). For example, if the pound is low in value against other currencies, this makes UK products cheaper in other currencies, which should stimulate export demand.

Import spending (M)

This represents spending on foreign products and is linked to the overall levels of consumption in a country, because it represents the spending that 'leaks' from an economy abroad. The amount of money that goes abroad depends on factors such as the range and quality of products produced domestically compared with products produced overseas, the exchange rate, and whether barriers to trade exist. The marginal propensity to import (MPM) refers to the extra spending on imports out of each extra pound earned; the higher the MPM, the more of any earnings that are spent abroad.

Movements along versus shifts in aggregate demand

Aggregate demand is inversely related to price. As the general price level in an economy falls, customers can afford more products, given a level of nominal income and wealth. In real terms, households are better off if prices fall and so the quantity demanded of products increases. Therefore a change in prices leads to a movement along the aggregate demand.

A shift in aggregate demand will occur if, at each and every price, there is a change in quantity that individuals or organizations are willing and able to spend on products in the economy. This could be because of a change in consumption or a change in injections or withdrawals.

A shift to the right (i.e. an increase) in aggregate demand may occur for the following reasons.

■ *An increase in consumption* This may occur if households have greater confidence in the future of the economy, making them more willing to spend money. If the government is perceived to have effective economic policies and the economy is thought to be growing quickly, this might mean that customers worry less about the future and therefore may be more willing to spend more. An increase in spending might also occur if taxes on household incomes are reduced, increasing the amount of income consumers have left over after tax to spend (this is known as 'disposable income'), or if interest rates fall, making it cheaper to borrow.

■ *An increase in investment* This might occur if businesses have become more optimistic about the future state of the economy. If managers believe that demand for their products is likely to increase in the future because of a strong economy, they may be more likely to invest now in anticipation of higher rewards in the future. They will invest in equipment, machines, and transport to be able to produce more for the higher levels of demand anticipated. Investment might also increase if interest rates fall, because this reduces the cost of borrowing; with lower interest rates, it is cheaper to borrow and more investment projects become affordable. The precise effect of a change in interest rates on investment depends on how interest elastic investment demand is.

- *An increase in government spending* This might occur because of a change in government policy. In 2012 the Dutch government was voted out because of its austerity programme, as voters were looking for more intervention by the government to boost aggregate demand. The intention was to increase spending (or at least not reduce it as much), reducing the downward effect on aggregate demand.

- *An increase in exports or a reduction in imports* Exports might increase if incomes abroad increase or the exchange rate is lower, which makes UK goods and services cheaper in foreign currency.

Throughout much of the early 2000s demand in the UK economy was growing. These were years of growth as demand rose relatively fast each year. However, in the last few years the growth in demand has been slow, and at times it has fallen. You can see this by the reduction in orders for firms' products, the closures in the high street, and the rise in unemployment as businesses cut back. The government would like aggregate demand to increase, but is reluctant to spend more because of the amount of borrowing it is already doing. Its solution is to attempt to encourage other sectors of the economy to push up demand. This is known as 'rebalancing the economy', and the government aims to place more emphasis on the private sector and less on the public sector. For example, the government hopes to encourage exports and business investment. It is less keen to promote more consumption spending, because in the past this has resulted in households increasing their debt, which has led to difficulties in future repayments.

Policies developed by governments to influence the elements of aggregate demand are called **demand-side policies**. Policies to reduce aggregate demand are called **deflationary**; policies to boost aggregate demand are called **reflationary**. From a manager's perspective the aggregate demand model highlights that demand for goods and services will not only come from households but also come from governments, foreign buyers, and other businesses, and that it is liable to change, which in turn will influence demand for their products.

The multiplier

If there is an increase in aggregate demand this can have a multiplier effect on the output of the economy. This is because an initial injection into an economy will lead to further rounds of spending. The size of the multiplier will depend on the marginal propensity to consume. Assume that the marginal propensity to consume is 0.8. This means that for each extra £1, 80 pence (0.8) is spent on consuming products domestically. Assume that there is an injection of £100 million into an economy—for example, if the government decides to invest in the infrastructure of the economy, such as a major building project. The businesses that build these projects will earn £100 million; this will go to staff for wages, to suppliers for materials, and to investors as profits. Each of these groups is likely to spend some of their extra earnings. If 0.8 is spent, this will create another £80 million of demand for other goods and services. Staff may be buying food and consumer electronics, investors may use their profits to buy products, and the suppliers will be replenishing stocks. Therefore this £80 million creates more demand in the economy which will become income for whoever supplies these products (e.g. the producers of the food, the consumer electronics, and the stocks). A proportion of this £80 million, say £64 million ($0.8 \times £80m$) has now been earned and will be spent on further goods and services, and this multiplier process continues.

Therefore the initial injection of £100 million has created a spending of:

$$£100m + £80m + £64m + \cdots$$

This series of rounds of spending will eventually add up to £500 million. At each stage 0.8 of the income earned is spent, leading to income for others of which 0.8 is again spent. The higher the marginal propensity to consume the more that is spent at each stage and the larger the multiplier.

The multiplier is given by:

$$1/(1 - MPC)$$

For example, if the MPC is 0.5 the multiplier is $1/(1 - 0.5) = 1/0.5 = 2$. Any injection into the economy leads to an increase in output that is twice as big.

If the MPC is bigger (say 0.8) the multiplier will also be bigger: $1/(1 - 0.8) = 1/0.2 = 5$. An initial injection into the economy leads to an increase in output that is five times as great. So in the earlier example an initial injection of £100 million leads to a total increase of £500 million.

Whether the multiplier will take full effect will depend on the extent to which money that is earned is then spent. Some of the effect may be on additional output, but some may simply lead to higher prices; this depends on the capacity of the economy and aggregate supply. If there is not much capacity, an increase in spending will affect prices more than output. The conditions affecting aggregate supply are examined next.

 You and economics

You have noticed lower levels of demand in the economy in recent years. Shops in the high street are sitting empty, there have been cut-backs in almost every government department you can mention—the armed forces, the police, and the civil service—and a lot more people are unemployed in your area. You and your friends are not sure whether you will get a job at the end of your degree course, given the labour market (although you hope that your choice of degree will make you more employable) and all your friends and family seem worried about the future of the economy in the next few years. You can see the problem—if people are worried, they are likely to save rather than spend and this can make the situation worse.

An increase in elements of aggregate demand, such as consumption, investment, government spending, and exports, will shift the aggregate demand outwards, showing more demand at any price level (see Figure 12.12).

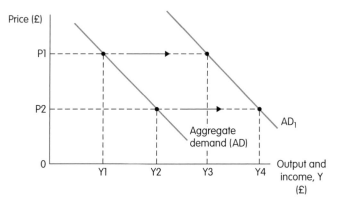

Figure 12.12 The aggregate demand curve

Aggregate supply

The aggregate supply schedule shows the amount of final goods and services that an economy can produce at each and every price, all other things unchanged, given the resources available in an economy at any given moment. The aggregate supply curve is generally upward-sloping: as the price level increases, firms can afford to produce more, and a higher price is needed to cover higher costs. A change in price is shown as a movement along the aggregate supply curve; it leads to a change in the quantity supplied. The amount that an economy can produce is a critical element of the economic well-being of a country; no matter what demand there is, a country needs the ability to produce the products.

The position of the aggregate supply curve depends on the availability and quality of resources in the economy at any given moment. For example:

- the number of people of working age in the population and the skills of these employees—this can be affected by factors such as demographic change, school-leaving age, the education system, and retirement age;
- the level of investment and the quality of technology—this can be affected by interest rates, expectations of future returns, and government incentives to encourage investment;
- the amount and quality of land—this may be affected by the availability of natural resources and the way the land is used (e.g. the way in which agricultural land is farmed).

With more, or better quality, resources, aggregate supply should increase. For example, with more investment in capital equipment, better technology, or an increase in the supply of labour, more output could be produced. This would be shown by a shift of the aggregate supply curve to the right. At each and every price, more can be produced. **Supply-side policies** are aimed at increasing the amount an economy can produce. To grow over time the aggregate supply must increase.

 ## Economics and employability

Tell us your name and a bit about your role at EEF.

My job title is 'Economist' and my main responsibilities are pretty varied. The organization I work for is the representative body for manufacturers in the UK, so my work involves developing an understanding of how the economic and policy environment affects manufacturers, and then communicating this to policy-makers and the press.

In practice this means that I am involved in a series of research reports, and I speak directly with manufacturers on a regular basis. As an economics team we use our research to inform our views on economic policy, and we lobby government on relevant policy areas. I also regularly blog and tweet about manufacturing.

In what ways is an understanding of economics useful in your work?

An understanding of economics is pretty fundamental to what I do! For example, most of our policy arguments are based around understanding the incentives that would encourage companies to invest and grow in the UK.

In what ways does economic change affect your clients?

Economic change doesn't affect my work directly, but it affects EEF's member companies. For example, the recent credit crunch meant that access to credit became constrained, and in many cases it became harder for companies to borrow the money that they needed to grow.

Did you study economics at university as part of your studies, and, if so, how has it helped you in your work?

I studied economics as part of Philosophy, Politics and Economics (PPE) and I couldn't do my job without it! In particular, I think that the fact that I regularly write on EEF's blog means that I need to have a broad understanding of macroeconomic issues (rather than some of the more micro manufacturing-specific issues that I have learnt on the job).

What skills are important in your role?

A wide range of skills: the ability to take a view on the economic situation based on both qualitative and quantitative evidence; the ability to work to tight time-scales; the ability to communicate with a wide range of audiences—and communicate often quite technical issues in a simple way; the ability to understand arguments, and their flaws, quickly; also, the ability to work with a wide range of people is key.

? *Think about it ...*   12.4

1. What do you think determines how many people are willing and able to work at each wage level?

2. If one business produces more, what impact does this have on the aggregate supply in the economy?

3. What do you think influences the number of businesses that start up in an economy each year?

The price elasticity of aggregate supply

The price elasticity of aggregate supply shows how responsive the quantity supplied in the economy is to changes in the price level. It is shown by the slope of the aggregate supply curve (see Figure 12.13). This is important, because if aggregate demand changes, the price elasticity of supply shows how much of the effect is on output and how much is on prices.

At low levels of output, for which there are many spare resources in the economy and the level of unemployment is high, aggregate supply is likely to be very sensitive to price. A relatively small increase in price may lead to significant increases in output, because managers are eager to start producing more and the extra costs of doing so are not high as resources are readily available and have been sitting idle. For example, if there is office space available, and people ready and waiting to work, businesses can increase output without needing a large increase in price to cover the extra costs. Resources are under-employed, making supply relatively easy to increase. This means that when the economy is operating well below capacity (the economy's potential output), aggregate supply is price elastic (for example, between Y1 and Y2).

However, as the economy expands it becomes increasingly difficult to produce more because resources are in greater demand and the price of factors of production, such as

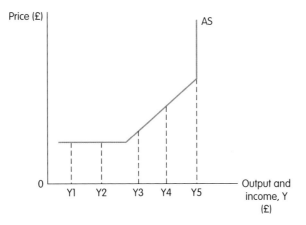

Figure 12.13 Aggregate supply

labour and land, has to increase because of the higher demand. More firms are competing for limited resources. Therefore the aggregate supply curve becomes steeper because larger increases in price are needed to bring about a given increase in output.

At Y5, the economy is at full employment. This means that resources are fully employed and the economy is producing at its full capacity; it has reached its potential output. Businesses cannot produce any more, given the existing level of resources. Supply in the economy at this point is totally price inelastic. Whatever happens to price, the quantity of products supplied cannot increase. Full employment means that, in the labour market, all those willing and able to work are working. Note, however, that this does not mean that unemployment is zero, because there will always be some people unwilling or unable to work at a given wage.

? *Think about it …* 12.5

Do you think that aggregate supply in your economy is likely to be price elastic or inelastic at the moment? Explain your reasoning.

*Data analysis* 12.3

1. If a 2 per cent price increase led to a 6 per cent increase in the quantity supplied, what is the price elasticity of supply? Is supply price elastic or inelastic? Explain your answer.
2. If the price elasticity of supply was +0.6, what would be the effect on the quantity supplied of a 3 per cent increase in prices?
3. Explain why aggregate supply might be price elastic or inelastic.

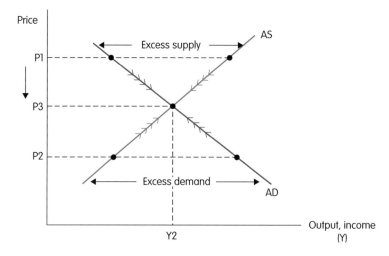

Figure 12.14 Equilibrium in the economy

Macroeconomic equilibrium: aggregate demand and supply

In the macroeconomy, just as in one specific market, the price level should adjust to bring about equilibrium. If the general price level is at P1, for example, there is excess supply in the economy (see Figure 12.14) given the aggregate demand and supply conditions. Producers are willing and able to produce more than is demanded. This puts downward pressure on prices; as prices fall, this reduces the quantity that businesses want to produce and increases the quantity demanded. This process continues until equilibrium is reached.

If the price is at P2, there will be excess demand in the economy and upward pressure on prices. As prices increase, this leads to an increase in the quantity supplied, because producers can afford to produce more, and a decrease in the quantity demanded, because products are more expensive. This process continues until equilibrium is reached.

Therefore equilibrium in the economy is determined by aggregate demand and supply conditions. Demand and supply in the economy can change as a result of factors beyond the control of the government, and therefore governments often have to respond to such changes to try to achieve their desired price and output targets.

Managers will be interested in future changes in the equilibrium of economies because this might affect factors such as the income of their target export markets or the costs of items bought in from abroad.

Shifts in aggregate demand and aggregate supply

Assume that an economy is at equilibrium at P1,Y1 in Figure 12.15. If there is an increase in aggregate demand in the economy, the aggregate demand schedule will shift to the right; more will be demanded at each and every price. This shift could be because of increased government spending, more household expenditure, and/or more spending

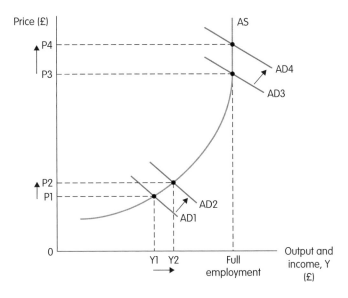

Figure 12.15 The effect of a change in the aggregate demand

from abroad. The consequence of this shift is that, at the old price level, there is excess demand; prices will increase, thereby reducing the quantity demanded and increasing the quantity supplied. The new equilibrium occurs with a higher price and a higher quantity demanded, as can be seen from the movement from P1,Y1 to P2,Y2.

An increase in aggregate demand is likely to lead to an increase in output in the economy and the price level. However, the relative impact of a shift on price and quantity will depend on the extent of the shift and the price elasticity of the aggregate supply.

At low levels of output, when aggregate supply is price elastic, an increase in aggregate demand leads to a significant increase in output relative to the price increase. As demand continues to increase, the demand for resources starts to bid up their costs more and, increasingly, the effect is on price rather than output (compare the effect on price and quantity of an increase in aggregate demand from AD3 to AD4 with that of an increase from AD1 to AD2). At full employment, when the economy is at maximum capacity, an increase in aggregate demand increases prices and does not affect the amount produced.

Therefore the price elasticity of the aggregate supply schedule is crucial in terms of the impact of an increase in aggregate demand. If the economy is in equilibrium below full capacity, governments may well want an increase in aggregate demand to boost output, and the impact on prices will not be significant. But as the economy approaches full employment, increases in demand simply lead to higher prices; more demand for products bids up prices of resources and makes the final goods and services more expensive.

Economists often disagree about the price elasticity of aggregate supply in an economy, and therefore about the effects and desirability of an increase in demand. **Keynesian economists** believe that the economy is often below full employment and that a government should intervene in such circumstances to boost aggregate demand. **Classical economists** believe that the economy is nearer to full employment and so any increase in aggregate demand is likely mainly to affect prices. This is a fundamental difference in economic thinking which leads to very different views of government policy. Keynesians stress the need for intervention and the role of government in boosting aggregate demand. Classical economists do not think this increases growth, which means that the emphasis should be on supply-side policies. The differences between Keynesians and classical economists centre on the speed with which markets clear. Classical economists believe markets work effectively and clear quickly. This means that the economy quickly returns to its long-run equilibrium; if the economy starts at its potential output it will quickly return to this, whatever shock happens, and so supply is inelastic.

? Think about it...   12.6

What is the effect on the equilibrium price and output in an economy of:

A: a shift to the right of aggregate demand?

B: a shift to the right of aggregate supply?

C: a shift to the left of aggregate demand?

D: a shift to the left of aggregate supply?

What is the likely effect on the equilibrium price and quantity in the economy of the following? Explain your answers.

A: Higher levels of productivity in the economy.

B: Lower incomes in export markets.

C: Cheaper borrowing for households.

D: Higher income tax rates.

E: A better trained work force.

F: Lower interest rates.

G: An increase in oil prices.

The global downturn 2008

The global downturn of 2008 and 2009 was on such a scale and occurred so swiftly that few managers (or indeed governments) were ready for it.

   The origins of the crash began in the USA in what is known as the 'sub-prime market'. US banks had been providing loans and mortgages to high risk individuals; these were potentially very profitable, but the risk of non-payment was high, making these loans 'less than prime' (i.e. sub-prime). An increase in loan incentives combined with a long-term trend of rising housing prices encouraged borrowers to apply for large mortgages, believing that they could meet the repayments and end up with property worth far more than they paid for it. Banks were willing to lend, thinking that an increase in house prices would ensure that they had sufficient collateral. This lending boosted aggregate demand and this grew faster than aggregate supply, increasing the value of assets such as property.

Problems occurred when US interest rates increased from 1 to 5.35 per cent between 2004 and 2006. This increased repayment costs and led to many borrowers defaulting on their loans. This meant that banks lost the money they lent. Given the global nature of business nowadays, it affected banks all over the world. US banks had bundled together millions of mortgages and sold them on to other banks in other countries; this reduced their own exposure to some extent, but had extended the risk to banks worldwide. Therefore the defaults affected financial institutions globally. Warning signs appeared in July 2007, when the investment bank Bear Stearns announced that many of its investors had lost their money. It gradually became clear quite how many banks all over the world were affected. This, in turn, contributed to an unwillingness to lend, which became known as the 'credit crunch'. Banks were reluctant to lend to businesses and households because they were afraid that the borrowers would default; they were also reluctant to lend to each other. Typically, banks lend to each other whenever one needs support; every bank will have times when the repayments that it receives on its loans do not come at the right time relative to requests from their customers to withdraw their funds. In these instances, banks borrow off each other. At a time when some banks began declaring huge losses, organizations within the financial system became wary of lending to each other. For example, in September 2008 Lehman Brothers announced a loss of US$3,900 million for the three months to August; it collapsed soon after this, sending shock waves all over the world and throughout the global financial system. The collapse in lending led to a major reduction in aggregate demand in economies worldwide.

Households and firms were unable to borrow as much as they wanted, which significantly reduced their spending and investment. In the UK, the recession became official in January 2009, following two quarters of negative growth. The global downturn affected many aspects of economies, including the following:

- share prices tumbled, reducing the value of individuals' savings and pensions;
- house prices fell, reducing the value of the largest asset of most households;
- many businesses closed or cut back, leading to millions of people worldwide looking for jobs.

The impact of such changes led to great concerns as individuals worried about their jobs, their savings, and their future when they retired. The value of millions of assets was reduced within months. The effects of 2008 are still reverberating around the world. In 2012 the UK economy shrank again and there were continued concerns over when the recovery would take place. In the next chapter we examine government economic policies and consider what governments might do to return to faster economic growth.

Summary

Macroeconomics involves the analysis of the economy as a whole, rather than one particular market. The total demand in the economy is known as 'aggregate demand'; the total supply in the economy is known as 'aggregate supply'. Equilibrium in the economy occurs when aggregate demand equals aggregate supply. Changes in the state of the economy will have major implications for businesses. An increase in aggregate demand will affect sales, and may also affect the ease of attracting resources if there are more firms competing for them. Changes in aggregate supply may affect price levels generally and the ease of recruitment. On both the demand and supply sides, macroeconomic changes can affect the success of every business. Macro-factors are beyond the control of managers, which makes it even more important to monitor their development and be prepared for them, if possible.

Checklist

Having read this chapter, you should now understand:

- [ ] the circular flow of income;
- [ ] gross domestic product;
- [ ] gross national product;
- [ ] the meaning of aggregate demand;
- [ ] the meaning of consumption and investment;
- [ ] the meaning of government spending;
- [ ] the meaning of exports and imports;
- [ ] the multiplier;
- [ ] the marginal propensity to consume;
- [ ] the meaning of aggregate supply.

Short answer questions

1. What is meant by an injection into the economy? Give an example.
2. What is meant by a withdrawal from the economy? Give an example.
3. What is meant by aggregate demand? What is the difference between GDP and GNP?
4. What is meant by aggregate supply?
5. Give two reasons why investment might increase.
6. What is meant by real GDP per capita?
7. What is meant by the multiplier?
8. What is the effect of an increase in aggregate demand on the equilibrium price and output if aggregate supply is totally price inelastic?

9. Give two reasons why aggregate demand might increase.

10. Give two reasons why aggregate supply might increase.

Discussion questions

1. To what extent do you think increasing GDP is a good target for governments?

2. Should governments try and increase aggregate demand?

3. What do you think determines how much households spend on consumption?

One step further

Visit our Online Resource Centre at **www.oxfordtextbooks.co.uk/orc/gillespiebusiness2e/** to test your understanding, watch video walk-throughs, and access further information on topics covered in this chapter.

Government macroeconomic policy

13

Learning objectives

By the end of this chapter you should understand:

- ☑ typical government economic objectives;
- ☑ what is meant by fiscal policy;
- ☑ automatic and discretionary fiscal policy;
- ☑ deflationary and inflationary gaps;
- ☑ the difference between a budget deficit and national debt;
- ☑ what is meant by monetary policy;
- ☑ how fiscal and monetary policy can affect the economy;
- ☑ the meaning of supply-side and demand-side policies;
- ☑ the difficulties of using these policies effectively.

Case study

'What I don't understand is why the government seems so set on cutting spending. I can see that this saves money in the short term but surely it damages the economy, and if the economy does badly so does the government. If I was the government I would just print money whenever anyone needed it. This leads to more jobs and spending and then everyone's happy. I've never really understood why the government worries if it is in debt or not. It controls the printing presses so why not just print more money if you need it? It's the same when people start worrying about inflation—if prices are going up then the government should print money so everyone can still afford things and there's no problem.

'As far as I can see the government needs to get far more involved and start taking responsibility for the economy. It's all very well and good to say we are in a recession but they need to get us out of it. Call me simple but they've got the resources and just need to get on with pumping money into the economy,' said Harry, an artist, to his wife, Margo.

'Yes dear,' replied Margo, an economist, 'if only life were that simple.'

Questions

1. What do you think the UK government spends its money on?

2. Where do you think the UK government gets its money from?

3. Do you think that the government should print money if the economy is only growing slowly? Why might this be a problem?

4. What else do you think a government could do apart from spend more to help an economy grow faster?

5. To what extent do you think the success of an economy depends on its government?

Introduction

All governments will have various macroeconomic objectives and will intervene in the economy to try to achieve these. For example, the government may want to achieve:

- **full employment** in the economy, so that all those willing and able to work at the given wage are working;

- **economic growth,** so that the income of the economy is increasing each year;

- **stable prices,** so that any price increases are relatively low and are predictable;

■ **an appropriate level of export spending relative to imports**—for example a government may be worried if the country is spending too much on importing products and is not exporting enough, so it may aim to balance these inflows and outflows.

Controlling the economy is very important for a government because of its impact on the voters. A government will want to maximize the welfare of its citizens and this will include their economic well-being. 'It's the economy stupid' was a phrase in Bill Clinton's campaign for US President against George Bush in 1992. Although Bush had seemed in a strong position because of his foreign policy, weaknesses in the economy enabled Clinton to attack Bush's record and be elected. This highlighted how important providing a stable and positive economic environment is to a government wanting to be re-elected.

From a manager's perspective, he/she will also want a government that provides an economic environment allowing businesses to trade easily, encourages growth, and helps planning. Decisions by a government on its priorities will influence the combinations of policies it uses, and this in turn will affect a firm's costs and demand.

 ## You and economics

It is coming up to election time and you have been listening to all the politicians. They all seem to promise the same things: more jobs, more growth and a higher standard of living for everyone. You have read their literature, and they all seem to say that they can bring about more exports, less unemployment, and a higher GDP. All well and good to promise, but how will they do this? Some argue that the key is for the government to intervene more; others seem to think that the key is to let the markets work without government getting so involved. If only you knew who to believe.

 ## Economics and employability

Tell us your name and a bit about your role.
I work for a major UK financial services organization in the Markets and International Banking Division. My role is Director, Strategy.

In what ways is an understanding of economics useful in your work?
Economics is critical in terms of my understanding of markets, business climates, and growth. Macroeconomics rather than microeconomics tends to play a bigger role in the work I do.

In what ways does economic change affect your clients?
The types of clients I work with are corporate, small and medium sized enterprises, and financial institutions. For these clients, economic change has an enormous impact. For example, any change in monetary policy impacts upon borrowing costs and foreign exchange movements which, in turn,

affect clients' revenues and profitability. Changes in fiscal policy impact particular client sectors and therefore can make one economy more friendly than another (e.g. from a tax perspective). Economic change also has a big impact on clients' costs. For example, inflation impacts on input costs and labour costs.

Many of our financial institution clients will try to capitalize on economic change through entering into equity, foreign exchange, fixed income, and/or commodity transactions.

Did you study economics at university as part of your studies, and, if so, how has it helped you in your work?
I studied a macroeconomics course at university. I actually studied in America and, although my degree was in the hard sciences, I went to a liberal arts college and thus the curriculum required to graduate was much broader. I loved the course at the time. I then went on to study more economics during my MBA. Economics helps me enormously in my work and I'm always seeking to learn more.

What skills are important in your role?
A number of skills are essential in my role. A combination of numerical, analytical, and critical thinking skills is crucial. This is combined with an ability to work under pressure and to very tight deadlines, whilst maintaining attention to detail. Finally, an understanding of economics, finance, and financial markets is key.

Government economic policies

To achieve its objectives, a government can use fiscal and monetary policies (see Figure 13.1).

- *Fiscal policies* involve changes in government spending, and the taxation and benefit system, to affect the aggregate supply and demand in the economy.
- *Monetary policies* involve the use of interest rates and control over the amount of money in the economy.

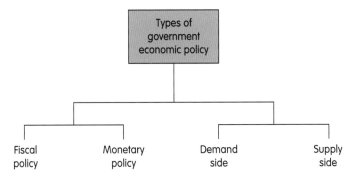

Figure 13.1 Types of government economic policy

Fiscal or monetary decisions may be 'demand-side' policies aimed at changing the level of aggregate demand or 'supply-side policies' aimed at influencing aggregate supply (see Chapter 12). These different types of government policy are examined in more detail below.

Demand-side policies are policies adopted by a government to influence aggregate demand in the economy. For example, if the economy is below full employment, the government may want to boost demand to increase output. It may do this by trying to increase injections into the economy (investment, exports, or government spending) or reducing withdrawals (savings, taxation, and import spending). However, if the economy is at full employment and demand is still growing, the effect of this is likely to pull up prices. In this instance, to prevent further price increases, the government may want to reduce aggregate demand using deflationary policies or hold it at existing levels. Whether or not it is appropriate to use demand-side policies depends, in part, on where the economy is at that instant.

Fiscal policy

When using **fiscal policy** a government may do the following.

- *Change its own levels of spending* This could be spending on final goods and services. For example, it may cut back its investment in transport or education. However, at any point in time the government will be committed to certain plans that it has already made, and it will not be able to change these easily. Any changes in government spending are likely to take time to be approved; they may also take years to have the full multiplier effect. A decision to invest in a new building programme, for example, may lead to spending that occurs over many years as the project is actually built. Just think of the planning and long-term investment required to get ready for the London Olympics in 2012. Changes in central government spending are set out in the budget each year. These will affect aggregate demand as they are an injection into the economy; they can also affect aggregate supply if, for example, they are used to encourage investment and research and development.

- *Change the taxation and benefit system* Changes in these will affect the amount of disposable income households have for consumption and the amount of retained profits businesses have for investment. Taxes and benefits will also affect aggregate supply by influencing factors such as the desire to work and likely profits from an investment.

There are numerous taxes in the economy that can be changed to influence demand:

- direct taxes, which are taxes such as income tax and corporation tax, which are taken directly from the income of individuals or organizations;

- indirect taxes, which are taxes such as value added tax (VAT), fuel duty, and excise duty (on alcohol and tobacco) which are paid when products are bought;

- council taxes, which are taxes that depend on the value of your house and are paid to the local authorities.

In relation to the tax system the government can change factors such as the following.

- The levels at which these taxes are paid—for example, it could increase the amount that you can inherit without paying inheritance tax.

- The range of goods and services that are liable to tax—for example, a government could reduce the number of goods on which indirect taxes are charged. Currently, in the UK, you do not pay VAT on most foods but you do pay it on crisps; the government could reduce this tax rate. Changes in what is taxed will affect the composition of spending.

- The rate at which tax is paid—for example, to reduce spending by households, the government might increase the rate of income tax paid. This would leave households with less income after tax and so it is likely to reduce their spending.

A government could also change the benefits and subsidies system by:

- increasing or decreasing the number of benefits available to individuals—for example, there could be higher benefits for carers of sick relatives;

- offering more or less benefits to people when they are ill or unemployed;

- increasing or decreasing the number of subsidies available to organizations—for example, to encourage the employment of the long-term unemployed or investment in 'green' technology;

- offering more or less finance for businesses investing in research and development;

- making it easier or more difficult for individuals to qualify for benefits.

Changes such as these can redistribute income in the economy and affect spending. For example, a high income earner would probably save much of each extra pound (because they have already bought essentials) whereas a low income earner probably spends most of each extra pound (i.e. has a high marginal propensity to consume). This means that if the government took one pound from high income earners, consumption would not fall much; if it then gave it to a low income earner as a benefit, spending in the economy would rise overall.

Changes in tax and benefits will also affect the incentive to work, to expand, and to develop new products which will influence supply in the economy.

 ## You and economics

You have just started your job and received your first monthly salary cheque—not quite what you had expected. You had foolishly divided your salary by twelve, but had forgotten to take off income tax, national insurance, and the voluntary pension contributions that you signed up to. This hasn't left you with anything like as much as you had hoped! You have been looking at buying a flat and just realized the costs involved—not only the legal fees and the cost of surveys but also Stamp Duty. You may need to rent for a bit longer!

Data analysis 13.1

In a progressive tax system, the average rate of tax increases with higher levels of income; in a regressive tax system, the average rate of tax actually falls with higher incomes. For example, VAT is regressive because everyone pays the same amount on an item regardless of his/her income level (see Figure 13.2).

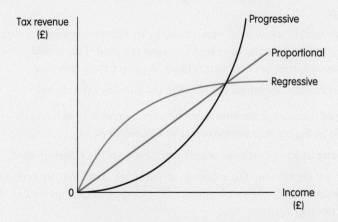

Figure 13.2 Progressive, proportional, and regressive taxation systems

Consider a tax system in which income up to £50,000 is taxed at 20 per cent and income earned over £50,000 is taxed at 40 per cent.

1. If your income is £40,000, how much tax do you pay? What is the average tax paid per pound?
2. If your income is £80,000, how much tax do you pay? What is the average tax paid per pound?
3. Is this tax system progressive or regressive? Explain your answer.
4. Why might a government want to have a progressive tax system? What will determine how progressive it is?

The government's budget position

All governments intervene in an economy to some extent to provide various services; these can include defence, education, healthcare, and transport. The government intervenes in the market system in areas in which it feels there are market failures or imperfections.

To finance its spending, a government will have to raise revenue and/or borrow. Revenue is raised through a variety of taxes and charges, such as income tax and taxes on the sale of products. Borrowing can be undertaken by selling bonds, which are effectively

IOUs. These bonds are mainly sold to financial institutions, such as banks. They have a final repayment date and pay interest annually.

The difference between a government's spending and income in any year is shown by its **budget position** and this is an important aspect of fiscal policy. A budget deficit means that the spending is greater than the revenue raised and so the government has to borrow. A budget surplus means that the income is greater than the spending. In the recession of 2008 and its aftermath, many governments felt that they had to spend more to try to boost demand in their economies because there was less spending by households and businesses; at the same time, with fewer people working and paying taxes, and lower company profits being taxed, the income of the government was lower, leading to higher budget deficits.

The budget position in the UK is shown by the 'public sector net cash requirement' (PSNCR), which shows the deficit or surplus for a given year. The total amount owed at any moment is called the 'national debt'. It is important to understand this distinction. A deficit occurs over a year, whereas the debt is the total amount owed ever, and so is usually a much bigger number. A government could have a huge debt and yet not have a deficit in a given year.

After 2008 there were major discussions in many countries about how to deal with government deficits and government debt. Some argued that it was essential to reduce the level of debt because the interest repayments were crippling and a waste of resources. They argued that it was much better to pay back the debt and regain control of the government's finances. If a government achieved a reduction in its deficit, debt lenders would have more confidence in its ability to repay and therefore the borrowing rate on any lending that did occur would be lower. If the government continued to borrow at high levels there would be fears that it could not repay; therefore lenders might charge even more because of the risk. High borrowing costs would make it more difficult for governments to repay loans, which would cause greater financial difficulties. Therefore there was general agreement in most countries that it was necessary for governments to reduce their deficits. This would involve cuts in spending and increases in taxes, and was likely to be politically unpopular. Whilst the principle of austerity and cutbacks might be accepted, there was widespread disagreement about how fast and how severe the cuts should be. By 2012, when government cutbacks were really beginning to take effect, several economists were arguing that these cutbacks were making the situation worse and that governments needed to ease up and promote growth through more expansionist policies. Those who disagreed highlighted that whilst the principles of economics might be accepted, the interpretation of how to apply these and what policies to adopt were still generating considerable controversy. By reducing the deficit and reducing aggregate demand are you leading to more unemployment and less tax revenue from spending and income, thereby making the problem worse? Would spending more boost income and generate more revenue from taxation, thereby paying for spending? These types of debate have been common, especially in the USA and most European countries. Following these debates and trying to estimate which policies will be adopted is clearly significant for managers.

£ Business analysis   13.1

Which of the following is most likely to directly shift the long-run aggregate supply curve outwards?

A: Growth in export demand.

B: A major increase in government spending on welfare benefits.

C: Improvements in the banking system to provide more funds for investment.

D: An improvement in consumer demand.

}{ People and economics: Paul Krugman

Paul Krugman is Professor of Economics and International Affairs at Princeton University and a columnist for the *New York Times*. He received his BA from Yale University in 1974 and his PhD from Massachusetts Institute of Technology (MIT) in 1977. In 1991 the American Economic Association awarded him its John Bates Clark medal, a prize given every two years to 'that economist under forty who is adjudged to have made a significant contribution to economic knowledge'. In 2008 Krugman won the Nobel Prize in Economics. His current academic research is focused on economic and currency crises. He is a major critic of the current austerity programmes of many governments.

Automatic and discretionary changes in fiscal policy

When analysing the underlying fiscal policy of a government, it is important to distinguish between changes in the budget position that occur automatically, because of changes in the level of output and income, and those that change because of deliberate changes in policy, which are called 'discretionary changes'.

If an economy declines, and there is negative growth and more unemployment, this means that, automatically, the government will receive less tax revenue (because there are less earnings and less spending) and will have to spend more on benefits (for example, to the unemployed). This means that the budget position will automatically worsen without any deliberate change in fiscal policy. If, on top of this, the government increases its spending and cuts the rate of tax, this will further worsen the budget position, but this reflects deliberate discretionary changes to try to boost demand. The UK government intervened extensively in 2008 and 2009 to try to prevent a major recession; the automatic effects of recession plus the discretionary changes meant that, by July 2009, government borrowing for that year reached £175,000 million—that is, 12.4 per cent of GDP.

As national income grows, tax revenue automatically increases and benefit spending falls. This improves the net tax revenue position. Therefore an improvement in national income such as Y1 to Y2 in Figure 13.3 automatically improves the budget position; a decline in income such as Y2 to Y1 automatically worsens it. But a government may make discretionary changes as well: a decision to pump more money into the economy would shift the spending line up; a decision to cut taxation would lower the slope of the net tax revenue line, because less would be earned at each level of income. Changes in the budget position due to changes in income alone are automatic; discretionary changes change the position of the spending or net tax revenue line.

In Figure 13.4, a discretionary increase in government spending (from B to C at income level Y2) and a cut in the rate of tax (which reduces the tax revenue from A to D) worsens the budget position because of changes in government policy. At Y2, the surplus position of AB worsens to a deficit of CD.

When reading about the deficit you may see that the Treasury refers to the 'structural deficit'. This is an important concept because it is the budget position with the automatic effects of changes in national income stripped out—that is, it shows the underlying budget position.

? Think about it... 13.1

Is an increase in government spending likely to be good or bad for business?

£ Business analysis 13.2

In 2012 the shadow Chancellor from the Labour Party, Ed Balls, argued that Britain faced a decade of slow economic growth. He argued that the government's austerity programme needed to be balanced with more focus on jobs and growth. He said that a cut in VAT and taxes on bankers' bonuses could be used to fund new measures to help the young unemployed.

However, Prime Minister David Cameron said that he was not going to abandon the spending cuts because this would increase the budget deficit and total debt, which would lead to higher interest rates so the government would not be able to borrow the money needed to finance this. Cameron accepted that there would be short-term difficulties but believed that the debt of households, banks, and government needed reducing and the economy needed to rebalance to become less dependent on financial services.

Discuss these two differing views of how the government might respond to slow or negative economic growth.

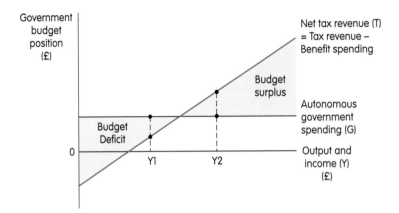

Figure 13.3 Budget deficits and budget surpluses

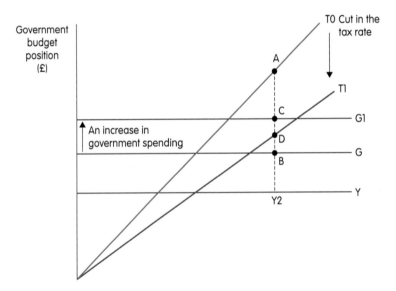

Figure 13.4 Discretionary changes in fiscal policy

Monetary policy

As well as, or instead of, changing its spending and taxation and benefits (which are fiscal measures), a government can also try to influence the money supply in the economy and the interest rates. This is known as **monetary policy** and in the UK is the responsibility of the Bank of England.

Money supply

When thinking about the amount of money in an economy, we obviously have to define what we mean by 'money'. A good starting point is to think about what functions money performs.

- *It acts as a medium of exchange* This means that money is something that is accepted widely by people and can be used in transactions—that is, it can be used to buy items and will be accepted by the seller.

- *It acts a unit of account* This means that we use money to measure the value of items. It enables us to convert the value of something into a number and then compare it with the value of other items.

- *It is a store of value* This means that people are willing to hold on to money in the belief that it will retain its value and still be valuable in the future. Rather than having to use it or exchange it immediately, people are willing to store it.

These features of 'money' can be demonstrated by many different items. Obviously, notes and coins perform these functions, but so do the funds that you have in your bank account. These funds may not physically exist (that is, the amount of 'money' shown on bank statements is far greater than the amount of cash that exists), but you can still use it via cheques, transfers and bank cards to buy things and to hold value.

There are, in fact, many definitions of money. Narrow definitions focus on very liquid assets, such as cash and accounts from which you can draw your money out quickly. Broader definitions include funds in accounts or investments, from which you have to give notice to withdraw. The key point is that the money supply depends a great deal on the banking system, because many of the funds it holds are part of what we now use as 'money'. Therefore the banking system can affect the size of the money supply through its lending.

When money is placed in a bank, a proportion of it is kept to meet future requests for withdrawals and the rest is lent out. This is how banks make their profits: by lending out money at a higher rate of interest than the rate that they pay to depositors. The money lent by banks will be spent by the borrowers (for example, on new consumer electronics or an extension to a house) and then these funds are likely to be deposited again in the banking system by the person who received them. Assume that you borrow £10,000 to build an extension to your house; this pays the builder and his/her suppliers, and they are likely to deposit this money in their banks. A proportion of this money is again kept back by the banks to meet requests for withdrawals, and the rest is lent out to more borrowers, further increasing the amount of money in the economy. (Notice that, in this case, the same physical money may be passing from one group to another, increasing the money available in the economy because of the lending by the bank.)

The repeated lending by banks highlights the money multiplier. This shows that any initial deposit in a bank leads to a much bigger overall increase in the money supply. Assume that 90 per cent of any money deposited is lent out. An initial deposit of £100 would lead to £10 being held in reserve to meet customers' demands and £90 being lent out. This then comes back into the banking system and £9 (10 per cent) is held in reserve and £81 is lent out. This will again be spent and end up in the banking system with £8.1 kept back and £72.9 lent out, and so the process continues.

Therefore for an initial deposit of £100 the effect on the money supply is:

$$£100 + £90 + £81 + £72.9 + \cdots$$

This eventually adds up to £1,000.

The money multiplier can be calculated using the expression:

1/(Proportion held in reserve)

Therefore if 10 per cent is held in reserve, the money multiplier is:

(1/0.1) = 10

and so a deposit of £100 leads to a money supply of £100 × 10 = £1,000.

You and economics

How much money have you got? Imagine someone asking you that. Your first inclination might be to see how much you have in your pocket or your wallet—that's obviously money. But if you needed to buy something you might also take some money out of your bank. And if you had to, you could use the savings account your parents set up for you when you were small. And if you were desperate, you could sell the few premium bonds your grandmother bought you when you were a baby. If the absolute worst came to the worst, you could sell your amplifier. These are all different forms of money, but they vary in their liquidity. Cash is most liquid because it is ready to spend there and then. The other assets can be turned into cash, but this will take differing lengths of time. Whatever happens, you hope that things don't get so bad that you have to turn your guitar and amp into cash.

Worked example

Assume that banks keep 0.1 of any deposit in reserve. This means that if £1,000 is deposited, £100 is kept back and £900 is lent out. When this £900 is spent and deposited back into the banking system, £90 will be kept back and £810 lent out. This will again end up in the banking system, and around £81 will be kept back and £729 lent out.

This process continues, meaning that an initial deposit of £1,000 leads to an increase in lending (and therefore the amount of money in the economy) of:

£1,000 + £900 + £810 + £729 + ⋯

This will add up to £10,000.

The size of the money multiplier is calculated using:

$$\frac{1}{\text{Reserve ratio}}$$

In this case, this is:

$$\frac{1}{0.1} = 10$$

The more that is held in reserve, the less is lent out at each stage and the lower the impact of a deposit on the money supply. A reserve ratio of 0.5 means that the money multiplier is:

$$\frac{1}{0.5} = 2$$

To limit the growth of the money supply in an economy, a government or its bank needs to control this lending process. Therefore it might:

■ encourage or instruct banks to keep more funds in reserve, which restricts their lending and so slows up the growth of money in the economy;

■ place restrictions on borrowing to reduce the demand for loans;

■ sell government bonds (IOUs) to take money out of the banking system (this is called **open market operations**).

If a central bank wanted to increase the money supply, it could reduce the amount banks have to hold in reserve or it could sell bonds, which would draw money out of the banking system. On occasion the government may have to intervene directly in the banking system. This happened in the UK during the credit crisis in 2007 when the bank Northern Rock approached the Bank of England for funds, and eventually the UK government had to take it into public ownership to keep it solvent (it was later bought by Virgin Money in 2012). In October 2008 the British government had to take a stake of nearly 60 per cent in the Royal Bank of Scotland to provide sufficient funds to keep the business financially viable. It also supported Lloyds TSB and HBOS, providing a total of £37 billion worth of capital. Further funds were injected in January 2009 to help restart personal and corporate lending. This was used to create a state-backed insurance scheme to allow banks to insure against existing loans going into default to restore banks' confidence.

 Business analysis   13.3

In May 2012 China cut the amount of funds that banks have to hold in reserve in an attempt to boost the economy. It was the third time the central bank had made such a move in six months.

This followed recent economic data suggesting that the Chinese economy was slowing down. The People's Bank of China said that banks would have to hold half a percentage point less in reserve.

This meant they would have to hold 20 per cent of their assets in cash reserves. This should enable the banks to spend billions of yuan.

Why might the government in China want the banks to lend more?

Why might lending not increase?

People and economics: Milton Friedman

Milton Friedman (1912–2006) was an American economist who taught at the University of Chicago. He received the Nobel Prize and is known for his research in areas such as consumption and monetary policy. *The Economist* magazine described him as 'the most influential economist of the second half of the 20th century . . . possibly of all of it'.

During the 1960s Friedman promoted an alternative macroeconomic policy to Keynesianism known as 'monetarism'. He argued that there was a 'natural rate of unemployment' and that governments could only increase employment above this rate (e.g. by increasing aggregate demand) at the risk of causing inflation to accelerate. He argued that inflation was always and everywhere a monetary phenomenon. He was called a monetarist. His beliefs strongly influenced the economic policies of the Conservative government led by Margaret Thatcher in 1979.

Interest rates

Rather than controlling the amount of money available via the banking system, monetary policy may focus on the cost of borrowing money (that is, the interest rate) to influence the **demand for money**. Interest rates in the UK are controlled by the Bank of England. The interest rate is the price of money—that is, it represents the cost of borrowing money and the reward for saving. By changing the interest rate, the Bank of England aims to control aggregate demand. In fact, the Bank of England changes the rate at which it lends, which is known as the base rate; this then affects the amount that other banks have to pay and therefore what they charge their customers.

There are, in fact, many different interest rates. For example, there is a difference between the rate for borrowing and saving. Banks will charge borrowers more than they pay savers (see Figure 13.5), which is how they make their profits; the borrowing interest rate is generally higher than the saving rate.

The precise amount charged to borrowers will depend on factors such as:

- the amount being borrowed—the more that a bank is lending, the less it may charge, as it will still make high levels of profit;
- the risk involved (for example, the track record of those who are asking to borrow money), because the higher the risk (for example, if there is little collateral to guarantee the loan), the more a bank will charge.

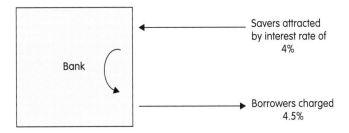

Figure 13.5 Banks and interest rates

■ Interest rate decisions are taken by the Bank of England's Monetary Policy Committee (MPC). The MPC has to judge what interest rate is necessary to meet the target for overall inflation in the economy. The inflation target is set each year by the Chancellor of the Exchequer. For many years, the target in the UK has been 2 per cent inflation.

 ## Business analysis   13.4

In 2012 lending via three websites that link savers directly with borrowers, thereby bypassing the banking system, reached £250 million.

The biggest of these sites is Zopa, which has lent more than £200 million since it started in 2005. Funding Circle, specializing in business loans, has reached £34 million, and RateSetter has reached £24 million. The government said it would lend these types of firm £100 million to help expand their own lending to businesses. Lenders via Zopa can receive returns on £5,000 of 7.4 per cent a year before tax (but after taking into account Zopa's 1 per cent charge), which is substantially more than is available on a savings account at a bank. Borrowers are paying up to 5 per cent less than they would be charged by the bank.

Zopa puts loan applicants through credit checks and divides people's savings into £10 chunks which are spread between borrowers to minimize any risk. On average, lenders have lost 0.5 per cent of their money as a result of borrowers defaulting.

Do you think that this form of lending and borrowing poses a threat to the banking system?

The interest rate and aggregate demand

The Bank of England is the final provider of cash to the banking system in the UK, and it is able to choose the interest rate at which it will provide funds to the other banks each day. The interest rate at which the Bank supplies these funds is quickly passed throughout the financial system, influencing interest rates for the whole economy—that is, if the Bank of England increases the rate at which it lends to other banks, they will charge lenders more as well to cover their costs. Banks need to borrow from the Bank of England because, on any given day, there may be more requests from depositors for funds than they have readily available, as they have lent the money out. To reduce inflation in the economy, the MPC will increase interest rates to dampen aggregate demand.

As can be seen in Figure 13.6 an increase in interest rates will affect the following.

- The rate at which financial institutions lend to businesses and households—higher interest rates will discourage borrowing and spending.

- The price of financial assets, such as shares—higher interest rates mean that there are higher rewards from saving. This is likely to reduce demand for shares and other assets, and thereby lower their price. This reduces the wealth of companies and households, and will probably reduce their spending.

- A high interest rate in the UK is also likely to attract funds from abroad as foreign investors seek high returns for their money. This increases demand for the UK currency, which increases the value of the pound. A stronger currency makes imports cheaper in pounds, which reduces the pressure from costs for higher prices; it also makes exports more expensive, which dampens aggregate demand, reducing the pressure to pull up prices. Both these effects should limit the rate at which prices increase.

The precise effects of changes in interest rates are difficult to determine. Some of the effects are likely to work through the economy more quickly than others, but there are certainly time lags for others. For example, higher rates may not immediately lead to a fall in household borrowing, but gradually consumers may reduce their overdrafts and loans, or at least not increase them further. According to the Bank of England, the maximum impact

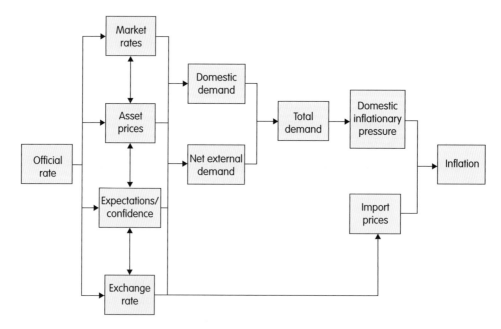

Figure 13.6 Interest rates and demand in the economy

of a change in interest rates on consumer price inflation takes up to about two years. Therefore interest rates have to be set based on judgements about what inflation might be—that is, the outlook over the coming few years—not what it is today.

 ## Business analysis   13.5

In March 2009, the MPC voted to reduce the official bank rate (that is, the interest rate charged to other banks) to 0.5 per cent. This was the lowest that it had ever been in the UK, and it was still at this rate over three years later.

The world economy appeared to be undergoing an unusually sharp downturn. Measures of business and consumer confidence had fallen markedly. World trade growth was likely to be the weakest for a significant period of time.

1. Explain how a cut in the interest rate might help the UK economy in the circumstances described in the passage above.
2. Show the possible effects on prices and output in the economy of a cut in interest rates using aggregate supply and aggregate demand diagrams.

Recent monetary policy

For many years controlling the money supply was seen as an important role of the Bank of England. There was a belief that the economy was relatively close to its potential output and therefore could not easily produce more. If the money supply grew too quickly, this would lead to too much spending which would result in inflation as output could not keep up. Milton Friedman famously said that 'inflation was always and everywhere a monetary phenomenon'. He argued that if the money supply grew too fast, inflation would result, and therefore monetary growth needed to be controlled. (This is examined in more detail in Chapter 14.)

However, in recent years, with the fears over low levels of demand in many economies, there has been discussion about how to increase spending. To do this the Bank of England has reduced the interest rate to its lowest level ever, with the aim of encouraging borrowing and spending. However, this has not had a significant enough effect and therefore the Bank has had to inject more money into the system via **quantitative easing**. This was done by the Bank of England in 2009, when it injected £200 billion into the financial system followed by £75 billion in October 2011 and another £50 billion in February 2012. By September 2012 the Bank of England had committed a total of £375 billion to quantitative easing. The aim of this was to increase the amount of money in the banking system, which it was hoped would then be lent to households and businesses to spend and increase aggregate demand. Quantitative easing occurs when the bank buys up assets—particularly government bonds—such as banks and pension funds. Usually, if the government wanted to buy up any assets, it would issue further bonds, borrowing money on the international money markets. This means that, although it has injected money into the system, it has also taken money out by selling bonds to balance this. With quantitative easing, it does not do this; it only pays for the bonds by creating funds electronically and transferring 'new' money across to the investors. A similar approach was used in Japan in the 1990s and reduced the effects of the recession. It is essentially simply 'creating' money to boost demand.

Fiscal versus monetary policies

In the preceding sections we have examined how fiscal and monetary policies can be used by governments to affect the economy. Governments will vary in their view of whether fiscal or monetary policies are more effective. Government policies will always include some elements of both fiscal policy and monetary policy; for example, a policy will always include some spending and some taxation. But the question is whether spending, tax, interest rates, or banking regulations are the best way in which to control aggregate demand. In the 1950s and 1960s, the general view was that fiscal policy could be used to 'fine tune' the economy. A boost to government spending or a change in tax rates could effectively change the level of demand to a desired level. This was known as a 'Keynesian approach', after the economist John Maynard Keynes. But fiscal policy does have problems—not least that changes cannot be made quickly, but rely on new policies being introduced in the annual budget. Even then, an increase in the spending programme may take years to actually come online.

In the middle to late 1970s, many countries were faced with high inflation and high unemployment, and fiscal policies did not seem to be working. The focus of government policy in many countries switched to monetary policy to influence the amount of money in the economy and the overall level of demand; in particular, in recent years, interest rates were used to try to achieve government objectives. Interest rate changes can be made regularly and are the Bank of England's responsibility, in order to remove any political influence. However, there is still a time lag, and predicting the precise impact on the economy can be difficult.

In response to the global recession of 2008, most governments have had to use a combination of expansionist fiscal and monetary policy. Increased spending by the government increases the money supply, and low interest rates have been used to prevent a major decline in demand. The need for more stimuli to the economy has led to a greater role for fiscal policy through increased government spending.

 Business analysis   13.6

In May 2012 a report by the International Monetary Fund (IMF) stated that the UK's continuing economic weakness meant that authorities should consider more quantitative easing (QE) and even cutting interest rates further. It said that if growth failed to pick up, the government would have to consider delaying its fiscal spending cuts. The IMF argued that the economic stresses in parts of Europe could significantly affect the UK. The IMF felt that UK growth was too slow.

In particular the IMF thought that the Bank of England should do more now to help the recovery, possibly even cut interest rates from their current very low level and inject more money into the economy. It also argued that more expansionist fiscal measures, such as temporary tax cuts and greater spending on infrastructure, should be used.

On the positive side, the IMF report said that the UK government had made a great deal of progress towards making its budget position more sustainable.

Do you think that the UK government has got it right when it comes to economic policy?

Demand-side policies

Fiscal and monetary policy measures can be used to shift aggregate demand; these are known as demand-side policies. If demand is below the level for full employment there is a 'deflationary gap', and in this case the government would want to reflate the economy. This could be by increasing its spending, cutting taxation and benefits, lowering interest rates, or expanding the money supply. If demand is too high for the potential output, this is called an 'inflationary gap' and the government will want to reduce demand. It can do this by a restrictive fiscal policy and tight monetary policy restricting money supply growth.

Supply-side policies

Supply-side policies are government policies (mainly microeconomic) designed to help markets and industries work more efficiently. Supply-side policies aim to increase aggregate supply and economic growth.

Supply-side policies aim to help markets more efficiently so the economy can move onto its production possibility frontier (PPF) or shift the PPF outwards, shifting the aggregate supply curve to the right (see Figure 13.7). These policies are unlikely to be a priority when demand is very low (for example, at Y1); at full employment, demand-side policies are inflationary unless supply increases as well. Supply-side policies are likely to be regarded as more significant as the economy gets nearer to capacity. Increasing supply enables demand to rise without being inflationary: for example, if demand increases from AD3 to AD4, this is not inflationary if supply also increases from AS to AS1.

The majority of supply-side policies focus on making product markets or the labour market more efficient and increasing the supply of resources and goods and services to the economy.

Business economics

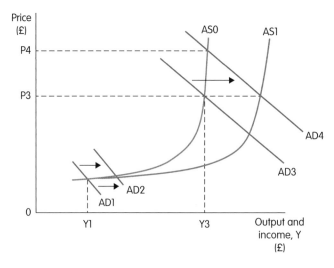

Figure 13.7 Supply-side policies shift the aggregate supply to the right

Product markets

The aim of supply-side policies in product markets is to make markets for goods and services more competitive, and to increase the pressure on firms to be efficient, productive, and innovative. With more competition, businesses will need to meet customer needs more effectively. This should lead to better quality products and a constant search for improvements.

These policies include the following.

■ *Competition policy* This policy is used to regulate large firms and ensure that they do not abuse their market power—for example, ensuring that price fixing is not occurring, that monopolies do not exploit customers, and that smaller new businesses have the opportunity to compete. Greater competition should lead to more innovation and a search for greater efficiency.

■ *Privatization* This involves selling assets from the public sector to the private sector. This should put pressure on managers by investors to improve the performance of their businesses compared with when they were in the government sector because they will be answering to private owners wanting rewards. Under private ownership the rewards can be kept by the businesses themselves, which may give an incentive to be more efficient and profitable, In the last twenty-five years, many UK businesses have been privatized, including British Airways, British Steel, British Telecom, and British Gas. Privatization often breaks up government monopolies and allows more competition in a market, putting further pressure on organizations to be more efficient.

■ *Deregulation* This occurs when regulations are removed to enable more firms to compete, thereby encouraging better customer service and innovation. Markets such as bus transport, telecommunications, and gas supply have been opened up to competition in the UK in the last thirty years, allowing more firms to provide the service and removing barriers to competition.

- *Encouraging free trade between countries* This provides more competition from abroad and puts pressure on businesses to be more efficient.

- *Encouraging business start-ups* Entrepreneurs can create competitive pressure and generate new ideas.

- *Providing incentives for innovation* For example, by subsidizing or providing tax breaks, businesses can be encouraged to undertake research and development into new products and processes.

- *Reducing bureaucracy* to enable businesses to start up and grow more easily. Regulations can increase costs and reduce the flexibility of businesses to exploit market opportunities.

? Think about it...   13.2

1. What determines the impact of greater competition in a market on a particular business?

2. How might greater competition in an economy affect different stakeholders?

Labour markets

Supply-side policies in the labour market are aimed at increasing the supply of labour and making labour markets generally more flexible, so that they can respond to changes in demand more easily.

Policies in labour markets include the following.

- *Reforming trade unions to restrict their power* Some economists argue that unions can push up the wage beyond equilibrium level by threatening industrial action, such as strikes. Less union power may increase the supply of labour, increasing the resources available in the economy and the aggregate supply.

- *Spending more on training and education, so that workers are in a better position to accept jobs* This can be important, for example, when helping employees to move from one industry to another and in preventing structural unemployment by reducing occupational immobility.

- *Changing the tax and benefits systems to ensure that working is an attractive option* For example, lower income taxes and lower benefits may provide a greater incentive to work rather than to stay at home. Cutting tax rates for lower paid workers may help to reduce the extent of the 'unemployment trap', which occurs when people calculate that they may be no better off working than if they remain unemployed.

- *Improving the housing market* to make it easier for people to move to where there are jobs. Between the mid-1990s and the end of 2007 there was a boom in demand for housing in the UK thanks to easy credit. Supply was limited due to tight planning controls and the result was high house price inflation, making it difficult for many people to get started on the housing ladder, to move to take their first job, or to move into particularly expensive areas.

Supply-side policies should be linked to the expected levels of aggregate demand. After all, if supply-side policies lead to more products being produced, this is only valuable if the demand is there to buy what is being offered.

In Figure 13.8, the line JA shows the number of people willing and able to accept a job at each real wage. LF shows the number of people in the labour force—that is, the number who could work at each real wage. The labour force slopes to the right slightly because, as the real wage increases, some people re-enter the labour market; for example, they decide that leisure is too expensive, given a high real wage, and decide that they want to work.

The line JA also slopes to the right because more people will want to accept a job at higher real wages; the lines JA and LF converge (see Figure 13.9) because the number of people willing to wait in the labour force for a better offer will decrease as the real wage gets higher. At very high real wages, most of those in the labour force will accept a job. The demand for labour is downward-sloping because fewer people will be demanded at higher real wages.

Equilibrium in the labour market is originally at W1. At this wage rate, the number of people accepting jobs is L1; the number in the labour force is L2. This means that L1, L2 is the natural rate of unemployment (that is, all those who are unemployed are voluntarily unemployed).

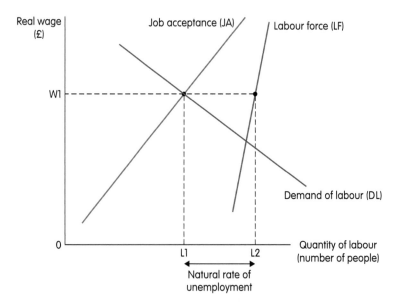

Figure 13.8 The natural rate of unemployment

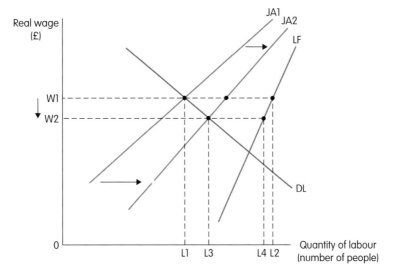

Figure 13.9 An increase in the number of people accepting jobs

Supply-side policies in the labour market should shift the job acceptance to the right; for example, at each and every real wage, more people can accept a job if they are better trained and aware of what vacancies exist. The new equilibrium is at W2 with a lower natural rate of L3, L4. More people are employed, increasing the capacity of the economy.

An increase in aggregate supply as a result of effective supply-side policies will be shown by an outward shift of the aggregate supply schedule. This should increase the quantity produced and put downward pressure on prices, because the quantity of products available has increased.

Supply-side changes in recent years include the following.

- Reform of disability benefit schemes (2007, 2009, 2011) to try and ensure that everyone who could be working is working. The intention of these reforms was to limit the inflows into incapacity benefits by the early monitoring of the health status of applicants. Claimants are being reassessed using the Work Capability Assessment.

- Efforts to improve the educational achievements of young people (2007, 2009, 2011).

- In 2011 the government introduced a pupil premium for disadvantaged students and increased the number of apprenticeships. The Education Maintenance Allowance was abolished in 2011 and replaced by a smaller targeted bursary programme administered by schools and sixth-form colleges. The aim is to increase the skills of the work-force.

- Improvements in public infrastructure: there have been substantial investments in infrastructure in recent years, although with the need to cut government spending this is set to fall quite sharply. Better communications, transport links, and services should enable faster growth.

- Making it easier to use land to build and develop: the 2011 National Planning Policy Framework aims to simplify the planning process and the New Homes Bonus aims to incentivize local communities to allow development. Red tape and bureaucracy are often blamed for limiting growth initiatives; in this case difficulty in getting planning permission can slow up new investment projects.

■ Improving work incentives for low-paid lone parents and second-income earners: in 2013 Universal Credit replaced a number of in-work benefits and tax credits, reducing complexity and improving work incentives for lone parents and second earners. This should increase the labour supply.

An increase in aggregate supply represents an outward shift in the production possibility frontier (see Figure 13.10).

 Go online to access a video walk-through of analysing demand- and supply-side polices.

Supply-side versus demand-side policies

The decision as to whether you should focus on supply-side or demand-side policies depends mainly on your view of where the economy is at the moment. If you think that the economy is in equilibrium, but a long way below full employment, the emphasis will probably be on demand-side policies to get the economy to produce at its capacity. If you think that the economy is near or at full employment, then growth will only occur by increasing capacity, which occurs with supply-side policies; there is no point relying on boosting aggregate demand, because firms are already producing what they can.

A big issue determining whether or not the economy is close to its potential output is how fast markets clear. Assume, for example, that an economy is in long-run equilibrium at its potential output and then demand falls. This will put downward pressure on prices, and if wages stay at the old level, in real terms employees are more expensive. This will

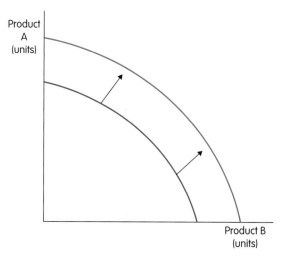

Figure 13.10 An outward shift in the production possibility frontier

reduce the quantity demanded of labour and increase the number unemployed. The economy will be operating below full employment. If this unemployment leads to lower wages, the real wage gradually returns to its long-run equilibrium level. The economy is back in long-run equilibrium with lower prices and wages. However, wages may be 'sticky' downwards and not fall for some time; this means that unemployment continues for a long period. Some believe that you cannot wait for the long run to happen—Keynes famously argued that it was not worth waiting for the long run because 'in the long run we are all dead!' In this case governments must intervene to boost demand rather than wait for wages to fall. This boost in demand would bring prices up again and restore real wages to their old level.

Keynesian and monetarist views of the economy

Different economists will make different assumptions about the economy, and this will lead to their own priorities and recommendations regarding government policy. Economic approaches include the following.

- Based on the work of John Maynard Keynes, Keynesians argue that markets do not clear quickly and the economy can get stuck below full employment. This creates a role for an interventionist government to pump money into the economy to stimulate demand and get the economy back towards full employment.

- Monetarists argue that an excess in the money supply is inflationary because they believe that the economy is at full employment and that more money going around the economy pulls up prices. They argue that governments need to control the rate at which the money supply grows to prevent inflation. The implication of this is that if governments are to focus on intervening, it would be on efforts to boost aggregate supply.

}{ *People and economics: John Maynard Keynes*

After the outbreak of the First World War, John Maynard Keynes (1883–1946) joined the Treasury. Following the peace settlement in the Treaty of Versailles, Keynes published *The Economic Consequences of the Peace*, in which he criticized the massive war reparations that the Allies demanded from Germany and predicted that it would lead to a desire for revenge amongst Germans. His best-known work, *The General Theory of Employment, Interest and Money*, was published in 1936. This highlighted how the economy could settle below full employment and put the case for expansionist government fiscal policy. In 1944, Keynes led the British delegation to the Bretton Woods Conference in the USA, where he played a major part in planning the World Bank and the International Monetary Fund.

Problems for the government intervening in an economy

The main economic objectives of a government are likely to involve economic growth, full employment, stable prices, and a healthy level of exports relative to imports. But achieving these can be extremely difficult. In part, this is because information about the state of the economy is often weeks or months out of date—just think of the vast information-gathering exercise involved in trying to calculate how much is being earned in an economy. With imperfect information, it is easy to make the wrong decisions. This is made worse by the time lag between making a decision, its coming into effect, and its making an impact on the economy. For example, the government may decide that it wants to invest in the economy and put together a programme of greater spending on healthcare. This has to go into the Budget, be voted on, and then put into action. The spending programme may take years to happen, and it may take even longer for this to feed through into more jobs and greater spending by construction firms and their employees. By the time the effects work through, the position of the economy may have changed dramatically. Like managers, politicians and their economic advisers are dealing in a world of imperfect information, but their decisions affect millions of businesses, employees, and households—no simple task.

Summary

Equilibrium occurs in an economy when planned injections equal withdrawals, which means that aggregate demand equals aggregate supply. The government can try to influence aggregate demand and supply using fiscal and monetary policies. Whether the focus is on aggregate demand or aggregate supply depends, in part, on the government's political stance and also on the extent to which the economy is at or near full employment.

Checklist

Having read this chapter, you should now understand:

- [ ] typical government economic objectives;
- [ ] what is meant by fiscal policy;
- [ ] automatic and discretionary fiscal policy;
- [ ] deflationary and inflationary gaps;
- [ ] the difference between a budget deficit and national debt;
- [ ] what is meant by monetary policy;
- [ ] how fiscal and monetary policy can affect the economy;
- [ ] the meaning of supply-side and demand-side policies;
- [ ] the difficulties of using these policies effectively.

Organizations and economics

HM Treasury

Her Majesty's Treasury (commonly known as HM Treasury) is the UK's economics and finance ministry. It is responsible for developing and implementing the government's fiscal policy. The Chancellor of the Exchequer is responsible for the work of the Treasury.

Source: http://www.hm-treasury.gov.uk

Standard and Poor's (S&P)

With offices in twenty-three countries and a history that dates back more than 150 years, Standard & Poor's is known to investors worldwide as a leader of financial market intelligence.

For example S&P rates government debt in terms of the risk of its not being able to meet its repayments. If the S&P rating falls, this is likely to make it more expensive for a government to borrow. Other credit agencies include Moody's and Fitch.

Source: http://www.standardandpoors.com/

Office for Budget Responsibility (OBR)

The Office for Budget Responsibility was formed in May 2010 to make an independent assessment of the public finances and the economy, the public sector balance sheet, and the long-term sustainability of the public finances. The Budget Responsibility and National Audit Act 2011 requires the OBR to publish two economic and fiscal forecasts for each financial year, one of which is to be the official forecast on which the Chancellor sets out the government's fiscal policy in the Budget. The Budget is the single most important economic and financial statement made each year by the Chancellor of the Exchequer to Parliament and the country.

Source: http://www.hm-treasury.gov.uk

Bank of England

The Bank of England is the central bank of the UK. It was founded in 1694, nationalized on 1 March 1946, and gained independence in 1997. The Bank's role is to promote and maintain monetary and financial stability. The Bank is the government's banker as well as the banker to the banking system. It also manages the UK's foreign and gold reserves. The Bank has had a monopoly on the issue of banknotes in England and Wales since the early twentieth century. Since 1997 it has had statutory responsibility for setting the UK's official interest rate to the general public through its banknotes and, more recently, its interest rate decisions.

Source: http://www.bankofengland.co.uk/

Organization for Economic Co-operation and Development (OECD)

The aim of the OECD is to promote policies to improve the economic and social well-being of people around the world. It provides a forum where governments work together to exchange ideas and find solutions to common problems related to economic, social, and environmental change. It measures productivity and global flows of trade and investment. It analyses and compares data to predict future trends. It also compares issues such as tax systems, the leisure time people take in different countries, schools systems, and pensions.

Source: http://www.oecd.org/

Short answer questions

1. What is meant by fiscal policy?
2. What is the difference between automatic and discretionary fiscal policy?
3. What is a budget deficit?
4. What is meant by an austerity programme?
5. What is meant by monetary policy?
6. What are typical government economic objectives?
7. What is meant by quantitative easing?
8. Analyse the effect of a fall in interest rates on the economy.
9. Explain two demand-side policies that a government might use to increase aggregate demand.
10. Explain two supply-side policies that a government might use to increase aggregate supply.

Discussion questions

1. Does it matter if a government is in debt?
2. To what extent is a budget deficit a good indicator of an expansionist government fiscal policy?
3. Is fiscal policy a better way of controlling the economy than monetary policy?

One step further

Visit our Online Resource Centre at **www.oxfordtextbooks.co.uk/orc/gillespiebusiness2e/** to test your understanding, watch video walk-throughs, and access further information on topics covered in this chapter.

Macroeconomic issues: unemployment and inflation

14

Learning objectives

In this chapter, we examine some of the key issues in macroeconomics.

By the end of this chapter, you should:

- ✓ understand the causes of unemployment;
- ✓ appreciate the costs of unemployment;
- ✓ understand the causes of inflation;
- ✓ appreciate the consequences of inflation;
- ✓ understand the possible short-run and long-run relationship between inflation and unemployment;
- ✓ the Phillips curve;
- ✓ adaptive and rational expectations.

© Case study

Rupa had been working as a fashion retail assistant for five years since she left school. She enjoyed the job and was hoping for a promotion. Therefore it came as something of a shock when she heard on the radio that her business was about to close! She had known that things had not been going particularly well from the updates the store manager had given them over the last few months. The uncertainty in the economy and the squeeze on household incomes from rising prices at a time when most people were enduring a pay freeze meant that households were being far more careful with their money. Where they could, many people seemed to be making do with what they had rather than buying new clothes.

However, Rupa had no idea that things were this bad and couldn't believe that she had not been told about the closure by her manager first. According to the news, the company had gone into administration blaming 'adverse trading conditions'.

Rupa was understandably worried because she had recently taken out a large mortgage. She had been encouraged to move into a bigger flat because interest rates were so low at the time; even so she had stretched herself financially. If she was now redundant, there was no way she could afford it. And unfortunately her partner would not be able to help out much. He had worked in a local call centre for a couple of years, but this business had been transferred abroad where costs were much lower. He had got a job since then working taking calls in a taxi business, but he was only working a few hours a week and struggling to find anyone who could offer him more work.

She was not confident that she would find work either. 'No one's hiring at the moment,' said her friend Jade, 'and the way the economy's looking they won't be for some time. The only jobs out there at the moment are for computer programmers and accountants, and we just don't have the skills or qualifications they need.' Rupa wondered if she would have to move to find work, but she knew the chances were that she would not be able to afford to move to where the jobs were anyway.

Questions

1. What are the causes of unemployment identified in the case?

2. If you were the government, what policies could you introduce to help reduce unemployment? Do you think it should concentrate on demand-side or supply-side policies?

3. According to the case real incomes have been falling, why are employees' nominal incomes not rising as fast as prices?

4. What do you think causes inflation?

Introduction

The macroeconomic environment can create opportunities and threats for businesses. In a booming economy, demand may be growing fast, creating more sales opportunities. In a declining economy, a business may have to consider redundancies and selling off assets. If prices are stable, planning will be easier than if they are changing rapidly. Therefore the state of the economy will affect the ease of doing business and the likelihood of success. It will also affect the extent to which a country attracts investment from overseas. Not surprisingly, economic change often makes headline news because it has a direct effect on jobs, households' standard of living, and economic growth.

The most common indicators of the health of an economy are:

- the rate of economic growth;

- the rate of unemployment;

- the rate of change of the price level;

- the trade position (this measures the difference between a country's earnings from goods and services from abroad and spending on imports).

When managers are considering economic conditions domestically or, indeed, considering entering overseas markets, they should monitor these key macroeconomic indicators carefully. Managers will be interested in the present situation and also forecasts of these factors, because they will have a significant effect on the trading environment. They will affect a whole range of management decisions, such as:

- which markets to target;

- whether to invest in more capacity;

- whether to agree to a pay increase;

- whether or not to recruit;

- where to locate production.

For example, one of the noticeable trends in recent years has been the growth of economies such as China and India, creating major export opportunities for companies such as Burberry and Unilever whilst also enabling cheaper production overseas by many manufacturers such as Dyson. More recently, the uncertainty about the state of the Eurozone has affected investment levels, as businesses are less willing to commit resources until they have a clearer sense of what will happen with this currency.

In the next two chapters we consider the four main economic objectives of government, beginning with unemployment and inflation.

? Think about it...   14.1

Explain why you think each of the following objectives might be desirable:

- low economic growth;

- stable prices;
- reasonable level of exports relative to imports;
- low unemployment.

Would you say one of these targets was more important than the others in your economy at the moment?

What other indicators might you use to judge the performance of an economy?

 # *Data analysis*   14.1

Table 14.1 Positions of different economies, June 2012

	Trade balance over last year ($bn)	Annual change in GDP (%)	Consumer prices (%)	Unemployment (%)
UK	−162	−0.1	+2.8	8.2
China	+165	+8.1	+3.7	4.1
USA	−753	+2	+2.2	8.2
Germany	+223	+1.7	+2.1	6.7
Netherlands	+56	−1.1	+2.3	6.2
Greece	−33	−6.2	−0.1	21.7

1. Based on the data in Table 14.1, which economy do you think is doing best if the targets are economic growth, stable prices, low unemployment, and a healthy trade position? Explain your answer.
2. What other data might be useful to make a decision?

Unemployment

Unemployment measures the number of people actively seeking work who are not employed at a given moment. Unemployment represents a wasted resource in an economy because it means that there are people who are not working who could be adding to production. They also receive benefits, which takes money away from other areas of the economy such as education. Not surprisingly, then, governments are eager to find ways of reducing the level of unemployment in the economy. From a business perspective, if fewer people are working, this is likely to reduce incomes in the economy and therefore, for many businesses, this is likely to reduce sales opportunities. From a political perspective, high unemployment may well be unpopular and lose votes. A famous advertising campaign run by the Conservative Party in 1979 stated 'Labour isn't working' and highlighted the high unemployment levels at the time; this was said to play a big role in helping the Conservatives to win the election. Reducing unemployment can win votes but also releases productive resources into the economy, enabling more growth.

Measuring unemployment

The two main ways of measuring unemployment are the Labour Force Survey (LFS) by the International Labour Organization (ILO) and the claimant count. The LFS is based on a random sample taken throughout the country. This is conducted every three months using around 53,000 households. The survey collects information about the personal circumstances and work of everyone living in these households.

Under the LFS guidelines, all people aged 16 years and over can be classified into one of three states: 'in employment', 'unemployed', or 'economically inactive'.

- Unemployed people have no job, want a job, have actively sought work in the last four weeks, and are available to start work in the next two weeks, or are out of work, have found a job, and are waiting to start it in the next two weeks.

- In general, anybody who carries out at least one hour's paid work in a week or is temporarily away from a job (for example, on holiday) is in employment. This means people may count as employed but actually want to work more hours.

- Those who are out of work, but do not meet the criteria of unemployment, are economically inactive.

The claimant count measures the number of people eligible for unemployment benefits. By changing the rules rewarding who can and who cannot claim benefits, this figure can change quite significantly, leading to major differences between the claimant count and the findings of the LFS.

? *Think about it…*   14.2

1. Do you think that someone who works only one hour a week should be regarded as in employment? Why might this suggest that underlying unemployment is actually much higher than reported figures?

2. Do you think that the Labour Force Survey or the claimant count is a better way of measuring unemployment? Explain the possible reasons why the claimant count and the ILO Labour Force Survey data may differ in Figure 14.1.

3. Analyse the possible effects of the data in Figure 14.1 on UK businesses.

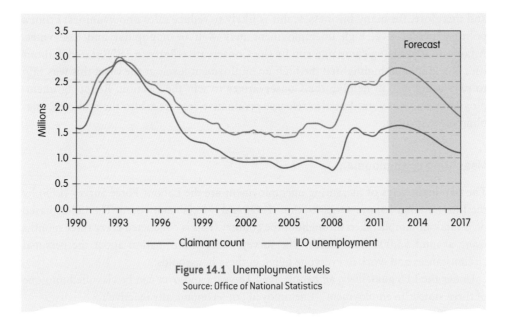

Figure 14.1 Unemployment levels
Source: Office of National Statistics

 Business analysis   14.1

According to the Trades Union Congress (TUC), the true levels of unemployment in the UK are much bigger (possibly double) than the figures reported by the government.

This is because the UK bases its jobless data on the number of adults who are out of work and have actively sought a new job over the past six weeks. But what about people who want work but have not actively sought work recently, who might number over two million? And what about those 'underemployed' adults who are in part-time work and cannot find full-time work?

Does it matter if the published unemployment figures underestimate the true levels of unemployment?

Causes of unemployment

Unemployment occurs for a number of reasons, including the following.

- *Real wages are too high* One possible problem in the labour market is that nominal wages may not be very flexible, particularly downwards. This may be because wages (or certainly salaries) are often agreed for at least a year so cannot change easily in between. Secondly, employees are often reluctant to accept a nominal pay cut or even accept a smaller increase in pay than the year before. This means that real wages in an economy can end up too high because the nominal wage has not fallen in line with prices. This prices labour out of a job because employees are too expensive. In theory, unemployment caused by high real wages will put downward pressure on wages and eventually the market will return to equilibrium (at W1 in Figure 14.2).

■ *A lack of demand in the economy due to low levels of aggregate demand* This is known as **cyclical (demand-deficient) unemployment** because it will occur in the

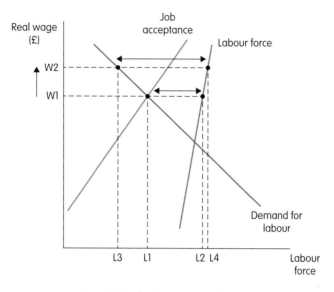

Figure 14.2 Real wage unemployment

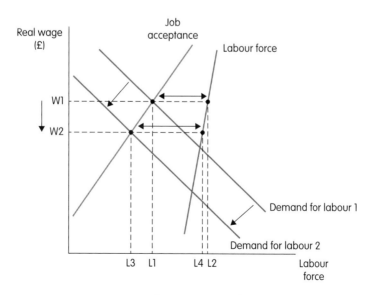

Figure 14.3 Cyclical (demand-deficient) unemployment

recession and slump periods of the economic cycle (see Figure 14.3). People are unemployed because the jobs simply are not there. Labour is a derived demand—with less demand for goods and services there will be less demand for labour. Shops have closed, factories have been shut, and businesses have stopped hiring, so even if you want to work it is difficult to find an opportunity. In this instance, a government might intervene to try to boost the level of aggregate demand. This would aim to increase demand for goods and services, and encourage businesses to expand and employ more people. The government may aim to encourage consumption in the economy, to boost injections (such as investment, government spending, and exports), and/or reduce withdrawals (such as spending on imports, reducing taxes, or reducing savings).

- *A change in the structure of the economy, so that some people lack the skills that they need to move from the declining sectors into the growth areas* This is called 'structural unemployment' because the structure of the economy has changed. For example, there has been a decline in manufacturing as the economy has moved into the service sector. Individuals have lost their jobs in one sector but may not have the skills to gain employment in the growth area. In this case the government would need to use supply-side policies to help to retrain employees and ease the transition.

- *Seasonal changes reducing demand for staff in some sectors, such as fruit picking or the hotel industry* This is unlikely to affect huge numbers of employees, and these people are likely to find work again the following season and so are not a major concern.

- *People not willing to accept a job at the given wage* This could be because of the unemployment trap, whereby people end up worse off by working because they start incurring taxes and lose their benefits, and so may earn less than they receive by remaining unemployed. In this situation, the government may use supply-side policies by reducing the benefits that are given to those who are unemployed and having lower taxes at low incomes.

- *A restriction in the supply of labour due to employees wanting to push up wages, perhaps via a trade union* By restricting the supply of labour, those in work earn more, but fewer people are employed than would be the case in a free market (see Figure 14.4). In this case, the government may try to reduce the power of unions, perhaps through legislation.

? Think about it...   14.3

In the recent recession unemployment has risen significantly, but by less than expected given the major falls in aggregate demand. Why do you think this might be?

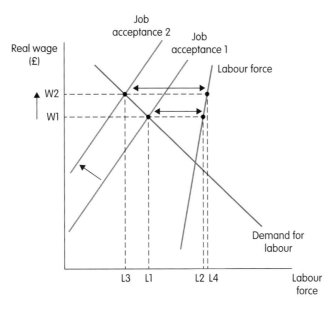

Figure 14.4 Trade unions restricting the supply of labour

Unemployment flows

When analysing unemployment it is important to consider not just the number of people and composition of people unemployed at any one moment, but also the flow of people into and out of the unemployment pool. If people are flowing in and out quite quickly, this may not be as bad as people becoming unemployed and staying there for years. One of the recent concerns about unemployment in the UK is the high proportion of people who have been unemployed long term. The longer you are out of work, the harder you may find it to get a job as you gradually lose your skills and may become less employable.

 Business analysis 14.2

In 2012 an estimated five million people in the UK of working age were on out-of-work benefits—1.4 million of them had been on benefits for nearly a decade. In that year the government Department for Work and Pensions introduced radical reforms of the welfare system to cut billions of pounds from the benefits budget.

Out-of-work benefit bills were capped at £26,000 a year, and a single universal credit for millions of people was introduced (replacing many other different benefits).

However, the Minister for Welfare and Pensions, Ian Duncan Smith, said that what the UK really needed was a cultural change to get people stuck on benefits working.

Why do you think unemployment was so high in the UK in 2012?

What sort of cultural change do you think might reduce unemployment?

Voluntary and involuntary unemployment

Another important distinction to make when analysing unemployment is between 'voluntary' and 'involuntary' unemployment. **Voluntary unemployment** occurs when all those willing and able to accept a job at the given real wage are working; there will still be some people unemployed if they lack the desire or the necessary skills to work. **Involuntary unemployment** occurs when people are willing and able to work, but there is not enough demand; this occurs when the economy is in a slump, for example.

The natural rate of unemployment

The natural rate of unemployment is the equilibrium rate of unemployment—that is, the rate of unemployment for which the aggregate supply of labour equals the aggregate demand for labour, and the labour market is in long-run equilibrium. At the natural rate of unemployment, all those willing and able to work at the given real wage rate are

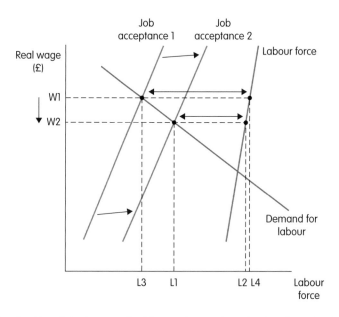

Figure 14.5 Supply-side policies increase the job acceptance rate and reduce the natural rate of unemployment

employed. This means that all unemployment is 'voluntary' (that is, employees are not willing or not able to work) and there is no involuntary unemployment.

To reduce the natural rate of unemployment, the government may focus on supply-side policies to make the labour market work more efficiently and bring about market equilibrium. For example it might:

- help train the unemployed so that they have the skills to get a job;

- provide better information so that the unemployed know what jobs are available;

- reduce benefits available to those not working to encourage them to accept work;

- reduce the taxes on working, such as income tax and national insurance contributions, to provide more incentive for people to work;

- help with issues such as childcare and caring for relatives to enable people to accept work.

 Business analysis   14.3

Unemployment rates in various countries in June 2012 were as follows:

USA	8.2%
China	4.1%
UK	8.2%
Eurozone	11%
Germany	6.7%
Greece	21.7%
Spain	24.3%
Thailand	0.7%
Netherlands	6.2%

Discuss the possible reasons for the differences in unemployment rates in these countries?

What difference might these unemployment rates mean to managers of businesses operating in these countries?

What actions might a government take to reduce these unemployment rates?

The consequences of unemployment

Involuntary unemployment represents a waste of resources and means that the economy is below full employment. This means that the economy is operating within the production possibility frontier and is productively inefficient because it is not using its

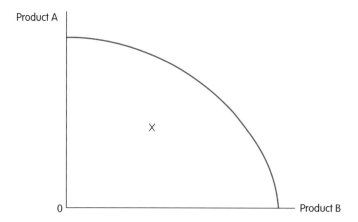

Figure 14.6 Operating within the production possibility frontier due to unemployment

resources fully to maximize the production of goods and services (see Figure 14.6). This means the economy is not at its potential output.

Unemployment also:

- reduces the tax income for the government because fewer people are working, which reduces the finance available for public sector projects and automatically worsens the budget position;

- involves a higher level of benefits, which may take finance away from other important areas of the economy, and therefore has an opportunity cost and again automatically worsens the budget position—if the government has a budget deficit it then has to finance this which may involve borrowing and debt repayments which is not necessarily a good use of government funds;

- is often associated with social costs, such as crime—if an individual's standard of living is low and he/she is frustrated at not getting a job, this may lead to antisocial behaviour.

 You and economics

You have been gaining some work experience with a computer programming company based in Brighton. It produces the backgrounds to some of the best-selling games in recent years. It specializes in city landscapes, providing the scenarios where various games such as car chases can take place. The business has been doing well whilst you are there and is trying to recruit new programmers. Even though unemployment in the country is extremely high, the business is struggling to find someone to fill the vacancy. The salary it offers is not really enough for someone to move to the area as house prices are high, so its catchment area is the commuting distance where there are not that many people with the skills it wants. Even with high unemployment, businesses can struggle to recruit because of skills gaps.

Business analysis 14.4

In 2012 UK business leaders urged government ministers to do more to help companies create a 'pro-employment landscape' as a change to employment law came into force.

The change in the law was that employees now have to work for two years rather than one before they are protected from unfair dismissal.

The TUC, the trades union organization, said that the change in the law could increase job insecurity and lead to a 'hire-and-fire' culture. But the CBI said that the change would give employers confidence to take on more staff.

Do you think that reducing employees' protection at work helps create jobs?

What two measures would you introduce to reduce unemployment in your country?

Analysing unemployment within different labour markets

Understanding unemployment levels and patterns is important to managers because it affects their ability to recruit, as well as reflecting the state of the economy as a whole. High levels of unemployment mean that there is less upward pressure on wages and makes it easier to recruit.

But simply looking at the overall figure of unemployment does not necessarily reflect the state of the labour markets in which a specific manager is most interested. For example, a particular business may be recruiting skilled engineers or surgeons, and therefore the trends in the overall unemployment rates in a country might not reflect what is happening in those particular labour markets. For example, in 2012 Australia changed its immigration laws to make it easier for electricians, plumbers, and construction workers to enter the country because of labour shortages, even though it still had a national unemployment rate of 5.1 per cent.

Significant differences between the unemployment rates in different regions may also need to be taken into account. For a business that recruits locally, the local unemployment rate matters more than the national figure.

? Think about it ... 14.4

1. Find out the unemployment levels in your country. How much do these levels vary between skills and regions? How much have they changed over time?

2. Is unemployment the major economic issue in your country? Explain your view.

Economics and employability

What is your name and can you tell us a bit about your role at Allen Associates?

I am Kate Allen, Managing Director of Allen Associates. We recruit for permanent and temporary roles at all levels in the marketing, PA/admin, HR and finance sectors. As well as running the business, I work on the HR Division and oversee the Finance Division.

In what ways is an understanding of economics useful in your work?

A view of the wider marketplace helps us understand our clients, the economic pressures they are currently experiencing, and how things might change in the future. This helps us prepare for changes in our clients' recruitment requirements.

How does economic change affect your work and your clients?

In every way! The jobs market is in a constant state of flux, driven by and responding to marketplace changes all the time. We have to be very adaptable in what we offer our clients in terms of flexible staffing solutions to meet their immediate needs, which can change daily. We also help them plan for the longer term so that they are in a strong position for the future. Having the most talented people already in place helps them respond quickly to opportunities presented by positive economic change.

Did you study economics at university as part of your studies?

I have a degree in English and History. I studied some economics as part of the Chartered Institute of Personnel and Development (CIPD) Diploma Foundation Course. However, if I had my time again I would certainly have benefited from, and been very interested in, studying for a more practical business degree. At some stage in the future, when the business is less dependent on me on a day-to-day basis, I would love to explore the possibility of doing an MBA.

What skills are important in your role?

All the skills related to running a successful business and managing people well are important. These include setting goals for the business, good written and verbal communications, being organized, and continually supporting, developing, and training our staff in their roles.

The ability to build and develop our business's reputation is really important. We are now in our fifteenth year and a significant proportion of our new business comes from recommendations by happy clients.

Networking skills also remain hugely important to our business growth. It's a continuous effort but can be rewarding and fun. We're well connected with local businesses as they are our current and our future clients.

Inflation

Inflation occurs when there is a sustained increase in the general price level over a period of time. With inflation of 2 per cent, for example, prices in general are increasing by 2 per cent over the year. This does not mean that all prices are increasing at this rate: some may increase by more and some by less, but on average they are increasing by 2 per cent.

When we measure real changes in variables, this means that they have been adjusted for inflation; for example, real wages and real GDP show how much these have changed, taking account of prices. For example, if your nominal income doubles but prices do as well, in real terms your purchasing power is the same. A business that makes 2 per cent more profits but finds that the costs of resources are now 4 per cent higher has suffered in real terms.

How to measure inflation

In the UK, the Retail Prices Index (RPI) measures what is happening to prices in a typical basket of goods and services for a household. It takes account of the relative importance of different items in terms of spending and calculates overall how much prices increase. This is called a weighted index, with the weights allocated to items reflecting the proportion of income spent on them.

The Consumer Prices Index (CPI) is similar, but does not include mortgage repayments when calculated; this means that the two measures can give different results (for example, if mortgage rates are cut this is reflected in the RPI but not in the CPI, so the RPI will be lower than the CPI).

The causes of inflation include the following.

■ **Demand pull inflation** At any moment in an economy, aggregate demand may be growing faster than aggregate supply. In this situation, businesses are likely to increase their prices given the ever higher levels of demand.

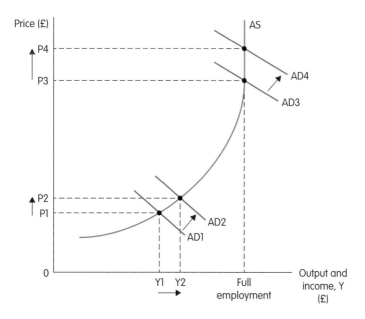

Figure 14.7 The effect of a change in the aggregate demand

As illustrated in Figure 14.7, an increase in aggregate demand usually leads to a higher price and quantity. Supply becomes more price inelastic as it approaches its capacity; the effect is on price more than output (for example, when aggregate demand increases from AD3 to AD4, compared with from AD1 to AD2, there is more impact on inflation). From a business perspective demand pull inflation is associated with high levels of demand and you are likely to be running down stocks, creating waiting lists, and expanding as and when you can. Therefore demand pull inflation is associated with a buoyant economy and higher profit margins.

In a situation of demand pull inflation a government will want to reduce aggregate demand (or at least restrict its growth in line with aggregate supply) to control price increases. In the UK, the Bank of England's Monetary Policy Committee (MPC) uses interest rates to influence spending in order to control demand and therefore prices. Higher interest rates will deter borrowing and spending by households and investment by businesses, leading to a fall in aggregate demand; this should prevent prices from increasing further.

- **Cost push inflation** The price level in an economy is inevitably sensitive to the level of costs: if costs increase, perhaps because of wage increases unrelated to productivity gains or higher imported prices of inputs such as oil, businesses may be forced to push up their prices to maintain their profits. Higher costs shift the aggregate supply curve upwards because a higher price is needed for any given level of output. This leads to higher prices in the economy. For example, in January 2011 the UK government increased VAT rates from 17.5 to 20 per cent, increasing firms' costs. Cost push inflation causes problems for businesses; their costs may be rising and managers may be wary of increasing prices, and therefore profit margins may be squeezed.

? Think about it...   14.5

Why might wage increases linked to productivity gains not be inflationary?

As illustrated in Figure 14.8, an increase in costs means that a higher price is required to produce any level of output. This leads to an upward shift of the aggregate supply curve. The effect of an increase in costs will usually be lower output and a higher price.

In this situation, the government will aim to reduce costs, perhaps by intervening with the exchange rate to increase its value to reduce import costs (this would also dampen demand by reducing demand for exports), or by introducing limits on wage and price increases.

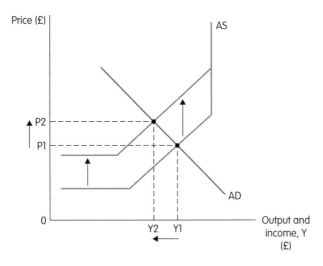

Figure 14.8 The effect of an inward shift of the aggregate supply due to higher costs

 Business analysis   14.5

Inflation rates in various countries in June 2012 were as follows:

USA	2.2%
China	3.7%
UK	2.8%
Eurozone	2.4%
Germany	2.1%
Greece	−0.1%
Spain	1.9%
Thailand	3.2%
Netherlands	2.3%

Discuss the possible reasons for the differences in inflation rates in these countries?

What difference might these unemployment rates mean to managers of businesses operating in these countries?

Monetarists and inflation

Monetarists argue that inflation is caused by the money supply growing too fast. If more money is circulating around the economy, this leads to more demand. So it is demand pull inflation but is always caused by excessive money supply growth. Monetarists believe that the economy is near or at its potential output and therefore aggregate supply cannot easily increase. This leads to inflation. Therefore the role of government is to control the growth of the money supply so the growth in demand matches the growth of aggregate supply. This view of inflation was promoted by Milton Friedman in the 1970s and influenced the economic policy of Margaret Thatcher in the early years of the Conservative government elected in 1979. Monetarists argue that if prices increase for any reason other than an increase in the money supply (e.g. higher costs), if the money supply is kept constant the result would be less spending (because there is the same amount of money but higher prices) and hence less output and more unemployment; this would put downward pressure on costs forcing them back down. Inflation would only occur in this instance if the money supplied was expanded to let it happen.

The monetarist view can be explained using the Fisher equation of exchange:

$$MV = PT$$

where M is money supply, V is velocity of circulation (how fast money moves around the economy), P is the average price level, and T is the number of transactions.

For example, if the money supply is £20,000 and the velocity is 2, the money spent is £20,000 × 2 = £40,000. Then, if 400 units are available, the average price level is £100.

The Fisher equation MV = PT is an identity rather than an equation because it must be true. The amount spent (the left-hand side of the identity) must equal the amount received (the right-hand side of the identity).

If the velocity of circulation is relatively constant and the number of transactions is constant (because the economy is at its potential output), an increase in the money supply will lead to in higher prices (inflation). This is the basis of Friedman's view that inflation is caused by excessive money supply growth.

However, if the number of transactions could be increased because there is spare capacity in the economy, an increase in the money supply could lead to more output and not necessarily increase prices. For example, assume that:

$$£20,000 \times 2 = £200 \times 2,000$$

If the money supply doubles and the number of transactions doubles, prices stay the same:

$$£40,000 \times 2 = £200 \times 4,000$$

Again, we can see how assumptions about how close the economy is to its capacity have a fundamental impact on an economist's view of the effect of changes in different variables.

){ *People and economics: Fisher*

Irving Fisher (1867–1947) was a US economist whose work on the quantity theory of money and interest rates contributed to monetarist thinking. Milton Friedman called Fisher 'the greatest economist the United States has ever produced'.

You and economics

You have been in your job for a year now and were hoping for a significant pay increase this year. Unfortunately, your boss has just sent an email round to everyone stating that there will be no increases for anyone this year because of 'difficult trading conditions'. This means that it is going to be a difficult year—your commuting costs have increased a lot, every time you go shopping it seems to cost more, and even though you have been cutting back where you can it has been a struggle. You are sure that prices will continue to rise, so with no pay increase this year this means no summer holiday!

 ## Business analysis   14.6

Analyse the possible effects on UK businesses of the changes in inflation shown in Figure 14.9.

Discuss the possible causes of inflation over this period.

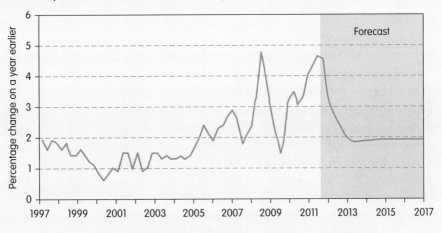

Figure 14.9 CPI inflation forecast
Source: Office of National Statistics, Office of Budget Responsibility

Deflation

If prices are falling, this is known as 'deflation' (i.e. negative inflation); this can happen if aggregate demand is falling. This has been a problem in Japan in the last decade. Falling prices mean that profit margins of businesses may be squeezed, and this leaves less funds for the owners and for investment. Managers may seek to reduce costs to cope with falling prices. This may be through policies aimed at reducing waste, getting better prices from suppliers, and seeking productivity improvements (perhaps by employing less staff).

Deflation also causes difficulties because there is an incentive for people to hold on to their money for longer rather than spend it. Households may decide to save their money because it will earn interest, and they can then buy even more later on when prices have fallen. The increase in saving and fall in demand puts further downward pressure on prices, giving even further incentive to households to save.

The problems of inflation

Inflation is significant because it can have the following effects.

- *Making planning more difficult* If inflation is unpredictable, for example, when managers are setting budgets they will be unsure what their costs will be and this makes it difficult to forecast profits or cash flow. Unanticipated inflation is likely to deter investment because of the uncertainty that it brings. Lower investment may damage the long-term growth of the economy.

- *Reducing consumers' real incomes* If prices are increasing faster than individuals' incomes, they are worse off in real terms: they cannot buy as many products, which can affect future sales for many businesses. The impact of inflation on real incomes will depend on employees' bargaining power—some groups will suffer more than others. For example, pensioners often have relatively little power compared with some members of trade unions and therefore tend to suffer from falling real incomes. The effect of relatively high inflation and low wage growth in the years after 2008 in the UK severely squeezed real household income.

- *Influencing wage demands* If inflation is predicted to be 3 per cent, for example, employees are likely to demand at least this increase in wages to protect the purchasing power of their earnings. If you had intended to offer your employees a pay increase of only 2 per cent, they will be worse off in real terms and this might affect your relations with them as they bargain for more. It might even lead to industrial action if employees continue to want more money than you are prepared to offer. If you do increase their pay, this will lead to even higher costs, which might lead to higher prices, which then leads to higher demand for pay—a phenomenon known as the 'wage–price spiral' (see Figure 14.10).

- *Squeezing profit margins* If inflation occurs, a business may find that its costs are rising by more than it feels it can increase the prices of its products. This means that its profit margins may be squeezed, reducing funds for investors and for further investment.

- *Reducing the international competitiveness of an economy* If inflation is higher in one country than it is in others, its products are relatively more expensive, which could reduce its exports.

The effects of inflation on individuals and businesses depend partly on whether it is anticipated or unanticipated.

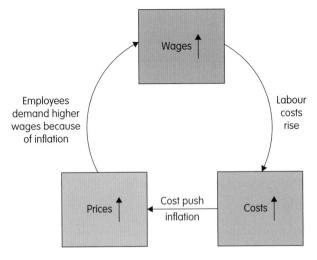

Figure 14.10 The wage–price spiral

- *Anticipated inflation* If individuals and businesses know that inflation is occurring, they can try to take suitable steps to prepare. For example, employees may bargain for pay increases to maintain their real wages. Individuals may look for savings accounts that offer interest rates that match or exceed the expected inflation rate. Businesses can adjust their prices and try to negotiate with suppliers to keep prices fixed. If interest rates and wages are increasing with inflation, in real terms, they are staying constant.

- *Unanticipated inflation* This is inflation that is not expected and for which no plans have been made. This may have more damaging effects than anticipated inflation because it causes uncertainty, which reduces spending decisions; it also means that some people will be caught out by higher than expected inflation, making them worse off.

? *Think about it ...*   **14.6**

1. What is inflation in your country at the moment?

2. Is it perceived as a major economic problem?

3. What actions do you think that the government could take to reduce it?

4. Inflation measures the cost of living. If the cost of living goes up, does the standard of living necessarily fall?

5. How might an increase in inflation affect business planning?

Analysing inflation

While the CPI and RPI give some idea of what is happening to prices generally in the shops, managers will tend to be more interested in what is happening to prices within their own businesses and sector, and therefore the general measure of inflation may not be appropriate. This is because the headline inflation figure is calculated by measuring the changes in prices in a 'typical basket of goods' bought by a household. Given that the types of purchase of most business are not in a typical basket of goods, this means that the relative inflation rates for your business can be significantly different from the general rate.

Controlling inflation

The right way to control inflation will depend on the underlying cause.

If the cause is cost push the government might do the following.

- Attempt to increase the external value of the currency (the exchange rate) to make imported components cheaper. It may do this by buying its currency with its own foreign currency reserves, increasing demand, or increasing interest rates to attract foreign capital inflows.

- Develop supply-side policies to shift the aggregate supply to the right and offset the costs increases.

- Limit pay and wage increases—it can do this within the public sector with its own pay deals and if necessary introduce legislation to try and limit wage increases (these are called income policies). These can often be unpopular and cause industrial conflict, as wages are being held constant when prices are likely to continue to rise in the short run, reducing real wages.

If the underlying cause of inflation is too much demand, the government can focus on demand-reducing (deflationary) policies such as reducing its own spending or increasing taxation rates.

The main weapon that has been used to control inflation in the UK in recent years is the interest rate. The Monetary Policy Committee is an independent organization that is a part of the Bank of England with the remit of restricting inflation to 2 per cent a year.

Inflation and unemployment

In 1958 A.W. Phillips published research which suggested that there was a trade-off between inflation and unemployment. This seemed to make some intuitive sense—efforts by the government to increase aggregate demand, for example, would lead to more spending in the economy which would reduce unemployment, but at the same time start to pull prices up to create demand pull inflation. However, further research suggested that this trade-off between inflation and unemployment was a short-term relationship only.

}{ *People and economics: A.W. Phillips*

William Phillips (1914–1975) was a New Zealand economist who lectured at the London School of
Economics (LSE), but later worked at the Australian National University and the University of
Auckland. His most famous work was analysis of wage rate and unemployment data suggesting a
trade-off between the two. This led to further analysis of the possible short- and long-run
relationships between inflation and unemployment.

Some economists argue that there is in fact no trade-off if the labour market works well.
Assume that the economy is in long-run equilibrium at full employment at P1L1 and then
aggregate demand increases (see Figure 14.11). This will lead to excess demand and pull
up prices causing demand pull inflation. If employees notice this and demand higher
wages, this restores the real wage to the same level as it was originally. The labour market
and the economy are back where they started with higher prices. An increase in aggregate
demand has simply increased prices and moved the economy from P1L1 to P2L1.

Now assume that the economy is in long-run equilibrium at P2L1 and aggregate
demand falls (see Figure 14.12). This lack of demand reduces prices and with less demand
and lower prices employees accept the need for lower wages. The wage rate falls to
match the fall in prices so that the real wage remains the same as it was originally and the
economy is again back at its long-run equilibrium, now at P1L1. A fall in aggregate

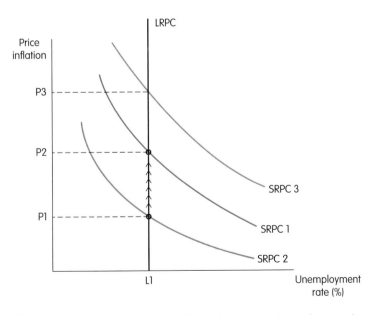

Figure 14.11 Higher aggregate demand leads to higher prices but no change in unemployment: SRPC,
short-run Phillips curve; LRPC, long-run Phillips curve

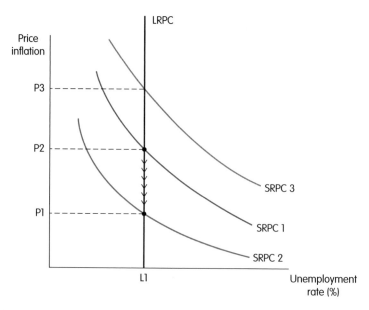

Figure 14.12 The effect of a fall in aggregate demand on unemployment if wages and prices adjust quickly: SRPC, short-run Phillips curve; LRPC, long-run Phillips curve

demand has led to lower wages and prices. Based on this model of the economy where the labour market clears quickly the aggregate supply is vertical and changes in aggregate demand affect the price level but not output and employment. Therefore government policies to change demand are not very effective except in relation to the price level.

However, Keynesians believe that the labour market is much slower to clear following a change in prices. Assume that there is a fall in demand in the economy (see Figure 14.13). This will reduce prices but nominal wages may not adjust downwards. This is because employees may have signed contracts, and so it is not possible to reduce their wages in the short term. It is also possible that employees do not immediately notice the lower prices and so are reluctant to accept lower wages. The result is that prices have fallen but wages have not, and so the real wage is now higher. Employees are expensive and so fewer are demanded, meaning that unemployment rises above its natural rate of L1. The economy is on a short-run Phillips curve at P2L2.

Over time, it is possible that wages will fall. This will restore the real wage rate to what it was, and the economy moves back to P2L1. This is because:

- there is downward pressure on wages caused by the higher levels of unemployment;
- employees will notice the lower prices and so be more willing to accept a pay cut;
- managers will be able to renegotiate contracts.

This process takes the economy back to the long-run equilibrium position of P2L1. In the long run, lower demand has led to lower inflation and has kept the same long-run rate of unemployment; however, in the process of adjustment unemployment has risen. Keynesians argue that this process of real wage adjustment could take a long time and so

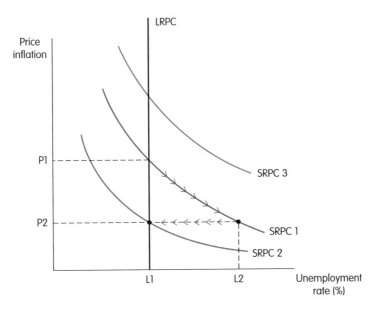

Figure 14.13 The effect of a fall in aggregate demand on unemployment if wages and prices take time to adjust: SRPC, short-run Phillips curve; LRPC, long-run Phillips curve

the economy could get stuck at P2L2, below the potential output of the economy, for some time, in which case it is possible to argue that the government should intervene to boost aggregate demand. This will bring prices back up, reducing the real wage and making employees less expensive again; the economy returns to P1L1 with higher prices but lower unemployment than P2L2.

Assume now that the economy is back at it long-term equilibrium at P1L1 and the government increases demand (see Figure 14.14). This would pull up prices, and if wages were slow to adjust the real wages of employees would be lower. The workforce would be relatively cheap and more could be employed. The economy would be above its potential output with lower than long-run unemployment. The economy would move from P1L1 to P3L3.

However, over time, given the high demand for workers and the higher prices, employees would demand higher pay, increasing the real wage to long-run equilibrium. The economy returns to P3L1 with the same long-run output but higher prices.

Keynesians and classical economists

The fundamental difference between Keynesian and classical economists lies in the efficiency of the labour market and its impact on output and employment in the economy. The more classical you are, the faster you think that the labour market clears; the more Keynesian you are, the more sluggish you think it is (see Figures 14.15 and 14.16). You can also see now why there is so much focus by some economists and policy-makers on

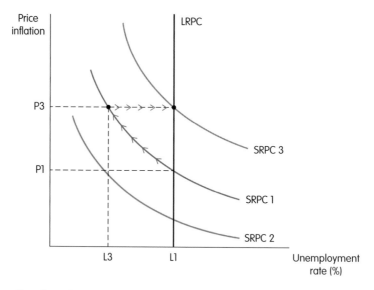

Figure 14.14 The effect of an increase in aggregate demand on unemployment if wages and prices take time to adjust: SRPC, short-run Phillips curve; LRPC, long-run Phillips curve

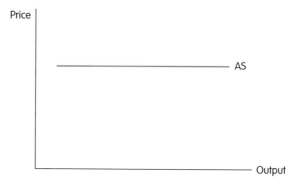

Figure 14.15 The extreme Keynesian view of aggregate supply (AS) in the short run. Aggregate supply is price elastic

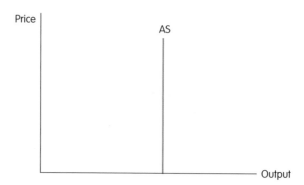

Figure 14.16 The extreme classical view of aggregate supply (AS)

making the labour market work better—for example, trying to increase information open to employees about job availability so that this puts pressure on wages when there is unemployment, and reducing the power of trade unions to stop them acting as a block to downward wage movement.

In the classical model of the economy markets clear quickly and therefore demand-side policies have little impact. Governments should concentrate on supply-side policies and shifting the natural rate of unemployment inwards.

Can the government reduce unemployment below its natural rate?

Increasing government spending could reduce unemployment by pulling up prices and reducing real wages (for example, the economy moves from P1L1 to P3L3 in Figure 14.14). However, when nominal wages eventually catch up with the price increases the natural rate of unemployment is restored with higher inflation. Employees would now expect this higher rate of inflation and demand this in terms of wage increases. To reduce unemployment below the natural rate again, the government could boost demand further and pull up prices again at a faster rate. For example, if employees had anticipated 3 per cent you could increase demand until inflation was 5 per cent. This would work in the short term until employees started bargaining for 5 per cent pay increases. In this case the government would need ever-accelerating increases in prices to keep prices rising faster than nominal wages in order to keep the real wage down. This would suggest that over time the only way for the government to keep unemployment below its natural rate would be to have ever-increasing inflation; this is not an appealing thought to any government in terms of its impact on the domestic economy and international competitiveness.

However, even if governments did adopt such policies, its effectiveness relies on using adaptive expectations. If inflation is 3 per cent, employees eventually bargain for a 3 per cent pay increase. If the government then expands demand and creates inflation of 5 per cent, employees will eventually demand a 5 per cent pay increase, so then the government needs inflation of, say, 8 per cent to reduce real wages, and so on. If employees keep looking backwards to what has happened and base their demands on this, in theory governments could keep one step ahead of them with ever higher inflation. However, the rational expectations model suggests that even this would not work. Rational expectations suggest that employees take all the information available into account when making their decisions and so would soon anticipate government policy. The government may 'fool' employees once or twice with higher inflation, but employees will soon realize this and anticipate this policy and will bargain ahead for higher wages. This suggests that the government cannot reduce inflation below the natural rate of unemployment even in the short run. The implication is that it should focus on supply-side policies and try to reduce the natural rate of unemployment (see Figure 14.17).

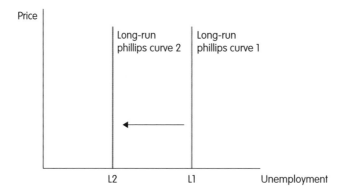

Figure 14.17 Supply-side policies to reduce the natural rate of unemployment

 Think about it ...   14.7

To what extent do you base your views of the future on the past?

Go online to access a video walk-through on analysing the Phillips curve.

Summary

The four main economic objectives of a government generally include low levels of unemployment and stable prices. Low inflation is important because it contributes to a more stable business environment and therefore helps planning and investment. Managers need to estimate costs, and inflation will affect their profit margins, their competitiveness overseas, and their desire to expand. Unemployment is important because it represents a waste of resource and inefficiency. High levels of unemployment may make recruitment easier (depending on the skills and location of those unemployed), but is usually associated with lower levels of demand. These issues are particularly pertinent in the present business climate in the UK where there has been high unemployment and relatively high cost push inflation. This has squeezed businesses on the demand and cost side, and led to many delaying expansion plans and rethinking their strategies.

Checklist

Having read this chapter, you should now understand:

- [ ] inflation and possible causes of inflation;
- [ ] deflation;
- [ ] unemployment and possible causes of unemployment;

- [ ] voluntary and involuntary unemployment;
- [ ] government actions to achieve unemployment and inflation objectives;
- [ ] the possible trade-off of inflation and unemployment;
- [ ] the Phillips curve;
- [ ] adaptive and rational expectations.

Organizations and economics

International Labour Organization (ILO)

The ILO brings together representatives of governments, employers, and workers to jointly develop policies and programmes promoting Decent Work for All. The areas it seeks to improve include the hours that people work, the rights of employees at work, fair pay, and the right to be represented in the workplace.

Source: http://www.ilo.org

Monetary Policy Committee (MPC)

The Bank of England's Monetary Policy Committee (MPC) has nine members: the Governor, the two Deputy Governors, the Bank's Chief Economist, the Executive Director for Markets, and four external members appointed directly by the Chancellor of the Exchequer. The appointment of external members is designed to ensure that the MPC benefits from thinking and expertise in addition to that gained inside the Bank of England. If the MPC, which meets monthly, is concerned about inflation exceeding its target, it will use higher interest rates to dampen aggregate demand and bring inflation down over time. If inflation is too low, the MPC can use lower interest rates to stimulate borrowing.

Source: http://www.bankofengland.co.uk/monetarypolicy/overview.htm

Short answer questions

1. Explain two possible causes of unemployment.
2. Explain the possible consequences of high unemployment levels for a business.
3. Explain how the government might attempt to reduce unemployment.
4. Explain two costs of high unemployment.
5. How is inflation measured?
6. If inflation falls from 3 to 2 per cent, what is happening to prices?
7. Explain how the government might attempt to reduce inflation.
8. What is deflation?
9. Explain two problems caused by inflation.
10. What is the Monetary Policy Committee?

Discussion questions

1. What is the best way for a government to reduce unemployment? Justify your answer.

2. To what extent do high levels of unemployment matter?

3. What is the best way for a government to reduce inflation? Justify your answer.

One step further

Visit our Online Resource Centre at **www.oxfordtextbooks.co.uk/orc/gillespiebusiness2e/** to test your understanding, watch video walk-throughs, and access further information on topics covered in this chapter.

Macroeconomic issues: growth and balance of payments

15

Learning objectives

In this chapter, we examine some of the key issues in macroeconomics.

By the end of this chapter, you should:

- ✓ understand the causes of economic growth;

- ✓ understand the benefits and costs of economic growth;

- ✓ understand the meaning of the balance of payments;

- ✓ understand the causes of a balance of payments current account deficit;

- ✓ understand the problems of a current account deficit.

Case study

'I think this year will be one of cut-backs,' said my mother, although she used to say this at the start of most years when she had finished paying for Christmas. This time she seemed to mean it. 'Things at work are a bit uncertain and they've delayed the new expansion of head office that they were planning. We have lost several big clients abroad who have closed down or are cutting back. It's such a pity as we were doing really well overseas in the last few years thanks to the weaker pound. When we do get a chance to bid for a new order we're finding we can't compete on price at the moment. Our products are good but the inflation over the last few years, plus high wage costs and all the regulations we have to meet, mean we are priced out of the market.

'Domestically things aren't much better. The government has tended to be quite a big customer for us but its austerity programme has almost wiped out those orders. Add to this the general lack of demand in the domestic economy and it's no wonder we're worried.'

Questions

1. How does uncertainty affect the growth of the economy?

2. What is meant by an austerity programme?

3. How do government cut-backs affect UK businesses?

4. Discuss the factors that you think influence the amount of exports businesses can make.

5. Do you think that trade is beneficial to the UK?

6. Discuss the reasons why some UK businesses might shift production abroad.

7. What effect do you think a weak pound has on the economy?

Introduction

In this chapter we examine two more typical government economic objectives: growth and a healthy current account on the balance of payments. We will consider the significance of these objectives and their implications for government policy and business decision-making.

Economic growth

Achieving economic growth is often an important target for governments. The growth of an economy is usually measured by changes in GDP. Achieving more growth means that the income of the economy rises, and this improves the standard of living in financial

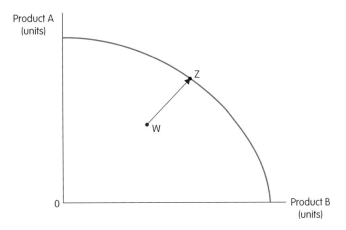

Figure 15.1 Economic growth and the production possibility frontier

terms. For many people the income of an economy is an important measure of its success, and so governments are keen to keep GDP increasing each year.

Historically, the average growth rate in GDP in the UK is between 2 and 3 per cent a year. This means that managers can expect the income of the UK to increase in size by approximately this proportion each year over time; this has implications for likely levels of demand, and therefore the desired levels of capacity and production for businesses.

To achieve economic growth, a government may attempt to increase the level of aggregate demand and/or aggregate supply. Increasing aggregate demand will take the economy nearer to full employment and this is shown in Figure 15.1 as a movement from W to Z; it is taking the economy from a position of underemployment of resources to one of full employment.

This form of economic growth is helping the economy to get back to its maximum output and reach the production possibility frontier. It is filling the 'output gap', which is the gap between where an economy actually is and where it could be—that is, the difference between its actual output and its potential output. Estimates of the size of the output gap in the UK are shown in Figure 15.2.

 Business analysis   15.1

Figure 15.2 suggests that the UK has been up to 4 per cent below its potential output. Why do you think this might be, and what do you think are the possible consequences of this?

To boost aggregate demand, a government might use expansionist fiscal and monetary policies to boost injections $(I + G + X)$ into the economy or reduce withdrawals $(S + T + M)$. For example, the government might:

■ increase its spending—for example, spending more on final goods and services such as healthcare and education;

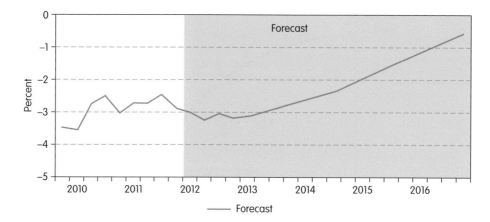

Figure 15.2 The UK output gap: estimates on a quarterly basis, based on the latest National Accounts data and expressed as actual output less trend output as a percentage of trend output (non-oil basis)

Source: Office of Budget Responsibility

- cut direct taxes to give households or firms more income, which should encourage spending;
- lower interest rates to encourage borrowing by households and businesses;
- encourage the banks to lend more.

These demand-side policies were analysed in more detail in Chapter 13.

? Think about it ...   **15.1**

Why are some countries so rich and others so poor?

Why do growth rates vary across countries and over time?

What are the policies that can change growth in the short and long run?

Supply-side policies for growth

Growth may also occur by increasing the potential output of the economy. This would be achieved by increasing its resources, improving technology and productivity. This can be seen as an increase in aggregate supply and an outward shift of the production possibility frontier (see Figure 15.3).

Supply-side policies may include incentives to encourage more start-ups, more innovation, investment, and competition in goods and services markets. New technology and greater use of capital equipment can increase productivity. Governments can help to

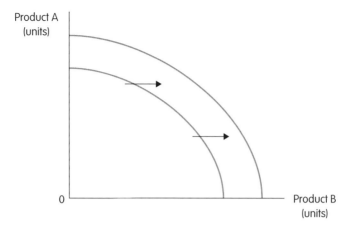

Figure 15.3 Supply-side policies leading to an outward shift of the production possibility frontier

create a more stable economic environment which is good for investment; it can also pro-vide incentives for research and regulate markets to prevent monopoly power. In the labour market the government can provide more incentives to work (for example, by reducing benefits) and, through the education system, provide a better skilled and better educated workforce. Supply-side policies were examined in more detail in Chapter 13.

The German economy has been a striking example of strong growth in recent years, and this has been due to its success in a number of supply-side areas. Germany has a well-developed manufacturing sector of medium-sized businesses competing against each other; these businesses are quite highly unionized, and in recent years the unions have appreciated the need for wage restraint to control costs and maintain international com-petitiveness. The education and training system in Germany provides a better skilled workforce than in the UK; in Germany, there is a well developed vocational training route developing key skills. German businesses have also invested more heavily in research and development to promote innovation. UK business spending on research and development (R&D) is low by international standards—Organisation for Economic Co-operation and Development (OECD) data for 2007 reported that UK business spend-ing on R&D was 1.1 per cent of GDP compared with 1.8 per cent in Germany—and while most other countries have increased their spending over the past decade, in the UK it has declined as a proportion of GDP. This suggests that to boost its growth the UK needs to focus on key areas such its education system, investment in innovation, and other ways of boosting productivity.

? Think about it...   15.2

Why might managers be reluctant to invest in research and development?

Business analysis   15.2

In the last 20 years the Indian economy has opened up more to the market system. The privatization of various state enterprises, fewer barriers to foreign investment and the removal of regulations that protected existing businesses have all led to more competition. This has helped to boost supply and lead to growth of more than 7 per cent a year in the last decade. India has made use of the fact that it has a large English-speaking population to become a significant exporter of information technology and software employees.

Explain India's rapid growth in recent years.

What do you think will determine its ability to continue to grow fast in the future?

You and economics

You are nearly finished at university and are hoping for a good job at the end of it. After all, you haven't spent several years studying and thousands of pounds for nothing—you want a return at the end of it. You hope to work hard to start paying off debts, get a flat in the first years, a new car, more exciting holidays and generally a better standard of living. And the longer you work, the more you expect to have a better lifestyle—after all that's what you work for, isn't it? So you want to be in a growing economy where your earnings rise, your property holds its value (or hopefully increases), and you can accumulate enough to pay for a reasonable retirement. The idea of an economy that is not growing (let alone one that is shrinking) is not something you want to think about!

Economic cycle

Although there may be an underlying trend in the growth rate of an economy, the actual growth year on year may not be that stable. In fact, economies tend to follow a cyclical pattern, which is known as the 'economic (or business) cycle'. While the trend rate of the UK economy may be a growth of between 2 and 3 per cent, in any given year it can be significantly higher or lower than this. Around the overall trend, there will often be periods of boom, recession, slump, and recovery (see Figure 15.4).

- A *boom* occurs when an economy is growing at a fast rate. This tends to be associated with low levels of unemployment, because there are plenty of jobs around, and a

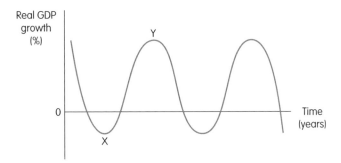

Figure 15.4 Boom, recession, slump, and recovery

shortage of land and office accommodation, because of the demand to produce more. A boom involves faster growth in aggregate demand and demand for most products tends to be high (although inferior products may suffer); this leads to an increased demand for factors of production. Given higher levels of demand, a manager will want to consider whether to expand and increase capacity. Order books should be full and businesses, in general, should be growing. Given the high levels of demand, it may be possible to increase prices.

■ A *recession* occurs when an economy is shrinking. This means that GDP growth is actually negative. The official definition of a recession in the UK is two quarters of negative economic growth. A recession tends to be associated with high levels of unemployment because of a lack of aggregate demand and spare capacity in the UK. With falling levels of demand, a business may consider laying off staff temporarily or even making redundancies if the fall in demand is believed to be long term. The business may also reduce capacity either by selling off land or capital, or by mothballing facilities until they are needed again. A recession officially began in the UK in January 2009; by August 2009, unemployment had risen by over 800,000, the average value of a house had fallen by nearly £20,000, nearly 56,000 homes had been repossessed, nearly 35,000 businesses had closed, and over 176,000 people had become insolvent. In 2012, the UK returned to a recession after –0.2 per cent GDP growth in the first three months of the year and –0.3 per cent at the end of 2011. This is known as a double-dip recession.

■ A *slump* occurs when the recession is severe and prolonged, leading to very high levels of unemployment. In this situation, confidence in the economy is low and there are high levels of spare capacity.

■ A *recovery* occurs when the economy begins to pick up and starts to grow after a slump. As it recovers, businesses begin to invest, consumers begin to gain confidence, and unemployment levels begin to fall.

In Figure 15.4, real GDP growth is negative at X and the economy is shrinking. The economy is in a slump. After this the economy begins to recover. At Y the economy is growing fast and in a boom.

Business analysis 15.3

In February 2012 the Bank of England stated that the UK economy would zigzag, going in and out of growth, but would avoid a recession provided that the Eurozone did not worsen. The Governor of the Bank of England said that the government cut-backs and the weaknesses of the UK's overseas trading partners were both limiting growth.

To what extent do you think the growth of the UK economy can be controlled by the government?

Business analysis 15.4

In May 2009 Robert Shiller, Professor of Economics at Yale University, warned that recent improvements in share prices should not be seen as evidence of a bounce in the economy: 'You don't know whether the argument with your wife is really over or not. Is the problem something that your spouse will bring up again and again.' In the 1930s and 1980s, for example, economies seemed to recover before dipping again, causing a W-shaped recession.

Other shapes of recessions are:

- V-shaped, as occurred in the UK in the early 1990s—the recession was short-lived and then the economy accelerated quickly;
- U-shaped, as occurred in the UK in 1980–1—this is similar to the V shape, but the decline and recovery are more prolonged;
- L-shaped, as experienced by Japan in the 1990s—this occurs when an economy stays stuck in a recession for a long time.

Why does it matter whether the recession is V-shaped, U-shaped, or L-shaped?

People and economics: Nikolai Kondratiev

The Russian economist Nikolai Kondratiev wrote *The Major Economic Cycles* in 1925 in which he claimed to identify long cycles in economies, which lasted for 50–60 years. However, Kondratiev's work was seen as a criticism of the Russian government and its ability to control the economy; in 1938 he was sentenced to a Soviet Gulag and received the death penalty.

Economics and employability

Tell us your name and a bit about your role at Mission Burrito.

My name is Jan Rasmussen and I am the founder, owner, and managing director of Mission Burrito, a chain of five Mexican restaurants. Over the last four years, since their launch, my responsibilities have ranged from handling the day-to-day operation of cooking and cash-handling, to strategic planning and raising funds for growth.

In what ways is an understanding of economics useful in your work?

As the business owner, my aims are to maximize both operating profitability and overall company valuation. Virtually every action and decision within the business has an economic factor, and these all have to be understood to add up to successful growth. A business is a very small cog in the larger social environment and economics governs most of the interactions.

To what extent do economies of scale matter in your business?

Economies of scale matter immensely in the restaurant business. The obvious effect of lowering prices of raw materials through bulk buying is actually less of a factor than the ability to share central costs over more operating units. Producing the very first operating manual takes many hundreds of man hours, but copying it to produce the second one takes minutes.

Why is average revenue important to you?

The restaurant industry is characterized by high fixed costs (they are expensive to run even if no customers come in) and high profit margins on sales (75 per cent is a general target), so setting the right price is essential, as it getting the quality of the food right. Getting customers through the door and maximizing their average spend (i.e. the average revenue per customer) while they are there is the priority.

Did you study economics at university as part of your studies, and, if so, how has it helped you in your work? If not, do you wish you had and why?

I studied economics and accountancy as part of my engineering degree. Both these continue to be extremely useful as they help me to see and explain all aspects of my business in a logical way and balance the emotional 'gut reaction' that so often takes over in decision-making.

What skills are important in your role?

As I lead the entrepreneurial drive of my company, my primary skills are to have ideas and get things done. For me, the key skill is to find a way to get on well with other people. I think I usually deal with at least five people a day who will have a significant effect on the business. Whether you need a million pounds of funding or a spare part delivered the same day, if you are honest, reliable, and realistic I find that it's much more likely to happen.

Business and the economic cycle

Managers need to be aware of the present level of income in the economy and the expected rate of growth in the future because this is likely to affect:

- the levels of demand for the business;
- the ease of recruiting staff;
- the likely demand for pay by staff;
- the ability to increase prices.

For example, if the economy moves into recession, it is easier for managers to recruit staff and there is likely to be less pressure from staff to increase their wages because they will be worried about their jobs. But managers will worry about whether there is sufficient demand for their product, and this will depend, in part, on the nature of the product, the sensitivity of demand to income changes, and their marketing actions.

Some businesses are cyclical. The demand for their product follows the level of income in the economy, and therefore the economic cycle, very closely. For example, the construction industry will suffer heavily in a recession and do well in a boom. But some industries are counter-cyclical—that is, they do better in a recession. For example, company administrators that take over failing businesses will be busier in a poor economic climate. In the UK recession of 2008 and the following years of slow growth and then recession again, discount stores such as Aldi, Primark, and Poundland found that their sales grew relatively quickly as customers traded down.

In a recession businesses will also look to control costs as tightly as possible because of the downward pressure on prices. Managers will look to ensure that the business is as lean as possible. If demand is lower than usual, other reactions may include the following:

- staff overtime may be reduced (because it is often paid at a higher rate than the standard hours) or people who leave may not be replaced (this is called natural wastage) (HR response);
- tighter budgets may be set for staff (finance response);
- new markets abroad may be pursued or more basic product lines introduced (marketing response);
- waste will be reduced and more effort made to get it right first time (operations response).

Time lag for businesses to respond

When looking at economic indicators, you will often find that data such as unemployment figures and stock levels respond to changes in the demand in the economy after a period of time. Assume that demand starts to fall in an economy—perhaps because of a fall in consumption or government spending. At first managers may be uncertain if this is likely to last and so may keep production at the previous levels and try to maintain staffing levels. The result is likely to be higher stock levels and lower profits. However, over time they realize that demand is staying low and start to make cut-backs. This leads to a fall in investment and more unemployment. This adds to the fall in demand and can contribute to a recession.

At some point expectations will change and managers will believe that the economy is going to come out of recession; this may be because of government policy changes. More positive expectations of the future of the economy can lead to an increase in investment. This is likely to be tentative at first—managers will use up stocks rather than increase production levels, and they will try and use existing staff rather than commit to more staff because of the impact on costs. Eventually investment will increase, boosting demand and helping to bring the economy out of the recession and into a recovery with less unemployment.

?   *Think about it...*   15.3

1. How might the economic cycle affect business planning?

2. Which other businesses can you think of that might benefit in a recession?

3. Find the growth figures for your own economy. At what stage of the economic cycle do you think this is?

Growth and the global economy

The increasing amount of trade between countries over time has increased the interdependence of nations. Changes in the economic position of the USA, the world's largest economy, has knock-on effects on economies all over the world. Quite how linked economies are was seen in the global economic crisis of 2008 when slow growth in many regions reduced export demand in other countries. Governments sought to help each other to sustain global demand; for example, in 2010 the UK government helped bail out Ireland with a contribution of over £7 billion. The UK Chancellor of the Exchequer said that Ireland was the UK's closest neighbour and it was in Britain's national interest for the Irish economy to be successful.

The high level of global interdependence was also evident during the Eurozone crisis of 2012 when problems in countries such as Greece, Ireland, and Spain worried their trading partners and led to slower growth there as well because of lower levels of demand. Stronger countries, such as Germany and France, had to help bail out other Eurozone countries with financial problems. Meanwhile the Chinese economy, known for its fast growth, was affected by the levels of uncertainty in Europe which was its greatest export market; as a result, in 2012 the Chinese government reduced interest rates for the first time in four years to stimulate their own growth. Increasingly, governments and managers cannot act in isolation and need to be aware of changes happening in the economies around them.

Business analysis   15.5

The government's economic policy objective is to achieve strong, sustainable, and balanced growth. In November 2010, the Chancellor of the Exchequer and the Secretary of State for Business, Innovation, and Skills launched the Growth Review to undertake a thorough assessment of how government can help create the conditions for growth.

The Growth Review focused on four ambitions for the UK economy:

- to create the most competitive tax system in the G20 (the G20 is a group of twenty developed economies);
- to make the UK the best place in Europe to start, finance, and grow a business;
- to encourage investment and exports as a route to a more balanced economy;
- to create a more educated workforce that is the most flexible in Europe.

1. How might a government encourage investment?
2. How could a government make a country a better place to start, finance, and grow a business?
3. How can government develop a better educated workforce?

Source: http://www.hm-treasury.gov.uk/ukecon_growth_index.htm

The benefits and costs of economic growth

Economic growth shows the rate at which the income of an economy is increasing. If national income grows faster than the population, this will result in a higher income per person. This, in turn, should mean a higher standard of living for the country's citizens. Many people measure their own success and the success of an economy in terms of their income and possessions, so a growth in GDP per person is often a government target. With higher incomes, people may spend more, which creates opportunities for business. In particular, there will be changes in consumption patterns as households trade up—for example, from a bicycle to a moped, or from a moped to car. Many businesses operating in the more mature economies, including the USA and the UK, are seeing new markets being created in emerging economies, such as Brazil and China, in which fast growth opens up much greater sales possibilities. Managers must monitor the growth of their own economy and growth rates overseas to identify strategic opportunities.

Economic growth also means that the tax revenues of governments should automatically increase (because more people are earning and firms are making more profits) and there is less spending on benefits as unemployment is lower. These changes should automatically improve the government's financial position, potentially allowing more spending on merit and public goods.

However, economic growth can also bring problems to a country, such as negative externalities—for example, there may be pollution and damage to the environment because of more deliveries and more output. There has been growing concern in recent years about the negative impact of economic growth on the environment. This has put pressure on governments to control the levels of pollution generated by businesses as they expand and to promote sustainable growth, considering the impact of expansion on natural resources. According to the OECD:

> The United Kingdom started to pursue policies to reduce greenhouse gas emissions at a relatively early date and now has a comprehensive set of measures in place. It has set clear targets for emission reductions consistent with international goals of limiting global warming ... On the international stage, it has been an active protagonist of a global deal to limit human-induced climate change. ... The United Kingdom is likely to reduce emissions by more than its target under the Kyoto Protocol, outperforming many OECD countries in the latter respect.

Economic growth may also be unsustainable in the long term. Growth may use up resources that are non-renewable, such as oil, and over-exploit natural resources, such as fish and trees, by using them up faster than they are being replaced. Sustainable development was defined in 1987 by the Brundtland Commission on Environment and Development as 'development that meets the needs of the present without compromising the ability of future generations to meet their own needs'. Fast growth now may be at the expense of the future welfare of society. Some economists argue that when the external costs of growth are considered, increasing GDP is not necessarily desirable. It could be that a society is now willing to sacrifice economic growth as measured by GDP growth in return for reducing the impact of the economy on the environment and the long-term quality of life.

? 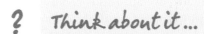 15.4

The UK's ability to achieve some of its environmental targets is likely to have been helped by the recession. Why might this be?

@

Your uncle is a very successful investment banker. He studied hard at school, got a good degree, and then worked his way up within the bank. In some ways he has a fantastic lifestyle—two cars, big house, some great holidays abroad, property in France, never seems short of money—he is undoubtedly 'well off'. On the other hand, he seems to work crazy hours and you can see that his job is quite stressful. When a big deal is being negotiated he can get, quite, short-tempered and he is often working so hard that his family don't see him much. Although there are elements of his life you wish you had, there are parts that you are glad you don't!

Balance of payments

The growth of an economy is increasingly linked to how other countries are doing. Countries such as the UK rely heavily on trade as a source of demand-stimulating growth. After 2010 the coalition government in the UK aimed to reduce levels of government spending so that it could cut its deficit but maintain the overall level of demand by encouraging investment by businesses and increasing exports. Its aim is for a more balanced economy with a smaller role for the state and a greater role for business and trade. Therefore businesses and governments will be interested in how well the country is competing internationally and how to improve competitiveness. The trading position of an economy is measured by its balance of payments, and so this provides an important indicator of an economy's international performance.

The **balance of payments** records the value of transactions between one country and the rest of the world over a given time period, usually a year. It measures the earnings from exports and the spending on imports during that period. In a free-floating exchange rate system the balance of payments will equal zero overall. This is because the value of the currency changes to ensure that the quantity supplied equals the quantity demanded. This means that the number of pounds leaving a country equals the number of pounds entering, and so the overall balance of payments is zero; there is no net flow of currency either way. However, what may be very significant is what is happening within these overall flows—that is, what is happening to elements within the balance of payments.

In Figure 15.5a, at ER1 the exchange rate is too high and therefore there is excess supply of the currency. The exchange rate will fall to the equilibrium at ER3. In Figure 15.5b, at ER2 the exchange rate is too low and there is excess demand; there will be upward pressure on the exchange rate. At ER3 the quantity demanded of the currency equals the quantity supplied; inflow equals outflow and so the balance of payments is zero.

In a fixed exchange rate regime the government intervenes to stabilize the value of the currency. If it is set above the free market equilibrium, such as ER1 in Figure 15.5a, the government needs to intervene to prevent it falling. The government can do this by buying up the excess supply of the currency (Q2Q3) using its foreign currency reserves. The government is buying its own currency in return for foreign currency it has stored. In this case the balance of payments is actually in deficit (negative) because more of the currency

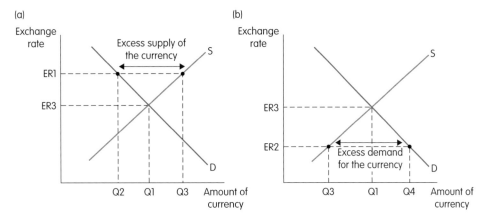

Figure 15.5 Exchange rate

is being sold than is being bought in the free market. However, this is soaked up by the government buying it, which is recorded as a positive number so:

Balance of payments (negative Q2Q3) + Official financing (positive Q2Q3) = 0

If the exchange rate is fixed at a lower rate than equilibrium, such as ER2 in Figure 15.5b, there will be excess demand for the currency. This means that a greater quantity is demanded of the currency than is supplied. This would put upward pressure on the currency, but to prevent this occurring the government sells its own currency in return for foreign currency (and therefore increases its foreign currency reserves). In this case the balance of payments is in surplus (positive), but the government is selling its currency (which is recorded as a negative number). Therefore:

Balance of payments (positive Q3Q4) + Official financing (negative Q3Q4) = 0

The elements of the balance of payments

Governments will worry not only about the overall balance-of-payments position, but they will also be concerned about its composition. Even if the balance of payments is zero because the inflows and outflows of currency are equal, a government may be concerned about the scale and direction of particular types of flow. Therefore it is important to understand the elements within the balance of payments.

Economic transactions that make up the balance of payments include:

■ exports and imports of goods such as oil, agricultural products, other raw materials, machinery and transport equipment, computers, and clothing—for example, the UK has tended to import more goods than it exports;

■ exports and imports of services such as international transport, travel, financial, and business services—for example, the UK exports more services than it imports;

■ income flows, such as dividends and interest earned by non-residents on investments in the UK and by UK residents investing abroad;

- financial flows, such as investment in shares and loans;
- transfers, such as foreign aid and funds brought by migrants to the UK.

A government will analyse the trends within the overall balance of payments. For example, it may be concerned if there is a large deficit in relation to goods or services (i.e the spending on imports is greater than the earnings from exports) because this may suggest that the country's businesses are uncompetitive in these areas. The **balance of trade** specifically measures the difference between a country's exports of goods and services, and its imports of goods and services, ignoring all financial transfers, investments, and the like. A country is said to have a 'trade deficit' if it is importing more than it exports. It has a 'trade surplus' if the export revenue is greater than the spending on imports. The UK has had a major deficit in goods for over twenty years, but a surplus in services, reflecting that it is relatively efficient at producing services, such as banking and insurance, and relatively inefficient at producing manufactured goods.

The current account of the balance of payments comprises the balance of trade in goods and services plus the net investment incomes from overseas assets (for example, interest payments, profits, and dividends from assets) and the net balance of private transfers between countries and government transfers (for example, UK government payments to help fund the various spending programmes of the European Union (EU)). This is a very common measure of the competitiveness of a country's producers relative to the rest of the world.

For the UK, the net investment income is positive, reflecting major investments overseas by British businesses and individuals. The transfer balance is negative; one reason for this is that the UK government is a net contributor to the EU budget.

Business analysis   15.6

In 2011 the UK Secretary of State for Business, Vince Cable, spoke of a recent visit by the Chinese Vice Premier: 'We both share the same aim: to develop closer bilateral commercial relations. Yet with UK exports still less than 1 per cent of China's imports, we can—and must—do better. We need also to further capitalize on the rapid internationalization of Chinese companies to sell the benefits of the UK as an attractive business environment for Chinese companies. We are already a favoured destination for Chinese outward investment but the volumes are low.'

How might the UK government help British businesses to export more to China?

How might the UK government encourage more inward investment from China to Britain?

Source: http://www.bis.gov.uk

A current account deficit

Whilst the balance of payments might 'balance' overall, within this the current account may be in surplus or in deficit. The current account is the difference between the value of exports of goods and services and the value of imports of goods and services over a period of time. A deficit means that the country is spending more on importing goods and services than it is earning from exporting—although the current account also includes net income (such as interest and dividends) and transfers from abroad (such as foreign aid), these are usually a small fraction of the total.

The amount that a country spends on imports will depend on factors such as the following.

- Its income level because this will affect its total spending, including spending on foreign goods and services—higher income and spending levels attract imports.

- the marginal propensity to import (MPM) which measures the extra spending out of each extra pound—the greater the marginal propensity to import, the greater the spending on imports for any level of income.

- Its own resources—for example, Nigeria is a major importer of petrol. Although it has major oil reserves, it has not developed its refining industry and so has to export oil to be refined which is then imported back in as petrol.

The amount that a country earns from exports will depend on the following factors.

- The income levels and the marginal propensity to import in countries overseas.

- The competitiveness of a country's products; this may depend on factors such as its unit costs and quality. This in turn will depend on factors such as the spending on research and development and the extent to which they benefit from economies of scale.

- The access and targeting of markets—for example, many economies have gained from the growth of the BRIC economies (Brazil, Russia, India, and China), but this requires businesses to target these countries to make the most of their export opportunities. UK businesses have been relatively slow to exploit the opportunities in these markets.

As can be seen in Figure 15.6, as domestic income levels increase, this increases spending on imports; exports are assumed to independent of the domestic income (they depend on the incomes of other countries).

At higher levels of income the country is likely to run a balance-of-payments current account deficit because of higher import spending. If there is a greater propensity to import, this means that there are more imports at any income level and this could create a larger deficit as shown at income Y1 where the deficit increases from 'ab' to 'ac'.

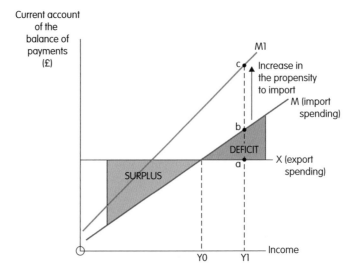

Figure 15.6 Export spending is assumed to be independent of income; import spending rises with income. As income increases, the economy moves towards a current account deficit. With a higher propensity to import, more is imported at each income level.

 Business analysis   15.7

- Singapore has a highly developed and successful free market economy. It has an open business environment, stable prices, and a GDP per person equal to that of the four largest Western European countries. The economy depends strongly on exports—particularly consumer electronics, IT products, and pharmaceuticals—and on a growing service sector. The economy contracted by 1.0 per cent in 2009 as a result of the global financial crisis, but rebounded by 14.8 per cent in 2010 and 4.9 per cent in 2011 on the strength of renewed exports. Over the longer term, the government hopes to establish a new growth path that focuses on raising productivity, which has sunk to a compound annual growth rate of just 1.8 per cent in the last decade. Singapore has attracted major investments in pharmaceuticals and medical technology production, and efforts will continue to establish Singapore as Southeast Asia's financial and high-tech hub.

- Zimbabwe's economy is growing despite continuing political uncertainty. Following a decade of contraction from 1998 to 2008, Zimbabwe's economy recorded estimated real growth of 6 per cent in 2011. However, the government of Zimbabwe still faces a number of difficult economic problems, including infrastructure and regulatory deficiencies, ongoing indigenization pressure, policy uncertainty, a large external debt burden, and insufficient formal employment. Zimbabwe's involvement in the war in the Democratic Republic of the Congo between 1998 and 2002 drained hundreds of millions of dollars from the economy. The government's subsequent land reform programme, characterized by chaos and violence, badly damaged the commercial farming sector, the traditional source of exports and foreign exchange and the provider of 400,000 jobs, turning Zimbabwe into a net importer of food products. Until early 2009, the Reserve Bank of Zimbabwe routinely printed money to fund the budget deficit, causing hyperinflation. Changes in early 2009—which allowed currencies such as the Botswana pula, the South Africa rand, and the US dollar to be used locally—ended hyperinflation and restored price stability, but exposed structural weaknesses that continue to inhibit broad-based growth.

1. These two economies are very different in terms of economic success. Why do you think this might be?
2. What type of business might have an export market in Singapore?
3. What problems might you have trading in Zimbabwe?
4. How might the success of Singapore and the problems in Zimbabwe affect businesses in your economy?

Source: Adapted from *CIA Factbook*, 2012. Reproduced with kind permission.

Problems with a current account deficit

When countries run large current account deficits this may be a concern as it may highlight uncompetitiveness. As the International Monetary Fund (IMF) says:

> It can lead businesses, trade unions, and parliamentarians ... to point accusing fingers at trading partners and make charges about unfair practices. Tension between the United States and China about which country is primarily responsible for the trade imbalance between the two has thrown the spotlight on the broader consequences for the international financial system when some countries run large and persistent current account deficits and others accumulate big surpluses.

The trade problems between the USA and China have arisen in recent years as a result of large current account deficits in the USA and large surpluses in China. US producers have accused the Chinese of deliberately keeping its currency undervalued to promote exports and put pressure on the government to let the yuan increase in value. Several US producers have called for protectionist measures to make it more difficult for Chinese firms to export to the USA (protectionism is examined in more detail in Chapter 16).

When a country runs a current account deficit, it means that it is spending more on goods and services from abroad than it is earning from these overseas. How can it afford these? By the inflows that are coming in on the financial account (so that overall the balance of payments is zero). This means that with a current account deficit a country is building up liabilities to the rest of the world with money flowing in on the financial account being used to buy imports. Eventually, these liabilities need to be paid back. So what is important is what is happening with these flows. If they are just being spent on consumption and this is not helping the country become more productive and competitive, the current account deficit is a problem. A country needs to be willing and able to (eventually) generate sufficient current account surpluses to repay what it has borrowed. Therefore, according to the IMF, whether a country should run a current account deficit (borrow more) depends on the extent of its existing foreign liabilities (its external debt) and on whether the borrowing will be financing investment that has a higher marginal product than the interest rate (or rate of return) the country has to pay on its foreign liabilities. For example, a deficit may not be such an issue if it is being used to import parts and materials to build up a particular sector of the economy which will generate profitable exports in the future. However, if the deficit simply reflects the imports of goods and services because the country is uncompetitive and there is no investment to improve the country's trading position in the long term, then the problem may be more serious.

 ## Business analysis   15.8

All other things being equal, which one of the combinations A, B, C, and D, shown in Table 15.1, is most likely to worsen the UK's current account position?

Table 15.1 Identify the combination that worsens the UK's current account position

	UK inflation rate	Exchange rate	UK unemployment
A	Higher	Lower	Lower
B	Higher	Higher	Lower
C	Lower	Lower	Higher
D	Lower	Higher	Higher

Reducing a current account deficit

If a government is worried about a current account deficit because it might suggest uncompetitiveness, it may adopt the following types of policy.

- *Expenditure-reducing policies* These are policies that aim to reduce the total spending in the country. For example, a government may try to reduce aggregate demand by increasing direct taxes, reducing government spending, or increasing interest rates. With less spending overall in an economy, there should be less money spent on imports, which should reduce the deficit. But the consequence is also less spending throughout the economy, which may lead to slower growth and higher unemployment. This highlights how government objectives may conflict. By reducing growth in the economy spending on imports may be reduced, improving the current account position, but at the same time it may damage any employment targets.

- *Expenditure-switching policies* These are policies specifically aimed at reducing the spending on imports. These could include measures that protect domestic businesses against foreign competitors. For example, it might introduce a tax (tariff) on foreign products that makes them relatively more expensive, making customers switch away, or a quota limiting the total number of foreign products sold in a country. But the consequence of these protectionist policies is less choice and more expensive products for customers. It may also lead to retaliation from other countries, and potentially spark a trade war.

? *Think about it ...*   15.6

What determines the effectiveness of a tax on foreign producers in terms of reducing spending on imports?

The effects of a depreciation of a currency

A government might also try to stimulate exports and reduce import spending by reducing the value of its currency. This is called a depreciation of the currency (if the currency was previously fixed and then is fixed at a lower level, this is called devaluation). The government can lower the external value of its currency by cutting interest rates and/or selling its own currency:

- lower interest rates will make the country less attractive for foreign investors—this will reduce capital inflows and limit demand for the currency (depending on the expected returns elsewhere);

- selling its currency in return for foreign currency increases the supply, which leads to an excess supply at the original exchange rate and puts downward pressure on its value.

When a currency falls in value, the country's products become cheaper in terms of foreign currency, making the country more competitive. This should lead to an increase in the quantity demanded of exports and an increase in spending on exports. The extent of the increase in export earnings will depend on the price elasticity of demand for exports—the more price elastic demand is, the greater the increase in export sales and earnings. The price elasticity will depend on factors such as the availability of substitutes, the ease of switching to alternative suppliers, and how buyers' income is spent on the purchase.

However, the decrease in the value of the currency also increases the price of imports in the domestic currency. As we have seen in Chapter 8, the effect on spending on imports depends on the price elasticity of demand for imports. If demand for imports is price elastic, sales will fall by more than the price increase (in percentages) and total spending on imports will fall.

This means that if demand for exports is sensitive to price, a fall in the value of the currency will boost export earnings significantly; if demand for imports is price elastic, import spending will fall and so, overall, the current account position will improve.

The importance of the price elasticity of demand for exports and imports is highlighted by the **Marshall–Lerner condition**, which states that if the price elasticity of demand for exports (PED exports) plus the price elasticity of demand for imports (PED imports) is greater than 1, a fall in the value of a currency will improve the current account of the balance of payments, that is:

PED exports + PED imports must be greater or equal to 1

? Think about it...   15.7

If the Marshall–Lerner condition is not met, what do you think happens to a country's current account position on the balance of payments if its currency falls in value? Explain your answer.

Assume that the pound falls in value. In the short term, demand for exports and imports is likely to be price inelastic. Customers have established buying patterns and may be reluctant to switch to other suppliers, and it may take time to find reliable alternatives. Because the pound has fallen UK exports are cheaper in foreign currency and this should increase demand; however, if demand is price inelastic the impact on sales will be limited and so export earnings will not rise significantly. Meanwhile, although imports are more expensive in pounds, UK customers will not want to or be able to switch away much in the short term and so end up paying more for imports. Therefore in the short run the current account is likely to worsen when the pound falls in value because of the relatively small impact on export revenue and an increase in import spending. This can be seen by the move from T1 to T2 on Figure 15.7.

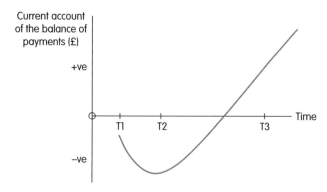

Figure 15.7 The J-curve effect: short term

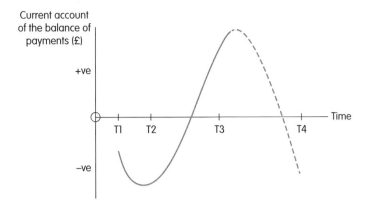

Figure 15.8 The J-curve effect: long term

Over time, however, customers abroad will be attracted by the cheaper UK goods and services and switch to them; this makes demand more price elastic and UK earnings from exports should rise significantly. At the same time UK firms switch away from the more expensive imports over time and so import spending falls. This means that the current account position should improve over time. This gives rise to what is known as the J-curve effect. This can be seen from the movement from T2 to T3.

Over the long term (after T3) the position is likely to worsen again (see Figure 15.8). This is because the higher price of imports increases costs and leads to cost push inflation. Higher UK prices offsets the advantage gained by the falling pound because it pushes up prices again abroad. The cost push inflation gradually erodes the competitive gains of the falling pound. This suggests that depreciation of the currency takes time to improve the current account position and will not be effective in the long run. The long-run effect may be for the deficit to return and for there to be higher inflation in the country caused by higher imported costs.

 Data analysis   *15.1*

A 10 per cent decrease in the value of a currency leads to a 5 per cent rise in export sales and a 2 per cent decrease in import sales.

1. What are the price elasticities for exports and imports?

2. Is the Marshall–Lerner condition met?

Conflicting government economic objectives

While the action required to improve a country's economic position may seem clear in some areas, the difficulty often comes in trying to achieve all economic objectives simultaneously. For example, an increase in demand may lead to upward pressure on prices and create demand pull inflation. However, faster economic growth may lead to more spending on imports, worsening the current account position. Therefore juggling different demands may cause problems for economic policy-makers. This, of course, is why normative economics is so contentious.

?   Think about it...   15.8

What might the consequences be of the key government economic objectives of:

- boosting aggregate demand to reduce unemployment?
- reducing aggregate demand to reduce spending on imports?

Forecasting economic change

Managers clearly want to try to know what is likely to happen to economic variables, such as national income, unemployment, inflation, and the levels of exports and imports, in their key markets. This means not only examining past trends, but also forecasting what will happen to these variables in the future. Managers' strategies will want to take account of emerging opportunities and threats, some of which will be created by economic change. Therefore forecasting the economy is an important part of business planning and environmental analysis.

Forecasts may be produced based on past trends and models that have been developed. However, an economy is made up of millions of markets, households, and businesses making decisions that can affect each other through a series of complex relationships. Not surprisingly, accurately predicting the economy is far from easy.

 #   Data analysis   15.2

Figure 15.9 shows the UK government's estimates of the economy's growth, and highlights that it cannot predict it exactly. The darker the shading, the more likely it is that this will be the actual figure. Notice how the further ahead the projection is, the greater the uncertainty that exists.

How useful do you think the data in Figure 15.9 is to managers operating in the UK?

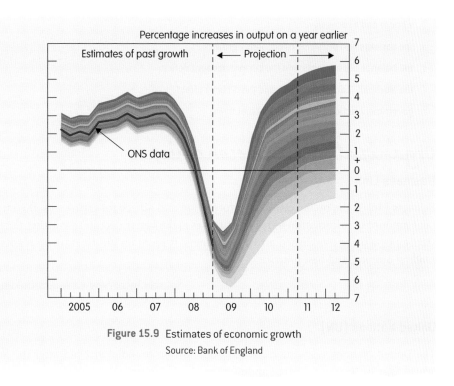

Figure 15.9 Estimates of economic growth
Source: Bank of England

Summary

The main economic indicators that a manager may examine to analyse an economy include GDP and the balance of payments. Changes in these can indicate shifts in aggregate demand and supply, and the international competitiveness of a country. Managers need to understand the causes and possible consequences of such changes, but forecasting future economic changes is far from easy.

The growth of a country can be important in terms of potential demand; the balance of payments position may reflect the success of businesses in exporting their products and exploiting overseas market opportunities. These issues are particularly relevant in the present business climate where growth in the UK has been very hesitant, making managers reluctant to invest, and where finding new markets overseas has been viewed by the UK government and by managers as a critical element of renewed growth.

Checklist

Having read this chapter, you should now understand:

- [ ] economic growth;
- [ ] the economic cycle;

☐ a boom and a recession;

☐ the benefits and problems of economic growth;

☐ the balance of payments and the current account deficit;

☐ the Marshall–Lerner condition and the J-curve effect;

☐ government actions to achieve its objectives.

Organizations and economics

Business Link

Business Link is the online centre of information and advice for businesses. It contains a huge amount of information to help businesses make better decisions, whether they are a start-up or a more established growing business. It provides information on regulations, funding options, and best practice.

Source: http://www.businesslink.gov.uk/

United Nations (UN)

The United Nations is an international organization founded in 1945 after the Second World War by 51 countries committed to maintaining international peace and security, developing friendly relations among nations, and promoting social progress, better living standards, and human rights. The UN works on a broad range of fundamental issues, ranging from sustainable development, environment and refugee protection, disaster relief, counter-terrorism, disarmament, and non-proliferation, to promoting democracy, human rights, gender equality and the advancement of women, governance, economic and social development, international health, clearing landmines, expanding food production, and more.

Source: http://www.un.org

UK Trade and Investment (UKTI)

UK Trade and Investment is a government organization that works with UK companies to help them succeed in international markets. It provides advice, guidance, finance, and network opportunities. At the same time it encourages the best overseas companies to consider the UK as a possible partner.

Source: http://www.ukti.gov.uk/

Short answer questions

1. What is meant by GDP?

2. Explain the possible implications of a recession for a business.

3. Explain the possible implications of a boom for a business. Distinguish between demand-side and supply-side policies.

4. How can a government stimulate economic growth?

5. What is the balance of payments?

6. Why does the balance of payments equal zero in a free-floating exchange rate system?

7. What is meant by a balance-of-payments current account surplus?

8. Explain the difference between expenditure-switching and expenditure-reducing policies.

9. What is the Marshall–Lerner condition?

10. What is the J-curve effect?

Discussion questions

1. To what extent will a fall in the value of a currency improve a country's current account position?

2. Should the USA worry about its large current account deficit?

3. Is faster growth a sensible aim for government?

One step further

Visit our Online Resource Centre at **www.oxfordtextbooks.co.uk/orc/gillespiebusiness2e/** to test your understanding, watch video walk-throughs, and access further information on topics covered in this chapter.

International business and trade

16

Learning objectives

By the end of this chapter, you should:

- [✓] understand the reasons for international trade;

- [✓] understand the benefits of international trade;

- [✓] be able to explain protectionism;

- [✓] be able to analyse the reasons for and arguments against protectionism.

Case study

John had worked for 15 years for a UK-based pottery business. He learned last week that production was to be moved to China and the company was to lay off several hundred staff as a result. John thought that this was an outrage and another example of a UK business forgetting its responsibilities and foolishly chasing short-term profits. Consumers will never support them for this, he thought. The managers, of course, sought to blame the owners, but John thought it was the managers' fault for not coming up with a better plan to keep production in the UK. But John wasn't just cross with the managers of his business; it was also the government's fault. Why didn't it stop this sort of thing happening? It could protect UK industry and save jobs, instead of which the Prime Minister always seemed to be abroad encouraging foreign trade and surely that would ultimately kill off UK firms?

Questions

1. Do you think that UK companies are right to switch production abroad to China?

2. Do you think that UK business managers have a responsibility to keep production in the UK?

3. Do you think that consumers care where something is made?

4. Do you think that the government should protect UK business from foreign competition?

5. Do you think that trade is good for UK business?

6. How important do you think that trade is for your economy?

Introduction

All countries are open economies to some extent. This means that businesses and households within an economy are involved in trade with other countries. As a manager, you may source some of your components from abroad; you may even produce abroad. You are also likely to sell some of your products overseas. Therefore understanding overseas markets from both a production and a marketing perspective is an important element of business. It has become increasingly important as economies become more inextricably linked to each other via trade so that the success of any one economy depends on others. For example, world trade in manufactured goods and services has grown far faster than

?   *Think about it...*   16.1

1. What do you think are the main exports of your country?

2. Do you think these have changed over time? If so, why do you think this is?

3. What are the main imports?

national incomes in the last fifty years, highlighting an increased global dependence on trade. The UK is a particularly open economy, which means that it is very dependent on trade, with sectors such as communications, finance, and entertainment generating high levels of export revenues; this makes understanding of international trade and international business issues particularly significant.

Why do countries trade?

International trade takes place when a business, household, or government in one country buys or sells a product from a business, household, or government in another country. An export occurs when a country earns revenue from a sale abroad; an import occurs when money leaves an economy to buy from overseas (see Figure 16.1).

International trade will happen when businesses and consumers within a country can get better value buying a product from abroad than producing it domestically. This occurs when businesses in one country have a **comparative advantage** over businesses in other countries. Comparative advantage exists when the opportunity cost of producing an item of the same quality is less than it is elsewhere; this means that businesses sacrifice fewer resources to produce an item than other organizations would do. When businesses have a comparative advantage, they are more efficient than their overseas rivals.

Assume that farmers in the UK wanted to grow bananas; it could be done, but the resources involved to create conditions favourable to banana growing would be so enormous that it would be very inefficient compared with buying these products from a country that naturally had the climate to grow this type of fruit. Similarly, a country such as China has enormous resources of relatively cheap unskilled labour, and so it makes sense for this economy to focus on producing products that use a lot of this resource, while another country may focus on sectors that build on its own resources and skills. For example, the UK specializes more on finance and the creative industries, in which it has specialist skills. But it is not only 'whole products' that are traded; take apart any laptop and you will find, for example, that the screen is made in one country, the DVD slot in another, the keyboard somewhere else, and the

Import spending on foreign products

Export revenue from sales abroad

Figure 16.1 International trade

hard drive somewhere else, and that all of these are assembled somewhere completely different as managers seek the best and cheapest place to produce particular elements of their products.

Of course, some products are easier to trade than others. Products such as razors, cigarettes, and perfumes are fairly global because they are essentially the same anywhere in the world. UK football has also become a global product, with a huge number of players and managers in the UK coming from overseas, and many clubs having foreign owners. Other products, such as foods and books, can become global successes, but need to be adapted to meet the tastes, culture, and interests of different regions. Services such as a bus journey, a haircut, and dental treatment cannot be exported because they are not physical items that can be moved globally (although the Sultan of Brunei is said to fly his favourite barber from Harrods in the UK to Brunei to cut his hair every few weeks!).

You and economics

Time for the weekly shop. Go to Sainsbury's and take your trolley around the store. Fill it with your usual weekly supplies: orange juice made from Spanish oranges, butter from New Zealand, bacon from Denmark, bananas from South America, tea from India, coffee from Colombia, and French wine. Thank goodness for trade—there wouldn't be much choice if you had to rely only on UK products.

Free trade

Free trade exists when there are no barriers to trade; this means that businesses can easily export or import products, without limits being placed on the nature or level of trade between countries. Free trade would occur if governments did not intervene and limit trade between countries.

The benefits of free trade are that countries and businesses can specialize in products in relation to which they have relatively low opportunity costs, and buy in other products or resources from abroad.

Free trade means that domestic businesses should produce products for which the cost per unit, given the nature of the product and the level of quality provided, is relatively low compared with businesses in other countries. This should mean that they are competitive and can export abroad.

By specializing and selling abroad, businesses can do the following.

- They can grow much faster than they could if they were only to sell domestically, because they have access to much larger markets overseas—this may enable them to benefit from economies of scale, thereby reducing unit costs even further. The domestic market may be saturated, or there may be restrictions on further growth domestically; international trade enables continued sales growth.

- They can buy other products from abroad where companies are specializing in areas of expertise at a lower price than the business could produce itself.

People and economics: David Ricardo

David Ricardo (1772–1823) was an English economist and a Member of Parliament. In his book the Principles of Political Economy and Taxation (1817) he set out the law of comparative advantage, which argued for free trade among countries. He believed that trade was mutually beneficial, even if one country is more productive than its partner in all areas, provided that each country specializes in the products where they have a relative advantage.

? *Think about it ...* **16.2**

1. Can you think of three types of economy of scale from which a business might gain if it were to expand by selling abroad?

2. A business sells its products for £20 and the unit cost is £15. If, through expansion overseas, the unit cost falls to £14, what has happened to its profit margin?

@ *You and economics*

You enjoy cooking and are much praised for creating new recipes. You have the ability to turn a range of fairly ordinary ingredients into a culinary masterpiece. You watch a lot of cooking programmes on TV, which has helped, but you seem to have a natural talent for cookery. However, you hate gardening—you find it boring and have a habit of killing any plant you try and care for. Your next door neighbour, however, is a natural gardener and seems to be able to grow anything. You strike a deal—you cook for her once a month in return for her looking after your small garden. You both specialize and trade occurs!

Trade also means that there will be greater competition within markets, which should encourage innovation and greater efficiency domestically. Businesses have to get better to survive. This should lead to more choice and better products for consumers. Given that businesses are consumers themselves, because they buy inputs, they will also gain from cheaper and better quality supplies. The growth of the internet has made it easier to find suppliers anywhere in the world; free trade enables you to buy these supplies unhindered.

Therefore trade can offer enormous benefits to businesses and households. However, success abroad cannot be guaranteed over time in any specific market. The ability to compete well in particular products can shift from one company to another when the market changes, or when new technologies make cheaper and better substitute products possible. Producers need to be ready to change and develop in response to new conditions and new opportunities. In 2009, Toshiba produced the last television made in the UK. John Logie Baird invented television in 1926, and for many years UK producers, such as Decca, dominated the worldwide industry. However, in the 1960s Japanese producers, such as Sony and Toshiba, entered the market and were able to produce better quality products at a lower price; over time, they took market share away from UK and US producers. But they continued to produce in the UK, because this was within the European Union (EU) and meant that they had easy access to European markets, until the costs of producing elsewhere became much more attractive. At that point, Toshiba shifted production to Poland, where costs were lower.

Although the possibility of the export market generates opportunities, international trade also brings threats to individual businesses. While free trade may be in the interest of businesses and households generally, individual firms or industries may suffer from more efficient production overseas in their sector, which attacks their market share. Open markets also mean that UK companies are vulnerable to being taken over by, or losing market share to, foreign companies.

Business analysis   16.1

In 2012 China's Bright Food Group bought a 60 per cent stake in Weetabix, which owns the breakfast cereal brand as well as Alpen and Ready Brek. The Northamptonshire-based firm was family owned until 2004, when it was bought by Lion Capital.

Bright Food chairman Zongnan Wang said: 'With Bright Food's strong resources and our expertise in both the Chinese and broader international markets, we are excellently placed to develop the Weetabix business.' The deal is the largest done by a Chinese company in the food and drink businesses. In 2011, Bright Food had revenues of $12.2 billion.

Do you think that foreign firms should be allowed to buy British brands?

Source: BBC

The benefits of trade

Assume, for simplicity, that there are two economies A and B; Table 16.1 shows the output of product X or product Y that could be achieved if the resources in the economy were split equally between the two industries X and Y.

Table 16.1 Output of countries A and B

	Product X	Product Y
Country A	40	10
Country B	30	20

The opportunity cost of product X in country A is 0.25 of a unit of Y, because this is how much would be sacrificed for each extra X if resources were moved out of industry Y. If resources were moved out of Y and into X, the country would lose 10 units of Y and gain 40 units of X, so one unit equals 0.25 units of Y. By comparison, the opportunity cost of one unit of Y is four units of X. If the resources were moved out of X and into Y, the country would gain 10 Ys and lose 40 Xs, so that one Y is equal to four Xs.

For country B, the opportunity cost of one unit of X is two-thirds of a unit of Y, and the opportunity costs of one unit of Y is 1.5 units of X (see Table 16.2).

Table 16.2 Opportunity cost ratios

	Product X	Product Y
Country A	0.25Y	4X
Country B	0.67Y	1.5X

Opportunity cost ratios

Therefore there are clear differences in the opportunity cost ratios for these two countries. For example, to produce a unit of X costs 0.25 units of Y in country A, but 0.67 units of Y in country B. Therefore country A is more efficient at producing X than country B, because it has a lower opportunity cost. If there is free trade, country B could buy these units from A for less than it could produce them itself.

The possible terms at which both countries could trade and benefit are given by the opportunity cost ratios, calculated as:

$$0.25Y < 1X < 0.67Y$$

If the rate of exchange of Xs for Ys when the two countries traded lies in this range, they could both benefit. Provided that country A sells each unit of X for more than 0.25 Ys, it will make a profit (that is, it will more than cover its opportunity cost); provided that country B can buy an X for less than 0.67 Ys, it will be cheaper than producing X itself. Therefore there are **terms of trade** that are mutually beneficial for both countries. A rate can be found that makes the seller a profit and saves the buyer money. This rate is known as the 'terms of trade'. For example, if the terms of trade were to be that one X is equal to 0.5 Ys, then country A could sell and make a profit of 0.25 Ys per sale; country B could buy and save 0.17 Ys per purchase.

If the resources were allocated to the industry in which each country has a comparative advantage (a lower opportunity cost), the overall outcome would be as shown in Table 16.3. Output has doubled in the industry to which all of the resources have been transferred. Total world output is 80 Xs and 40 Ys thanks to specialization. Before specialization occurred and resources were split between both industries in both countries, the total output was 70 Xs and 30 Ys. With each country concentrating on an industry in which its skills lie, the world output increases by 10 Xs and 10 Ys; by trading at suitable terms of trade with A selling Xs and B selling Ys, both countries can gain.

Table 16.3 Specialization

	Product X	Product Y
Country A	80	0
Country B	0	40
Total	80	40

Data analysis   16.1

Table 16.4 Trade

	Product X	Product Y
Country A	30	10
Country B	40	20

1. Calculate the opportunity cost ratios for each product for each country shown in Table 16.4.
2. What terms of trade might be mutually beneficial?

 ## Business analysis   16.2

China is now the world's largest manufacturing country and accounts for a fifth of global manufacturing. Its factories produce so cheaply that this has helped its trading partners to keep their inflation down because of the low costs of Chinese imports which, in turn, has helped keep prices low. However, this may not last much longer because of rising costs in China. Higher land prices, increasing safety and environmental laws, higher taxes, and especially high labour costs are pushing up the price of Chinese products.

For example, Foxconn, an electronics manufacturer which produces for many overseas consumer electronics companies, including Apple, put up salaries by 16–25 per cent in 2012. Given these rising costs, many manufacturers are looking at alternative locations to produce such as Vietnam. At the moment China often has the edge because it has a better supply chain and a more developed infrastructure, but it may not be long before businesses start to move into other regions if they are looking for low-cost manufacturing.

Do you think rising costs mean that China will stop exporting?

Therefore trade enables businesses to find cheaper resources and export markets that boost its sales. For the economy as a whole, it enables businesses, governments, and households to consume combinations of products outside its production possibility frontier (PPF).

Assume that an economy was originally producing and consuming at Z, where it has Q3 units of X and Q2 units of Y (see Figure 16.2). If it were to reallocate resources domestically from X to Y, it could move from Z to W on the PPF. Reallocation of resources leads to a loss of output of Q1,Q3 of X and an increase in output from Q2,Q4 of Y. But if these units (Q1,Q3) can be sold abroad at a profit, it may be able to gain, say, Q2,Q5. This means that, by trading, the economy can end up consuming at V, which is outside the PPF.

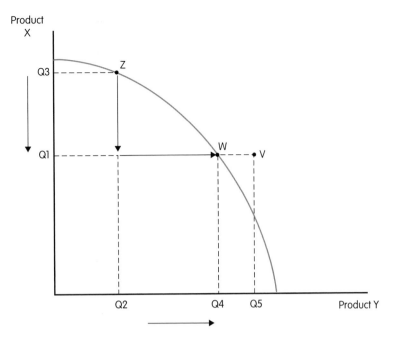

Figure 16.2 International trade and the production possibility frontier

The case for free trade seems to be proved by the experience of world trade and economic growth since the Second World War. During the first twenty-five years after the war, world economic growth averaged about 5 per cent per year—a high rate that was partly the result of these lower trade barriers. World trade grew even faster, averaging about 8 per cent during the period. Therefore the data seems to show a definite statistical link between free trade and economic growth.

 You and economics

Out shopping again, and time to inspect the labels to see where the various retailers and brands are based.

Table 16.5 Brands and retailers according to their geographic base

Brand	Country
Benetton	Italy
IKEA	Sweden
Nike	USA
Nivea	Germany
Tetley Tea	India (owned by the Tata group
Zara	Spain

Just serves to remind you how global business has become.

In other words, trade policies that allow the unrestricted flow of goods and services make markets more competitive, and should lead to the best products being available at the best price.

Exports

Exports are a key part of aggregate demand for many countries such as the UK. Export markets provide enormous opportunities for businesses to boost their sales. This is because doing so:

- provides access to bigger markets;
- provides access to faster growing markets;
- enables a business to grow even if the domestic market is saturated, or if they are not allowed to grow further domestically because of competition policy.

The exports from a country will depend on:

- the sectors in which it has comparative advantage—that is, the products in relation to which businesses are relatively efficient and which they should be able to sell abroad more cheaply than other companies can produce for themselves;
- the exchange rate—that is, the value of the currency will affect the price of a country's products abroad (a strong currency makes a country's exports expensive in terms of foreign currencies);
- the competitiveness of a country's businesses—for example, in terms of design and costs (high labour costs or raw material costs will push up prices, which could dampen competitiveness);
- incomes abroad—that is, the success of one economy is very dependent on the growth of others;
- whether barriers to trade exist—some governments may limit imports into their country using what are known as protectionist measures.

 Business analysis   16.3

The UK has consistently lost its share of total global exports over the past fifty years, especially in the last twenty years. In 1950 the UK accounted for more than 10 per cent of global exports; by 2009 this share had fallen to under 3 per cent. According to Ernst & Young, a significant reason for this poor performance has been the failure to penetrate emerging markets effectively and uncompetitiveness caused by an overvalued pound (although this has been helped in recent years by the depreciation of the pound). What is striking is the difference between the performance of goods and services, with the latter continuing to grow in importance especially IT and financial services.

The growth of emerging markets with rising living standards and an expanding middle class provides an excellent opportunity for exports, and UK firms need to focus more on these markets in areas where they have a comparative advantage.

German businesses have been much more successful at exporting to BRIC economies thanks to high productivity levels and more cost competitiveness. UK businesses now need to follow this lead.

In 1950, 12 per cent of UK exports went to Australia, Canada, India, and New Zealand combined accounted for just under 15 per cent. Over time, the Commonwealth has significantly declined in importance to UK exports, particularly since the UK joined the EU in 1973. Around 60 per cent of UK exports are now to EU countries. At the same time the UK has become more reliant on exports to other developed economies, such as Japan and the USA, and developed economies now account for 75 per cent of UK exports. BRIC economies, by comparison, seem to have been neglected—just 5 per cent of UK exports go to the BRIC economies, which compares unfavourably with BRIC shares of 10.6 per cent for Germany and 11.1 per cent for the USA.

Discuss the importance of the value of the currency in determining the competitiveness of a country's businesses.

What other factors do you think influence competitiveness?

What factors influence which countries businesses export to?

Source: Ernst & Young Special Report 2011: http://www.ey.com

 ## Economics and employability

Tell us your name and a bit about your role.
I'm a computer programmer at an investment bank working in foreign exchange derivatives.

In what ways is an understanding of economics useful in your work?
It's important for me to understand macroeconomic concepts and events, especially anything to do with central bank interest rate setting and economic indicators. Macroeconomic events such as a Japanese Central Bank intervention on the yen can cause spikes in activity in the systems we develop and form peak demands on our systems that we need to cater for.

In what ways does economic change affect your clients?

It affects them hugely as the more economic change there is, the more volatile currency exchange rates are. This means that clients may have to change their approach or risk-management with respect to their exposure to different currencies.

What skills are important in your role?

As you might expect, the key skills important in my role are software development skills. However, I've found that having strong communication skills is essential in my day-to-day work.

The importance of clusters

Michael Porter, a well-known business analyst, highlighted the importance of business clusters in determining the comparative advantage of a region or country in *The Competitive Advantage of Nations* (1990). A 'business cluster' is a geographical concentration of interlinked businesses, suppliers, and associated organizations in a particular sector. These organizations can share expertise and resources, and can collaborate and benefit from synergy. Clusters, claims Porter, improve innovation and productivity. Successful clusters include Silicon Valley in the USA, the City of London as a financial centre, and Northern California and Bordeaux in France as wine regions.

The benefits of clusters can change over time. For example, the cluster of car industry service firms that developed near Birmingham in the UK when the city was a major car producer has now become an important element in the development of Formula One and other specialist vehicle businesses.

According to Porter:

The UK needs to mount a sustained programme of cluster development to create a more conducive environment for productivity growth and innovation through the collective action of companies and other institutions ... It will be essential to mobilise businesses and business institutions that are willing and able to engage in the upgrading of their clusters.

}{ *People and economics: Michael Porter*

Michael Porter (born 1947) is the Bishop William Lawrence University Professor at Harvard Business School. He is a leading authority on company strategy and the competitiveness of nations and regions. Michael Porter's work is recognized in many governments, corporations, and academic circles globally. He chairs Harvard Business School's programme dedicated to newly appointed chief executive officers of very large corporations. His work includes five forces analysis, factors influencing the competitiveness of nations, and analysing the causes of competitive advantages of businesses.

? *Think about it ...*   16.3

Protectionism

Although there are many potential benefits of free trade, in reality many barriers to trade between countries do exist—this is known as **protectionism**.

Protectionism occurs when a government prevents or limits the flow of products from one country to another, for the following reasons.

- *To protect jobs in a particular industry that is suffering* Over time, the competitive advantage of one country in an industry may fall as new competitors come along; this means that resources have to be shifted into other sectors in which a new comparative advantage may be emerging. This reallocation can take time and can create unemployment as resources try to shift (for example, employees may lack the necessary skills to move easily from one sector to another). During this period, a government may decide to protect the declining sector to ease, or even halt, the transition process.

- *To retaliate against actions taken by the other government to limit trade* For example, if the US government were to place restrictions on European wheat being sold into the USA, then European governments might place similar restrictions on US wheat being sold into Europe. This is done for political, rather than economic, reasons. Over the years, there have numerous trade wars over products such as steel, bananas, and T-shirts.

- *To protect strategic industries that may be thought of as essential to the safety of the economy* For example, the weapons sector may be protected and the government may want to protect some of the food sector to ensure supplies in times of war. Once again, this is a political, rather than an economic, reason for protectionism.

- *To protect infant industries* When new industries are developing in an economy (perhaps a new technology-based industry), they will lack the expertise and economies of scale of countries that have been building in this area for a while. Some governments argue that they need to protect their 'infant industries' to help them to grow and be able to compete on equal terms. However, the danger is that the protectionist measures are never removed, enabling inefficient domestic producers to continue in production. Also, if these industries are viable in the long term, they should be able to raise finance from the private sector. If the government needs to intervene, it suggests either that there are problems in the private-sector financial markets or that the government may be financing industries that are not viable. Providing financial assistance can encourage inefficiency if firms come to rely on such aid, and do not make the changes and improvements necessary to compete in global markets.

Whilst protectionism might appeal to a government in that it enables it to be seen to be acting and doing something—and this may win votes from electors—it does not necessarily benefit their economies. In many cases, the arguments for protectionism are political, not economic, and, in fact, the long-term effect is often damaging to the economy. This is because households and firms end up having less choice of products (because they must rely more on domestic production), and because they will pay more for these products than they could buy them for abroad. By protecting domestic firms, governments are, in effect, subsidizing these businesses and enabling them to be inefficient. But big businesses in some industries are often well organized and can place a great deal of pressure on the government to protect them. Consumers, by contrast, tend not to be well organized and do not group together to give themselves bargaining power; therefore their interests can be easily overlooked by governments.

Forms of protectionism

There are many different barriers to trade, including the following measures.

- *Tariffs* These occur when a government places a tax on foreign products; this increases their price and therefore domestic customers will tend to switch away towards domestic products. The extent to which customers switch away will depend on the price elasticity of demand.

- *Quotas* These limit the number of foreign products allowed into an economy. This means that domestic customers have to use domestic businesses if they want to consume more than a given quantity. The lack of competition allows inefficient domestic producers to survive.

- *Administrative regulations* A country can introduce administrative regulations, such as different safety standards, or rules about which ports or airports can be used to import products (which, in effect, limits the quantity that can enter a country in a given time). Indonesia, for example, has specified that certain categories of good, such as clothes, shoes, and toys, can only be imported through five ports, thereby restricting quantities coming in. Argentina recently imposed discretionary licensing requirements on car parts, textiles, televisions, toys, shoes, and leather goods; licences for all of these used to be granted automatically. Some countries have imposed outright import bans, often justified by a tightening of safety rules or by environmental concerns. For example, China has stopped imports of a wide range of European food and drink, including Irish pork, Italian brandy, and Spanish dairy products. The Indian government has banned Chinese toys.

- *Subsidies* A government can subsidize its own businesses, which reduces their costs and enables them to undercut some foreign producers. Again, this is subsidizing inefficient local producers who could not otherwise compete against foreign businesses. The funds for these subsidies have to be raised from somewhere and the consequences of this (for example, in the form of higher taxes) have to be considered when looking at the overall effects of subsidizing. However, from a consumer's point of view, a subsidy does have the advantage of not directly increasing the price of the products (unlike a tariff). Protectionist subsidies that governments have used include funding for peanut farmers in the USA and subsidies for sugar beet farmers in the EU.

One issue that has arisen in recent years is the protectionism that it is claimed that developed countries use in relation to developing countries. Many poorer nations claim that richer nations demand access to their resources, but make it difficult for developing countries to sell their products in the richer economies.

 ## Business analysis 16.4

In 2012 the USA announced that it would impose tariffs of about 30 per cent on imports of solar panels from China. The ruling came after several US solar panel manufacturers, led by SolarWorld, asked the government to penalize Chinese companies for dumping low-priced products on US markets. Critics of the decision claimed that the less expensive imports had helped make solar panels more affordable for US customers. The trade disputes between the USA and China are long-standing and based on the US claim that China has kept the value of its currency artificially low to boost its exports.

Analyse how China might keep the value of its currency low.

Analyse how the low value of a currency might make Chinese products more competitive.

Is a trade war with China a good thing?

 ## You and economics

When you were last in the city centre you noticed a demonstration by a political group you had not heard of before arguing that the government needed to protect British jobs. From the fliers it seemed as if they believed that workers from overseas were taking UK jobs. It's true that you have noticed a number of people from abroad working in your area, but that strikes you as a good thing because it is helping the economy and generating output and income. When you had finished your studies before university you took time out to travel and work in several countries in Europe and you wouldn't have missed that for the world. And after university you are hoping that you can get a job with a multinational, and one of the attractions of this would be spending some time working in different places around the globe. Your only regret is that you didn't study Mandarin and Spanish at school because these would have been so useful these days.

 ## Think about it... 16.4

Do you think the movement of foreign workers into the UK is good for the UK economy?

The effect of a tariff

A tax placed on foreign products will increase the costs of overseas producers. Assume that there is a world price P1 for a product and then a tariff is added; this would shift the supply upwards, meaning that a higher price needs to be paid for the product on the world market (P2 in Figure 16.3). The effect of this is to lower the quantity of products demanded, but increase the quantity supplied by domestic producers.

The effect of the tariff is:

■ to raise the price in the market from P1 to P2 (so that domestic businesses and households pay more for products), which reduces the consumer surplus by ABCD;

■ to allow inefficient domestic producers to produce when they could not have done without the tariff (because the higher price enables them to cover their higher costs), meaning that the domestic producer surplus increases by area A, and B represents the payment for inefficiency;

■ to transfer money from consumers to the government, because of the tax paid on the foreign goods (area C).

When analysing the overall effect of a tariff, it is also important to consider what happens to this tax revenue and how it is used elsewhere in the economy.

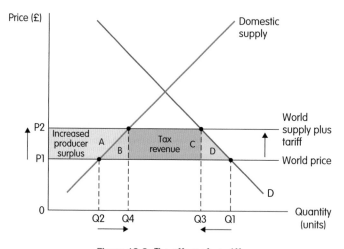

Figure 16.3 The effect of a tariff

The effects of introducing a quota

In the free market, the world price is P1 and the quantity consumed is Q2. A quota limits the amount of imports to Q3,Q4 and, as a result, with less quantity available, the world price increases to P2 (see Figure 16.4). This increases the amount produced domestically to Q3. As with a tariff, a quota allows inefficient domestic producers to survive.

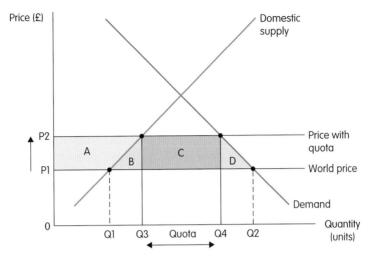

Figure 16.4 The effect of a quota

Trading blocs: free trade areas and customs unions

To promote more free trade among themselves, some countries have joined together to create areas in which any barriers to trade are removed (or are to be removed over time). These are called 'trading blocs'.

If there is an agreement between countries simply to remove barriers between them, but to allow members to adopt whatever policies they want with other non-member countries, this is known as a 'free trade area'. If the member countries have free trade between them and also agree to have a common policy, such as a tariff, against all non-member countries, this is known as a 'customs union'.

The European Union, for example, is a customs union made up of twenty-seven countries with freedom of movement of goods, services, people, and capital between them. The EU has a population of nearly half a billion, providing a large market for UK producers, as well as a good source of supplies. The lack of trade barriers means that the EU represents a huge potential market for UK producers that is relatively easy to enter. It provides a market for over 50 per cent of UK exports.

Other examples of free trade areas include:

- the North American Free Trade Agreement (NAFTA), which was negotiated in 1994 involving the governments of Canada, Mexico, and the USA, and which covers environmental and labour issues, as well as trade and investment;

- the Central American Free Trade Area (CAFTA), which includes Costa Rica, Dominican Republic, El Salvador, Guatemala, Honduras, and Nicaragua;

- Mercado Común del Sur, or the Southern Common Market (Mercosur), which is a free trade area between Argentina, Brazil, Paraguay, Uruguay, and Venezuela;

- the Association of South-East Asian Nations (ASEAN), which aims to bolster economic growth among its ten members—that is, Brunei, Burma, Cambodia, Indonesia,

Laos, Malaysia, the Philippines, Singapore, Thailand, and Vietnam—and to promote peace and stability across the region. ASEAN aims to create a single market by scrapping tariffs and removing barriers to trade.

? Think about it ...   **16.5**

What do you think determines whether a country is willing to join a trading bloc or not?

Trade creation and trade diversion

Within a customs union, member countries usually trade more among themselves because of the reduced barriers to trade. 'Trade creation' occurs when, having joined a free trade area with trade barriers removed, producers can buy products more cheaply from suppliers in member countries than from domestic suppliers. For example, the removal of tariffs may make supplies available more cheaply from member states than from local suppliers.

Trade diversion may also occur when a country joins a customs union. This is when trade is switched from other lower-cost countries towards more expensive members of the agreement; products may be cheaper from outside the customs union, but the tariff makes them more expensive, so producers switch to member-country producers. The result is that producers may now pay more than they would have done before the country joined the customs union.

Assume that a product from a member country costs £10, but would cost £9 from a non-member without a tariff. If the tariff increases the non-member's price to £12, you will switch to the £10 option, even though the product is more expensive than it would have been before joining the union—this is 'trade diversion'.

 # Data analysis   **16.2**

Table 16.6 Value of goods exported (US$ bn) 2009

	UK	Germany	France	Italy
BRIC	18.7	102.5	25.0	25.8
EU	194.6	696.3	298.1	233.9
North America	58.1	82.7	30.7	26.7
Other	81.8	239.2	130.3	120.5
Total	353.4	1120.7	484.1	407.0

Source: IMF Direction of Trade Statistics

Table 16.7 Value of service exports (US$ bn) 2009

	UK	Germany	France	Italy
BRIC	12.3	12.7	9.7	3.5
EU	114.7	129.5	80.5	78.6
North America	66.0	34.1	24.5	11.1
Other	93.9	68.9	48.9	26.2
Total	285.9	246.2	163.6	119.3

Source: IMF Direction of Trade Statistics

Using the data in Tables 16.5 and 16.6, calculate the percentage of goods and services exported by these EU members to other EU countries.

Comment on the possible significance of the data above for UK managers.

Discuss the factors that influence where a country exports to.

Organizations affecting world trade

The importance of world trade to the growth of the world economy and the increasing trade links that exist between countries mean that trade is a key economic issue. As a result, governments often belong to various trade agreements, or join customs unions to enable their countries to benefit from importing and exporting. There are also various international organizations that exist to facilitate trade, and to try and ensure that it continues to grow and that economies remain relatively stable.

? **Think about it ...** 16.6

Why do you think that industries such as steel and agriculture are often protected?

The World Trade Organization

The World Trade Organization (WTO) was established on 1 January 1995, but grew out of the General Agreement on Tariffs and Trade (GATT) which was started in 1948. The aim of the WTO is to reduce barriers to trade worldwide. Whereas GATT had mainly dealt with trade in goods, the WTO and its agreements now cover trade in services and in traded inventions, creations, and designs (i.e. intellectual property).

Since GATT was created, there have been nine rounds of trade negotiations between member countries. At first, these focused on lowering tariffs (customs duties) on imported goods. As a result of these negotiations, by the mid-1990s, industrial countries' tariff rates on industrial goods had fallen steadily to less than 4 per cent.

The WTO provides:

- a forum in which governments can negotiate trade agreements;
- a place in which to settle trade disputes;
- enforcement of agreed trade rules.

The principles of WTO include the following.

- *Most-favoured nation (MFN)* Under the WTO agreements, countries cannot usually discriminate between their trading partners. If a member country grants another country a special favour (such as a lower customs rate for one of their products), it has to do the same for all other WTO members.
- *National treatment* Treating foreigners and locals equally means that imported and locally produced goods should be treated equally. The same should apply to foreign and domestic services, and to foreign and local trademarks, copyrights, and patents.

In the WTO, when countries agree to open their markets for goods or services, they 'bind' their commitments. For goods, these binding commitments amount to ceilings on customs tariff rates. One of the achievements of the Uruguay Round of multilateral trade talks was to increase the amount of trade under binding commitments. In agriculture, 100 per cent of products now have bound tariffs. The result of all this is a substantially higher degree of market security for traders and investors.

The International Monetary Fund

The International Monetary Fund (IMF) is an organization of 186 countries, working to:

- bring about greater global monetary cooperation;
- secure financial stability;
- facilitate international trade;
- promote high employment and sustainable economic growth;
- reduce poverty around the world.

The IMF monitors the economic position of countries and provides economic policy advice. It also lends to countries that are in difficulty, and provides technical assistance and training to help countries to improve their economic management.

The IMF is funded by a charge, known as a 'quota', which is paid by member nations. The quota is based on a country's wealth and determines voting power within the organization—those making higher contributions have greater voting rights. The IMF acts as a lender of last resort, providing its foreign exchange reserves for short periods to any member in difficulties. Past interventions by the IMF have included providing funds for countries caught up in the 1997 Asian financial crisis, and loans to help South American countries such as Argentina and Brazil stave off debt default crises. It is currently contributing to the second international bailout of Greece, and discussing further loans to Hungary. The IMF can also grant emergency loans following natural disasters; these have included the 2004 Asian tsunami.

In recent years developing countries have complained about what they say is their lack of influence in the IMF. Under the present voting system the USA has 17 per cent of the vote in the IMF, whereas India, with more than three times the population of the US, has less than 3 per cent.

The World Bank

The World Bank's predecessor—the International Bank for Reconstruction and Development—was set up to drive recovery after the Second World War. It is now the world's leading development organization, working for growth and poverty reduction. It is owned by the governments of its 187 member states. The World Bank channels loans and grants, and advises low- and middle-income countries.

The euro and the Eurozone crisis

The euro is the common currency adopted by several countries within the European Union. Its members are Austria, Belgium, Cyprus, Estonia, Finland, France, Germany, Greece, Ireland, Italy, Luxembourg, Malta, The Netherlands, Portugal, Slovakia, Slovenia, and Spain.

The advantages to a business of having a single currency include the following:

- it is easier to compare sellers' prices;
- there are no transaction costs for converting currency;
- there are no worries about the currency increasing or decreasing in value against other Eurozone partners, which makes planning easier.

However, the future of the Eurozone began to come under real strain after the began to come under real strain after the 2008 global crisis when it became clear that some member countries, such as Greece, had very high levels of debt (either the government had debt or banks, firms and households did). In countries such as Spain and Italy high wage settlements over the decade before also meant the economies were uncompetitive. Worries about the ability of these countries to repay their debt meant that they became high risk economies. Those that were willing to lend to such countries wanted higher returns; this increased the costs of repayment and potentially made the countries an even great risk. This put downward pressure on the euro and worried stronger economies such as Germany which found that the value of its currency was being determined by the weak financial position of others. To try and save the euro a new fiscal agreement was made in which Eurozone leaders have agreed to limit their government's 'structural' borrowing (i.e. their underlying financial deficit excluding the impact of the recession) to just 0.5 per cent of their economy's output each year. They will also limit their total borrowing to 3 per cent. These rules are supposed to stop them accumulating too much debt, and avoid another financial crisis. The financial conditions placed on these countries required governments such as Greece to make some very painful cuts, which were politically very unpopular (for example, unemployment in Spain was over 20 per cent so further cuts were resisted). At the time of writing it was still not clear if these governments would be able to see through the financial changes demanded of them or whether they would be forced to leave the euro.

In fact the Eurozone members already had a fiscal agreement which should have prevented many of these problems, but it had been broken by several member countries. Germany was the first big country to break the 3 per cent rule; Italy regularly broke it. Only Spain stuck to the rules between 1999 when the Eurozone was created until the recession of 2008. Greece never stuck to the 3 per cent rule—it manipulated its borrowing statistics to look better than they were to get into the euro in the first place!

 ## Business analysis   16.5

Between 2011 and 2012 the European Central Bank (ECB) lent over €1,019 billion in low-interest loans to banks across the EU. The loans were aimed at helping the banks have more liquidity. UK lender HSBC borrowed about £350 million; Lloyds Banking Group also borrowed around £11.4 billion.

Do you think that the ECB should help banks with their liquidity?

Assessing overseas markets for international business

Selling abroad can be a means of growing your business. Many multinationals, such as Sony and Unilever, have been targeting the emerging economies, such as China and India, as a critical part of their long-term strategy because this is where they see fast sales growth coming from rather than the more mature markets of Europe or the USA.

As with any market, assessing an international market will involve forecasting its size and growth, and calculating the likely costs of entry. Managers need to estimate the likely return on the investment to determine whether it is desirable. Factors such as the market share and power of existing firms, their likely reaction to a new entrant, and the risk involved in competing will all be worth considering. In international markets, understanding the cultural issues of a market may prove particularly difficult because of greater differences in buying habits, management styles, and ways of doing business. International business may also involve exchange rate issues, which can make planning more difficult. An increase in the value of your currency may make your products more expensive in foreign currencies and this may reduce sales; it would also make imports from overseas competitors cheaper in pounds, which might make domestic customers switch to them. Given the instability of some currencies and the significant changes in value there can be in relatively short periods of time, this can make business planning very difficult and means that a significant influence on business success can be out of managers' direct control.

Entering overseas markets

Initially, many businesses sell abroad by exporting some of their products. For example, they may receive enquiries from abroad and send their products in response to these requests. At this stage, there is no risk involved in selling abroad. But if interest in selling abroad continues, managers might consider the following options.

- *Using an agent to represent the business abroad* This means hiring someone who understands the market well and who may be able to generate more business for you. The agent will usually take a percentage of the sales.

- *Forming a partnership or venture with a local business* For example, the overseas business might help you to distribute, or you might share product development. Again, the advantage is using a business that knows the market well, which reduces the risk of operating in unfamiliar markets.

- *Taking over an existing business in that country* This can be a fast way of entering a market, but inevitably it is quite risky because of the cost and expense of buying an existing business, and the possible operational and cultural issues involved in acquiring and running a new company.

- *Setting up your own operations abroad* This is the most risky option because it involves major investment and relies on your understanding of local conditions.

The method of entering a market that is chosen by a manager will depend on factors such as the likely level of sales and return, the extent to which the market is unfamiliar, and the degree of risk that a manager is willing to take.

 Business analysis   16.6

In 2008, Coca Cola made a US$2,500 million bid for the Chinese juice company Huiyan. China is the world's fastest growing drinks market. The bid was three times the existing share price just before the offer was made. In the first half of 2008 Huiyan had a 44 per cent market share by sales value in China's pure juice sector and 42 per cent of the nectar sector, according to data from research firm ACNielsen. The deal was eventually prevented by the Chinese government, which wanted to protect its own firms.

1. Why would Coca Cola want to buy Huiyan and be willing to pay so much for it?
2. Why would the Chinese government not want to allow a bid such as this?

The business implications of trade

Trade opens up new markets and therefore new opportunities for business. The EU, for example, is a customs union, which means that there is free movement of goods, services, people, and money among member countries. This makes trade easier because there are no barriers within it—if you can sell a product in Liverpool, you can also export it and sell it in Berlin, Barcelona, and Toulouse.

Trade also creates opportunities in the form of cheaper production bases and cheaper materials. By producing in China, for example, a UK manufacturer pays far lower wages on average, and this brings down the costs and increases profits. This is why companies such as Hornby and Dyson have switched production overseas, and why other companies outsource aspects of their production, such as their call centres, abroad. The fixed costs of production will be lower if rents and overheads are lower.

But trade also brings threats to individual businesses. While free trade may be in the interest of businesses and households generally, individual firms or industries may suffer due to more efficient production overseas in their sector, which attacks their market share. Open markets also mean that UK companies are vulnerable to being taken over by foreign companies. Many 'UK' businesses are actually foreign-owned (such as Jaguar being owned by the Indian business Tata, BAA and O_2 by the Spanish business Ferrovial, P&O by Dubai Ports, and Manchester United by American Malcolm Glazer, and the American company Kraft buying Cadbury).

Trade and the recession

In the recent global recession, world trade slowed down. With lower incomes, households, firms, and governments bought fewer products from abroad. This contributed to

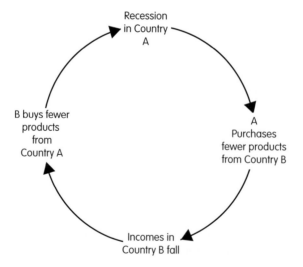

Figure 16.5 The growth of economies is increasingly interrelated

slower growth in these countries, which reduced their ability to import. The recession highlighted how interconnected countries are, with a decline in one having a major knock-on effect on its trading partners (see Figure 16.5).

The recession led to high levels of unemployment in many countries, and demand from producers for subsidies and protectionist measures. (For more on the recession, see Chapter 12.) While there may be some economic arguments for protectionism, the pressure was mainly political, as businesses demanded help so that jobs would not be lost.

Summary

Trade between countries is based on the principle of comparative advantage. This means that countries' trade will relate to the sectors in which they have a comparative advantage—that is, a lower opportunity cost. Protectionism occurs when a government tries to protect its own businesses. In a free trade area, barriers to trade are removed. Trade creates opportunities and threats for managers. Trade is hugely important to businesses, on both the supply side and the demand side. Inputs are bought in from abroad, production is outsourced to overseas companies, and products are sold in foreign markets. Therefore understanding what drives trade is vitally important to managers.

Checklist

Having read this chapter, you should now understand:

- [ ] free trade;
- [ ] comparative advantage;
- [ ] opportunity cost;
- [ ] the meaning of clusters;
- [ ] the meaning of terms of trade;
- [ ] the meaning of protectionism;
- [ ] the meaning of a quota;
- [ ] the meaning of a tariff.

Organizations and economics

European Central Bank

Since 1 January 1999 the European Central Bank (ECB) has been responsible for conducting monetary policy for the Eurozone—the world's largest economy after the USA.

Source: http://www.ecb.int

G8

Since 1975, the heads of state or government of the major industrial democracies have met annually to deal with the major economic and political issues facing their domestic societies and the international community as a whole. The six countries at the first summit, held at Rambouillet, France, in November 1975, were France, Germany, Italy, Japan, the UK, and the US (sometimes referred to as the G6). They were later joined by Canada and Russia.

The G8 Summits deal with macroeconomic management, international trade, and relations with developing countries. Microeconomic issues such as employment and the information highway, transnational issues such as the environment, crime and drugs, and a host of political–security issues ranging from human rights through regional security to arms control are also discussed.

Source: G8 information centre, the G8 research group: http://www.g7.utoronto.ca/

Short answer questions

1. Explain the link between comparative advantage and opportunity cost.
2. If the opportunity cost ratios for one unit of X are two units of Y in country A and three units of Y in country X, what are possible terms of trade? Explain your answer.
3. Does a high or a low exchange rate encourage exports? Explain your answer.
4. Distinguish between a tariff and a quota.
5. Explain how a tariff affects consumers.
6. Explain two reasons why governments introduce protectionist measures.
7. What is the difference between a free trade area and a customs union?
8. Explain two benefits of free trade to businesses.
9. Explain two threats of free trade to businesses.
10. Explain the possible benefits of clusters of businesses in the same industry within a country.

Discussion questions

1. Discuss the benefits of free trade to a country and the businesses within it.
2. Should governments introduce protectionist measures to save jobs within a country?
3. Discuss the effects of introducing a tariff on different stakeholders.

One step further

Visit our Online Resource Centre at **www.oxfordtextbooks.co.uk/orc/gillespiebusiness2e/** to test your understanding, watch video walk-throughs, and access further information on topics covered in this chapter.

Glossary

abnormal profit occurs when the total revenue is greater than the total costs

adding value occurs when the output created by the transformation process is worth more than the inputs used in this process

aggregate demand is the total planned demand for final goods and services in an economy at each price, all other factors unchanged

aggregate supply shows the total level of planned output in an economy at each and every price, all other factors unchanged, i.e. the extra benefit of a unit, to read: ... all other factors unchanged, i.e. the extra benefit of a unit

allocative efficiency occurs when the price paid by the customer equals the social marginal cost of producing the good

appreciation is when a currency increases in value against other currencies

asymmetric information occurs when there is a difference in the information available to each of the two parties involved in a transaction

average cost (or average total cost) is the cost per unit

average product of labour is the average output per worker

average revenue is the price of a unit (i.e. total revenue divided by total revenue divided by the number of units)

balance of payments measures the value of one country's transactions with the rest of the world over a given period

balance of trade measures the value of the difference between a country's exports and its imports in goods and services over a given period

barriers to entry factors that make entry to a market difficult (e.g. the need for a licence to operate)

budget position measures the difference between government revenue and spending over a given period

cartel occurs when businesses collude to set price and/or output

classical economists believe that wages and prices adjust to clear markets quickly and the economy settles at or near full employment

community surplus measures the sum of consumer surplus and producer surplus

comparative advantage is the advantage held by a country in the production of a product, i.e. it has a lower opportunity cost than other countries

complements are products with negative cross-price elasticity—that is, an increase in the price of one reduces the quantity demanded of the other

concentration ratio the n-firm concentration ratio measures the market share of the largest n firms

Consumer Price Index is a measure of inflation

consumer surplus is the difference between the price charged for a product and the utility that consumers derive from it

consumption is the level of planned spending by households on final goods and services

copyright provides legal protection for literary works, dramatic works, musical works, artistic works, recordings, and broadcasts

corporate social responsibility refers to behaviour that occurs if a business accepts responsibilities to society over and above its legal obligations

cost–benefit analysis is used by governments to assess investments by considering private and social costs and benefits

cost push inflation occurs when higher costs force producers to put up their prices

cross-price elasticity of demand measures the responsiveness of the demand for one product in relation to changes in the price of another, all other factors unchanged

crowding out is the reduction in private sector investment following an increase in government spending

cyclical (demand-deficient) unemployment occurs when people are unemployed because of a lack of demand in the economy

deflationary policies government initiatives to reduce the level of aggregate demand in an economy

demand curve shows the quantity demanded at each and every price, all other factors unchanged

demand pull inflation occurs when the aggregate demand is greater than the aggregate supply, thereby pulling up prices

demand-side policies focus on increasing aggregate demand

depreciation occurs when a currency loses value against other currencies

derived demand occurs when the demand for resources is derived from demand for the goods and services

diseconomies of scale (internal) occur when there are increases in the long-run average costs as the scale of production increases

dividend is the payment made to shareholders out of profits

dominant strategy refers to the actions taken by a player in a game regardless of the actions of other players

economies of scale (internal) occur when there are reductions in the long-run average costs as the scale of production increases

equilibrium price the price at which the quantity demanded equals the quantity supplied

euro (€) a single currency used by seventeen of the twenty-seven members of the European Union

European Union a customs union of twenty-seven European countries in which there is free trade between members and a common tariff against non-members

exchange rate the price of one currency in terms of another

expenditure-reducing policies are aimed at reducing aggregate demand to reduce spending on imports to improve the balance of payments current account

expenditure-switching policies are aimed at switching spending away from imports to improve the balance of payments current account

externality occurs when there is a difference between private and social costs and benefits; may be positive or negative

fiscal policy policy using government spending, taxation, and benefit rates to influence the economy

fixed costs costs that do not change with the amount of products produced

fixed exchange rate an exchange rate system in which the government intervenes to maintain the value of the currency

free goods goods for which provision involves no opportunity cost

free market allocates resources by allowing market forces of supply and demand to operate without any intervention

free trade occurs between countries when there are no barriers to trade

game theory an approach to oligopoly in which each firm's strategy depends on its expectations of how the others in the market will behave

Gini coefficient measures the extent of income inequality in an economy

gross domestic product (GDP) measures the value of final goods and services produced in an economy in a given period regardless of who owns them

gross national product (GNP) measures the value of final goods and services produced in an economy over a given period of time (usually a year)

income elasticity of demand measures the responsiveness of the demand for a product in relation to changes in income, all other factors unchanged

index numbers show the percentage change in a variable relative to a base number

indirect tax is a tax placed on producers (e.g. VAT)

inferior good is a good for which demand falls when income increases

inflation occurs when there is a persistent increase in the general price level in a given period

investment the purchase of capital goods such as machinery and factories

involuntary unemployment measures the number of people who are willing and able to work at the given real wage, but who are not in employment

just-in-time production production occurs when an order is received rather than in advance of demand

Keynesian economists believe that markets are slow to clear and therefore the economy can remain below full employment; this suggests that governments may want to intervene to increase aggregate demand

labour productivity measures the output per worker

law of diminishing marginal utility the extra benefit from consuming additional units of a good or service will eventually start to fall

law of diminishing returns states that as additional units of a variable factor are added to a fixed factor, the marginal output will fall

lean production aims to reduce all forms of waste in the production process

long run the period of time during which all of the factors of production are variable

Lorenz curve illustrates the income distribution of an economy

macroeconomics involves the study of the economy as a whole

marginal cost the extra cost of producing an extra unit

marginal efficiency of capital (MEC) shows the expected rate of return on investment projects

marginal physical product of labour the change in total output when an extra worker is employed

marginal propensity to consume (MPC) the proportion of each extra pound earned that is spent

marginal propensity to import the proportion of each extra pound earned spent on imports

marginal propensity to save the proportion of each extra pound earned that is saved

marginal revenue the extra revenue earned by selling another unit

marginal revenue product (MRP) measures the value of the output produced by employing an extra worker

marginal social cost the extra cost to society of producing a unit

marginal utility the extra satisfaction gained from consuming a unit

market capitalization the market value of a company's shares

market concentration measures the extent to which a market is dominated by a few firms

market segment a group of similar needs within an overall market

Marshall–Lerner condition if the price elasticity of demand for export plus the price elasticity of demand for imports is greater than 1, a depreciation of the currency will improve the current account of the balance of payments

merit good a good that the government believes has a higher benefit than individuals believe

microeconomics study of the economic behaviour of individual units of an economy

minimum efficient scale (MES) the first level of output at which long-run average costs stop falling with expansion

mixed economy allocates resources using a combination of market forces and government intervention

monetary policy uses control of the money supply and interest rates to influence the economy

monopolistic competition a market structure in which there are many firms, but each offers a differentiated product

monopoly occurs when a single firm dominates a market

multiplier shows how an increase in injections into an economy can have a multiplied effect on national income

natural rate of unemployment occurs when the labour market clears and the economy is at full employment

nominal (data) actual amounts received at a given time (compared with real data)

normal good a good for which demand increases when income increases

normal profit occurs when the total revenue equals the total costs

normative economics focuses on economic decisions based on values (cf. positive economics)

oligopoly a market structure in which a few firms dominate the market

opportunity cost the benefit foregone in the next best alternative

output gap measures the difference between the amount that an economy is able to produce if its resources are fully employed and the current level of demand

patent protects new inventions, covering how things work, what they do, how they do it, what they are made of, and how they are made

perfect competition a market situation with many firms, perfect information, freedom of entry and exit, and homogeneous products

PESTEL analysis provides a framework for managers when examining the external environment in terms of the political, economic, social, technological, environmental, and legal factors

Phillips curve shows the possible relationship between unemployment and inflation

planned (or command) economy occurs when the government allocates resources

positive economics focuses on economic decisions based on testable hypotheses (cf. normative economics)

price discrimination occurs when different prices are charged to different customers for the same product

price elasticity of demand measures the responsiveness of the demand for a product in relation to changes in its price, all other factors unchanged

price elasticity of supply measures changes in the quantity supplied relative to changes in prices, all other factors unchanged

producer surplus is the difference between the price paid to producers for products and the cost of producing the items

production possibility frontier (PPF) shows the maximum combination of products that an economy can produce, given its resources

productive efficiency occurs when more of one product can only be produced if less of another product is produced; it also occurs when a firm produces at the minimum of the average cost curve (i.e. at the lowest cost per unit possible)

productivity measures outputs relative to inputs (e.g. output per worker)

profit measures the difference between revenue and costs

profit margin measures profit as a percentage of sales revenue

protectionism occurs when a government protects its domestic firms against foreign competition

public goods products that are non-diminishable and non-excludable

public sector a sector in which organizations are owned by the government

quantitative easing involves using monetary policy techniques to increase the money supply

quota a limit on the number of foreign products allowed into a market or limits on the amount that a firm can produce

rational expectations an approach which assumes that people use all the information available to them at any given time to make rational decisions

real (data) amounts that are adjusted for inflation

recession occurs when there is negative growth in an economy for two successive quarters

reflationary policies government initiatives to increase the level of aggregate demand in an economy

resources inputs into a business which are used to produce outputs (e.g. land, labour, capital, and entrepreneurship)

short run period of time during which at least one factor of production is fixed

shortages occur when there is excess demand

shutdown point the price that just covers the average variable cost; if the price falls below this in the short run, the business will shut down

signalling occurs when people attempt to indicate their value to others

stakeholders individuals and organizations affected by a firm's activities

structural unemployment occurs when people are unemployed because of changes in the structure of the economy

substitutes products that have positive cross-price elasticity—that is, an increase in the price of one increases the quantity demanded of the other

supply curve shows the quantity that producers are willing and able to produce at each and every price, all other factors unchanged

supply-side policies policies focusing on increasing the supply in the economy by improving the way in which markets work

surplus occurs when there is excess supply in a market at the given price

tariffs taxes placed on foreign products

terms of trade measure prices of exports from a country compared with prices of imports into the country

total cost fixed costs plus variable costs

total revenue the value of sales (calculated as the price of a product multiplied by the quantity sold)

trade union an organization that represents employees

trademarks a trademark is a sign that can distinguish your goods and services from those of your competitors; it can be, for example, words, logos, or a combination of both

transaction costs costs associated with undertaking business activities or making decisions

utility refers to the satisfaction that a consumer would receive from consuming a product

variable costs costs that change with output

voluntary unemployment occurs when people who are looking for work are not yet willing to accept work at the given real wage rate

References

Baumol, W.J. (1959). *Business Behavior, Value and Growth*. New York: Macmillan.

Berle, A.A. and Means, G.C. (1933). *The Modern Corporation and Private Property*. New York: Macmillan.

Drucker, P. (1954). *The Practice of Management*. New York: Harper & Row.

Frank, R. (2008). *Microeconomics and Behavior* (7th edn.). NewYork: McGraw-Hill.

Greenspan, A. (2007). *The Age of Turbulence: Adventures in a New World*. New York: Penguin.

Kahneman, D. and Tversky, A. (1979). Prospect theory: an analysis of decision under risk. *Econometrica*, **47**, 263–92.

Kotler, P. (1983). *Principles of Marketing*. Englewood Cliffs, NJ: Prentice Hall.

Marris, R. (1964). *The Economic Theory of 'Managerial' Capitalism*. New York: Macmillan.

McCarthy, E.J. (1960). *Basic Marketing*. Homewood, IL: Irwin.

McKean, R.N. (1965). The unseen hand in government. *American Economic Review*, **55**, 496–506.

Phillips, A.W. (1958). The relation between unemployment and the rate of change of money wage rates in the United Kingdom, 1861–1957. *Economica*, **25**, 283–99.

Porter, M. (1985). *Competitive Advantage*. New York: Free Press.

Porter, M.E. (1990) *The Competitive Advantage of Nations*. New York: Free Press.

Schumpeter, J. (1942). *Capitalism, Socialism and Democracy*. New York: Harper & Brothers.

Simon, H.A. (1955). A behavioral model of rational choice. *Quarterly Journal of Economics*, **69**, 99–118.

Sweezy, P. (1939). Demand under conditions of oligopoly. *Journal of Political Economy*, **47**, 568–73.

Williamson, O.E. (1964). *The Economics of Discretionary Behavior: Managerial Objectives in a Theory of the Firm*. Englewood Cliffs, NJ: Prentice Hall.

Index